THE GUIDE

Architec
the Indian
Subcontinent

IN SUPPORT OF THE ARTS

 Steel Limited

The Guide to the Architecture of the Indian Subcontinent

**First published in Japan on September 20, 1996
by Toto Shuppan**

Toto Nogizaka Building,

2nd floor 1-24-3

Minami - Aoyama. Minato-ku,

Tokyo 102

JAPAN

Telephone: 03-3595-9689

Fax: 03-3595-945

Written and Photographed by Takeo Kamiya

Publisher: Atsushi Sato

Produced by: Gallery MA

Designed by: Akita design Kan Inc.

Cartography: J. Map

Printed by: All Nippon Printing Co. Ltd

ISBN- 4-88706-141-2

**English edition published in August 2003
Revised edition published in February 2004
Revised 2nd edition published on 1st July, 2009
Publisher: Architecture Autonomous**

House No. 674, Near Nisha's Play School

Torda, Salvador do Mundo

Bardez, Goa 403 101

INDIA

Telephone: 91-832-2410711, 2410715

Fax: 91-832-2410709, 2417535

e-mail: archauto@sancharnet.in

archauto03@yahoo.com

Translated by Geetha Parameswaran of Japan Centre

e-mail :tashi@bgl.vsnl.net.in

Printed at

Pragati Art Printers

17, Red Hills

Hyderabad 500 004

INDIA

Telephone: 91-40-2338 0000

Fax: 91-40-2339 0230

e-mail: info@pragati.com

WEBSITE: http://www.indoarch.org

THE GUIDE TO THE

Architecture of the Indian Subcontinent

written and photographed by **TAKEO KAMIYA, ARCHITECT**

translated by **GEETHA PARAMESWARAN**

edited by **ANNABEL LOPEZ & BEVINDA COLLACO**

in collaboration with
Jindal Art Foundation

Contents

How to use this book

Charmed by the architecture of India, after repeated travel over a period of 20 years, the author wrote The *Guide to the Architecture of the Indian Subcontinent*. Photographs are the main focus and the text explains these. Maps and drawings have been included where available. When browsing through this book, one gets the feeling of actually being in India. In all, 612 buildings from 287 cities, towns and villages of India are covered. The obviously important buildings, as well as those that are not usually visited, are covered by this book. There is also an information guide to the transport and lodging of each region, at the beginning of the chapter. An ideal route that covers the maximum number of places in the shortest time has been introduced. Please use it.

COMPOSITION OF THIS BOOK

The author divided India into five zones and the book into five chapters - North, South, East, West, and Central. Each chapter is subdivided into a number of states, with an architectural outline of each state. The buildings are introduced citywise, from the north to the south, with a city map for main cities.

ABOUT THE NOTATIONS

❶ Numbering in the maps of the areas corresponds with the numbers given to towns and also serves as an index. The o mark shows that the city is the state capital or an important city.

❷ Towns are broadly classified and the name of the place where the building is located, is also given.

❸ The building is classified giving the building name, year of construction, grouping, architect's name, etc.

❹ Stars show the grading the author has given the building and its fascinating quality, during his actual visit. A grey star is for the place name and a black star is for the building. A maximum of 3 stars are given as ranking.

❺ Grouping is done in a practical manner. Where religion is applicable, it has been called Buddhist, Hindu, Jain, Islamic and Sikh. Vernacular buildings of west India are Rajput, those of the Maratha regime are Maratha, British era are Colonial and those built after 1947 are Post Independence.

❻ Old names or any other names are mentioned in brackets.

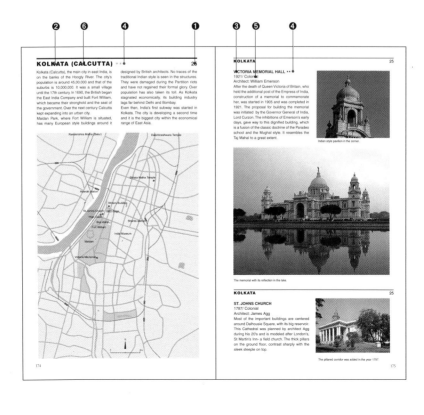

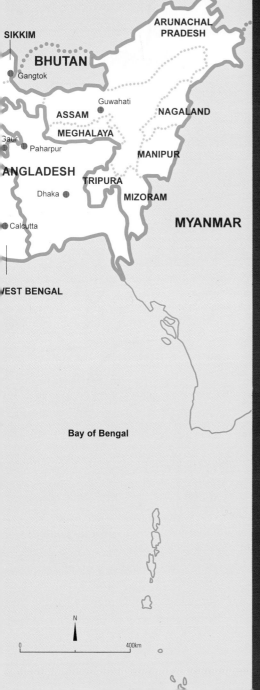

CHINA

SIKKIM

BHUTAN

Gangtok

ARUNACHAL
PRADESH

Guwahati

ASSAM

NAGALAND

MEGHALAYA

Gaur

Paharpur

MANIPUR

ANGLADESH

TRIPURA

Dhaka

MIZORAM

MYANMAR

Calcutta

EST BENGAL

Bay of Bengal

N

0   400km

Map Index

Note: Since Assam, in the far eastern region of India, shares its boundary with several countries, and there are independence movement struggles by minority ethnic groups, foreigners are not allowed to tour the area. The author could not conduct an extensive tour of the northeast so this area had to be omitted from the book. On the other hand, since Bangladesh was part of Bengal, it has been included in this book, as the legacy will not be understood properly if they are not together. Moreover, Mukhalingam of Andhra Pradesh architecturally belongs to the Orissa zone, and hence has been included in east India.

Editor's Note: In November 2000, several new states were created in India. In UP, the northern-most section covering the Kumaon and Garhwal hills became the new state of Uttaranchal. The new state of Jharkhand was created in what was southern Bihar and is an area of great natural beauty and mineral wealth. The southern part of Madhya Pradesh was carved out as Chhatisgarh, which is thickly forested and populated by tribal communities.

Map labels

Gangtok
Darjeeling
Bagdogra
Gauhati
Syedpur
Paharpur
Sylhet
Bogra
RAJSHAHI
Dhaka
Comilla
Jessore
Howrah (Calcutta)
Chittagong
Cox's Bazar
Bombay →
Rangoon →
Port Blair →

Key
Airways
Railway- Broad Gauge
Railway- Metre Gauge
Roadways
National Border
State Border

Port Blair →

Getting Around

AIRWAYS
Since India is a big country, one will need to fly to save time. Previously, there was only the state owned Indian Airlines, but in recent years, there are many private airlines that have aircraft flying to smaller towns. Here I should caution that the flight to the Himalayas and Ladakh often gets cancelled due to bad weather. It is better to reserve in advance on a well-established airline.

RAILWAYS
This is the oldest mode of transportation in India, and since there are not many electric trains, it will mean travelling in steam trains that have not changed in 50 years. Nevertheless, India has one of the most distinguished railroad systems in the world and the width of the rails is classified into broad gauge, narrow gauge and metre gauge. Many routes have been changed to broad gauge since this map was made. The express trains become sleepers at night, from 9 p m to 7 a m. The big terminals have counters exclusively for foreign tourists and they sell national and regional train timetables in English.

BUSES
There are many buses to a single destination and they are convenient since they are capable of taking small sharp turns. However, the seats are narrow, which results in quickly tiring the traveller. Try to get a seat in the front section of the bus. The good thing is, especially in south India, if you can enjoy the natural scenery, even a long journey is not boring. It is advisable to confirm the time and your seat reservation at the bus stand on the previous day. For your information, a long-distance bus does an average of only 30 km per hour.

TAXIS
Long distance taxi charges should be bargained and resolved every time. It is sound policy to contact a number of drivers and speak to them about the tour itinerary. There are times when you decide on the charge according to your tour itinerary and there are times when you pay by the kilometre. The rent-a-car system is not very popular in India.

RICKSHAWS
In the bigger cities one can travel around in taxis, but in small towns, it is easier to get around in a rickshaw. There are three types of rickshaws. The most primitive is the hand-pulled rickshaw, which can be seen only in Calcutta. Then there are cycle rickshaws that travel slowly and are appropriate if one wants to enjoy the hustle and bustle of the place. The rates are cheap and you can bargain before getting in. However, these rickshaws are getting fewer by the year and motor powered rickshaws, called autos, are becoming more popular. They are fast, make a lot of noise and are also the cause of considerable air pollution.

An Introduction to Indian Architecture

India nurtured various cultures in ancient times. Along with literature, fine art, music, dance and drama, architecture too, in all its grandeur, rose to great heights. It is not easy to explain Indian architecture; it is entirely different from that of Europe.

James Fergusson, the architectural historian, analysed Indian architecture for the first time in his book, *History of Indian and Eastern Architecture.* Fergusson recognized two types of architecture: **Architecture of Intellect**, with the Parthenon in Greece as its ideal, and **Architecture of Emotions**, with the Halebid Temple in India as the best of this form. He added that forms of architecture in the world lie between these two extremes. If there is something which could be referred to as 'complete architecture' it should exist somewhere in between these two monuments.

The Hoysaleshwara Temple at Halebid, dates back to the Hoysala dynasty that ruled over south India in the 12th century. This spectacular temple, built over a large area, is filled with sculptures both on the exterior and the interior. Fergusson says that this is a structure which appeals more to Man's senses than to his reasoning power. Most Hindu temples in India are filled with sculptures. The temples at Khajuraho and Konark also have images of men and women in various sexual poses. If this type of architecture represents the "doctrine of pleasure" then the Cistercian monasteries in Europe must represent the "doctrine of abstinence". When one compares the Cistercian monasteries that banned sculptures and murals as a hindrance to their meditation, then these Hindu temples seem to be the diametric opposite.

Islamic architecture plays a major role in India's architectural history. Idol worship is prohibited in Islam and there are absolutely no statues or murals inside mosques. The structure is a symmetrical, geometric shape and the space inside is bright, in contrast to Hindu temples.

Geographically, India is a large country with different climactic conditions from the north to the south; hence the style of the buildings across the country was also different. Moreover, ancient India did not ever have centralized rule. The Mauryas in the 3rd century BC and the Mughals between the 16th and 17th centuries reigned over most of India. These were the only times when most of the country came under central rule. Otherwise, different kings ruled over different parts of the country, until colonization, and all of them have contributed to the development of different cultures.

European architectural history is clearly defined according to the ages, into Roman, Greek, Gothic, Renaissance, Baroque, Rococo and modern, but Indian architecture cannot be compartmentalized in this way. This is because India is a complex nation geographically and historically, with a diverse architectural heritage.

Yet architecture in one region in India is not entirely different from the other. The Indian sub-continent is bounded by the sea on the south and the Himalayas and China in the north, and therefore has had little contact with the outside world. If one has to analyze it, *unity in diversity* is the key to Indian culture. Diverse geography, rulers, religions and eras, together created a fascinating architectural mosaic.

What strikes one when travelling in a taxi, is that the driver does not use a road map. Asking for the way in towns and villages, with people offering directions and advice, is how the trip continues. Instead of starting on a trip equipped with a detailed map, accumulating the whole in parts, is the Indian way. This is perhaps the basis for the construction method of vernacular architecture in the villages and even in the cities of India. While it would be wrong to say that Indian architecture is "lacking in totality", it would be more accurate to point out that Indian architecture is "rich in detail".

Geographical Divisions of Indian Architecture

The author may have wanted to introduce Indian architecture from the north to the south, but India is a vast country, from the snow-clad Himalayas in the north to the tropical south. The climate being entirely different, the architectural styles too are so varied, that a geographical classification may not be justified.

The regions could be listed alphabetically, but it will be easier if the buildings are classified geographically, according to regions. This kind of classification will also explain the difference in architecture.

A regional classification will also mean classification of states, because India is a multilingual country and people who speak a common language are concentrated in one region. These regions have been demarcated as states. For example, the meaning of Tamil Nadu is the 'country where the Tamil language is spoken'. Since people who speak a common language also share the same history and culture, as far as an architectural analysis goes, this is a relevant classification.

Further, since there are a large number of states, they have been classified under 5 groups, North, South, East, West and Central. In states sharing a common border, it may be difficult to distinguish the difference in architectural styles. This way the differences are very clearly demarcated in the 5 groups.

The Northern Group includes the regions of Kashmir and Ladakh, states of Himachal Pradesh, Punjab, Uttar Pradesh and Delhi.

Sikkim, Bihar, West Bengal, Orissa and Bangladesh form the second group. When India gained independence, it was partitioned into India, which has a majority Hindu population, and East and West Pakistan, which have a majority Muslim population. Eventually East Pakistan separated from West Pakistan and became an independent country, Bangladesh.

In this book, Bangladesh is considered an indivisible part of Bengal and has therefore been included here. It is desirable that most people travel to Bangladesh too, because Indian architecture is really the architecture of the Indian sub-continent. In this group, the temples of the Middle Ages in Orissa, and the terracotta temples of the early modern age in Bengal, are most conspicuous.

The third group consists of Rajasthan and Gujarat. Jain temples and mountain temple towns especially temples in Mount Abu and Ranakpur; the mosques in Ahmedabad, which show a local style of Islamic architecture; the magnificent palaces and castles of the Rajputs from the early modern age, are all represented here.

The fourth group,includes Madhya Pradesh, Maharashtra and the small state of Goa. The famous cave temples of Ajanta and Ellora will astonish tourists. There is a lot of cave architecture in the world, but nothing that can be compared with the cave temples in India. At the northern end are the stately structures of the Hindu temples of Khajuraho and at the southern end are the Christian churches in Goa.

The fifth group consists of the Dravidian states of Andhra Pradesh, Karnataka, Kerala and Tamil Nadu. In the north is Bijapur with its Muslim architecture. In Karnataka, during the Middle Ages, temple building has shown its original development in the architecture of the Hoysala period. Kerala has wooden structures in the unique style of the west coast.

Classification of Indian Architecture through the Ages

Before we introduce Indian architecture, let us take a look at the history of India. Although, in this book, Indian history has been broadly classified into Ancient Times, Middle Ages and Modern Age, it is not defined as clearly as is European history. With European architecture, historical terminology has been used, making it easier to conjure a mental image. The objective of this book is not to classify Indian history, but to view it from different methods of construction used over the ages.

Ancient Times

Indian civilization begins with the Indus civilization that dates back about 4000 years. The famous cities of Harappa and Mohenjadaro are now in Pakistan, while the ruins of Lothal are in India. Aryans from the west settled in India and developed "Vedic" literature as part of the Brahman religion. These became the Holy Books of the religion, which later came to be known as Hinduism.

During the 5th-6th centuries BC, Gautama Siddharta became Buddha and started Buddhism and Vardhamana became Mahavira and started Jainism. Buddhism had the support of the royal class and was adopted by the masses. As Buddhism spread across the country, so did its monasteries and temples. As Hinduism re-established itself strongly, the Buddhist presence disappeared from India in the 13th century.

Cave temples typically represent the architecture of Ancient Times. Naturally there must have been castles, palaces and houses during that time, but none of those remain, because buildings constructed of wood, rotted or burned easily. Temples were built of bricks, but when Buddhism died out, these were destroyed or pulled down due to a lack of protectors. However, cave temples and monasteries still exist today because they were carved out of rock - a much stronger material. There are around 1,200 such cave temples and monasteries left and 75 per cent of them belong to Buddhism.

Middle Ages

As they were not satisfied with cave temples, entire sculpted rock temples were built during the Middle Ages. A few still exist unto the present day. In contrast to the rock temples that imitated wooden temples of ancient times, the stone temples, built by laying cut stones one on top of another, came to be the model of sculpted stone construction.

But since these developed together, there is no line dividing the ages in terms of centuries. Construction of stone temples commenced in the 5th century, during the Gupta dynasty, but was standardized only during the 8th century. Many stone temples were built between the 7th and 9th centuries, but the temples carved out of rocks were constructed up till the 12th century. Hence according to the history of architecture, the transition from ancient times to the Middle Ages took many centuries.

Buddhism took the lead in construction during ancient times and in contrast, Hinduism took the lead during the Middle Ages followed by Jainism. The method of stone construction improved by leaps and bounds in north and south India. The style caught on and very soon the whole of India was filled with stone structures.

The Chandella dynasty in the north and the Chola dynasty in the south showed remarkable developments in architecture, by building magnificent temples, using stone. Islam entered India during the 11th century and established power in Delhi during the 13th century. Till the 16th century, the Turkish and Afghan dynasties continued to rule Delhi during a period referred to as the "Delhi Sultanate". Western styles of architecture, including techniques like domes were brought to India during this age and had a strong influence on building styles. This period called the Middle Ages, and the advent of the Mughals who conquered most of India, signalled the beginning of the Modern Age.

Modern Age
Mughal rule spread into more than half the sub-continent and the splendid Mughal style, which is a mix of the Indo-Islamic construction style, also blossomed. At that time, the Vijayanagara kingdom, which is predominantly Hindu, flourished in south India. At the same time, the Nayaks who were also Hindus ruled over some areas in the south. Both these dynasties appreciated technical developments with the main themes being large-scale construction, complex expressions and elaborate decorations. This phase is called the Modern Age. Emperor Akbar's Hindu-Islamic fusion in north India and the lavish Dravidian style of construction in the south are remarkable styles of this age.

Modern Age Indian architecture also includes the British era in India, until its Independence in 1947. British rule coincided with the decline of the Mughal era and the revival of Hinduism. The construction during this time was an adaptation of the Indian style in the colonial style brought from Europe. The direct impact of British architecture was seen from the second half of the 19th century, when research on Indian architectural history advanced and the Mughal style influenced colonial constructions. It is referred to as the Indo-Saracenic style.

The Present
As we plunge into the age of Modernism (post-Indian Independence), we have to say that architectural styles differed largely until then. A major influence on Indian architecture, post-Independence, was that of French architect, Le Corbusier, who designed Chandigarh and various buildings in Ahmedabad. Indian architects, educated in Europe and America also made a mark, but trying to transplant the architecture of Europe and America that was very different in history and style had its own problems. It is only right to call modern architecture "Cosmopolitan architecture".

The 600-odd buildings in the book, are grouped together according to their similarities. To enable the traveller to decide which place to visit, the buildings are given a star rating, from 0 to 3. The rating is based on the fascinating quality of the building. If a building has archaeological importance, but is in ruins, then it is given a low rating. Ratings are also given from 1 to 3, with regards to the region, the importance or number of buildings, natural scenery, etc. This is done as a subjective measure to help the traveller use this as a yardstick while planning his journey.

Publisher's Note

As a student of architecture in the 70's, I had a dream of doing documentation on the lines of this book. The thought of travelling around each and every part of India seemed so challenging and romantic, and the task so worthy. I would astonish the world with the amazing diversity of the architecture of my country. On beginning an architectural practice, this dream did not seem at all feasible but on each personal discovery of an architectural marvel, I invariably felt a sense of guilt.

Then in 2000 on a visit to Tokyo for the **East Wind Conference**, I was gifted the Japanese version of this marvellous book. The English version did not exist and shockingly there were no plans to bring one out. I begged, cajoled and finally succeeded through a letter campaign where K.T. Ravindran, P. R. Mehta and Amita Baig wrote to TOTO (the Japanese publishers) on the importance of bringing out the book in India.

This book deals with the monuments of the subcontinent, but the discussion must begin at a lower plane. Vernacular Architecture is our starting point and is similar to the flora and fauna of a region. It springs from the ground like the wild flowers, perfect in its use of material, siting and taming of the weather. It also embodies the local lifestyle and its process of evolution is completely unconscious.

However, when it came to building the monuments of a place - the religious buildings, palaces, tombs and civil structures, the Master Builder stepped in. These buildings were large and meant to impress, often symbolizing a particular faith or way of life. Unlike Vernacular Architecture, materials and craftsmen could be brought from a distance and of course ideas could come from as far as man had travelled. But often enough the inspiration was local and from the vernacular. For example, the shape of a haystack could inspire the crest of a temple.

Leaf through the book and marvel at the variety on display. It does not appear to come from a single country or lineage, but it can be argued that India is a vast country with a startlingly diverse geography, consisting of the Himalayas, high altitude deserts, rain forests and other more common features (only by Indian standards). But this only partly explains the variety.

India (unlike China) has rarely been a centrally ruled country. Moreover she has many religions and cultures co-existing and competing. It is this plurality, which greatly contributes to the excellence and variety on display. But there is also the genius of the Indian Master Builder whose approach to design was different. Unlike the Western architect who approached the subject from a total conception and moved down to the details, the Indian temple designer moved from both ends, simultaneously. The details playing a major role, affected the final outcome in a most startling way, creating monuments of great beauty and uniqueness. One impetus must have been the greatest tradition of Rock Cut Architecture on this earth, which trained his mind to think in a completely different dimension.

Strangely enough the greatest flowering of Islamic Architecture is in India. Though their main thrust was Islamic, they evolved in a completely different way from their place of origin, as they were interwoven with local Hindu traditions of the time. I believe it is these qualities which lured Takeo Kamiya to return each year over a 20-year period to complete this great documentation. Motivation and consistency of this quality is rare and it pleases me immensely that the Indian Institute of Architects has decided to honour him.

This book means a lot to me. To begin with it is a clarion call for all of us who have a stake in the preservation of our Architectural Heritage. These monuments are under great threat from the forces of "development" and commercialization and a complete absence of sensitivity. It is our duty to put into place sensible management plans for all these monuments.

Unfortunately, the forces of globalization have reduced architecture to a universal product. One cannot tell anymore where one is, by the buildings we see around us and there is sameness, which is creeping in. The variety in this book should be an inspiration for us architects to create more sympathetic and distinctive architecture. It would be a Modern Architecture no doubt; but one which reflects the spirit, climate and resources of a place.

I have a request to make to all the users of this book. It has been 26 years since the research of this book began and obviously aspects of the infrastructure of a place have changed. I'd really be grateful for feedback on this, so that the next edition can be corrected.

This English Edition would not have been possible without my collaborator and patroness of the Arts, Sangita Jindal. I must also thank Shri Jagmohan, Honourable Minister of Tourism and Culture and Ms. Rathi Vinay Jha and Mr. Amitabh Kant of the Ministry of Tourism. A special thanks to our amazing editor Annabel Lopez, who fortunately for me has supported all my quixotic projects.

Gerard da Cunha
archauto@sancharnet.in

Postscript:
This revised edition of *The Guide to the Architecture of the Indian Sub-continent*, has been made available through the painstaking efforts of Professor M A Dhaky, Director (Emiritus), American Institute of Indian Studies, Art and Archaeology, Gurgaon and Bevinda Collaco journalist and media consultant, who has edited the revised version. This book now has a dedicated website and can be accessed at **http://www.indoarch.org** books can also be ordered on-line.

JAMMU & KASHMIR

BUNIYAR
SRINAGAR
AVANTIPUR
MARTAND
PAYAR
ACHHABAL
VERINAG

TEMISGAN RIZONG
LIKIR
PHYANG
LAMAYURU LEH
ALCHI SHEY
SASPOL TIKSE
STOK CHEMRE
HEMIS

JAMMU
CHAMBA
BHARMAUR
HIMACHAL PRADESH
BAIJNATH MANALI
MASRUR NAGAR
KHOKHAN DIYAR
BAJAURA
SARAHAN (North) SUNGRA
RAMPUR
SHIMLA KAMRU
MANAN
PINJORE BALAG
HATKOTI
KHADARAN
SAINJ
SARAHAN (South)

Pakistan

AMRITSAR
Lahore

PUNJAB

CHANDIGARH

HARYANA

DELHI
DELHI

Alwar

BRINDAVAN
SIKANDRA
FATEHPUR SIKRI AGRA

West India
Jaipur

Gwalior

Jhansi

N

0   200km

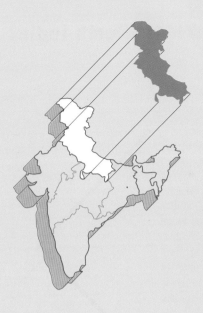

North India

China

Nepal

• Kathmandu

UTTAR PRADESH

50 LUCKNOW

JAUNPUR 51
53 SARNATH
ALLAHABAD 52 VARANASI 54

• Khajuraho

• Patna

Gaya •

East India

Middle India

TRAVEL INFORMATION (North India)

DELHI

New Delhi, the capital of India, has direct flights from Europe, Asia and the Gulf, so it is convenient as the starting point or the final destination of one's tour. Besides high-budget hotels, low-budget ones like Hotel Central Point, are also available. Reservations for these may not be made outside India, but the information counter at Delhi airport helps with hotels for various budgets and also with reservations. Visitors are advised to be cautious and deal only with authorised agents.

Connaught Place, the core business district, is convenient for shopping; also many airlines have their offices located here. There is a reservation counter inside Jeevan Bharati. One can make reservations for travel within the country at the Indian Airlines office, nearby. Galgotia Bookshop and the New Book Depot, stock books on architecture. Archaeological Survey of India's publications are on sale at the counter inside the National Museum. The bookshop will freight the books you buy, to your address back home, for a fee. Janpath Street has the offices of the Survey of India that sells maps of the region.

Delhi is historically, a very important city. One can sight-see in a taxi or by auto rickshaw. It is sometimes difficult however, to get transport to Delhi or New Delhi station to catch the night train. If you do get a taxi, be prepared to pay an exorbitant rate.

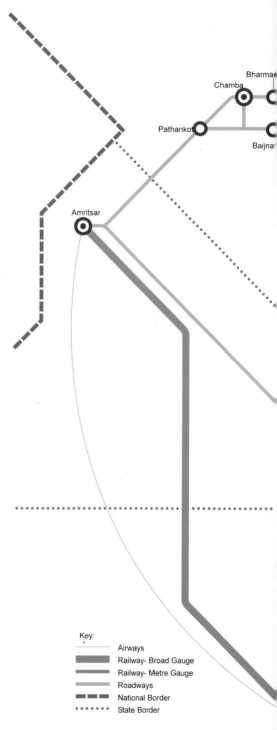

Hotel Centre Point

Key:
- Airways
- Railway- Broad Gauge
- Railway- Metre Gauge
- Roadways
- National Border
- State Border

Manali

Nagar

Kullu

Mandi

Sarahan (North)   Sungra

Rampur   Kamru

Shimla

Hatkoti

Chandigarh

Sarahan (South)

Delhi

PUNJAB

Chandigarh and Amritsar are two cities which are accessible by air and rail. Chandigarh is 3 hours from Delhi by the Shatabdi Express while Amritsar is five-and-a-half hours away. Express buses ply between the two cities.

Amritsar International is a good hotel, while in Chandigarh, hotels near Piccadilly are recommended. Foreigners are not allowed entry into Le Corbusier's Capitol complex.

HIMACHAL PRADESH

Girls in Nichiar

Broad gauge trains ply from Kalka. They are metre-gauge from Kalka to Shimla. One can also fly to Shimla which is five hours by road from Chandigarh and seven hours from Rampur. A taxi from Rampur to Sarahan takes one-and-a-half hours. It is advisable to stay at Hotel Shrikhand, near Bhima Kali Temple. One can hire a van to visit Kamru, Hatkoti and south Sarahan. Manali, is ten and a half hours by road from Shimla. Reservations for the Castle Hotel at Nagar, can be made at the tourist office in Kullu. Chamba in the west, is five hours from Pathankot, while Pathankot to Amritsar is a three-hour trip. Bharmaur is accessible by bus from Chamba, but a taxi is safer and a one-way ride takes three-and-a-half hours. While in Chamba, Hotel Irawati is a good place to stay at. A convenient midway halt for the above destinations is Mandi or Kullu. Take a bus or a taxi to the temples.

TRAVEL INFORMATION (North India)

KASHMIR

When Kashmir became a disputed territory in the 1980s, entry for foreigners into the area has been periodically banned. Visit Kashmir at any time of the year, except winters. Kashmir's climate is cooler than that of the rest of India and therefore the hot Indian summers (April-May) is peak season here. Kashmir has had negligible tourist traffic due to the turmoil. The army has taken up most of the hotels, but tourists can stay in the houseboats on Dal Lake. Staying in one of the deluxe houseboats is a rare and remarkable experience.

After negotiating the price at the taxi-stand, you can arrange for a daily taxi pick-up and visit the gardens and ruins of Kashmir. It is pleasant to have lunch surrounded by all the greenery with the sound of running water, so a packed lunch would be a good idea.

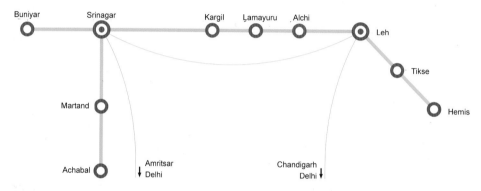

Green valleys offset by snow-clad mountains.

The mask dance at the Buddhist monastery.

LADAKH

The bus journey from Srinagar to Ladakh takes two days. The mountain passes are sealed off in winter so buses ply only between June and October. Ladakh can also be accessed by air, but be careful about altitude sickness, when flying in.

When in Ladakh, stay in Leh and perhaps one night in Kargil. Ga-Ldan Continental, in Leh is a good, simple hotel. The *gompas* (monasteries) can be visited every day by hiring a taxi from the taxi stand, for an agreed upon price. The rates are higher than in the plains as one has no bargaining power here. You are allowed inside the *gompas* for a fee but there is no charge for photography. All the monasteries can be seen in a day's trip, except for Lamayaru, for which a halt at Alchi, is essential. The only accommodation here is one of two inns standing adjacent to each other. It is better to stock up on food and water in Leh. If travelling by taxi from Srinagar, one can stop *en route* at Murbek. It is then possible to visit Lamayaru and stay overnight at Alchi; an expensive option, as it takes three nights to reach Leh. Drivers can also be hired in Kargil, but they will need the required travel permit.

AGRA

The Shatabdi Express runs from Delhi to Agra and back, on a day's trip. If on an architectural tour, stay in Agra or Sikandra for two days, then take in Fatehpur Sikri on the third day.

Agra has a number of starred hotels. Grand Hotel, which is medium budget, is fairly good. Autos provide for comfortable transportation so it is better to engage one for the entire day. Visit Fatehpur Sikri by taxi, but if one wishes to merely go there and back, take a bus. Meals in Fatehpur Sikri are available near Buland Gate. The Delhi-Agra-Jaipur triangle is connected by rail and bus routes. For Brindavan, take the bus to Mathura, (1 hour 30 minutes) and then return in a taxi, after visiting the museum.

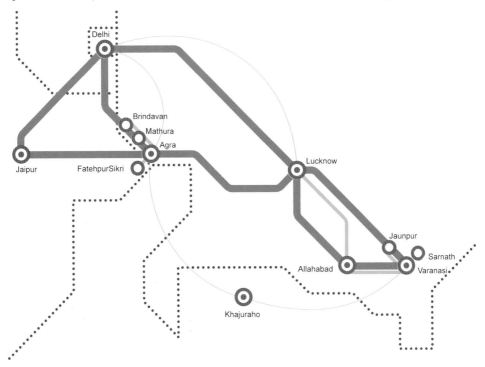

An idyllic sunset.

VARANASI

If you have a tight schedule, take the air-route, Delhi-Agra-Khajuraho-Varanasi. The Shatabdi Express from Delhi takes 6 hours, or one can fly to Lucknow and take the five hour bus/train journey to Allahabad. The Allahabad-Varanasi leg is 3 hours. Taking the overnight train from Lucknow saves time. A good choice of hotels is Hotel Gomti in Lucknow, President Hotel in Allahabad and the luxury hotel Clarks Varanasi, or the tourist bungalow in Varanasi. Both, are some distance away from the *ghats*. Sarnath, in the northern outskirts of the city is accessible by auto. You can go to Jaunpur by bus or taxi and return on the same day.

JAMMU & KASHMIR

The author has chosen to introduce Indian architecture from the geographic north of the country to the south, for the sake of convenience. The state of Jammu and Kashmir, India's northernmost state, has been taken up first. Two former kingdoms of Jammu and Kashmir were clubbed together to form this state. Srinagar in Kashmir, is the state's summer capital, while in winter the capital shifts to Jammu.

The valley of Kashmir is at a height of 1500 m, while the Himalayas tower to 8000 m. Kashmir enjoys a very cool climate in contrast to the sub-tropical climate of the rest of India. Blessed with greenery, it is one of the major summer resorts of India and is still referred to as, 'Paradise on Earth'.

Kashmir is noted for its wooden architecture. Here we are not referring to the architecture of the entire state of Jammu and Kashmir, but just Kashmir. Jammu, though attached to Kashmir to form a single state, is quite different in architectural character.

Ladakh is 3500 m above sea level. Leh is at 3520 m. The average height of the trans-Himalayas is 5000 m. Though a part of Kashmir, Ladakh is an entirely different region in terms of religion and culture. It has many similarities to Tibetan culture and is often known as 'Little Tibet'. In fact authentic Tibetan culture is seen more commonly in Ladakh, than in Tibet. After Tibet was annexed by China, Tibetan Buddhism commonly known as 'the Lama religion', was at odds with the communist principles of China. The Dalai Lama, spiritual leader of the Buddhists, fled Tibet and took refuge in Dharamsala in India in 1959.

Jammu and Kashmir shares its border with China, Pakistan and Afghanistan and hence is the cause of Indo-China and Indo-Pak border strife. Today, due to the political tensions in this region, whenever hostilities erupt, travel to the area is restricted.

❶ Lamayuru *Gompa*: A Buddhist monastery on a bleak Ladakh mountainside.
❷ A *mandapa* in the Alchi *Gompa*. A style of drawing which has its roots in India.
❸ Nishat Bagh, a Mughal garden in Kashmir.

An example of the classical Islamic architecture of Kashmir. Dastagir Sahib Tomb and Mosque.

Wangat

Paraspora

Ushkar

4 Buniyar

Pattan

Srinagar **1**

Dal Lake

Amarnath

Lodruva
Loduv

Payar
5

3 Avantipur

2 Martand

6 Achabal

7

Verinag

Jammu

KASHMIR

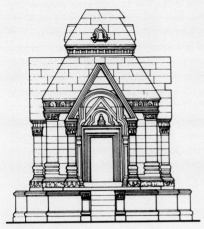

Elevation of the Pandrethan Temple, outside Srinagar(10th century)

Kashmir has seen an amalgamation of various cultures. The Buddhist culture flourished during the 3rd century BC when Emperor Ashoka reigned over India and Kashmir came under his rule. Kashmir is dotted with Buddhist ruins that belong to this age, but most of them are foundations of structures and there is no way of knowing what the buildings looked like.

Alexander introduced the Hellenic culture, during the 4th century BC. Gandhara region now in north Pakistan has Buddhist sculptures where Hellenic influences can be seen. Perhaps Hellenic culture also influenced the architecture of that time. Glimpses of it can be seen in temples built during the Hindu era, especially in the corridors surrounding the Hindu temples of Buniyar and Martand. Stone structures developed during the Hindu age. The roofs during this era differed from the roofs in the plains. Since Kashmir gets a lot of rain and snow, the roofs slope in a steep incline that makes them look like spires.

Islam spread during the 14th century and a large number of mosques were built. They are atypical in that they were built of wood with a spire covering them, instead of a dome. Wooden mosques are not seen anywhere else in India, except in Kashmir and Kerala. This is because Muslims adopted the traditional architectural style used for Hindu temples even though they changed the construction material. Another characteristic feature of that era is the gardens. Akbar conquered Kashmir in 1588 and floating gardens and river palaces were built for him. Jehangir (1605-27) captivated by Kashmir's beauty planted Chenar trees and built pleasure gardens.

Tourist sights in Kashmir are concentrated in and around Srinagar as the rest of Kashmir is largely mountainous terrain. One can now fly into Srinagar from Delhi or Jammu, but in the past the journey had to be made by horse-cart from Rawalpindi and could take an indefinite number of days. Chuta Ito wrote his impressions after reaching Kashmir. "Here I could get my first ever panoramic view of Kashmir. This is the first time I had ever seen such a vast landscape in its entirety. It looks like I have left this earth and entered Heaven." Since the 90's, this paradise has been witness to a great deal of turmoil due to insurgency and terrorism and the situation seems to be deteriorating. As a result, the numbers of tourists in the area have dwindled. Travel to this region has become very difficult and dangerous, but on the other hand, there's the definite benefit of enjoying the quiet serenity of Kashmir with no tourists around.

SRINAGAR ★ ★ ★

TOWN, DAL LAKE AND HOUSEBOATS

Srinagar on the edge of Dal Lake is Kashmir's most important town. Greenery in summer, snow in winter and the crystal clear lake are unforgettable sights. Some houseboats on Dal Lake are regular residences, while others are quaint hotels for tourists. Delicate arabesque patterns adorn the exteriors. The houseboats used as hotels, have a wide living-room, dining-room and three or four bedrooms with bathrooms attached. Meals are usually prepared by a housekeeper. An early morning riser is refreshed by the gentle, cool breeze blowing over the water. The morning sunshine sparkling on the lake and the mountains, makes the landscape look like an exquisite painting.

There is a network of roads besides which, the Jhelum River is also used as a transportation network, with people moving around in tiny boats called *shikaras*. There were nine wooden bridges over the Jhelum River but some were destroyed during the years of strife. Even mosques and houses are made of wood. Wooden houses four to five storeys high, like those in northern Europe, are seen crowded together; a rare sight, even in the plains.

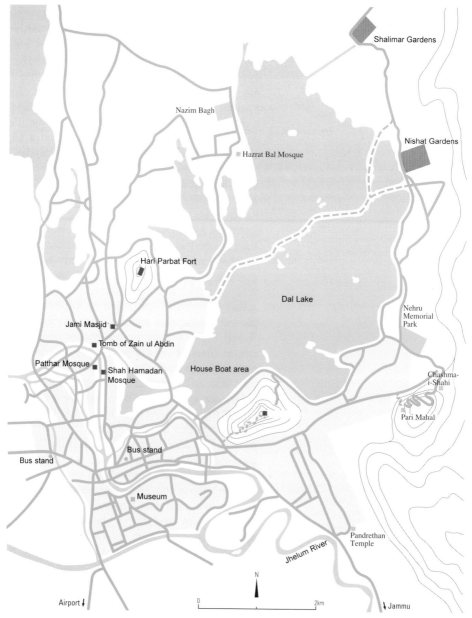

❶ Hari Parbat fort constructed by Akbar in 1588.
❷ Houseboats and the city from Shankaracharya Hill.
❸ The new wooden bridge built on the Jhelum River, with a row of houses in the background.
❹ Partial wooden houses built over stone and brickwork.
❺ Small houseboats that ply up and down the lake.
❻ People living in the row of houses use both, the roadways and waterways for transport.
❼ The bedroom in a houseboat.
❽ Gorgeous houseboats used as hotels for tourists are kept anchored in one place.
❾ The deck of a houseboat adorned with magnificent woodcarvings in the traditional style.

JAMI MASJID (FRIDAY MOSQUE) ★★★
1674/ Islam

Masjid is an Arabic word for mosque, in Spanish it is *maskita* and became *mosque* in French and English. *Jami* is a mosque for a larger gathering. It is also called *Jum'a* or *Jumma,* which means Friday mosque. Just as there is only one cathedral in each diocese in the Christian context, it was fundamental that there be only one *Jami* in each town. When the faithful collect for prayers and the capacity of the prayer hall is insufficient, believers overflow into the courtyard. There is no single space demarcated for prayers in a mosque.

The Jami Masjid is the most magnificent and fascinating of all wooden mosques in Kashmir. Originally built of wood in 1385 by Sultan Sikander Butshikan, it was destroyed in a fire some time later. It was rebuilt and this time the exterior walls were made of brick. The present mosque was built in 1674 and belongs to the era when Aurangazeb was emperor.

To the west of the courtyard, is an arched entrance called *iwan,* or *liwan* in Western India, built in the traditional style. This *iwan* faces Mecca and has a prayer room inside. However,

The minaret of the Jami Masjid.

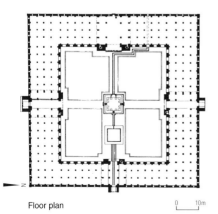

Floor plan

0   10m

it is not a Persian *iwan* but a cube with a pyramid roof. This style has been adopted from the Hindu temples in Kashmir. The spire acts as a minaret calling the faithful to assemble for prayers. The other three *iwans* are just simple entrances allowing access into the courtyard.

Inside the building is an imposing hall, which has pillars made from the trunks of 300 Himalayan cedars. Originally there must have been intricate carvings on the pillars. Thick laminated boards suspended across a huge span add an interesting architectural touch.

❶ The wall and entrance on the southern side.
❷ The courtyard and the *iwan* facing Mecca.
❸ The southern tower that also acts as the minaret.

31

❶ The interior of the prayer room.
❷ Wooden trabeated structure.
❸ A pair of wooden pillars.
❹ The prayer hall and the *Mihrab* in the central hall.
❺ A view of the ceiling in the central hall.

SHAH HAMADAN MOSQUE ★★
18th C/ Islamic

The first mosque which was built in 1395, was burned down twice, once in 1479 and then in 1731. The present mosque is an independent hall-like structure, very different from the courtyard type of mosque. The sculptured effect of this mosque when seen from the banks of the Jhelum is magnificent. Though the basic shape is a cube, it is still a Sufi (monastery). The interior has rich colours and the technique used is an art form called *papier-mâché*.

❶ A view from the banks of the Jhelum River.
❷ Later additions to the façade are very easily distinguishable.
❸ The interior of the prayer room.
❹ Colourful *papier-mâché* adorns the pillars and the ceiling.Trunks of trees are made into pillars.
❺ Walls and windows are made of wood.

SHALIMAR BAGH (GARDEN) ★★★
Around 1616/ Islamic

Mughal emperors habitually spent summers in Kashmir to escape from the intense heat of Delhi. A number of gardens which face Dal Lake and some on the other side of the lake still exist. Shalimar Garden, developed by Jehangir and later by his son Shahjahan, is the epitome of Islamic garden design brought to India by Babur. The linear water channel, formed by diverting the water from the mountain to the lake, is the central axis in this symmetrical garden. The row of square gardens are connected by canals with pavilions built over them. Seated in these pavilions, surrounded by lush greenery, lulled by the sound of flowing water, *chaddars* or waterfalls and fountains, it is easy to imagine that this is the 'Paradise in Heaven' described in the Koran.

A *zenana* (segregated area for women) at the far end of the garden built by Shahjahan, has a pavilion of black marble.

This pavilion also doubles as the *Diwan-i-Khas* where Mughal emperors gave private audience.

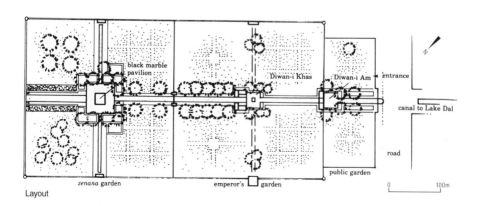

Layout

❶ The entrance to Shalimar Gardens.
❷ *Diwan-i-Khas* at the end of a sycamore tree-lined avenue.
❸ The pillars surrounding this pavilion are of black marble. The roof of the pavilion was constructed at a later date.
❹ Small pavilion which is the entrance to the *zenana*.
❺ A fountain seen through the black marble pavilion.
❻ Interior of the black marble pavilion.
❼ The water-channel running through the *Diwan-i-Khas*.
❽ Roof of the *Diwan-i-Khas* made of colourful *papier-mâché*.
❾ Waterfalls have been created using steps. Flowers and candles were kept in the niche behind the waterfalls.

NISHAT BAGH (GARDEN) ★★
1632/ Islamic

Nishat Bagh, built by Asaf Khan, elder brother of Empress Nur Jahan, is a symmetrical garden where the central axis is emphasized more than in square gardens. The step incorporated on either side of the central axis is reminiscent of the terraced gardens of the Italian Renaissance period. While Italian gardens were built as descending gardens, this garden has been built as an ascending garden. Earlier, this fairly large garden could only be approached by boat from the lake. Today unfortunately the pavilions are broken and weeds cover the waterways.

Up: A stone seat and *chaddar* (waterfall)
Middle: A view from the centre of a sloping terrace.
Down: A lookout tower at the top of the garden.

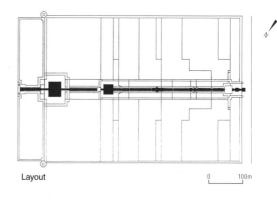

Layout

0   100m

SHANKARACHARYA TEMPLE
Around 8th C/ Hindu

This small temple sits on the summit of a hill approximately 90 m south of Dal Lake. This limestone temple has an octagonal terrace surrounding it, which could have been a corridor. The top of the temple which must have had a stone steeple is broken. It is said that this temple was originally a Buddhist temple.

Right: The top of the temple is closed.
Left: The entrance is up a flight of stairs.

TOMB OF ZAIN-UL-ABDIN
Around 1430/ Islamic

The Persian style tomb of Zain al Abidin's mother, was built of brick. It appears from the walls that this tomb was decorated with colourful glazed tiles. The Hindu style corridor in the precincts, indicates that the tomb could have been built on the foundations of a destroyed temple.

View of the tomb from the south.

PATTHAR MASJID ★
1623/ Islamic

After Kashmir was taken over by the Mughals, mosques were built everywhere. Stone construction received a new lease of life and Patthar Masjid, (Stone Mosque) was built with grey sandstone by Empress Nur Jahan. A departure from the traditional Kashmiri style, this mosque does not belong to this region.

Right: The central *iwan*.
Left: The interior of the prayer room.

SURYA TEMPLE ★★
750/ Hindu

Ruins of this temple dedicated to the Sun God (*Surya/Martanda*) worshipped since Rig Vedic times, lie in a valley 60 km southeast of Srinagar. Built by King Lalitaditya (Karkotaka dynasty) the 60 m x 80 m precinct is encircled by pillars and small halls. There is a tank in the temple complex and a room in front of the sacred room has features found only in temples constructed much later. In Kashmiri temples, the entrance is to the west and the *sanctum sanctorum* is to the east. On the *sanctum sanctorum* and other halls, a gabled roof crowns a 3-petal arch. The Hellenic style brought to India by Alexander was incorporated along with Gandhara sculptures thereby lending a unique character to Hindu temples.

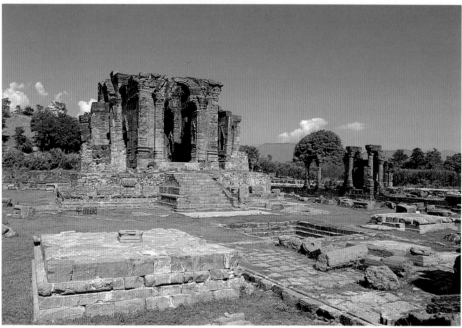

Full view of the temple precincts with the tank in the foreground.

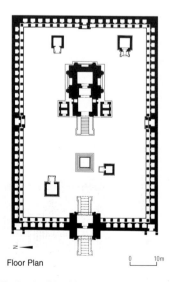

Floor Plan

0   10m

❶ The façade of the cloisters and small rooms.
❷ A close-up of a pillar in the cloister.
❸ Sculptures of deities in the main precincts.

AVANTISVAMIN AND AVANTISVARA TEMPLES
9th C/ Hindu

Avantivarman, capital of the Utpala Dynasty, boasts of two temples on the route to Martand from Srinagar. Only the foundation platform, surrounding walls and the lower part of the entrance of the two temples still exist. Although very similar in design to the temple of Martand, these temples are simple, with no front shrine. A striking feature here is the importance given to the entrance, which is the same as that given to a main shrine.

UP: A view of the Avantisvamin Temple.
DOWN: The entrance to the Avantisvamin Temple.

Source of image - P. Brown

VISHNU TEMPLE ✶
Around 900 AD/ Hindu

The best preserved temple in Kashmir, is situated 80 km west of Srinagar along the Jhelum River. Built with granite and on a small scale, most of the temple remains intact, except for the pyramid roof. Pillars surrounding the temple are very well preserved. Looking at this temple, one cannot help feeling that one is looking at ruins in Greece.

Right: Façade of temple with rooms and cloister.
Left: The front façade of the main shrine.

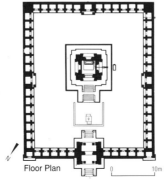

Floor Plan   0   10m

Part elevation of the temple.

PAYAR ⋆

SHIVA TEMPLE ⋆
11th C/ Hindu

Located in a village square, 20 km west of Avantipur, this temple dedicated to the *Shiva Lingam* is a quaint miniature of the Kashmiri style of construction.

All four sides of this serene shrine are open, with a gabled roof over each of the four entrances. The Hellenic style, on the cornice of the roof combined with sculptures of Hindu deities on the tympanum of the three-petal arch, presents an interesting effect.

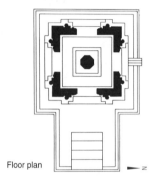

Floor plan

View of the temple from the rear.

ACHHABAL ⋆

BEGMABAD BAGH (GARDEN) ⋆
1640/ Islamic

Situated on the old highway between Anantnag and Verinag, is Begmabad Bagh, which acquired the name as it was built by the Empress Nur Jahan. Till today natural spring water runs in the fountains and canals. The profusion of sycamore trees in this Mughal garden, gives it a lively appearance. The original pavilion was destroyed and the existing one was built at a later date.

Right: Pavilions with water channels passing through.
Left: Waterfalls, fountains and *chaddar*s, in a continuous flow of water.

VERINAG ★

NILA NAG BAGH (GARDEN)
1620/ Islamic

Nila Nag Bagh was built by Jehangir, and later by his son Shah Jahan. A large water source is enclosed by an octagonal, pillared structure and water channels flow into a mountain rivulet in the valley. This small square garden is surrounded by mountains. Sycamores, poplars, lawns and flower beds, make this a pleasant and serene garden.

Colonnade surrounding the water source.

JAMMU ★

RAGHUNATH MANDIR
1857/ Hindu

Located right in the heart of Jammu town is Raghunatha Mandir, dedicated to Rama. It was built by the feudal Lord, Ranbir Singh. Each of the seven small shrines has their own four-point *shikhara*. As it is a fairly new temple, it is not very heavily embellished and the fading paint on it reminds one of the Byzantine abbeys in Russia.

❶ The pathway with the small shrines in a row.
❷ The gold plated *shikhara* of the main building.
❸ The temple reminiscent of a Byzantine abbey in Russia.

JAMMU

ANNEX OF THE NEW PALACE
Early 20th C/ Colonial

Amar Mahal (new palace) is located near Hotel Jammu Ashoka, a short distance from the old palace. A fascinating structure, irregular in plan, it has gabled roofs, projecting in many directions and a colonnade made of wood, on the lower floor.

LADAKH

Known as 'Little Tibet', Ladakh, part of the northernmost state of India is situated 3000-4000 m above sea level. Leh, the hub of Ladakh is as high as 3520 m. Ladakh's landscape is as bleak as a desert. Because of its altitude, Ladakh gets hardly any rainfall and hence has neither trees nor a blade of grass growing on the slopes of the rocky, Himalayan terrain. Flowing majestically between the mountains is a tributary of the Indus River. Water from melting snow collects at various places on the valley floor and small streams join the Indus River. While the slopes are barren, the valley where the Indus River flows is green.

In the valleys are villages where farms are visible as green tracts of land. This green stretch is so vivid against the bleak slopes that the place looks like Paradise. As the air clears, snow-capped mountains are visible in the distance and in the foreground are lambs grazing on the banks of streams. Regally overlooking all this from the top of the rocky mountains are the *gompas* (monasteries).

Entry into Ladakh was restricted because of the Indo-Chinese strife and it is only since 1974, that foreigners are being allowed into the region. Hotels are available only in Leh and the other regions do not have much by way of lodging.

Tourists are cautioned about altitude sickness. Flying in from Delhi or Srinagar is a time-saving option, but the sudden increase in altitude, causes altitude sickness. It is therefore advisable to relax in the hotel on the day of arrival. It is also possible to get to Leh by bus or taxi from Srinagar, which takes 2 days (1 night in Kargil). The natural scenery and architecture are splendid indeed. All the buildings including temples, have flat roofs as there is little rainfall. Like the climate, the main religion is also different from that of the rest of the country. Most of the people here are of Tibetan descent, though a few new residents are Muslim. Some of the temples and monasteries of Tibetan Buddhism, or, the 'Lama' religion, are quite exceptional.

❶ Wood, earth and willow houses of the Ladakh region.
❷ The murals on the walls inside Alchi Lhakhang Soma (new temple -13th century).
❸ Buddha statue on the rockface at Mulbekh, 8th-9th C.
❹ Goddess of Mercy in Sanka gompa, with 1000 hands.

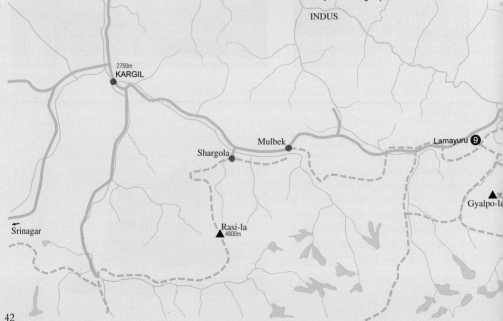

INDUS

2750m
KARGIL

Mulbek

Shargola

Lamayuru ❾

Gyalpo-la
39

Srinagar

Rasi-la
4800m

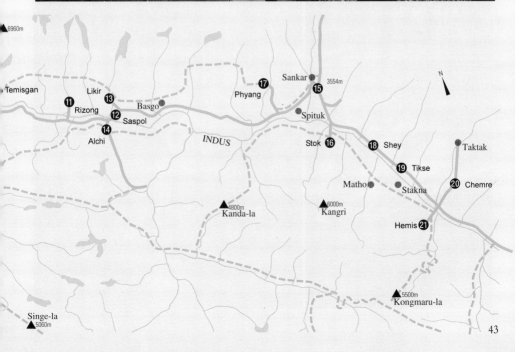

LAMAYURU ★★

GOMPA (MONASTERY) ★★
Around 11th C/ Buddhist

Ladakh situated 3000 m above sea level has a pitted, eroded landscape, resembling the surface of the moon. The noteworthy buildings in the region are monasteries. On approaching Ladakh from Srinagar, Lamayuru is the first monastery one encounters. It stands on bleak, rocky mountainous terrain, so typical of Ladakh.

At first sight, the monastery sprawled across the hill-side, appearing as large as a village, leaves one wonderstruck. The multi-storeyed structure with its *lhakhang* (temples), *dukhang* (assembly halls) and cells for the monks, is precariously perched on the steep slope. These buildings are built with a wooden framework, earthen walls and terraced roof piled with willow branches. According to the great sage, Naropa, *Sengge Sang*, the wooden 'Lion room' was built in the 11th C but the murals and pillars are new.

❶ Interior of the room with the Goddess of Mercy.
❷ The top part of the main building.
❸ Interior of the *Dukhang*.
❹ Pillar capital in the Lion room (Sengge Sang).

View of the gompa, 4,000 m above sea level, surrounded by mountains.

TEMISGAN ★

GOMPA (MONASTERY) ★
Around 16th C/ Buddhist

Temisgan village occupies a stretch of the riverbank, 5 km north of Nyurla on the road that connects Leh and Srinagar. The *gompa,* comprising three individual buildings on top of the mountains, was built during the 16th century. The most arresting of them is the small red building with the *Bodhisattva* enshrined within. *Avalokitesvara* is the Bodhisattva of compassion and *Tara* is the female form of Avalokitesvara and is depicted in 21 different forms.

Up: The *Bodhi Sattva* building on the mountain-top
Down: Porch of the *Padmasambhava* building, with a prayer wheel to the right.

RIDZONG ★★

11

GOMPA (MONASTERY) ★★
1840/ Buddhist

After 10 km on the road from Lamayuru to Saspol, a 30-minute trek reveals a monastery nestled between the mountains. Like the monastery of the Shinto group, the people living in the Rizong Gompa too are very isolated.

The large building on the steep slope houses more than a hundred monks. This well-planned structure, was built as late as the 19th century. White walls and brown windows give it a uniform appearance harmonized with nature. The building reminds one of modern terraced apartments.

The porch and the terrace of the *dukhang.*

Top: *Gompa* nestled between mountains. Down: Colourful Tenchun.

CAVE TEMPLES AND WALL PAINTINGS
13th-14th C/ Buddhist

While cave temples are scattered all over India, north India has very few. In Ladakh a cave temple can be found only in Saspol 65 km from Leh. Since the mountain is not rocky or firm, the cave is more like a natural cavern with pillar-and-beam or trabeated structure. The interiors of the cave have priceless murals of Mahayana Buddhism in very bright colours which are still very well preserved. Since the caves are too small to be prayer rooms (Chaitya caves), they may have been rooms for the monks to live in. Ruins of a castle still exist on the hilltop and the Chamba Gompa is in the village nearby. It is mandatory to engage a guide to tour this region.

❶ Group of caves below a line of white chortens.
❷ A mural in the second cave - Gautama Buddha and Tara the female Bodhisattva of Compassion.
❸ A mural in the 3rd cave - an image of Yabyum

GOMPA (MONASTERY) ⋆
11th C/ Buddhist

Likir Gompa rises on a hill 5 km north of Saspol on the highway. This gompa, established earlier than most others, is very highly revered and has hundreds of monks living in it. Formerly belonging to the Kargynd sect, they now belong to the Gelug-pa sect.

The complex comprising temples, assembly halls and monks' rooms, is not very old. The dukhang (assembly hall) is fascinating and faces a courtyard. Young monks guide visitors.

Right: Façade of the dukhang facing the courtyard.
Left: A distant view of the gompa.

GOMPA (MONASTERY) ★★★
11th-13th C/ Buddhist

Alchi monastery, (Rinchen Zangpo complex), lies in a village a short distance beyond the Indus River after Saspol. Unusually located in the plains and rather than on a hill, this perfect example of a Buddhist temple was protected from invasions and is very well preserved.

The five main spaces are *lhakhang Soma* (new room), *sumtsek* (3-storeyed room), *dukhang* (day room), *lotsawal lhakhang* (translation room) and *manjushri lhakhang* (room of the Buddhist saint of Wisdom). The *sumtsek* and *dukhang* belong to the the 11th-12th centuries and the others to the 13th century.

In the 9th century civil war broke out in Tibet, many *zamir* monks migrated to Ladakh and Tibetan Buddhism developed there. Rinchen Zangpo (958-1055 AD) translated the Buddhist scriptures and a room is dedicated to him.The *dukhang* where monks gather and recite sutras is the largest building with a pillared corridor, a front yard and a brightly coloured front door. The building dedicated to Dai Nichi Nyorai is called *Dai Nichi*. The *Lhakhang Soma* has a *chorten* in the centre and the four halls are filled with murals. There is a writing room where the *sutras* are studied and rooms for the monks. Alchi Gompa has a historic mural of the 11th century. One difference between Chinese and Indian Buddhist temples is that Indian temples do not have a master-plan, or a central axis.

A group of chortens in the village

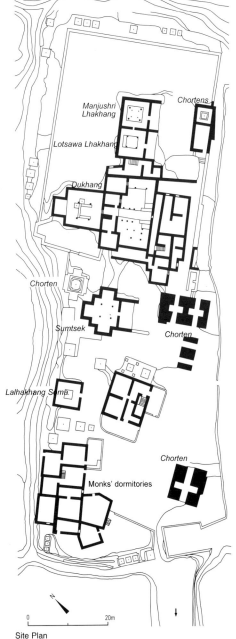
Site Plan

A distant view of the Alchi Gompa.

❶ Interior of the new shrine.
❷ Murals in the *Sumtsek*
❸ Murals in the new shrine
- the Buddha.
❹ The entrance to the shrine.
❺ The shrine dedicated to
Rinchen Zangpo.

SUMTSEK TEMPLE
11th C/ Buddhist ★★

As a rule, buildings in ancient India were built of wood. Sumtsek Temple built in the 11th century and still very much in use, is a perfect example of this architectural style. It reflects the delicate 'wooden' construction style that was used for temples in Kashmir. Glimpses of the Hellenic culture can be seen in Grecian carving, while the capitals of pillars are in the Ionic style. *Chortens* have been positioned in the middle of the square structure. The Sumtsek Temple has an atrium in the centre that rises up three levels. The skylight on top that lights up the interior is in the original style used in the construction of *gompas*.

The interior of the temple has walls covered with murals depicting *mandapas* and Buddhist motifs which demonstrate the religious ambience of the time.

The entrance to the three-storeyed temple.

❶ Wooden framework on the façade. ❷ Murals visible from the atrium. ❸ Head of Buddha seen only from the second level.

LEH ★ ★ ★

TOWN AND OLD PALACE
17th C/ Buddhist

Located on the banks of the river on a plateau amidst mountainous terrain is Ladakh's only city, Leh. Strategically situated, Leh was a prominent trading centre connecting Kashmir, Tibet and China. Leh Palace, a nine-storeyed structure was built during the 17th century by King Sengge Namgyal. Though the palace is now mostly in ruins, the prayer rooms and *gompa* inside reflect the accord with which religion and the government co-existed. The Potala Palace in Lhasa is built in the same architectural style as Leh Palace. The landscape around, dotted with houses with interior courtyards and almost no greenery looks like a desert. The town of Leh is sprawled on a slope, with houses similar to modern step-terrace apartments. Leh receives around 100 mm of rainfall and most of this is snow. As a result, all the houses have flat roofs. What gives accent to Leh, as you enter the city, are the white *chortens*. To the west of Leh town, located on a hilltop, is the white Shanti Stupa built in 1983 by the Japanese Myohouji sect.

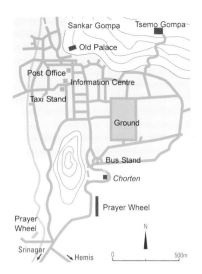

❶ Palace and *Tsemo gompa* overlooking Leh town. ❷ A *chorten* at the entrance to the Old Palace. ❸ Cluster of *chortens* at the southern entrance to Leh. ❹ *Tsemo gompa*, above the palace. ❺ Woodwork at the entrance of the Old Palace. ❻ Prayer wheel. ❼ Terraced houses, clinging to the slopes, with the Shanti Stupa in the background. ❽ View from the old palace.

LEH

SANKAR GOMPA (MONASTERY)
17th-18th C/ Buddhist ★

About 2 km outside Leh is a small, modern *gompa*. This elegant cluster of monks' rooms, surrounding a courtyard is simple but very different from other monasteries around. In contrast to the white walls of the monks' rooms, the *dukhang's* entrance and the capitals of pillars are all painted in gay, bright colours. The front door with murals on either side looks majestic.

The entrance to the prayer room.

STOK

ROYAL PALACE ★
1822/ Buddhist
Situated 17 km from Leh on the banks of the Indus, is a palace built by King Tsewang Namgyal. In 1834 it was annexed by the Dogra family and became the refuge for the overthrown royalty. The four-storeyed building with 77 rooms, still houses the royal family but one portion has been converted into a museum. The palace with a courtyard is very similar in style to the *gompas*.

Up: The palace has been constructed on terraced land, with steps leading up to it from the right.
Down: A courtyard, surrounded by wooden rooms.

The terrace of the palace.

PHYANG ★

GOMPA (MONASTERY) ★
Around 16th C/ Buddhist
Adjacent to the charming village of Phyang 16 km from Leh is the fascinating three-dimensional Kargynd Gompa. It has a large collection of Buddhist deities that are honoured at festivals. Access to the courtyard is through a tunnel-like staircase. The *dukhang* is accessed from the courtyard by a flight of stairs.

Stairway from the courtyard to the *Dukhang*

SHEY ★

18

GOMPA (MONASTERY) ★
16th-18th C/ Buddhist
Amidst wonderful scenery 16 km south-east of Leh, is a castle on a hill. This castle holds a *gompa*, smaller than other *gompas* in the region. It has a statue of Gautama Buddha which was built by King Tedan Namgyal. The building has a panoramic view of the Indus River and its valley. A large number of *chortens*, stand in a row in the wasteland opposite.

The castle on top of the hill.

GOMPA (MONASTERY) ★★
15th C/ Buddhist

About 5 km from Shey is a *gompa* of the Gelug-pa group. Spread over the hill, the gompa is strikingly similar to a miniature hill town in Italy. The rooms and monks' quarters house over 300 monks. A flight of stairs leads into a courtyard surrounded by a colourful corridor with rooms beyond. The sight of a giant gold painted Buddha is overwhelming.

❶ Rooms and monks' quarters spread over the hill.
❷ The room above the entrance, with the statue of Buddha.
❸ The corridor painted with colourful murals.

Head of the giant Buddha that rises into the atrium.

GOMPA (MONASTERY)
Buddhist ★

Chemre Gompa appearing as large as a mountain town is 15 km north of Hemis. A backdrop of barren mountains with neither grass nor trees is set off by the rich green of the Indus valley. Uniform buildings, white walled and flat roofed seem to be very precariously stacked on the mountain slope. A shaded entrance leads to rooms filled with murals. Thak Thok Gompa is 10 km from Chemre.

Right: A full view of the *gompa* from the valley.
Left: The *Dukhang* facing the front yard.

HEMIS ★ ★ ★

GOMPA (MONASTERY) ★★
17th C/ Buddhist

Hidden away 43 km south-east of Leh, is the important Hemis Gompa. It belongs to the Drugpa group which has connections with the Royal family. Monk Stagstang Raspa brought here by King Sengge Namgyal, established this monastery which has around 500 monks, even more children but absolutely no women in it.

Tradition has it that in Ladakh the oldest son is for the family while the second, is given to God. Padmasambhava's birthday is celebrated on a grand scale and the Mask Dance is enacted in the vast courtyard. The courtyard with corridors all around has to the north, a large building which houses two-prayer rooms, the *dukhang* and *tsokhang* . An interesting feature is the light, bathing the atrium of these spaces.

Façade of the *Dukhang* facing the southern courtyard.

The fascinating element of Ladakh's temple architecture is not its construction techniques, but the contrast created by light and shade along with the mysterious Buddhist statues and murals. There are a number of rooms opening onto the terrace above. In the *Tso-khang* room, Buddhist images are enshrined with the largest being that of the founder. A giant statue of the deity Tara is enshrined in the *Guru Lhakhang*.

Gompa partially hidden by rocks and boulders.

Tshog-khang where the golden Buddha is enshrined.

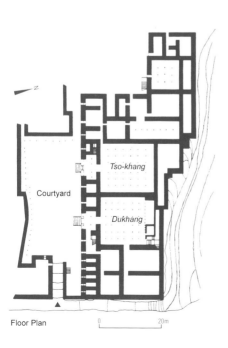

Floor Plan

Courtyard

Tso-khang

Dukhang

0   20m

Top:Roof of the *Dukhang*. Bottom:Interior of the Taksayn *gompa*.

HIMACHAL PRADESH

The state of Himachal Pradesh, with 55,673 sq km of mountainous terrain, shares its border with China. The plains extending from the state's southern boundary, give way to the hilly heights of the Himalayas. Since most of Himachal Pradesh gets good rainfall throughout the year, it is covered with green forests of Himalayan pine, a rare sight in India. The people of this region are gentle in character unlike the people in the plains who are aggressive. While Islam is the main religion in Kashmir and Ladakh has Buddhism, the main religion in Himachal Pradesh is Hinduism.

Given the mountainous terrain of Himachal Pradesh, most of the roads are steep with hair-pin bends and curves. Railway lines are almost non-existent. Access to some areas of Himachal Pradesh is therefore not very easy. If you do travel by road, negotiating the bends with just a wall between the road and the ravines is a thrilling experience.

The architecture of Himachal Pradesh is unique in character. Sloping roofs to cope with the heavy rainfall in the region, are a distinctive feature. Temples are built in an architectural style that is commonly used in the plains, but the *shikharas* (spires) are made of wood instead of stone. Buildings in the eastern part of the state have sloping roofs of an unusual shape. The roofs of houses in Ladakh are flat because of the low rainfall it receives, while in Kashmir, where the rainfall is heavier; the houses are covered by a straight sloping roof, as in Nepal. But in Himachal Pradesh, the sloping roofs have a slight curve which is very intriguing. They strongly resemble the *irimoya* roof form in Japan. They could not be a result of Chinese influence, because the Himalayas stand tall between China and this region. Nor could it be a Tibetan influence since there is no direct contact between Tibet and Himachal Pradesh. It is not likely that this style could have come in from Nepal, because the roofs there are not sloping like these and do not have a curve. This characteristic style, the origins of which still remain a mystery, is reflected not only in the temples and palaces but also in the vernacular architecture of the region.

Due to the inaccessibility of the region, there is very little documentation on the architecture of Himachal Pradesh, which is quite different from that of the rest of India.

The architectural style of east Himachal Pradesh, illustrated by W.Simpson.

View of Khadaran village surrounded by pine-forested mountains.

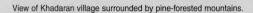

Udaipur

Keylang

Chamba 22   Kardang

Bharmaur 23   Gondhla

Chhatrarhi

Pathankot   Vashist

Dharamsala   Manali 28

                   Jagatsukh

Baijnath   29 Nagar

Masrur 24 Kangra   25

                   Kulu

          Khokhan 27

          Bajaura 30

                   26 Dhiyar

Mandi

                                        Sungra

                                   32

                        Nirmand   Nichar

                        Nithar 34   33 Sarahan (North) 31 Kamru

          Mamel   Rampur

          Kao   Behna

               Shimla   Jubbbal

          35   36   Manan   39

               Sainj 38 Balag   Hatkoti

                    37   Khadaran

                         40

                              41 Sarahan (South)

Chandigarh

TOWN & RANG MAHAL (PALACE)
18th-19th C/

Chamba 926 m above sea level, is perched on a ledge overlooking the Ravi River. True to its reputation it is a beautiful town. On one side of the river is a *maidan* (open ground) which is the focus of most recreational, cultural or commercial activities in the village. On the opposite bank on slightly raised ground, are temples, palaces, public buildings and a tourist bungalow. A long narrow stretch of land on the ridge has wooden buildings in a style rarely seen in the plains. The entrance to the town has an interesting building, which has rounded pillars in a Western style and a roof in the Himalayan style. It houses the offices of the Police Department.

The large palace was built in the 18th century by Raja Umed Singh and was extended in the 19th century. Since the King was a vassal of the Mughals, the construction shows a definite Islamic style. At present it houses a school and other public facilities. The courtyard is used as a recreational area. Chamba is noted for its stone temples, built in a style that was used by the Pratihara dynasty during the 9th-10th century.

❶ A view of the city from the Himalayas.
❷ The palace, as seen from the *maidan.*
❸ The courtyard of the former palace. *(Rang Mahal)*
❹ The Police Institute.

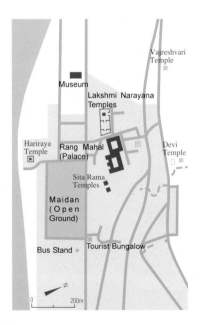

LAKSHMI NARAYANA TEMPLE
COMPLEX ★★ 14th C/ Hindu

Chamba valley is renowned for its *shikhara* style temples, prime examples of which can be found in Chamba town. The temple precincts are situated to the west of the palace. The *shikharas* visible in a single file from the entrance are of the six temples dedicated to Lakshmi Narayana, Radha Krishna, Chandra Gupta Mahadeva, Gauree Shankara, Triyambakeshwara and Lakshmi Damodara. A characteristic feature of these temples is the "sedge hat" style wooden roofs, an indigenous design that developed to protect the temples, given the easy availability of wood. The wall surfaces have deities and panels carved with mythological scenes.

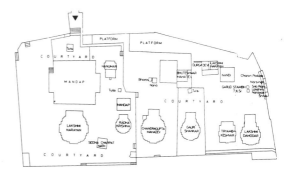

❶ The group of temples in a row.
❷ The rooftops of the *shikhara* style temple group.
❸ The facade of the Gauree Shankara Temple.
❹ Carvings on the wall of the Lakshmi Narayana Temple.

LAKSHMI NARAYAN TEMPLE
14th C/ Hindu ★

The last temple in this row is dedicated to Damodara, which is another name for Krishna. It is a small symmetrical temple with a porch. The octagonal roof harmonizes with the rest of the edifice. A disc-like stone *amalaka* on the roof gives the temple a two-tiered appearance. Since slate is abundant in the area, it is used as roofing for houses and temples.

Left: A full view of the Lakshmi Narayan temple.

Right: The intricately carved stone wall.

BHARMAUR (BRAHMOR)★★   23

LAKSHANA DEVI TEMPLE
(LAKHNA TEMPLE)
Circa 700/ Hindu★

Larkana Devi temple, with a collapsed front portion is one of the oldest temples existing today. The entrance has closely sculpted statues of local deities and the *mandapa* has a very interesting ceiling, which is repeated in most temples in India. Cross-beams have been fixed from the four corners and they shorten in progressive rows.

The wooden entrance.

The ceiling of the *mandapa*, with a lotus sculpted in the centre.

HINDU TEMPLES
9th-10th C/ Hindu ★

A two-and-a-half-hour drive from Chamba down a deep valley, one can see the town unfolding above the terraced paddy fields on a steep slope. Stone temples and wooden temples stand together, right in the middle of the town. The Narasimha Temple and the Mani Maheshwara Temple are in the Pratihara style of the 10th century. Both these temples are in the style of half temples with just the *garbhagriha* and *mandapa*. The wooden temple of Larkana Devi was built at a later date.

A view of the village and the temples.

The group of wood and stone temples.

MASRUR ★ 24

MONOLITHIC TEMPLE
Around 8th C AD/ Hindu

The simple rock cut temple in Masrur, one of two that exist in north India, is sculpted from rock and merges with the cliffs in the surroundings. The rocky outcrops were not perpendicular to the ground, so the top of the temple fell down and not much has been done to restore it. The exterior and the sacred rooms are decorated with carving.

Reflection of the temples in the tank..

VAIDYANATHA TEMPLE
1204 AD/ Hindu ★

Hindu temples were built on a standard design with a *garbhagriha (*sacred room) where Gods are deified, and the *mandapa* at the front. The *garbhagriha* is topped with the *shikhara*, while a pyramidal roof covers the *mandapa* in north Indian style. Vaidyanath Temple is a typical example of this style but the roof of the *mandapa* is a later addition.

TRIYUGINARAIN (TIRYGI NARAYANA) TEMPLE ★
17th-18th C/ Hindu

A 3-tiered roof on the temple.

Temples of Himachal Pradesh could have wooden roofs because of the abundant availability of trees in the region. To distinguish between houses and temples, the temple roofs were built very high.Though made of slate, the three-tiered roof of the Tiryugi Narayana Temple is one such example.

ADI BRAHMA TEMPLE
1753/ Hindu ★

In Khokhan village, located 15 km from Kulu on the Beas riverbank, is a rare temple crowned with a four-tiered roof. These roofs (also called *pagodas*) are seen in a variety of styles. In Khokhan, the top part of the *pagoda* is crowned with a ridge pole instead of the usual ridge-like projection. At mid-level, a style that resembles Nepal's *pagodas* has been incorporated. The height of the roof is over 20 m. The slant in the *pagoda* could be because it was added to the flat roof at a later date.

❶ There is a room built on the 2nd floor, with no access to it.
❷ The top part of the four-tiered *pagoda*.
❸ The entrance on the ground floor.

OLD VILLAGE
Hindu

Manali town, is a picturesque resort in the Kulu valley and the village, where the old houses reflect the Himalayan style of architecture, is worth a visit. In the vernacular Himalayan style the houses followed a standard design. The ground floor was built with stones, the floor above with wood which had a cantilevered balcony and the roof over the structure was made of slate.

❶ The old houses in the village.
❷ A wooden entrance in a stone wall.
❸ A group of wooden houses.

Wood carving in the old houses..

HIDIMBA DEVI TEMPLE ★
1553 (approx.)/ Hindu

Deep in a pine forest 2 km from Manali is the large wooden Dhungri Temple, dedicated to Goddess Hidimba. Its three-tiered roof of Himalayan pine planks is surmounted by a gold-plated disc. The first floor walls are made of earth. The sculptures on the lintel of the entrance and windows are in a style seen in the temples at Bharmaur.

Left: The temple surrounded by Himalayan pines.
Right: Detail of the wooden entrance

Perched some 100 m up a steep slope, off the Kulu Manali road is picturesque Nagar which showcases a variety of architectural styles found in the Himalayas. The palace has been converted into a hotel. The walls are an excellent example of the traditional Himalayan style of wooden architecture, where layers of wood, alternate with broken stones. The wall appears striped and corners where the planks meet, look like pillars. This rather uneconomical style was popular because this region was rich in forest wealth.

Nagar Castle Hotel.

STONE TEMPLE
Hindu ★

Naggar, once the capital of the Kulu kingdom still boasts a number of stone temples. Gauree Shankara Temple (11th-12th century) the oldest, has a statue of *Nandi* (Bull) indicating that it is dedicated to Shiva. It is a simple temple with a *shikhara* in the Nagari style (northern style).

Jagannatha Temple, very close to the Palace Hotel is very appealing. The squat *shikhara* has a 'sedge hat' roof in wood but the customary *amalaka* is missing.

The Krishna Temple which stands magnificently on a mountain peak, has a large wooden roof over the *garbhagriha*. The *mandapa* in front was built later.

Images of Trimurthy (Brahma, Vishnu and Shiva) are sculpted on the walls of all three temples.

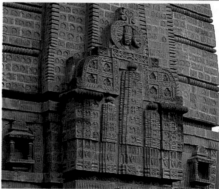

The Gauree Shankara Temple in the village below.

UP: Krishna Temple perched on a mountain peak.
Middle: The carved surface of a wall of Krishna Temple.
Below: The Jagannatha Temple near the Palace Hotel.

TRIPURASUNDARI TEMPLE ★★

Hindu

Tripura Sundari (Goddess of 3 worlds/Goddess Durga) temple with its *pagoda* style roof, resembles the Hidimba temple to a great extent. At its apex is a three-tiered roof of white wood, last constructed in 1990. When rain damages the roof and it is beyond repair, a new roof is made with Himalayan pines.

The walls constructed from wood and stones have a cantilevered balcony at the second floor level, which extends on all four sides and forms part of the *Pradakshina pada* (a circumbulatory for walking around the temple). The balcony has wooden tassels hanging from it, a characteristic feature of the architecture of Himachal Pradesh. Lions and monkeys are carved at the four corners of the structure, on the first floor and second floor, respectively. The carving on the window frames is more artistic than that on the entrance.

❶ The rear of the temple.
❷ The apex of the wooden roof.
❸ The balcony cantilevered from the second floor with wooden tassels trim.
❹ The old wooden window frame that was replaced.

BAJAURA ★

VISHVESHWARA MAHADEVA TEMPLE ★
9th C/ Hindu

The *shikhara* in the *Nagari* style of this simple, ancient, but well preserved temple is a legacy of the Pratihara dynasty. Shallow porches on all sides have statues of Vishnu, Ganesh and Durga in niches on the west, south and north respectively, while the entrance is on the east. The roof has an *amalaka* but no sedge-hat. The pot and foliage motif on the base and capital of the pillars is a very common Indian design.

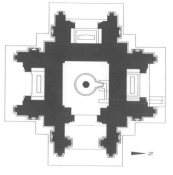

Right: The pot and leaf design decoration.
Left: Temple at the edge of the village.

Floor plan

KAMRU ★★ ★★

BADRINATHA TEMPLE ★
/Hindu

Sungra town is situated 20 km from Baspa River, which is about 210 km from Shimla. High on the mountains 2600 m above sea level is Kamru village. It served as the capital of the Bushahr kingdom until the capital was shifted to Sarahan. The castle above the village is now a part of the temple precincts. The style of these temples resembles the Japanese architectural style. The five-storeyed main shrine is located on the top-most ridge, an unusual site in Himachal Pradesh. Its sloping roofed tower is quite unique.

The main shrine with its sloping roofed tower rises above the others.

MAHESHWARA TEMPLE ★★
/Hindu

Taking the mountain route off the highway near the Sutlej River, the Maheshwara temple is a 20 km drive away. This 3-storeyed wooden temple with a pagoda style roof, stands against a backdrop of ravines and mountains. It resembles the Middle Ages churches of northern Europe. Also, just as forested northern Europe incorporated southern stone buildings into its architectural repertoire, Himachal Pradesh too, adopted stone architecture from the plains and merged it with traditional wooden architecture. This style which is a synergy of two different architectural styles has resulted in varied forms. Similarities in the architectural development of northern Europe and Himachal Pradesh, which are geographically far apart is very interesting. A *mandapa* in front of the main shrine is topped with a disc-shaped *shikhara*. The open second floor has a striking *irimoya* on the *mandapa*.

❶ Temple precincts. Nichyar Temple seen in the background.
❷ The wooden panels on the wall.
❸ The *pagoda*-like *shikhara*.
❹ The small stone shrine in the precincts.
❺ An *irimoya* on the *mandapa*.

SARAHAN (NORTHERN) ★ ★

BHIMAKALI TEMPLE ★★★
18-19th C/ Hindu

Sarahan is now just an insignificant village on a mountain, 50 km from Rampur. It was once the capital of the Bushahr kingdom. Bhimakali Temple is located at an altitude of 1920 m and blends with the surroundings creating an unforgettable scene. It was originally a castle with a temple, since there was no separation of religion and politics. Now the whole structure is part of the temple precincts. The precincts are in three tiers, with roofs built separately on the buildings. The original building with the sloping roof was designed to have two tiers. Since the walls of the original shrine fatigued with age, a new shrine was built nearby. The third and fourth floors of the new shrine are dedicated to Goddess Kali and the old shrine is used as a treasure house. The reason why the temples are so tall is because they were built as part of the palace. There is no clear demarcation between the temple tower and the palace tower, because there are many temples which are not related to the palace. The main shrine uses a technique seen in the Himalayan region where layers of wood alternate with layers of broken stone, giving the walls a striped effect. The top-most floor is cantilevered and roofed with slate. A Japanese style *irimoya* is placed on top. There are either two *irimoya* placed near each other or placed in a cross shape. A small roof is added over this. These roofs look like variations of the roofs on temples in Japan.

❶ The temple as seen from the mountains.
❷ The exterior of the temples.
❸ The entrance building leading from the second courtyard into the third courtyard.
❹ The same entrance building as seen from the second courtyard.

Full view of the Bhimakali temple.

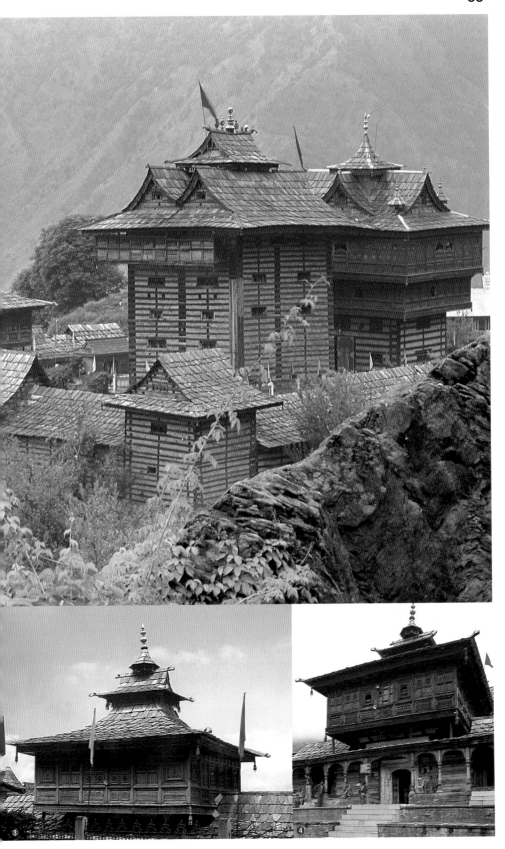

❺ The decorative new temple.
❻ Entrance from the 2nd courtyard into the 3rd courtyard.
❼ The elaborate embellishment on the walls of the new temple.
❽ The technique used to construct the walls of the former temple.
❾ The silver-plated entrance door.
❿ Window of the old shrine.

OLD AND NEW PALACE ★
1917/ Hindu

The capital of the Bushahr kingdom shifted from Kamru to Sarahan and this has resulted in Sarahan having two palaces. The traditional styled old palace is still occupied by the royal family. The walls of this palace have arabesque patterns which the new temple has emulated. The English style new palace closely resembles the palace in Rampur. The slate roof has been changed into a tin and stone roof.

The new palace. A view of Srikhand Mahadev

A section of the wall of the old palace.

RAMPUR ★   34

ROYAL PALACE
1919/ Hindu

Rampur at 924 m above sea level and 130 km from Shimla, is the commercial hub in the Sutlej River basin. This winter palace of the Bushahr kingdom is a blend of Western and traditional building styles. The predominately European ground floor has a wooden second floor, over which is a traditional roof. The octagonal pavilion reflects the preferences of the people.

The pavilion and the palace.

COLONIAL BUILDINGS
19-20th C/ Colonial

Shimla, capital of Himachal Pradesh and a famous hill-station, is situated 2213 m above sea level. It was the summer capital of the British from 1865. Situated on a ridge, it has a main street called the Mall, which is too narrow for a car to enter. It stretches the length of the town. During British rule, Indians were banned from the 3 km Mall at the eastern end of which is the church and library, while the western end has the viceregal lodge. The City Office and Railway Ministry buildings are outstanding examples of Colonial architecture that exist today.

❶ Christ Church (1844, designed by J. T. Boileau).
❷ The church and the library.
❸ Library (1910/ designed by J. Ransom).
❹ The City Office (1910).

RASHTRAPATI NIWAS ★
(Viceregal Lodge)
1888/ Colonial
By Henri Irwin

This palace was built for the Viceroy to India, Lord Dufferin who ruled over India and was also known as the Deputy Emperor. There are viceregal lodges in Calcutta and New Delhi too. Irwin, who also designed the Victoria Memorial hall in Chennai (Madras), has designed an authentic English building here. It presently houses the Indian Institute of Advanced Studies (IIAS).

Up: West facade Down: View of viceregal palace.

DURGA TEMPLE ★
Hindu

About 50 km down the road from Rampur to Shimla is the road to Manan. Of the two temples located here, one is the Durga temple built in the *pagoda* style. The *mandapa* of this temple has two *irimoya* roofs and the *garbhagriha* has a roof made of slate. The interior is minutely sculpted with Hindu deities and tribal Gods. The extremely colourful paintings enhance the ambience of the place.

Right: A temple built in the *pagoda* style.
Left: The colourful interior of the temple.

MANANESHWARA (MAGNESHWAR) TEMPLE ★
Hindu

This temple atop a hill is dedicated to Mananeshwara (Shiva). Here too the *irimoya* are in a row in the lower room and since they are very gaily painted the temple looks like a palace. Origins of the temple tower are not known and it was perhaps used as a fortress, as in the Caucasus regime of Russia. The temple tower looks like a pandal (structure used for festivals).

Up: The angular structure, which envelopes the roof.
Down: The top part of the temple roof.

Detail of the decoration under the eaves.

ROYAL PALACE ★★
19th C/ Hindu

Rajputs, warriors from west India, extended their kingdom up to the Gangetic plains. They established small kingdoms in every region in Himachal Pradesh between 8th-9th century. King Chandra Gupta, who built the temple in Khajuraho, was also a Rajput. This branch advanced into the Himalayas and established the Deyok kingdom. Sainj palace, 30 km on the road from Shimla is still occupied by Chandra Gupta's descendants. The palace, a natural fortress is surrounded by a valley on three sides and as added protection, has very strong front walls. The 3-tiered hall in the centre of the palace with an atrium is surrounded by wooden rooms. The square hall of the prayer room is skilfully designed to receive light from the atrium. Previously, this was not a palace, but a building used during festivals.

❶ The palace with an open space in front of it. ❷ The atrium in the central hall. ❸ The balcony facing the front.

SHIVA TEMPLE ⋆
/Hindu

On the mountain road 10 km from Sainj is Balag which has a rare temple with a sedge-hat shaped tower, made of stone and a *mandapa* of wood. Traces of Himalayan and Aryan culture can be seen in the sculptures of tribal deities on the walls of the temple. There is a small shrine in the precincts, with a stone *shikhara*. There is another small temple tower nearby.

❶ Full view of Shiva Temple.
❷ Murals on the wall.
❸ A small temple tower.

A Hindu, Shiva Temple.

HATESHWARI TEMPLE AND SHIVA TEMPLE ⋆
/Hindu

In the Jubbal ravines, 85 km from Deog, is an ancient group of temples. This pilgrim place has the Shiva Temple with its prominent sedge-hat roof and a cluster of shrines with *shikharas*. The façade of the Shiva Temple is extremely striking.

The double-storeyed Hateswari Temple, built between the 6th-9th century has stone walls and a wooden roof. Besides these two, there are several stone temples in the vicinity.

A bird's eye view of the temple

Up: Hateshwari Temple. Down: Shiva Temple with a row of small towers.

VILLAGE AND RAIREMOOL DEVI TEMPLE

This really beautiful, but not easily accessible temple is best reached by getting to Deba town, 20 km from Senji, taking the mountain road from there for 5 km, alighting and walking for 30 minutes. It cannot be reached without a guide. As you walk, you get tantalising glimpses of the village through the pine trees. The traditional buildings have walls of stone and white wood, with black stone roofs. Against this picturesque backdrop stands the Rairemool Devi Temple, with its sloping roof and high *irimoya* style roof. The village square has a group of single-storeyed buildings and the main temple. Hindu deities have been carved in the tribal style on the low level walls. There is a very steep staircase going up to the tower, but non-believers are not allowed inside.

❶ Village with a deep ravine. ❷ & ❸ Main temple with a projecting balcony. ❹ Sculptures at the single-storeyed temple's entrance.

BIJAT (BIJLESHWAR MAHADEV) TEMPLE★★
Hindu

After crossing Khadaran, although the road deteriorates considerably, driving is a thrill with just a low wall dividing the road from the ravine far below. Drivers are cautioned to proceed at a very slow speed. Down this road 50 km from Khadaran, is the town of Sarahan. Known as Southern Sarahan, it is not the same Sarahan where the Bhimakali temple is situated.

In the vicinity of the courtyard of the complex are two identical buildings connected to each other by the entrance into the courtyard. For some reason, a new building was constructed and "Vijeta" or Vishnu was shifted here. Looking carefully, it is obvious that the building on the right, with a very shaky wooden staircase, is the older of the two.

The sculptures on the entrance to the southern tower.

❶ The twin buildings facing the courtyard. ❷ The buildings facing each other in the courtyard. ❸ Details of the southern tower.

PUNJAB

The Indus (Sindhu) and Ganga (Ganges), are two main rivers that flow through India. Indus is the base from which the English name "India" is derived. The civilization that flourished in the valley is known as the Indus Valley Civilization and the people and their language were known as Sindhu.

In Persian, "s" is silent, so 'Sindhu' was distorted to 'Hindu'. In Europe, Sindhu with its silent 's', when translated, became 'Indou' in French, and 'India', in English. That was 'how 'Sindhu' changed to 'India', which became the official name of this country after Independence. Indians however, prefer to refer to their country as Bharat, which is always written in parenthesis, next to India in any Indian atlas.

As the Indus River had five tributaries in its upstream basin, the region was called Punjab or the land of five rivers. 'Punj' meaning 'five' and 'ab' meaning 'water'. This land was very fertile and rich with agricultural produce. At the time of Partition, east Punjab became a state of India, while west Punjab went to Pakistan. Lahore the main city of Punjab and the old capital of the Mughal Era became part of Pakistan.

Pandit Jawaharlal Nehru, the first Prime Minister of India, decided to plan a new city as the capital of Punjab. Le Corbusier, the famous architect selected for the job, designed Chandigarh as the new state capital.

Subsequently this state was divided into Punjab, where Punjabi-speaking Sikhs lived, and Haryana, where Hindi-speaking Hindus lived. Chandigarh which lies in-between, became the capital for both the states.

The main religion in Punjab is Sikhism which was started in the 16th century, by Guru Nanak. This religion is a combination of Islam's Sufism (one God and equality of all) and Hinduism (trust in God). It was aimed at removing the caste discrimination that was so prevalent in Hinduism.

The Sikh religion was established in the early 19th century, and a warrior class of people was formed. Their place of worship is called the *gurudwara*. Since Sikhism is a fairly new religion, they did not develop their own style of architecture. They adopted the Mughal architectural style.

Sikh believers grow their hair and wear a turban around the head. Visitors are requested to cover their heads, whenever they enter a *gurudwara*.

The main temple of the Sikhs - The Golden Temple (Hari Mandir), Amritsar.

HARI MANDIR (GOLDEN TEMPLE) ★★
1764/ Sikh

Amritsar was a small village during Guru Nanak's lifetime, but by the second half of the 16th century, during the lifetime of the fourth Guru Amar Das it became the most important city for Sikhs. A *gurudwara* was established in 1589 during the lifetime of the fifth Guru, Arjun Singh. Ahmad Shah Durrani of Afghanistan destroyed it when he invaded India and the present temple was rebuilt in 1764. Later in 1802, Maharaja Ranjit Singh established the Sikh kingdom and plated the roof with gold and what was originally Hari Mandir (temple of God), came to be called the Golden Temple. It is the presence of this temple that has made Amritsar the Holy City for all Sikhs.

The main building is rather small and is built in the middle of a tank which is 120m x 150m. This gives it the appearance of floating on water. Believers enter the gate at the edge of the tank *Amrita Sarovar* (tank of nectar) from which the name for the city was derived and cross over a bridge to enter the temple. A white marble terrace about 15 m wide surround the tank.

The temple and its surrounding precincts, all made of marble along with the water in the tank, appear pure, different and extraordinary. The entire precinct with water all around it, is magnificent.

The central building is designed in the latter Mughal style. It is open on all four sides, does not have any doors that can be closed and does not have any dark spaces. It accentuates the doctrine that all humans are equal. Sitting in the bright hall with the open stairwell, listening to *kirtans* (songs) to the accompaniment of the *tabla* and the harmonium, is supreme bliss.

❶ Crossing over the bridge to the gold plated, Hari Mandir.
❷ The top portion of the white building that surrounds the precinct has a classic appearance.
❸ There are existing battle marks in various places, from the time the Indian Army attacked the militants.
❹ Access to the bridge is through a two-storeyed building with a marble entrance.

WORKS OF LE CORBUSIER ★★
1950-69/ Post Independence

In 1950, three years after the Partition of India and Pakistan, it was decided that a new capital city should be built for Punjab in India. The architect selected for this purpose, Charles Edouard Jeanneret (1887-1969), popularly known as Le Corbusier, was the flag-bearer for the concept of modernism that arose in Europe. Actually, designing a whole new city was unthinkable in Europe. CIAM (*Congres de Internationeaux Architecture Moderne*) put this idea into practice in Brazil and Chandigarh in the third world. Le Corbusier dispatched his cousin, architect Pierre Jeanneret to India, to supervise the designing of the city.

Secretariat, (Government Building) designed by Le Corbusier.

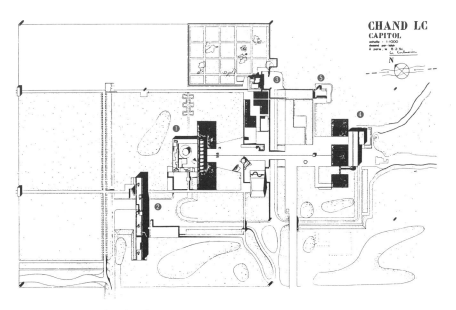

Site Plan of Capitol Complex (Civic Centre)
❶ Legislative Assembly. ❷ The Secretariat. ❸ Proposed Governor's residence. ❹ High Court ❺ Open-hand monument.

CHANDIGARH

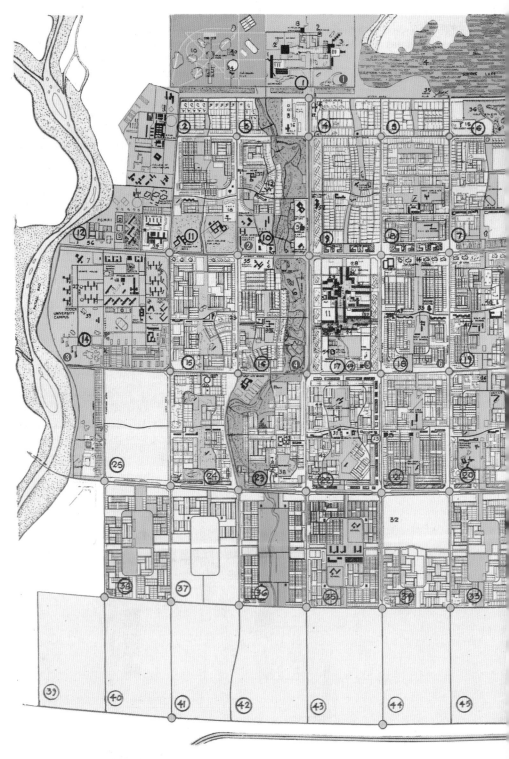

Le-Corbusier's Master Plan.
❶ Sector No.1 (1-9 Capitol Complex)/Left side
(10- Rajendra Garden) - Right Side 4 (Sukhna Lake)/ On the west side behind Rock Garden.
❷ Sector No. 10 (5: Museum and Fine Arts College) ❸ Sector No. 14 (7: Punjab University campus)
❹ Sector No.16 (6: RockGarden) ❺ Sector No.17 (11: Shopping Sector) 49: Bus terminal and tourist office
❻ Sector No.18 (33: Tagore theatre) ❼ Eastern outskirts (51:) Railway station (direct train from Delhi)

82

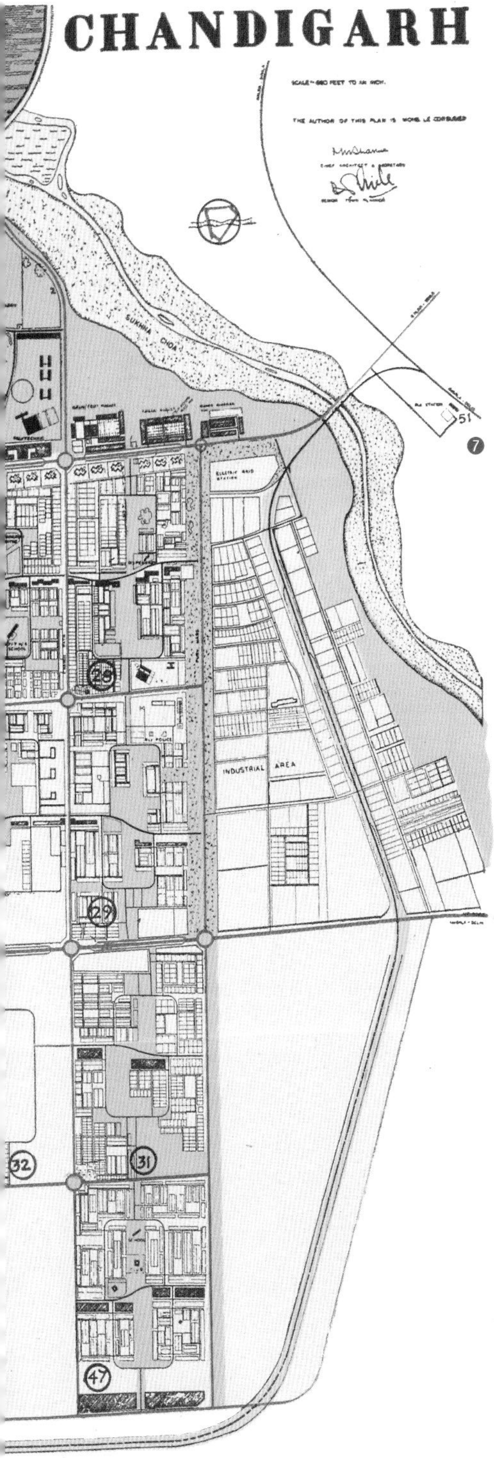

The city was originally divided into 47 sectors and the Capitol Complex as well as Civic Centre were meant to be the focal point. A green belt penetrates the centre to the south while in the heart of the city, Sector 17 has been designed as the business district. The orderly design, wide roads and well-planned facilities with a leaning towards modernism, makes it an ideal 'garden city'. Chandigarh is regarded as a bible for modern architects. It has become a symbol of youth for India and its people are proud of its state-of-the-art-city status. The city became a tourist spot with long queues of people waiting to see the Rock Garden.

Chandigarh is very different from traditional cities. The chasm between social levels is broad, as is evident in the sparsely populated northern sectors as compared to the southern part. A large colony, 'Kumhar Colony' or porters' colony was developed towards the southern end. This colony has degenerated into a slum.

There is criticism about Chandigarh's design but Corbusier's design caters very well to Indian sensibilities. The large *brise-soleil* (sun screen) and their three-dimensional effect, along with the interior spaces, present a fantastic picture, without going against traditional Indian architecture.

The museum that was built later is in the same series as that of the museum in Ahmedabad and the National Western Museum in Tokyo. Pierre Jeanneret, designed the housing by and large.

The business area being developed.

The slum on the outskirts of the city.

CHANDIGARH
It is pronounced as Chandigarh in India. Le Corbusier who is French, pronounced it as 'Shayandegar'.

1. Vidhan Sabha (1960)-Legislative Assembly.
2. Entrance door of the Legislative Assembly building with Le Corbusier's mural.
3. The Open Hand Monument.
4. Museum - 1968.
5. The Fine Arts College - 1969.
6. Office of the City Museum.
7. Gandhi Bhavan (Inside the University)
8. High Court (1986)
9. The Central Hall in the High Court.

ROCK GARDEN
1976/ Opened Post Independence
by Nek Chand

The rock-garden serves as a counterbalance to the very functional, geometric city of Chandigarh. It is a rock garden with self-styled, uninhibited sculptures.

The creator Nek Chand, is not a sculptor by profession, but was an inspector with the State Roadways. He collected unused, waste material in the city and went about creating the sculptures, one by one until he had completed a large collection of sculptures. Each sculpture created was methodically installed on a base with a platform and a foundation. The effect is satisfying and resembles Sam's Tower in the USA.

Up: A style, very similar to Gaudi's. Down: Statues of unused materials.

PINJORE ★   44

YADAVINDRA GARDEN ★
17th C/ Islamic

Mughal gardens spread all around Srinagar but 30 km on the road to Pinjore from Chandigarh is an open terraced Mughal garden, built by Aurangazeb's foster-brother Fidai-Khan.

Entrances to the ascending gardens of Kashmir are at the lower level. The Yadavindra Gardens are descending gardens where the entrance is at the top of the hill. The visitor enters at the top and walks down subsequent terraces.

The full view of the garden is thus a different experience from the one derived in Kashmir.

The water canal in the centre of the garden, passes through seven open terraces and pavilions and is decorated with *chaddars* and fountains. It must be pointed out though, that the pavilions in the Yadavindra Garden are of a poor quality.

Up: The third open terrace.   Down: The fourth open terrace.

DELHI

Delhi is a unique capital city in that it is essentially made up of two distinct cities: Delhi and New Delhi. Delhi was the seat of power for seven different dynasties. These dynasties left their mark in the form of an architectural legacy that is as varied as it is wonderful. In this, Delhi is different from the three other major Indian cities of, Mumbai, Kolkata and Chennai which were developed during the British colonization. They do not have too many old buildings since their structures are fairly new.

The earliest surviving mosque in India is the Quwwat-ul-Islam Mosque dating back to 1198. In 1192 Qutb-ud-din Aibak started the Slave Dynasty, so called because he was a slave of Muhammed Ghori.

Until the 16th century there were two Muslim dynasties ruling Delhi. The Sultans were the monarchs ruling during this time and this is referred to as the 'Sultan dynasty of Delhi'. Siri was the capital of the Khalji

Humayun's Tomb - Gateway to Mughal architecture.

dynasty. Tughluqabad or Ferozabad became the capital of the Tughluq dynasty. Now there are just ruins as evidence of these two dynasties.

During the Mughal era most of India was brought under their rule. Delhi was made their capital and, along with Agra, these were the most important cities. Most of the structures of this time still remain. The city that Shahjahan developed is now called Old Delhi.

When the British came to India, they annexed most of the region for the East India Company. Until the 18th century, Kolkata was their capital. But in 1911, they shifted their capital to Delhi.

Edwin Lutyens and Herbert Baker designed New Delhi under the instructions of the Viceroy. In 1931, the main establishment for the vice-regal offices was constructed. Sixteen years later when India attained Independence in 1947, New Delhi was retained as the capital of the country and the main seat of the new Government.

Delhi was a Union Territory under the direct governance of the Centre, but it has now been converted into a state. Delhi's population is currently, 10 million.

DELHI ★★★

QUTB COMPLEX (QUWWAT-UL-ISLAM MOSQUE) ★★

1193-14th C/ Islamic

Quwwat-ul-Islam Mosque (Power of Islam), was the first Islamic structure built in India. A temple at that site was destroyed by Qutb-ud-din-Aibak and the materials were used to construct a mosque. Idol worship is banned in Islam, so all the decorative statues on the pillars were destroyed. The technique of arch construction originated in the Middle East and the craftsmen who built the mosque did not know the technique of making true arches. The next generation of craftsmen grew proficient in traditional Muslim construction techniques, which can be seen in the tomb of Iltutmish and in Alai Darwaza.

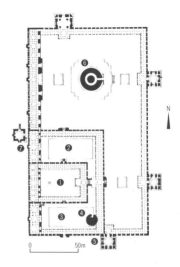

Floor Plan showing the development of the Quwwat-ul-Islam ❶ The earlier mosque. ❷ Later developments ❸ Further developments. ❹ Qutb Minar. ❺ Alai Darwaza. ❻ The incomplete minaret. ❼ Grave of Iltutmish.

Minaret and Alai Darwaza seen from the small pavilion in Qutb region.

The 5th century stupa in the middle is not Islamic, but has been brought here from elsewhere.

Interior of the grave of Iltutmish (1236).

QUTB MINAR (MINARET) ★★

A *minar* is usually attached to a mosque to call the faithful to prayers, however Qutb Minar was designed as a victory memorial. Part of the oldest mosque of India, it is 72.5 m tall and the shaft has alternating, round and triangular ribs. Iltutmish who succeeded Aibak, built this *minar* modelled after the Jamu minaret of Afghanistan, from the 3rd floor upwards and even after that, it was extended. 379 steps lead to the top, but the *minar* was closed to the public after a stampede.

Scripts from the Koran, carved on the surface.

Every floor of the *minar* has a projecting balcony.

KHIRKI MASJID

1375/ Islamic

This is an early Arab mosque. It looks like a fortress from the outside. There are four small courtyards inside with raised floors and a hall lined with columns. There is not much decoration here but the sturdy columns support an authentic archaic arch, which closer approximates what is now recognized as authentic Islamic architecture.

Right: One of the square entrances.
Left: Inner courtyard in the mosque.

TUGLUQABAD AND TOMB OF GHIYAS-UD-DIN ★
1321-25/ Islamic

The third capital of Delhi, Tughluqabad, houses the tomb of Ghiyas-ud-din Tughluq. Now, only the fort walls remain. The tomb is well preserved in a small fortress enclosure outside the main fort walls. The sloping red sandstone walls and white dome on top, make this structure a simple but a sturdy one. It can be called a prototype of Buhari Ismail's (10th century) mausoleum.

Up: Ghiyas-ud-din's mausoleum. Down: Fort of Tughluqabad.

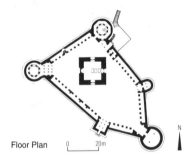

Floor Plan   0   20m   N

TOMBS OF THE LODI DYNASTY ★
15th-16th C/ Islamic

The tombs in Lodi Gardens, were built when the Sultan era was drawing to a close. The interior and exterior sides of the walls are decorative, but they look rather crude. They lack even the sturdy simplicity of Ghias-ud -din's tomb. New styles of design had to wait for the Mughal era. *Gumbad* is the word for tomb in Persian, and a tomb with a dome roof is also called a *Gumbad*.

Sikander Lodi's tomb (1517).

Up:Sheesh Gumbad (end 15th C). Down: Tomb-Muhammad Shah (1444)

PURANA QUILA ★
16th C/ Islamic

This fort was constructed a hundred years before Lal Qila and is hence called *Purana Qila* (old fort).

It was built by Humayun the second Mughal Emperor, but he was attacked by his Afghan rival Ṣher Shah Suri who began building his capital Shergarh on the same site. Humayun defeated Suri and improved on it. At each changing of hands, the structure improved and became better.

✦ Sher Mandal is a small octagonal structure, which was used as a library. It is said, that in 1556, when Humayun was climbing its steps, he fell down and died.

✦ Quila-i-Kuhna Masjid was built in 1541 by Sher Shah, in the style of his home town. There is a fantastic *Mihrab* inside.

Up: Sher Mandal. Down: Quila-i-Kuhna Mosque.

TOMB OF SAFDARJANG ★
1774/ Islamic

Mirza Mukhim Abdul Mansur Khan was the Governor of Oudh during the reign of the Mughal Emperor, Muhammed Shah. He was noted for driving away enemies and hence acquired the name Safdarjung. The mausoleum was built by his son, Nawab Shuja-ud-Daulah, on Safdarjung's death in 1754.

This large mausoleum with gardens on all four sides, was one of the last constructions of the Mughal empire. Though it bears some resemblance to the Taj Mahal, it has barely captured the essence of the Taj Mahal. It has adhered to the style of the Taj Mahal, but the magic is missing.

Up: Mausoleum with gardens on four sides. Down: Ceiling of the tomb.

TOMB OF HUMAYUN ★★★
1565/By Mirak Mirza Ghiyas

One of the earliest constructions of the Mughal era is Humayun's Tomb, a large complex, with a garden divided into quadrants (*char bagh*) and the mausoleum in the middle. Humayun designed it as a garden for the public and after his death, his senior Queen, Haji Begum, built his tomb there. It took 9 years to complete. The tomb is in the centre of a 10-hectare plot, measures 90 m x 90 m and is 38 m in height. Built with red sandstone and marble, it has a dome and became the prototype for Mughal mausoleums. In true Persian style, there is an *iwan* in the centre of each side. The shape of the mausoleum is square, a sign of the influence of Jain architecture on the Mughals.

Also called a *cenotaph,* the actual tomb is in a basement under a chamber. This concept was brought down from central Asia by Mughals, who are Mongol descendants. The two layered, or double-shelled dome, with the top separate from the interior, is reminiscent of Samarkand or Bukhara. The exterior becomes pronounced, while the interior gets a sculptured effect. Mughals preferred sculpture to painting. Humayun's grave is a Persian structure with four *iwans* surrounding a courtyard. The arches with their backs to each other have the same pattern carved on the front.

Several Moghul princes and princesses and Haji Begum herself lie around Humayun's tomb including Shah Jahan's son, Dara Shikoh.

❶ Humayun's Tomb in the middle of the square garden.
❷ The garden divided into quadrants.
❸ The pattern on the wall with a combination of red sandstone and marble.
❹ The arches face outward with their backs to each other.

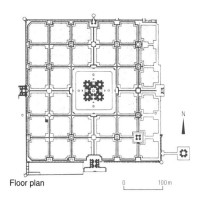

Floor plan

0   100 m

The west entrance leading to the parking lot.

The upper portion of the mausoleum with the handrail for the staircase in the foreground.

LAL QUILA (RED FORT) ★★
17th C/ Islamic

Delhi was developed by Shahjahan and hence called Shahjahanabad. *Lal Quila* or Red Fort gets its name from the red colour of the sandstone used for its walls.

Construction of the fort started in 1639 and in 1648, the capital shifted from Agra to Delhi. The inside of the fort was a town and even now, the road that leads to Lahore Gate, is lined with shops as in a castle market. The army occupies most of the area inside the fort. Both, Lahore and Delhi gates are masterpieces. The small *chhatris* (pavilions) on the roof emphasize the 'Indianess' of the structure. The palace complex has the customary *Diwan-i-Am* and *Diwan-i-Khas*. The structures are single-storeyed and may not be prime examples of Mughal architecture, but they highlight the care given to detail in Mughal construction. An example of this is the royal prayer room, Moti Masjid, a small marble structure built in 1659 by Aurangzeb. Within the fort is a beautiful square garden with pavilions at various places. One of them has the inscription '*if there is a Paradise on earth it is here! It is here!! It is here!!!*' There is a huge marble fountain on the grounds and a water channel runs from the palace to the garden.

❶ Façade of Lahore Gate
❷ Moti Masjid
❸ Diwan-i-Am
❹ Interior of Diwan-i-Khas
❺ Delhi Gate made of red sandstone
❻ Diwan-i-Khas
❼ Interior of Rang Mahal
❽ Fountain in Rang Mahal

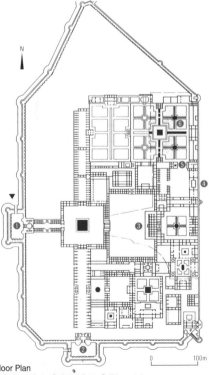

N

0   100m

Floor Plan
❶ Lahore Gate ❷ Delhi Gate ❸ Diwan-i-Am
❹ Diwan-i-Khas ❺ Moti Masjid ❻ Square garden

JAMI MASJID (FRIDAY MOSQUE) ★★
1658/ Islamic

Jami Masjid, 500 m from Lal Quila, built by Shahjahan, is the largest mosque in India. It stands on a rise with a huge flight of stairs from 3 sides. This inspiring structure can be seen from a great distance. The two minarets are more than 39 m high. There is a fountain in the 900 sq m courtyard.

The prayer room to the west of the courtyard, facing Mecca, is a combination of red sandstone and marble and has three domes crowning it. It is eleven spans wide, while its length is barely two spans. This is quite different from Christian churches that are longer in length, than in width. There is an arcade all around the prayer room which was originally a continuation of the prayer room, but has now been sealed off as an independent structure. The construction style is similar to that of Humayun's Tomb, which reflects the differences in Indian and Arabian ethnicity. The sister mosque of the Jami Masjid, called Badshahi Mosque, constructed by Aurangzeb, is located in Lahore.

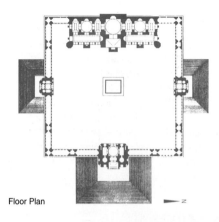

Floor Plan

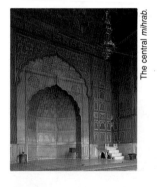

The central *mihrab*.

A view of the prayer room from the eastern arcade.

JANTAR MANTAR (OBSERVATORY) ★
1724/ Rajput

This observatory was constructed by Sawai Jai Singh II, to complement the astronomical calendar. It has a time clock and a constellation, meridian and astronomical observatory. These resemble constructions of the modern age. He later constructed the same in Ujjain, Mathura, Benares, Jaipur, etc.

Celestial observatories.

The British designed New Delhi when they shifted their capital from Calcutta. Shahjahanabad (Lal Quila and the area around), were then called Old Delhi. Old Delhi lies to the north of New Delhi, but the whole area is targeted for the development of the city, there is therefore no difference between Old and New Delhi. For convenience, buildings of the Mughal era have been referred to as Delhi and the buildings built during the British era and later, have been referred to as New Delhi.

Commercial complex around Connaught place.

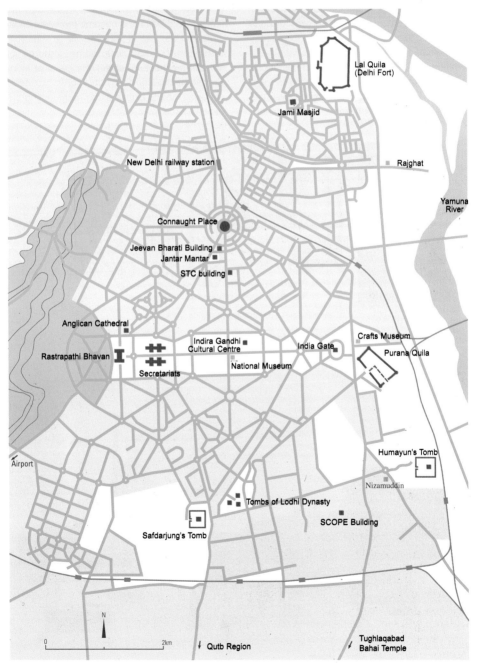

RASHTRAPATI BHAVAN
(VICEROY'S HOUSE) ★★

1929/ Colonial

by Edwin Lutyens

Southern facade of Rashtrapati Bhavan.

When the British Empire decided to shift its capital to Delhi, an English architect Edwin Lutyens, was invited to design the new city. He began planning in 1911 and finished in 1931, barely 19 years before Le Corbusier started Chandigarh. Later, Chandigarh developed with functional buildings, beautifully landscaped and internationally styled. It was so successful that Lutyens' work went into oblivion. Later, Modernism was forgotten, but Lutyens' designs were recognized for their worth and even today students of architecture study them.

Rashtrapati Bhavan (Viceroy's house) is at one end of Rajpath Marg, which leads on to India Gate and is perpendicular to Janpath. With this as the central axis, a hexagonal road pattern has been created. Connaught Place was the link with Old Delhi and became the commercial centre. Rashtrapati Bhavan is a classical European building with some features of Mughal architectural style. This blend of Indo-English architecture is not a great success, especially the Buddhist stupa surmounting the central dome, which is very European in style.

India Gate, by Lutyens.
(Memorial for martyrs of war)

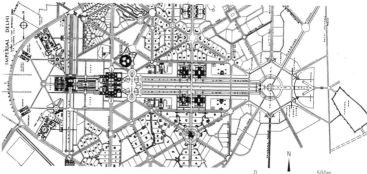

The central part of the master plan of New Delhi.

Rashtrapati Bhavan as seen from the square.

SECRETARIATS ★★
1931/ Colonial
by Herbert Baker
Lutyens asked his architect and friend, Herbert Baker to help him design the city of Delhi. Herbert Baker designed many important buildings in Delhi. The Secretariat is a set of twin buildings that face each other in front of Rashtrapati Bhavan. The inspiration for this design could have been the Royal Navy School in Greenwich, designed by Christopher Wren. Baker's desire was to design a structure in the western classical style. The Parliament House in the vicinity, is also his creation.

Up: Central part of the Secretariat. Left: Two buildings of the Secretariat facing each other. Right: Central hall in the Secretariat.

ANGLICAN CATHEDRAL ★
1928 Colonial
By Henri Alexander Nesbitt Medd
While designing the British National Church, the design that evolved, did not have influences of the Indian traditional style, at all. The simple structure is very neat and graceful. According to Medd, this design was inspired by Palladio's church Il Retentore in Venice.

JEEVAN BHARATHI BUILDING ★
1986/ Post Independence
by Charles Correa

In Connaught Place, where there are predominately colonial buildings, a giant of a building in mirror and space frames was built. Twin buildings are conceived with a pergola and a *darwaza* (gate). Pedestrians can walk directly onto the deck, from the bus terminal at the rear.

Up: The whole structure can be seen from Connaught Place.
Dow: The half-mirror mural and *pagoda*.

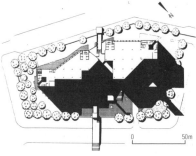

0   50m

Floor Plan

BAHAI HOUSE OF WORSHIP ★
1981/ Post Independence
by Fariburz Sahba

Bahaulla founded the Bahai religion in Iran, in the 19th century. Later it spread all over the world and a number of temples were built. Fariburz Sahba, an Iranian architect, designed the famous temple in Delhi using the lotus motif, as the lotus is a revered flower in India. The roof of the building is shaped like a lotus flower. With the blue sky for a backdrop, the snowy white lotus image is most appropriate for a religion that preaches peace. It is known as the Lotus Temple. The form of this structure bears a strong resemblance to the Sydney Opera House in Australia.

The prayer room shaped like a lotus.

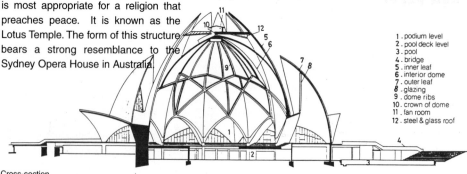

1 . podium level
2 . pool deck level
3 . pool
4 . bridge
5 . inner leaf
6 . interior dome
7 . outer leaf
8 . glazing
9 . dome ribs
10 . crown of dome
11 . fan room
12 . steel & glass roof

Cross-section

STATE TRADING CORPORATION BUILDING ★
1989/ Post Independence
By Raj Rewal

Born in 1934, Raj Rewal, put his heart and soul into designing, using his European and American education and inspiration drawn from traditional Indian architecture. The large State Trading Corporation (STC) building, a blend of red and yellow sandstone, draws inspiration from Mughal architecture. Raj Rewal implemented the use of space in the streets of Jaisalmer in his housing projects. STC building is the best example of his style.

View from the road.

The office building - a superb structure.

SCOPE OFFICE COMPLEX ★
1989/ Post Independence
By Raj Rewal

This is a large building covering 75,000 sq m. Here Raj Rewal has created a rich building and the style makes one forget the boredom of city life. Each of the buildings have their own unique character, while at the same time, stand together, to form a composite whole.

A view of the office complex

INDIRA GANDHI NATIONAL CENTRE FOR THE ARTS
1984 Post Independence
Ralph Lerner

This large culture centre, built in 1984, at Rajpath, was a memorial for the Prime Minister, Indira Gandhi who was assassinated. In 1986, an international competition was held and Ralph Lerner's design was accepted. He has tried to interpret traditional Indian designs in today's context.

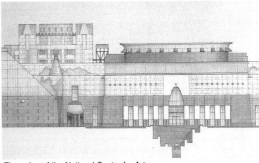

Floor plan of the National Centre for Arts.

The Indus and the Ganga are two perennial rivers in India. The Indus flows westwards and enters the Arabian Sea, while the Ganga flows eastwards and enters the Bay of Bengal. The state of Uttar Pradesh lies in the great Indo-Gangetic plain on the banks of the Ganga. The land irrigated by river water is very fertile and this state along with Punjab comprise the granary of India. Uttar Pradesh is a densely populated state.

Ganges is the English name for the river, Ganga. In India, where water is insufficient, rivers are sacred. The Ganga is considered the most sacred of rivers and according to Hindu mythology the Ganga which flowed when God created the world, is the physical and spiritual life source of the country.

This is symbolized in Varanasi (Benares), which is on the banks of the river Ganga. Every Hindu aspires to go to Varanasi at least once in his lifetime, to take a bath in the holy Ganga and drink the water. Just above Varanasi, the Ganga branches into the Yamuna River which flows south through Agra and reaches Delhi. These two rivers, the Ganga and Yamuna are revered and statues of river goddesses Ganga and Yamuna, can be seen at the main entrance or at the entrance of the *garbha griha* of many temples. In the 12th century, when this region came under Islamic rule, many temples were destroyed and mosques were erected in their place.

There was a lot of religious strife, which still persists in Ayodhya, north of Varanasi. Religion, all along has been giving mental peace to humanity, but if there is an intolerance of other religions, there can only be discord in society. Vandalizing a religious building that belongs to another community is a tragedy indeed.

The Mughals who ruled over most of India, made Agra and Delhi their capital and the third Mughal emperor, Akbar, tried to bring harmony between the two religions. He even created a new religion called 'Din-i-ilahi' which was a blend of Hinduism and Islam. In architecture too, he tried to blend practical sciences of Hinduism with the Islamic architectural styles. He incorporated the trabeated or pillar and beam construction technology of the Hindu architectural style and developed his own unique style of construction and design. This is reflected in his tomb in Sikandra, outside Agra, and in the new city that he built, called Fatehpur Sikri. It evokes even more interest than the Taj Mahal, which was pure Persian in style.

Jami Masjid in Fatehpur Sikri

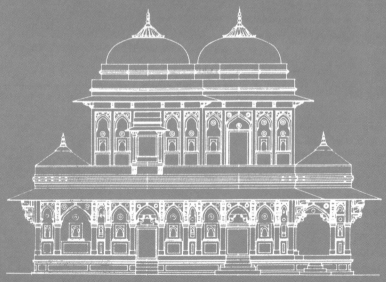

An elevation of Birbal's house in Fatehpur Sikri.

Vishnu, one of the gods worshipped by Hindus, came to earth ten times and one of these reincarnations was Krishna, a favourite of the Hindus. Mathura has gone down in history as the birthplace of Krishna. Brindaban, 9 km from Mathura, is a sacred place of the believers and is visited by many pilgrims. Buddhist and Jain temples were built here during ancient times but were later destroyed. Since the temple in Brindaban (16th century) is close to Delhi and Mathura, Islamic architectural styles have crept into the design, making it quite unique.

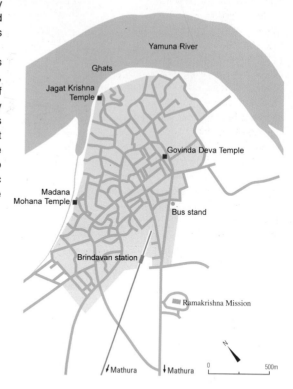

The ghat facing the Yamuna River.

JAGAT KRISHNA TEMPLE ★
16th C/ Hindu

This temple resembling a Pre-Roman church of North Spain stands silent at the edge of the town. The Yamuna River at the rear and the ghats as a backdrop, make the temple look fantastic. Earlier, the temple had an open porch in front. Carved on the tympanum above the entrance are Krishna and animals revered by Hindus. If these sculptures were removed it would be difficult to believe this was a Hindu temple.

Right: The cubic form of the temple.
Left: The big *amalaka* crowning the *shikhara*.

GOVINDADEVA TEMPLE ★★
1590/ Hindu

Many temples were built during Mughal emperor Akbar's reign, which was a peaceful and harmonious era. Raja Man Singh I of Amber built a red sandstone temple for Govindadeva (Krishna). This temple does not have a *shikhara* over the *mandapa* as it was destroyed by the Mughals. With its many arches and no sculptures to adorn it, the *mandapa* looks like a mosque. The framework of the sides and the balcony are Indian in style and the joints show powerful molding. The exterior, with the pronounced horizontal lines, is unique. The destroyed tower over the *mandapa* perhaps resembled the tower over Jagat Kishore Temple.

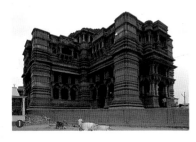

❶ The outside of the *mandapa*.
❷ The exterior view of the building.
❸ *Mandapa* interior with cross arches.

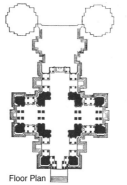

Floor Plan

Cross-section of the shrine

MADANA MOHANA TEMPLE
16th Century/ Hindu

This temple, in the same style as the Jagat Kishore Temple is also dedicated to Krishna. It appears that many rooms have been added on later to this complex structure. Especially, the double-storeyed entrance gate appears out of place. The wall of the octagonal *shikhara* is done in lattice work and a medallion has been installed, but there is no statue within.

Entrance Gate and *shikhara* of main shrine

Agra, just 200 km from Delhi, is an important architectural and tourist destination. The world famous Taj Mahal and Agra Fort, on the banks of the Yamuna River, are indicative of Agra's prominence at one time. Sikander Lodi made it his capital in 1501. Babur, defeated Sikander Lodi in the Battle of Panipat and started the Mughal Empire in 1526. The Mughal Gardens that he constructed still exist in the city. Agra became famous as the capital city of the Mughals during Akbar's reign, when it was also called Akbarabad. When Aurangazeb shifted his capital from Agra to Delhi, further development of the city stopped. Later, in 1803, the British ruled over Agra.

Along with Sikandra and Fatehpur-Sikri, the one time capital, Agra was the region where the best of Islamic architecture blossomed.

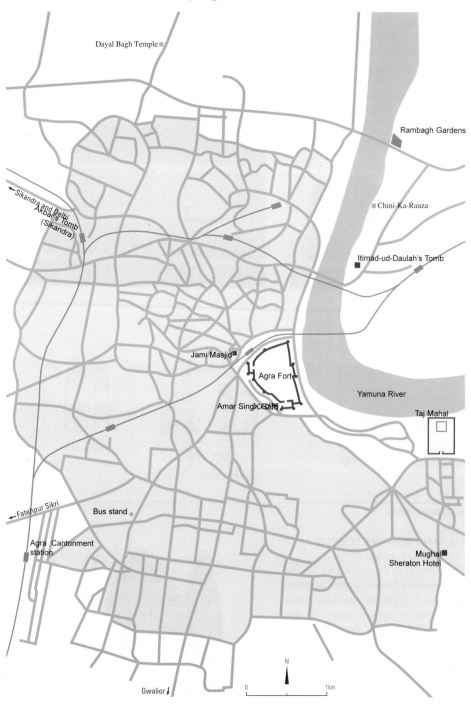

Dayal Bagh Temple

Rambagh Gardens

Sikandra and Delhi
Akbar's Tomb
(Sikandra)

Chini-Ka-Rauza

Itimad-ud-Daulah's Tomb

Jami Masjid

Agra Fort

Yamuna River

Amar Singh Gate

Taj Mahal

Fatehpur Sikri

Bus stand

Agra Cantonment station

Mughal
Sheraton Hotel

N

Gwalior

0   1km

AGRA FORT ★★
16th~17th C/ Islamic

The most important fort built during the Mughal era is Agra Fort constructed by Akbar from 1565 to 1573. A fort with the river at the rear is a defence strategy also seen in Delhi. This fort is also in red sandstone and is called Red Fort. Akbar erected the walls, gates and the first buildings within the walls. Shahjahan built the imperial quarters and the mosque. A century later, Aurangzeb built the outer walls of the fort. The mosque is very close to the entrance gate, as in Lahore and Delhi.

Within the fort is one large mosque and two smaller mosques. The larger mosque, Moti Masjid made of marble, is the crown of Mughal architecture. It is a tragedy that it has been closed to the public in recent years. Of the two smaller mosques, Mina Mosque is an extremely small, royal prayer-house while Nagina Mosque was used by the royal ladies as a prayer-house (*zenana*).

As in other palace complexes, this one too, has a *Diwan-i-Khas* and a *Diwan-i-Am*, which are pillared halls. Shah Jahan's residence (Haas-Mahal) has a square garden, Anguri Bagh. It has flowerbeds, waterways and fountains.

Jahangiri Mahal and the golden pavilion, both architectural marvels are perfect examples of the synergy of Hindu and Muslim architecture, which will later be reflected in Fatehpur-Sikri too.

The last structure built was a curved roof structure. When the Mughals annexed Bengal as their granary, this traditional design of Bengal was incorporated into palace buildings. It is called the *Bangaldar* roof. It would later be widely incorporated into Rajput palaces.

Amar Singh Gate glistens in the evening sunlight. The thin long holes are gun points.

Akbar Gate inside Amar Singh Gate

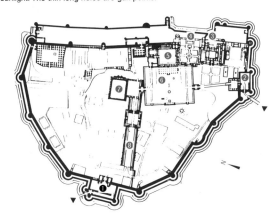

❶ Delhi Gate ❷ Amar Singh Gate and Akbar Gate
❸ Jahangir Palace ❹ The pavilions for relaxation
❺ Diwan-i-Khas ❻ Diwan-i-Am
❼ Moti Masjid ❽ Bazaar lined street

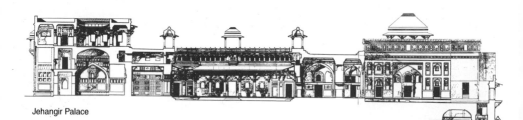

Jehangir Palace

❶ Jehangir Palace constructed during Akbar's reign.
❷ The detailed sculpture on the entrance of Jehangir's Palace courtyard.
❸ Jehangir Palace is not an arched structure, but a pillar and beam structure.
❹ The pavilion for relaxation, Haas Mahal and Anguri Bagh.·
❺ The interior of Moti Masjid - made of marble.
❻ The Nagina Mosque for the use of ladies (*Zenana*).
❼ The *Bangaldar* roof.
❽ Diwan-i-Am where an audience was given to the general public.

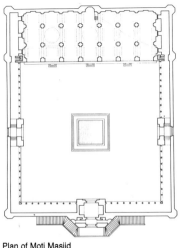

Plan of Moti Masjid

TOMB OF ITIMAD-UD-DAULAH ★★
1628/ Islamic

Itimad-ud-Daulah or 'Pillar of the Royal Family' was the pet name of Mirza Ghiyas Beg, minister in Jehangir's court. Since he was also the father of Empress Noor Jahan, this jewel-like tomb was built for him. The tomb has a geometric shape and is placed in a square garden. The tomb chamber is 21 m square. The central hall where the tomb is located is divided into 9 parts and there are steps in the corner leading to the four minarets. Stone decorations start from the spindle on the roof of the central hall and are symmetrically placed throughout the building. The white marble mausoleum is decorated with coloured stones. The crest and arabesque patterns created with inlay are awesome. The stone lattice screens *(jalis)* on the windows, especially the one on the wall of the platform where the cenotaph is kept, look like lace curtains.

An stone mural on the wall with inlay work.

The inlay stonework panel

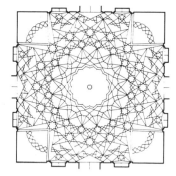
Drawing of the design of the central hall roof.

Facade of the Tomb of Itimad-ud-Daulah.

TAJ MAHAL ★★★
1653/ Islamic

Shahjahan became immortal, for building one of the wonders of the world, a monument of love, rather than for his prowess in controlling his empire as the fifth Mughal Emperor. Empress Mumtaz Mahal was the grand daughter of Itimad-ud-Daulah and was also called Taj Mahal (Peerless) in the Royal household. The couple loved each other so much that Mumtaz Mahal accompanied Shah Jahan to the battlefront after giving birth to their 13th child. During the expedition she died while giving birth to their 14th child. Shah Jahan wanted to immortalize her beauty and built a magnificent, stately, milky white mausoleum, which took 22 years and 20,000 people to build. Because of financial tension created by this venture, he was kept under house arrest by his son Aurangzeb. Shahjahan spent his last days gazing at the Taj Mahal, with his wife's memories for company.

The Mughal construction of tombs starting with Humayun's tomb, reached its zenith in this one. Its uniqueness is that it is placed at one end of a square garden. The Yamuna River flows in the background and the square garden is in front. As you enter there is nothing to hamper the vision of the white beauty in front. The tall dome, 55 m in height with brass spires, is taller than the minarets in the corners. The perfection of its proportions and a high standard of craftsmanship, have made people look upon this building with awe. Since the style is Persian, it cannot be called the best of Indian architecture. It is more a work of art than an architectural creation.

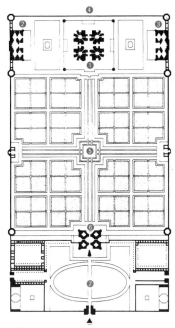

Site Plan
❶ The grave ❷ Funeral mosque ❸ Guest hall
❹ Yamuna River ❺ The tank in the centre
❻ Double-storeyed entrance ❼ Front garden

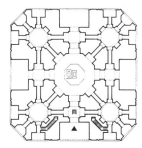

Floor plan

The reflection of the Taj Mahal in the tank

❶ Interior of the tomb (1820) ❷ Cross-section ❸ Naubat Khana ❹ A guesthouse for VIPs from abroad.

❺ Taj Mahal ❻ Double-storeyed entrance. ❼ *Chhatris* on the parapet. ❽ The 6.7 m high tomb.

RAM BAGH GARDENS
16th C/ Islamic

The first emperor of the Mughal dynasty, Babur, was an educated man. He loved the huge gardens he left behind in central Asia and wanted to build a geometrical, Islamic garden in India. This style was later developed on a grand scale in Kashmir. Babur built Ram Garden (originally Aram Garden) which was the resting place for his body before it was interred in Kabul.

Pavilion, which faces the Yamuna River.

JAMI MASJID (FRIDAY MOSQUE)
1648/ Islamic

This small mosque built by Shah Jahan, is similar to the Jami Masjid in Delhi but the quality of construction is not very impressive. This is because the dome is low, it does not have tall minarets and the red sandstone and marble do not blend with each other. However, the group of *chhatris* (domed roof-top pavilions) on the parapet are beautiful.

Façade on the courtyard side.

MUGHAL SHERATON HOTEL ★
1976/ Post Independence
by ARCOP - R. Khosla, R Sabikhi, K Gujral, A Verma, Ray Afleck, Ajoy Choudhary

This group of stone buildings, though not traditional in design, is built in a style of architecture that is commonly seen in Agra. The plan is like a *caravan sarai*. Red bricks have been used on the outer walls that remind one of red sand stone. The courtyard with its water body, looks like a Mughal garden. This building won the Aga Khan prize for interior decoration.

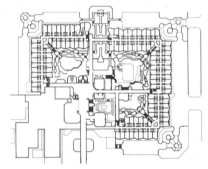

Plan of the first floor

Up: Guest room and courtyard made of bricks. Down: Interior of the lobby.

TOMB OF AKBAR ★★★
1613/ Islamic

At the beginning of the 16th century, Sikandra was the capital of the Lodi dynasty. There is no visible sign of the Lodi legacy in this area and even though Lodi ruled over this region, his tomb lies in Delhi.

Sikandra, 10 km north of Agra, now houses the majestic mausoleum of Emperor Akbar of the Mughal dynasty and its surrounding gardens.

Akbar was the Mughal Emperor who brought most of north India under his control. The Rajputs of the west co-operated with him and as a result, most of his reign was peaceful and culture flourished. Before his long reign of 50 years was completed, he ordered the building of his own tomb.

Akbar's style of construction is strongly reflected in this structure. His harmonization of Hindu and Islamic ideas was also put into practice in the sphere of architecture and has given rise to an interesting and novel style of construction.

The mausoleum is in the middle of a garden, where each of the sides measures 700 m. On each side is a magnificent entrance tower with minarets at each corner and a group of *chhatris* on top. The tomb itself is entirely different from other tombs. it is on a platform that is 150 m long on one side and is a pillar and beam structure 3 storeys high. Red sandstone has been used like wood with a pillar and beam framework which is found in wooden structures. Red sandstone rocks have been used like wooden pivots. Using stone as one would use wood for constructions, was a traditional Indian architectural technique. Akbar made effective use of this technique and this style is not seen anywhere else in the Islamic world, other than in India. In India, it is found only in Akbar's tomb

and in Fatehpur Sikri. A *chhatri* over four pillars makes up one module and there are ten such modules. The effect is so unique that it looks like something out of a fantasy. The top of the tomb is a courtyard surrounded by arcades and marble screens with Akbar's cenotaph in the centre. It is said that a dome was supposed to erected over the tomb, but it looks perfect as it is. Akbar's coffin is kept in an undecorated tomb in the basement.

The two-storeyed entrance in the south.

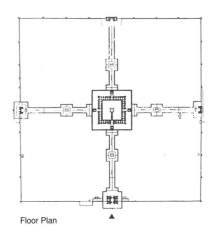
Floor Plan

The stone inlay in the two-storeyed entrance and the platform and tomb with an *Iwan* in the centre.

The courtyard at the top-most level

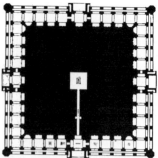

Floor Plan

Up: The mausoleum topped with a large number of *chhatris*. Down: A group of *chhatris*.

Cross-section

The tomb in the basement below.

The first floor hall with its vaulted ceiling decorated with colourful tiles (Entrance for steps leading to the basement).

117

FATEHPUR SIKRI ★ ★ ★

Legend has it that Emperor Akbar's son, Jehangir was born only after Akbar visited the Sufi saint, Salim Chishti, who was living in Sikri, and received his blessings. Ever grateful, Akbar decided to shift his capital from Agra to this place. At the same time, since he had also successfully annexed Gujarat, he called the city Fatehpur Sikri (Capital of Victory). The city is planned on a grid. The town below the castle, no longer exists. Zones for the mosque and palace were demarcated on the plateau and red sandstone was used for all structures. Apart from the castle walls, fortifications are minimal. One part of the city wall and the entrance still remain as evidence of plans to build a large city within. Before these plans could materialize, the city was abandoned in 1585, because the man-made lake to the northwest could not provide sufficient water for the entire city. As this Fatehpur Sikri was not affected by the war, it has survived as a display of its architectural style to later generations. The architectural style is very similar to that of Akbar's mausoleum in Sikandra and reflects Akbar's ideology of a fusion of religions, technology and practical sciences.

It is fascinating to see the effective use of pivots in stone, the same way they are executed in wood. This style of construction is not usually used in arch construction. This is seen only in stone temples built by Hindus and Jains, without using the principles of masonry construction. It takes great experience and a number of devices are required.

Islam was a foreign religion imported into India and it brought with it, its own rich, traditional culture. Under Islamic rule, traditional religion and art also prospered. Akbar who developed a new construction style by fusing both, Hindu and Islamic architectural styles, was a true advocate of this culture.

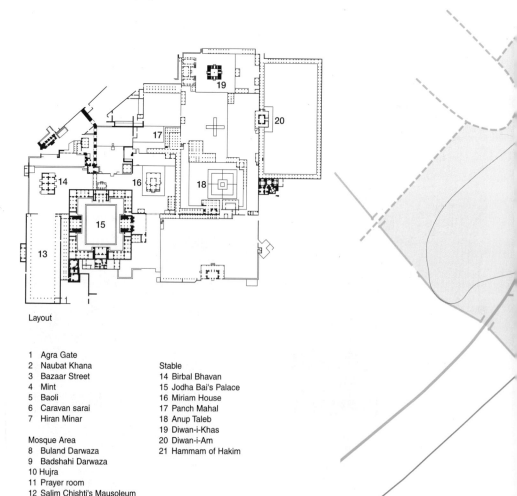

Layout

1	Agra Gate		
2	Naubat Khana		Stable
3	Bazaar Street	14	Birbal Bhavan
4	Mint	15	Jodha Bai's Palace
5	Baoli	16	Miriam House
6	Caravan sarai	17	Panch Mahal
7	Hiran Minar	18	Anup Taleb
		19	Diwan-i-Khas
	Mosque Area	20	Diwan-i-Am
8	Buland Darwaza	21	Hammam of Hakim
9	Badshahi Darwaza		
10	Hujra		
11	Prayer room		
12	Salim Chishti's Mausoleum		
13	Islam Khan's Mausoleum		

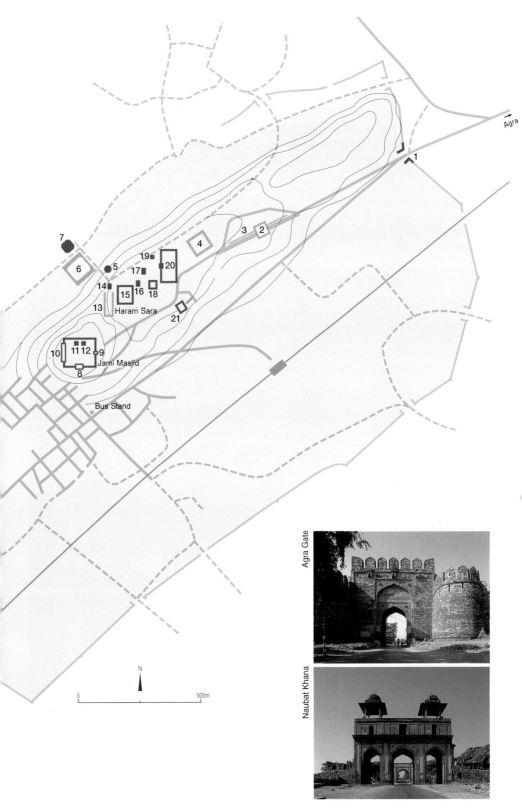

Agra

7

6

5

19

17

20

14

15 16 18

13

Haram Sara

21

4

3 2

1

10 11 12 9

8

Jami Masjid

Bus Stand

N

0   500m

Agra Gate

Naubat Khana

MOSQUE QUARTER ★★★
Middle of the 16th C/ Islamic

This large mosque has a prayer room that faces Mecca. There is an open ground in front of the mosque, which is too large to be called a mere courtyard. Two mausoleums for Sufi saints were built here and since the Sufi graves are called *dargahs* this mosque is also called Dargah.

BADSHAHI DARWAZA /1571/
Since all mosques face west, their entrances will usually face the east. Badshahi Darwaza which Akbar used, is one such entrance, crowned with *chhatris*.

BULAND DARWAZA ★★ /1576/
In 1573, Emperor Akbar annexed Gujarat and commemorated his victory by building a 54 m high gate in the south, which has steps leading to it, like one finds on hills. It is one of the best examples of Indo-Islamic architecture. The mosaic wall with its combination of red and yellow sandstone and marble is admirable.

JAMI MASJID (FRIDAY MOSQUE) ★★
1571/Islamic

This mosque served as the model for the Jami Masjid in Delhi, built 80 years later. However, the prayer room is smaller and the minarets are lower than those in Delhi. The mosque has a Persian *Iwan* in the centre. The red sandstone pillars and beams inside the mosque reflect the Indian fascination for complex construction. The *Quibla* wall (facing Mecca) in the central hall is decorated with mosaic patterns using different coloured stones. This mosque is a great example of Akbar's penchant for fusing Hinduism with Islam in his unique style.

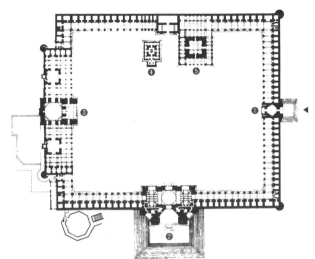

❶ Buland Darwaza
❷ Mosaic on the wall of Badshahi Darwaza.
❸ The corridors and Buland Darwaza.
❹ The central *Iwan* in the prayer room.
❺ *Mihrab* in the prayer room
❻ The interior of the prayer room.

Floor Plan
❶ Badshahi Darwaza **❷** Buland Darwaza **❸** Prayer room of the Friday Mosque **❹** The tomb of Salim Chishti **❺** Islam Khan Mausoleum

Cross-section

TOMB OF SHAIKH SALIM CHISHTI ★★
1570, 1606

Akbar built a mausoleum for Salim Chishti inside the mosque. At first, it was red sandstone and white marble, but was later rebuilt as a white marble mausoleum inside a red sandstone building. The broad stone eaves, supported by pillars on which rests the dome, is its characteristic feature. Islamic in style, it was adapted to India's rainy conditions and has elaborate details on pillars and lattice screens.

TOMB OF ISLAM KHAN

This structure is a mausoleum of red sandstone, which houses graves of Sufi saints.

❶ Tomb of Islam Khan.
❷ Tomb of Shaikh Salim Chishti.
❸ The elaborately decorated pillars and eaves.
❹❺ The *jali* (lattice screen) in marble.

PALACE QUARTERS ★★★
Middle of the16th C/ Islamic
The palace along with the mosque have been set on an east-west axis. The sandstone building sits in flying geese formation to adapt to the 45 degree slope. It has all the components of Akbar's architectural style - pillars, beams, broad eaves, *chhatris*, etc. At present only the stone edifice remains. During Akbar's reign, a gentle ambience was created with carpets, silk curtains, cushions and furniture.

JODHA BAI PALACE ★/1569
Akbar's residence was Jodh Bai Palace. The palace was divided into the area where the affairs of state were conducted and the living area (*Haram Sara*). The palace has a Persian style courtyard and each side has in the centre, the Indian style pillar and beam structure with broad eaves, instead of the arch *iwan*. The bedroom was on the second floor.

BIRBAL BHAVAN ★/1569
Since it is not known what some of the buildings were used for, there are many buildings with wrong names. As Jodha Bai Palace is also wrongly named, so is Birbal Bhavan. It transpires that maybe Akbar's wives lived here, not Birbal. The second floor has a stark look, but the interior is delicately carved all over.

Jodha Bai Palace

❶ Courtyard in Jodha Bai Palace. ❷ Birbal Bhavan. ❸ Interior of Birbal Bhavan. ❹ Window in Jodha Bai Palace.

PANCH MAHAL ★★
/1570

This unique building in the palace zone has pillars and beams and looks like a jungle gym. Perhaps it was used to watch a game; to keep cool in summer; or as a viewing platform. Chess was played in the open space, using humans as chessmen. The pillars reinforce the building against natural calamities.

MIRIAM'S HOUSE ★

This structure housed Empress Miriam. The queen mother may have also been living here. It is very similar in appearance to Birbal Bhavan, but the interior is very colourful.

DIWAN-I-AM
/1570

Diwan-i-Am was the place where the Emperor used to give audience to the public, to hear their grievances and deliver judgments. On the lower level is the wide Hakushu-type courtyard with an arcade around it.

❶ Panch Mahal (five-storeyed building).
❷ Miriam's house.
❸ *Diwan-i-Am* from the rear.
❹ The tank Anup Talao, with a platform in the centre.

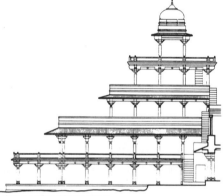

Cross-section of Panch Mahal.

Details of the pavilion near the tank.

HIRAN MINAR ★

Minars or minarets are not mere decorations but are lookout towers or lighthouses which stand independently. Attached to the shaft of Hiran Minar are numerous stone elephant's tusks which present a very strange sight. It was thought to commemorate Akbar's favourite elephant Hiran. Lamps were probably hung on the tusks to light the way for travellers.

HAMAM OF HAKIM

The noteworthy Muslim *hammam* (bathhouse) is in an area where three scholarly brothers lived. It has many rooms for saunas and baths.

DIWAN-I-KHAS ★★/1570

Diwan-i-Khas is a unique but strange building, built in Akbar's style of architecture. From the stairwell in the corners, two bridges intersect each other in the middle. A pillar with a banana cluster-like motif on its capital, supports these bridges. Legend has it that Akbar would sit on a platform where the bridges crossed and listen to wise men debating and pass judgments.

BAOLI ★

This is a group of wells in the west-Indian style, above which were a set of complex steps and a cool room.

❺ Hiran Minar
❻ *Diwan-i-Khas*
❼ The central pillar in the *Diwan-i-Khas*
❽ *Hammam* of Hakim
❾ *Baoli* (stepwell)

Lucknow, the capital of Uttar Pradesh was built by Nawab Asaf ud-Daulah of the Oudh dynasty, when he shifted his headquarters here. Lucknow was prominent as a cultural capital, but the its buildings all belong to the near past. This was the battleground during the 1857 uprising against the British. Of the two main groups in Islam called the *Shias* (majority) and *Sunnis* (minority), Lucknow is the heartland for the Indian *Shias*. This fact that is reflected in the buildings.

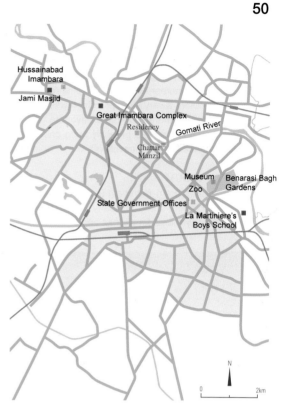

The marble mausoleum in the city.

JAMI MASJID (FRIDAY MOSQUE)
1845/ Islamic

Nawab Muhammed Ali Shah started constructing this mosque, but it was completed only after his death. Since it is a relatively new structure, it has many embellishments in the Mannerist style. The exterior has stucco instead of brick finish, which makes it appear darker, while the interior is bright and colourful.

Legislative Assembly

LA MARTINIERE'S BOYS SCHOOL ★ (CONSTANTIA)
18th C/ Colonial
by Claude Martin

French army officer, Claude Martin (1735-1800) built *Constancia* on the eastern outskirts after his retirement and it was converted into a boys' school after he died. A blend of a European palace, Akbar's mausoleum and Thirumalai Nayakan palace, it has European sculptures on the roof.

La Martiniere's Boys School

GREAT IMAMBARA COMPLEX
1784/ Islamic

The complex housing the Imambara Mosque, *baolis* and two gates was built by Asaf-ud-Daulah, when he shifted his capital here. Rumi Darwaza (Turkish entrance) is nearby. The day the Imam of the Sunni group died as a martyr in 638 AD is remembered every year as *Muharram*. It is on such days that these *imambaras* are used. Lucknow, with its large Muslim population has a number of *imambaras*. Although many have a domed roof, this one built in the Mughal style has a flat roof and the large space within has a more European flavour. Stepped wells are rare in this region.

Long façade of the large Imambara.

Floor Plan

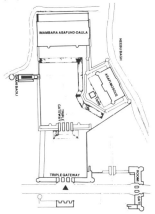

❶ Mosque and Rumi Gate seen from the large *imambara* ❷ The hall. At the far end is a replica of Hassan Hussain Ali's grave ❸ Rumi Gate ❹ Imambara Mosque strikingly similar to the Jami Masjid in Delhi.

The *baoli* (step well)

Jaunpur, built in 1360 by Feroze Shah Tughluq, later became the capital of the Sharqi dynasty. Many mosques and mausoleums built in the Indo-Muslim style during 14th-15th century still exist. Jaunpur came under Mughal rule in the 16th century. A special feature of these structures is that in front of the prayer room, in place of the *iwan* is a structure too shallow to be called an *iwan*, with high walls that look like the Pylon of ancient Egypt. The details are unrefined but graceful.

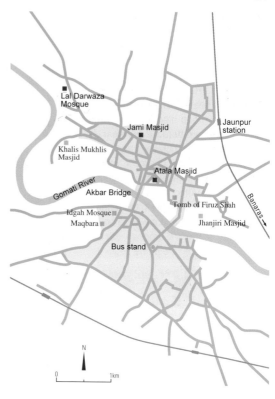

Entrance of the Jaunpur castle.

ATALA MASJID ★
1408/ Islamic

Earlier this mosque was a temple dedicated to Atala Devi. Pillars and beams from the temple were used in the mosque, but the layout with the four *iwans* is distinctly Persian. It is unusual that the *iwans*, other than the one in the prayer room, were not in the courtyard. The central arch is over 22m high.

Right: The pylon, like the *Iwan* is shallow in depth.
Left: The *Mihrab* where the brickwork is visible.

JAMI MASJID (FRIDAY MOSQUE) ★
1478/ Islamic

This mosque, built by the last king of the Sharqi dynasty, is the largest in Jaunpur. It is surrounded by a double storeyed arcade and like the exterior, the prayer hall is not polished. It has strong archaic features. The sloping wall surface of the *iwan* is 25 m high and even here the other *iwans* face outwards. Perhaps, this is an inborn trait in Indians to respect the outdoors.

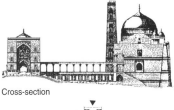

Cross-section

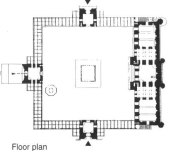

Floor plan

The *Iwan* facing the courtyard.

Up: The central prayer hall. Down: The arcade surrounding the courtyard.

LAL DARWAZA MASJID
1450/ Islamic

This very small mosque built by Bibi Raji queen of Sultan Muhammed, is called the Lal Darwaza (red door) Mosque, since it is painted red in colour. As it was a part of the Sultan's palace complex, it has a mezzanine floor for ladies in the prayer hall. The staircase to the mezzanine floor is through the *iwan* wall.

AKBARI BRIDGE
1568/ Islamic

Until the introduction of the Islamic architectural style, there were no bridges built in India. The age-old traditional Indian systems of building did not extend to construction of bridges. Among those built by the Mughals, the best example is the one built by Afzal Ali in Jaunpur, during Akbar's reign. Though not comparable with Iran's Hajyu Bridge, this 16-span bridge is very elaborate. Besides serving the purpose of a bridge, it also has restrooms and pavilions.

Akbar Bridge.

A single span of the bridge.

ALLAHABAD ⋆

52

KHUSRAU BAGH (GARDEN) ⋆
17th C/ Islamic

Khusrau Bagh, near the railway station, built in the Mughal period, was the summer house of Jehangir. Khusrau, Jehangir's son was killed for political reasons and his body was brought to Allahabad only seven years later. A mausoleum was built for him near those of his mother and sister. The mother's mausoleum does not have the step formation while the top portion has a pillared corridor that is very rare.

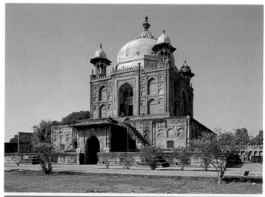

The water sluice in the courtyard.

Up: Khusrau's sister's mausoleum. Down: All three mausoleums.

MUIR COLLEGE
1878/ Colonial
By William Emerson

William Emerson began constructing in India when he was in his prime and became chairman of the Architect's Guild in Great Britain. When Emerson came to India, he was spellbound by Romanticism, which is reflected in Muir College, with its Eyptian minarets, Mughal domes and Gothic tracery, all used together. This building in the English style, is a structure that reflects William Emerson's personal style.

The top of the minaret.

Up: Muir college. Down: Arcade with Gothic tracery.

ALL SAINTS CATHEDRAL
1877~1893/ Colonial
by William Emerson

This cathedral was built in Allahabad as it was a capital city during British rule. Emerson ignored the traditional Indian styles of architecture and built it in the Gothic style. Construction was started in 1877, but funds ran short and the project kept getting delayed. The tower, on the top could not be completed due to a shortfall in the budget. The lower level has latticework in marble, in the Fatehpur Sikri style.

View of the facade.

The interior of the cathedral.

BUDDHIST MONASTERY AND DHAMEKH STUPA

3 BC~12 AD/ Buddhist

After he attained *Nirvana* Buddha preached at Sarnath, which is 8 km from Varanasi (Benares). Circa 500 AD, Sarnath had many temples, *stupas* and monasteries, and trainee monks gathered here. When Buddhism declined in the 12th century, it flourished again only in the 19th century. Just one structure with the ordinary courtyard-type plan exists today. This is the Dhamekh Stupa, which was built at the start of the 6th century. Built of bricks and finished with stone cladding, it stands 34 m high. The surface is sculpted with arabesques and geometric patterns. In 1931, the Mulgandha Kirti Vihar was built inside the ruins. A Japanese artist, Kosetsu Nosi has painted Buddhist scenes here.

Stone finish on the surface of the *Stupa*.

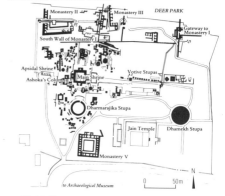

Sketch Map

❶ Dhamekh Stupa ❷ Mulgandha Temple ❸ Ruins of the monastery.

Varanasi, on the banks of the Ganga is one of the most sacred places of pilgrimage in India. Gautama Buddha visited this place which was called Kashi. This means that Varanasi's history must be at least 3000 years old. The buildings however date back to the 17th century. Unfortunately, while they have style and character, they are not excellent.

In the 12th century, Varanasi came under Islamic rule whose Mughal emperor was intolerant of other religions. He built a mosque, named after him, which has been the cause for unrest until today. In the 18th century, it was ruled by a Hindu feudal lord and was revived as the sacred place of Hindus. Now it is a religious and cultural city of 1,000,000 people. There are many temples in Benares but none stands out for its excellence. There is the Jantar Mantar (astronomical observatory), but it compares unfavourably with the ones in Jaipur or Delhi.

Today, what brings hordes of people to this place is the town with its collection of anonymous buildings and the *ghats* (stepped terraces on the banks of the river) that weave a religious spell. The sight of people worshipping the sun, while bathing at dawn, is unforgettable.

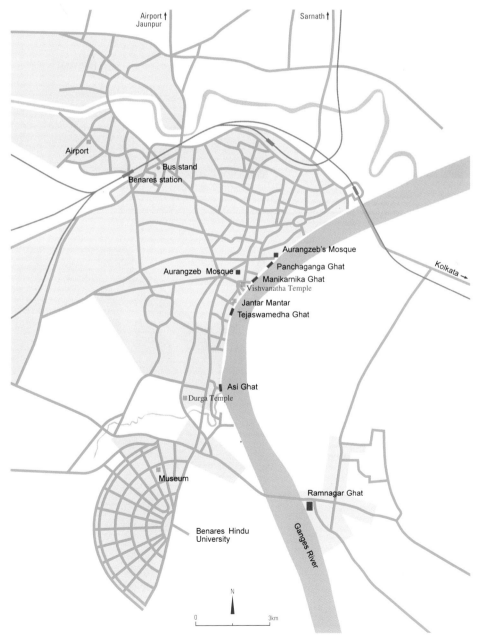

MOSQUES OF AURANGZEB
17th C/ Islamic

Aurangzeb built two mosques on the banks of the Ganga. For a lack of space, they are built in a confined area and their precincts are not very wide. The smaller mosque built on the site of a temple, is in the Mughal style. The larger mosque was built with material from Vishnunath Temple, though no historical records support the claim. It has stucco painting on it. The height of its minaret is 70 m from the riverbank and it acts as a good landmark.

The new Vishnunath Temple (golden temple) was built in the 18th century.

The Hindu golden temple.

Up: The small Aurangazeb Mosque. Down: The large Aurangzeb Mosque.

RAMNAGAR FORT ★
17th~18th C/ Rajput

The Ganges is so wide, that the town could not be built on the opposite bank. The Maharaja's palace (feudal lord who established himself in 1736) is built upstream. The 17th century fort runs parallel to the river and has temples and palaces surrounded by courtyards with guards, guarding it. The palace facing the main courtyard is a blend of corbelled brackets and Mughal style arches. It reminds one of Akbar's style of construction. The side along the river has an entrance gate, allowing access to those who arrive by boat.

The fort wall.

Entrance from the courtyard.

GHATS AND TOWNSCAPE ★★
Hindu

In India, the banks of a river are considered sacred and terraces or steps are built there. These steps that lead into the river are called *ghats*. In Benares, the *ghats* stretch for 3 km or more and each section has its own name. At dawn, people bathe while worshipping the sun. This spectacle, against a stony backdrop leaves a deep impression on the mind of a visitor.

A deep desire of Hindus is to die in Benares, be cremated on the *ghat* and the ashes to be immersed in the river. In Manikarnika Ghat, there is always a queue of bodies waiting to be burnt. The steps of the *ghats* lead to narrow lanes, which are tightly packed with houses, shops and temples. Cows, horses, squirrels, rats and birds all walk alongside people, creating an almost medieval ambience, with little distinction between man and beast.

Up: A view of the *ghats* at dawn, as seen from a boat. Down: The scene at dusk.

Up: The *ghats* viewed during the day, from a boat Down: Dasashvamedha Ghat.

The *ghats* with Aurangazeb's fort in the background.

Nepal

North India

VAISHALI
5

Banaras

7 6 PATNA
MANER

BARABAR HILL
SASARAM 8
NALANDA
9

11

BODHGAYA 10

BIHAR

Middle India

Silpur

RAJGIRI 35
UDAYGIRI

ORISSA
KHANDAGIRI & UDAYGIRI 34
BHUBANESHWAR 37
DHAULI 38 39
HARIPUR
CHAURASI 42
PURI 40 KONA

MUKHALINGAM 43

South India

East India

China

Bhutan

SIKKIM
TASHIDING ② LABRANG
PEMAYANGTSE ③ ④ ①
RUMTEK

KANTANAGAR
㉖

⑬ PANDUA
㉘ PAHARPUR

⑫ GAUR
KUSUMBHA
㉗
㉚ PUTHIA
⑯ BARANAGAR
⑭
MURSHIDABAD

BANGLADESH

㉙ PABNA

DHAKA ㉛ ㉜
SONARGAON
COMILLA ㉝

⑰ GHURISA
ARAKAR HADAL-NARAYANPUR
⑲
⑳ BISHNUPUR
⑮ BARDDHAMAN
㉑ KALNA
㉒ GUPTIPALA
㉓ BANSBERIA
WEST BENGAL
ATPUR ㉔
㉕ KOLKATA

N

0   200km

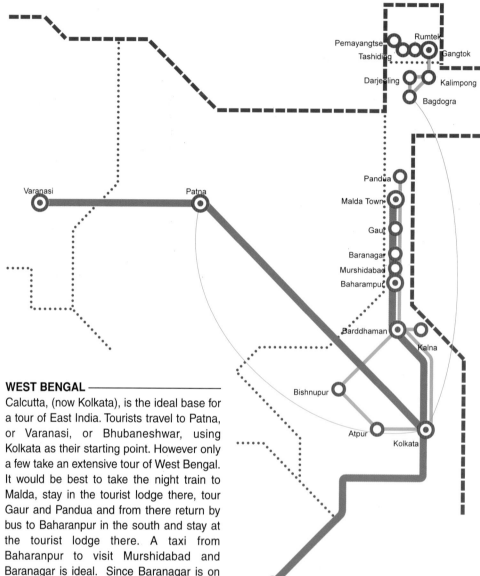

Pemayangtse
Rumtek
Tashiding
Gangtok
Darjeeling
Kalimpong
Bagdogra

Pandua
Malda Town
Gaur
Baranagar
Murshidabad
Baharampur
Barddhaman
Kalna

Varanasi
Patna

Bishnupur

Atpur
Kolkata

Bhubhaneshwar

WEST BENGAL

Calcutta, (now Kolkata), is the ideal base for a tour of East India. Tourists travel to Patna, or Varanasi, or Bhubaneshwar, using Kolkata as their starting point. However only a few take an extensive tour of West Bengal. It would be best to take the night train to Malda, stay in the tourist lodge there, tour Gaur and Pandua and from there return by bus to Baharanpur in the south and stay at the tourist lodge there. A taxi from Baharanpur to visit Murshidabad and Baranagar is ideal. Since Baranagar is on the banks of the Bhagirathi river, one can go by boat and take a rickshaw from there, too. From Baharampur, go to Barddhaman and from there to Kalna and Guptipala. Bishunupur is two hours away by bus or taxi. Stay in the tourist lodge there and visit the terracotta temples by rickshaw. From here, Kolkata is four hours away by bus or train. If you take a taxi, you can also visit Atpur. The hotels in these places are very basic. High and medium range hotels are available only in Kolkata, which also has low budget hotels. Some of the quality hotels are the Oberoi Grand, Lytton Hotel and Fairlawn Hotel.

Fairlawn Hotel

SIKKIM

Sikkim is inviting for its cool, mountainous towns and its intriguing Buddhist *gompas* (monasteries). Foreigners can get a free 15-day permit from the District Magistrate's office in Darjeeling or the Sikkim Tourism offices in Delhi, Kolkata and Siliguri. The easiest way to reach Sikkim is to fly from Kolkata to Bagdogra. Gangtok is a four-and-a-half-hour journey by road from the airport. Norhill Hotel, is one of the better quality hotels in Gangtok. Phodong, can be visited either by taxi, van or bus, but a trip to Pemayangtse will involve an overnight stay. Hotel Mount Pandim in Pemayangtse has rooms with spectacular views, but as there are no heaters, it is quite cold. From Gangtok, the *gompas* in Tashiding and a visit to Rumtek can be covered in the same trip. Kalimpong and Darjeeling though similar to Sikkim, lie in West Bengal. Gangtok to Kalimpong is 3 hours by road and Kalimpong to Darjeeling two-and-a-half hours. Travel to Kathmandu is possible from Darjeeling via Siliguri. Visas can be obtained at the border. The journey takes 24 hours.

BIHAR

Flying from Delhi to Kolkata and visiting Varanasi, Khajuraho, Bodhgaya and Agra is a recommended, short-duration itinerary. Surface transport will be necessary for visiting Buddhist sites. Fly to Patna from Kolkata or take a train (9 hours). Stay in Hotel Pataliputra is advised. A trip to Vaisali takes two hours, while getting to Maner takes 45 minutes. A one-way trip to Bodhgaya is possible, but one has to pay the return fare too. It takes one and a half hours to get to Nalanda. Those who are interested in Jainism can visit Pavapuri. Pavapuri to Rajgiri is a 30-minute journey. Bodhgaya via Gaya will take about two hours. Here you can stay in Hotel Centaur Hokke in Rajgiri and go to Gaya by bus. Hotel Bodhgaya Ashok in Bodhgaya is recommended. Barabar Hills, can be visited from Gaya by taxi. You can also cross the border and enter Benares and visit Sasaram. If you cannot catch the one and only early morning train you will have to stay in an hotel. Since the bus services are bad, it is advisable to take a taxi from Bodhgaya to Benares.

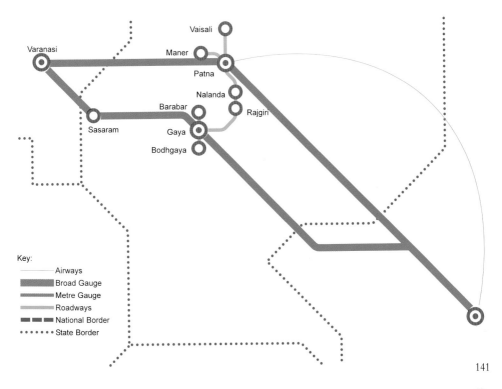

Key:
— Airways
— Broad Gauge
— Metre Gauge
— Roadways
■■■ National Border
•••••• State Border

TRAVEL INFORMATION (East India)

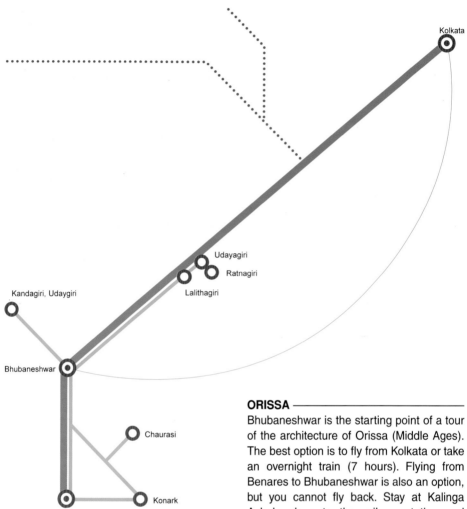

Kolkata

Udayagiri

Ratnagiri

Kandagiri, Udaygiri

Lalithagiri

Bhubaneshwar

Chaurasi

Puri

Konark

ORISSA

Bhubaneshwar is the starting point of a tour of the architecture of Orissa (Middle Ages). The best option is to fly from Kolkata or take an overnight train (7 hours). Flying from Benares to Bhubaneshwar is also an option, but you cannot fly back. Stay at Kalinga Ashok, close to the railway station and temples. Oberoi Bhubaneshwar, a high class hotel, is far from the temples and therefore not convenient. Hire a rickshaw for a couple of days and see the temples at leisure.

Khandagiri and Udayagiri can be seen in a single trip. Rajgiri is two and a half hours away and Udayagiri is 30 minutes away. Take a bus to Konark and Puri, but if you wish to visit Hirapur, Dauli and Chaurasi, which are *en route*, hire a taxi. Hirapur is 10 km away and can be reached by bus. It is around 100 km to Konark. There are simple tourist bungalows or travellers' lodges in Konark. If you stay overnight you can pray to the Sun God at dawn. Puri has good hotels, but non-believers are advised to just visit the place and catch the overnight train, back to Kolkata, since they are not allowed inside the temple.

Stone carvings in a niche on the wall.

BANGLADESH

You have to fly from Kolkata or from Kathmandu in Nepal, because the border between India and Bangladesh is closed.

Flying is a much easier option, because most of Bangladesh in the delta basin, is criss-crossed with tributaries. There are not many places to see and there are very few tourists. It is better to take a taxi from the Dhaka tourist office. Dhaka town can be seen by going around in a rickshaw or auto rickshaw and Sonargaon can be visited by taxi. Hotel Abakash is a good place to stay.

From Dhaka, fly to Syedpur and take taxis from there to Dinajpur and stay in hotel Al Rashid. One can take a bus trip to Kantanagar or walk the distance in an hour. You cannot get to the temple without a guide from the village. It is difficult to go from here to Paharpur.

From Jamalganj, the nearest station to the ruins, the view is incomparable, but the road is terrible. Instead, it is recommended that you go to Bogra, stay in Panjolan Hotel and take a trip to Paharpur. Bogra to Rajshahi is three hours by express bus. Panjolan Hotel is the best place to stay. Getting to Kusumbha, from here takes an hour-and-a half and Puthia is an hour away. You can relax in Puthia. Fly from Puthia to Dhaka. It takes 3 hours to get to Comilla, but there are no good hotels there. Take a rickshaw to see the ruins. From Comilla, either return to Dhaka or take the bus to Chittagong (4 hours), stay in Shaukat Hotel and fly back to Kolkata.

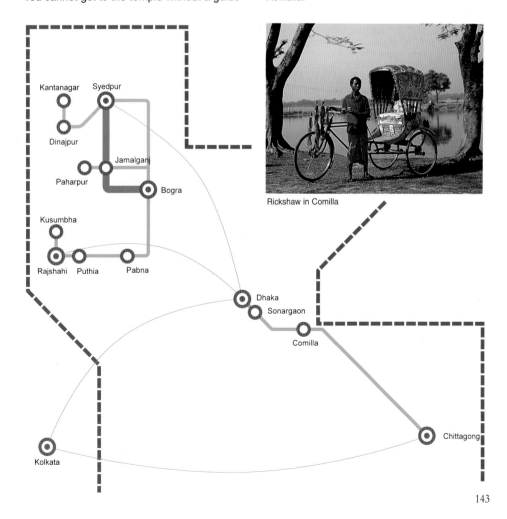

Rickshaw in Comilla

SIKKIM

Sikkim is a mountainous state whose borders touch Nepal, Tibet and Bhutan. The area is small and hilly and the population is around 400,000. Originally the Lepchya ethnic tribe lived here and later, a Tibetan tribe migrated in the 17th century. Noteworthy buildings are Buddhist *gompas* (monasteries) because the state has cultural links with Ladakhi and Tibetan Buddhism. Sikkim is very green and quite different from Ladakh because it is only 2,000 m above sea level. The monarchy that ruled since the 17th century, came to an end in the 19th century with the advent of British rule. In 1975, Sikkim was integrated as one of the states of India. Various tribes from Nepal migrated during the 19th century and are now a fairly large group. Darjeeling, famous for its tea, was gifted to the British and now belongs to West Bengal.

Travel permits for visiting Sikkim can be obtained when in Sikkim itself, but it is convenient to get one in Sikkim Tourism offices. When you take the bus or taxi from Bagtog airport to the capital Gangtok, the customs are located at the entrance to the town. Gangtok, which is blessed with natural beauty, lies to the east of Singtam, Pemayangtse and the monasteries are to the west. There is not much to see except for the interesting Namgyal Tibet Research Centre, built in the traditional style.

❶ Entrance to Sikkim (Rampo).
❷ Kanchenjunga at dawn.
❸ *Chorten*, Gangtok.
❹ Namgyal Tibet Research Centre for students, Gangtok.
❺ Interior of the *Kulu lagan*, Tashiding Gompa.

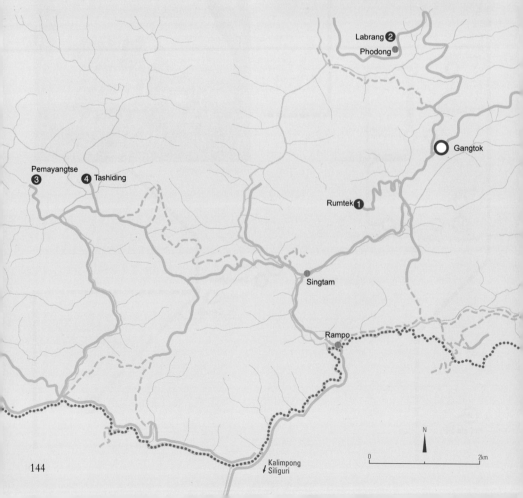

RUMTEK ★

GOMPA (MONASTERY) ★
20th C/ Buddhist

Rumtek Gompa 24 km from Gangtok, was started in the 11th century by Naropa's disciple Lama Marpa. It is the original *gompa* where the Kagyupa group (Akaboha) started and is still their main *gompa*. The 16th Gyalwa Karmapa, fled Tibet in 1959 after the Chinese invasion and built a replica of his Tibetan monastery, here. The main building in the traditional style is open to people of any caste who want to see the lifestyle in the monastery.

The colourful pillars.

Up: *Dukhang* Down: Prayer room facing a courtyard.

LABRANG ★

GOMPA (MONASTERY)
20th C/ Buddhist

In the mountains 40 km from Gangtok, are two *gompas*. The *Phodan* was built recently and is accessible by taxi. As you walk up the mountain you find the Raburian monastery which has its rear portion facing the valley. The roof of the *gompa* is not of a very good quality. The entrance and window frames are very delicate and are colourfully painted.

The full view.

The facade.

PEMAYANGTSE ★

18th C/ Buddhist

Deep in the mountains 115 km from Gangtok, 2085 m above sea-level, this is one of the two important *gompas* of Sikkim. Rebuilt after the original was destroyed by an earthquake in 1960, this *gompa* belongs to the Ninma group started by Padmasambhava. A closed corridor and smaller shrines surround the main shrine. The Mask Dance Festival or *Chaam* is celebrated annually.

❶ The various shrines of the *gompa*.
❷ The window of the young monks' quarters.
❸ The trim on the eaves of the main shrine.

The murals on the wall.

TASHIDING ★ ★

4

GOMPA (MONASTERY) ★
17th C/ Buddhist

This sacred *gompa* is located 13 km from Pemayangtse and 30 km from Tashding Bazar. The road is bad and you have to trek up the mountains for about 30 minutes to reach it. There are four shrines, Mani Lagan, Cheku Lagan, Gonkan and Gulu Lagan in this unsullied, serene place isolated from the ordinary world. There are many *chortens* in between these buildings. Though the layout dates back to the 18th century, the building is fairly new. The mere sight of Tashiding is thought to bring blessing.

Sacred inscriptions carved on the compound wall.

Up: The front view of the Gulu Lagan. Down: Interior of the Gulu Lagan.

BIHAR

States in India were created according to linguistic groupings. People speaking the same language share the same history, the same culture and even a similar architectural repertoire. Thus a statewise introduction of architecture is logical. East India comprises Assam in the far east, Bihar where Bihari is spoken, West Bengal where Bengali is spoken, and Orissa where Oriya is spoken. Even the architectural style of each of these states is as distinct as their state languages. Bihar does not have an architectural history, but is important as the place where Buddhism and Jainism originated.

During the 5th and 6th centuries, the kingdom of Magadha was the cultural centre of Bihar and *Rajgir* (*Rajagriha*) was the storehouse of scriptures. As in ancient Greece, philosophers came here in great numbers, started negating Brahminism and many dissidents arose. At this time Gautama Buddha (Shaka), who started Buddhism and Mahavira (Daiyuu), who started Jainism were born into *Kshatriya* families. They renounced the world and became ascetics when they were young men. They preached their doctrine after attaining *Nirvana*. Buddha taught moderation and Mahavira taught *ahimsa* (non-violence). Their centre of activity was Bihar and later these religions spread from here to other parts of India. During the 13th century, Buddhism almost disappeared from India. Apart from Tibetan Buddhism, not much is left by way of Buddhist architecture except for the Daibosatsuji Temple in Bodhgaya and the ruins of Nalanda.

While Jainism did not spread as Buddhism did, it is still a living, flourishing religion with an architectural culture of its own in west India. Vaishali in Bihar, is the birthplace of Mahavira and the Parasanad hills are a sacred place for Jains, but architecturally there is not much left here. From the 13th century Bihar came under the control of the Delhi sultans. They had developed a distinct architectural style, but they did not develop anything in the central provinces. It was the same during British rule. Patna the capital of Bihar is also the land of Pataliputra, which was the capital of the old Magadha Empire.

❶ Guridrakuda Mountain, Rajgir, where Buddha was born.
❷ The place of *Nirvana* and the *stupa* in Kushinagara.
❸ Temple group, Parasanad Hills, sacred place of Jains.
❹ Mahabodhi Temple in Bodhgaya where Buddha was enlightened.

STUPA AND STAMBHA
3rd C, BC/ Buddhist

A *stupa* and *stambha are* built in the place where Buddha spent his last rainy season in Vaisali. A *stupa* is a sepulchral mound containing a reliquary. A *stambha* is a memorial pillar and Emperor Ashoka built more than thirty such memorial pillars in different regions. A statue of an animal was often sculpted on top of the *stambha*. This style originated in Persia.

An animal statue tops the *stambha*

GOLGHAR (GOLA)
1786/ Colonial
By John Garstin

This dome which looks like an inverted rice bowl, was used as a storehouse during famines. It is 29 m x 25 m, built with brick and mortar and is devoid of decoration. It has a staircase to the top and a hole, through which grain was poured in. The design is an example of functionalism that was prevalent in the 18th century.

The Golghar built in 1786.

GURUDWARA (HAR MANDIR TAKHT)
Sikh

The main *gurudwara* (prayer house) of the Sikhs is in Punjab, but almost every place has one built in the Mughal style. They are either in marble or are painted white. Either way they reinforce the theme of purity. Anybody can go inside but the hair and head has to be covered with at least a handkerchief. Cigarettes are not allowed inside. There is no tank around this *gurudwara* as there is in the birthplace of the 10th Guru Gobind Singh. Har Mandir Takht is the record of the four great Sikh *takhts* or thrones.

Interior of the prayer room.

The whole edifice (five floors) as seen from the courtyard.

CHOTI DARGAH ★
1616/ Islamic

There are two *dargahs* 30 km west of Patna, which are the earliest examples of Islamic architecture here. Badi Dargah, the older *dargah* located near a lake, dates back to the 13th century, while the Choti Dargah belongs to the Mughal era and is similar in style to the ones in Agra and Fatehpur Sikri. The base of the dome has pillars, beams and broad eaves. There is a closed corridor and a small mosque in the precincts. The top of the large minaret in the southeast corner has broken.

Mughal style entrance.

Up: Choti Dargah   Down: Façade with pillars, beams and eaves.

LOMAS RISHI CAVE ★
3rd C, BC/ Ajivika

During Emperor Ashoka's reign, unique developments in Indian architecture started with the cave temples. There are seven cave temples on Barabar and Nagarjuna hills, 25 km from Gaya, still existing from the early days. These do not belong to the Buddhist religion but to a religion known as Ajivika which was prevalent in those days. The caves are small and simple, with very little decoration. There are sculptures on the façade of the Lomas Rishi Cave, which are very similar to wooden constructions of earlier times.

Interior of the Stama Cave.

Façade of the Lomas Rishi Cave.

NALANDA ★★

NALANDA UNIVERSITY ★★
6th-7th C/ Buddhist

After the death of Gautama Buddha, Buddhism spread swiftly, as the *Sanghas* (monks) joined forces with the ruling class. Temples and monasteries were built in various countries. From Gandhara in the west, to Bihar and Bengal in the east, especially in the Nalanda region 15 km from Rajgir, great Buddhist centres were established. Temples and ten monasteries came into being. Students from India, and from other countries came here to study and thus the earliest Buddhist university was established. A Chinese Buddhist monk Huen'tsang, came to Nalanda to study and collect scriptures. According to his book, about 1,000 monks were studying there at that time. The buildings were constructed with bricks and finished with plaster. It is hard to find a more orderly campus in ancient India. The monastery (*vihara*) measured 50-60 m on each side. The courtyard was surrounded by monks' rooms that were 2 or 3 storeys high. The third temple had a 31 m high *stupa*, a shrine and smaller *stupas*. Other temples have *chaitiyas* (sacred *stupas* and statues) enshrined in the middle. As the superstructure is broken, the shape and height of the original temple is not known.

❶ The group of monasteries can be seen from Temple 3. ❷ Temple 3 ❸ Temple 13

❹ Small *stupas* in Temple 3 ❺ Platform of Temple 12. ❻ Sculpture on a small *stupa*. ❼ Foundation platform of Temple 2 (Shaka)

Temple 3   Temple 12   Temple 13   Temple 14

1B

1A

Temple 1   4   6   7   8   9   10   11

0   50m

Layout of the complex   Temple 2

❽ The way to the first monastery ❾ Small *stupa* group in Temple 2.

BODHGAYA (BUDDHAGAYA) ★★ 10

MAHABODHI COMPLEX ★★
7th C/ Buddhist

Shaka renounced the world and started meditation under a peepal tree 10 km from Gaya. After he attained *Sambodhi*, he was called Buddha and the tree was called the *Bodhi* tree. This sacred place is called Bodhgaya; now a place for pilgrimage with temples, *stupas* and monasteries. The place where Buddha meditated, is now sacred. The surrounding stone wall dates back to the 2nd century. The large temple beside the *Bodhi* tree was built in the 7th century. Though half complete, it is important as a relic that depicts the exceptional quality of Buddhist construction. It was restored by Burmese Buddhists in 1877.

The original stone wall is now in the Bodhgaya museum and a replica is kept in place of the original. Buddhism weakened in India and was abandoned by the 15th century. It restarted only in the 19th century, during British rule.

The temple has four small towers in each corner and has the five-shrine style. The small towers were added in the 19th century. The main tower is made of bricks and finished with plaster. The original tower was curved like the *shikharas* of Hindu temples. Today, most Buddhist countries have constructed temples in Bodhgaya and it has become the meeting ground and extensive showcase for various Buddhist architectural styles.

Up: Main gate of the temple, with an *amalaka*.
Middle: Ancient sculptures seen on the surrounding stone fencing.
Down: Murals on the foundation platform. Every niche has a Buddhist statue.

The Bodhi tree behind the temple.

TOMB OF SHER SHAH SUR ★★
1545/ Islamic

Sher Shah Sur of the Sur dynasty, who battled for Delhi with the Mughal emperor Humayun, belonged to Bihar. He commanded architect Aliwal Khan to build his mausoleum in the middle of a lake. The square island did not conform with Mecca's direction, so four east-facing rooms were built in four corners of the 3-storeyed octagonal structure with pavilions built on all three storeys. The entire mausoleum with big and small *chattris* surrounding the dome presents a pure and unique geometric design.

Up: Pillared corridor built with an arch and dome framework.
Down: The mausoleum appears to be floating on the lake.

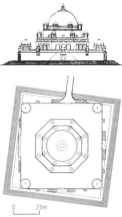

Elevation & Plan

TOMB OF HASSAN KHAN SUR
1535/ Islamic

Aliwal Khan, who trained in Delhi, designed the mausoleum of Hassan Khan, father of Sher Shah Sur. He made changes in the plan of the mausoleum in Delhi. He corrected the inward turning pillars of the octagonal Delhi mausoleum to straight pillars in this tomb thus lessening the severity of the design.

The tomb in the middle of the town.

WEST BENGAL

Bengal is situated in the alluvial plain of the Ganga. After independence from the British, Bengal was also divided into west and east. The west became the state of West Bengal, which is now a part of India and the east became East Pakistan and later Bangladesh. The land was divided on the basis of the religion of the people. The region where there was a majority of Hindus became a part of India and the region that had a majority of Muslims, became Pakistan. As in the case of Palestine, dividing the country and its people on the basis of their religion, was an unfortunate experience for India.

From ancient times to the Middle Ages, Buddhism was the main religion in Bengal. Today Buddhist ruins can still be found in Bangladesh. In the 12th century Bengal was taken over by the Hindu Sena dynasty. In the 13th century it came under Muslim rule. Even though the ruler was a Muslim, the citizens were steeped in Hindu culture, which is evident from the Bengali-type Hindu temples found in every nook and corner of West Bengal. West Bengal unlike Orissa, is located in the Delta plains and is not rich in stone for construction purposes. As a result, Bengali houses and temples were made of bricks. To make the temples monumental, raw clay panels were moulded, baked in the kiln and used as decorative cladding over brick walls. This is a unique terracotta style seen only in West Bengal. It is very similar to the Persian (Iran) style of using coloured tiles on walls, because they too lacked natural building stone. Unlike the temples in Orissa, Bengali temples are small and cannot be called very grand, but they reflect the Bengali lifestyle and are appealing structures. Vishnupur with its varied and beautiful terracotta and laterite temples, is a treasure trove of Bengali temples.

In the 18th century, when the British founded the East India Company they made Kolkata (Calcutta) their headquarters. Kolkata (Calcutta) was the capital of British India until they shifted their capital to Delhi. The British built many buildings here and left behind an architectural legacy. Shantiniketan, the university with its unique educational technique started by the first Nobel laureate in Asia, Rabindranath Tagore, is also situated here.

❶ Tagore's open-air university, Shantiniketan.
❷ Houses with *Bangaldar* roofs, Ghurisa.
❸ Fateh Khan's mausoleum with a *Bangaldar* roof, Gaur.
❹ The new city of Kolkata (Calcutta).
❺ A close-up of the eaves of the Gangeshwara Temple, Baranagar.

Gaur was the capital during the Buddhist and Hindu reign but no traces of these eras remain. Islamic culture flourished in West Bengal, especially in Gaur which was under Muslim rule in 1200 and was the capital of Bengal in the 1500's, but was abandoned in the 16th century when an epidemic ravaged the area. Ruins of the 15th-16th century are brick structures decorated with coloured tiles. Kotwali Darwaza ruins face Bangladesh.

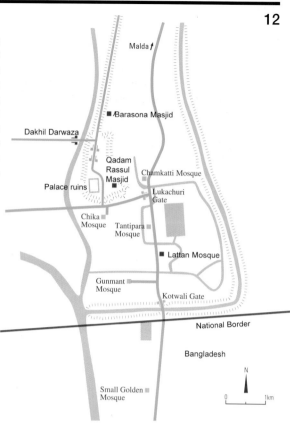

Malda

Barasona Masjid

Dakhil Darwaza

Qadam Rassul Masjid

Chamkatti Mosque

Palace ruins

Lukachuri Gate

Chika Mosque

Tantipara Mosque

Lattan Mosque

Gunmant Mosque

Kotwali Gate

National Border

Bangladesh

Small Golden Mosque

N

0   1km

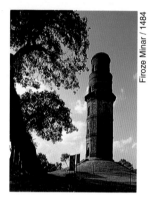

Firoze Minar / 1484

LATTAN MASJID ★
End of 15th C/ Islamic

One of the best preserved mosques in Gaur, it has a prayer room which is 9 m square and a domed ceiling. The rectangular front room has a ceiling that looks like the hull of a ship and is decorated with colourful lattice patterns. The front wall has colourful tiles but most of them have been destroyed. This mosque has the common half-dome of Bengal.

❶ The view from the *Mihrab*.
❷ The mural and the circular pillar in the corner.
❸ Tiles that have remained intact in some parts.

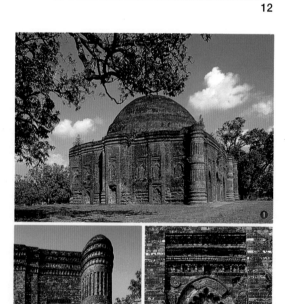

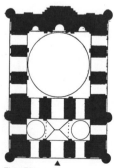

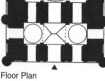

Floor Plan

158

DHAKIL DARWAZA
1425/ Islamic
Dhakil Darwaza, 500 m from Bara Sona Mosque, is the main gate of Gaur Fort, of which, only the walls remain. It has minarets on four sides and a pathway to the other side, which is 35 m long. The whole structure is made of bricks and the walls have decorative patterns made of terracotta.

The gate on the south.

BARASONA MASJID (GOLDEN MOSQUE)
1526/ Islamic
It is the Jami Masjid (Friday mosque) of Gaur town and the biggest of the existing mosques. The façade is 12 spans wide, while the prayer room inside measures 3 spans and the porch is 15 spans wide. Most of the prayer room is destroyed. It was made of bricks and finished with stones.

Right: The interior of the big porch.
Left:Damaged roof of the prayer house.

QADAM RASUL MASJID ★
1513/ Islamic
Qadam Rasul means footprints of Mohammed the Prophet and this mosque deifies these. The tomb of Fateh Khan is in the precincts (picture on page 156). The eaves on the exterior are not horizontal like other mosques but are sloping. Hindu temples built later in India replicated the octagonal pillars on both sides of the main entrance. The Madana Mohana Temple in Vishnupur and this mosque are surprisingly similar in design. It reflects the traditional Bengali architectural style with its curved, sloping roof. Hindu temples would also adopt this style later.

Up: View of the mosque from the square.
Down: The front facade.

Pandua 16 km from Malda, was as important a town as Gaur. It was created by the British East India Company and called English Bazaar. It was Bengal's capital from 1338 to 1500 but declined in prominence after the capital shifted to Gaur. The 15th century buildings are mostly of brick. The eaves have the *mukuri* (roof style) reflecting the traditional Bengali style.

Up: Choti Dargah-15th century. Down: Qutb Shahi Mosque-1585.

ADINA MASJID ★
1375/ Islamic

Adina Masjid is a very old mosque and measures 150 m x 90 m. It is similar to the great 8th century Umaiya Mosque of Damascus. The long prayer room in the middle, with a large span, is also Damascan in style. But after Adina, Arabian style mosques with surrounding courtyards were not constructed anymore in Bengal. Instead the later mosques became outward-facing structures.

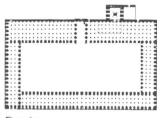

Floor plan

Up: Central *mihrab* and *mimbar*. Down: Prayer room in the mezzanine.

EKLAKHI TOMB
15th C/ Islamic
Since there is not much difference between the mosques and tombs of West Bengal, one is not sure whether the structure is a tomb or a mosque. If the symbolic dome is changed to the *shikhara* style tower, the structure will look like a Hindu temple. Both the structures used pillars, window frames and terracotta panels.

The front view with bent eaves and murals partitioned by lattice work.

MURSHIDABAD ★   14

PALACE AND IMAMBARA
1837, 1847/ Islamic
Murshidabad is located 10 km, north of Behrampur. It became prominent when Nawab (protector) Murshid Kuli Khan shifted the capital from Dhaka to this place in 1704 and his name was retained as the name of the city. Located here is an Italian style palace and a long *imambara*, also in the same style.

Imambara and signalling tower.

KATRA MOSQUE
1725/ Islamic
Katra Mosque is the Friday Mosque of Murshidabad. It is a large structure with two floors. The rooms are in a row and the four corners have minarets. The small rooms with domes are called *madrassa* (school) or *caravan sarai*. Originally there were five large domes, but now only two domes at the two ends are still standing.

The mosque with minarets at the side.

BARDDHAMAN (BURDWAN) ★   15

TOMB COMPLEX OF KHWAJA ANWAR-I-SHAHID
1698/ Islamic
On the outskirts of the town, within a large quiet garden, is a mosque and tomb surrounded by a large tank. There is a pavilion in the middle of the lake with a bridge to reach it from the front of the mosque. The main building is the tomb of the tax collector Anwar-i-Shahid. In both the sites, the rooms have split roofs, which is rare.

Pavilion and Anwar-i-Shahid's Tomb.

PANCHANAN SHIVA TEMPLE
Hindu

Ajimganj can be reached by crossing the river from Jiyaganj 10 km north of Mushirabad. Baranagar is very close to Ajimganj. *Bungalow* is a traditional Bengali house with a split, sloping roof. Baranagar has four *bungalow*-type temples. Split, sloping roofs are made with bamboos so that rainwater could drain off quickly during the monsoons. This technique when transformed to brick and plaster for temples came to be called *Ek Bangla*.

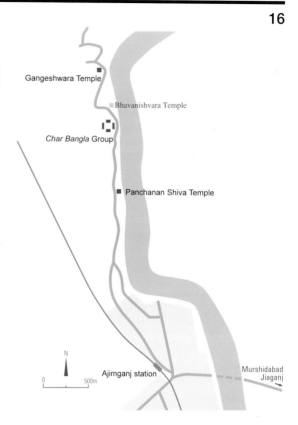

Gangeshwara Temple

Bhavanishvara Temple

Char Bangla Group

■ Panchanan Shiva Temple

N

0   500m

Ajimganj station

Murshidabad
Jiaganj

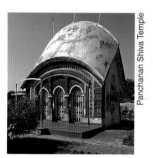

Panchanan Shiva Temple

GANGESHWARA TEMPLE ★
18th C/ Hindu

When two *ek banglas* are built next to each other, it is called a *jor bangla*. The front *jor bangla* is the porch and the rear one is the shrine. Gangeshwara Temple is a small temple measuring 7 m on each side. The detailing in this temple has been executed with great care. All the walls are decorated with fine terracotta panels (pic-page 157). As construction stone was scarce in the coastal plains, it was traditional in Bengal to carve on raw clay panels and then bake them for use as decorations on buildings. The red colour of the clay is also known as *bangla* colour.

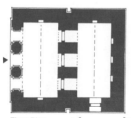

Floor Plan   0   3m

❶ Side entrance. ❷ Intersection of two *banglas*. ❸ Terracotta pillars.

CHAR BANGLA GROUP ★★
1760/ Hindu

Char Bangla temple group are four independent *bungalows* around a common courtyard facing inward. Temples in India generally faced outward since they were always well decorated. The Char Bangla temple group, without much exterior decoration, is reminiscent of Arabic pillared halls or Persian four-*iwan* mosques.

Each *ek bangla* has a facade which is decorated with terracotta sculptures and no porch. *Linga* the symbol of Shiva is deified in the shrine. The trident which is the weapon of Shiva, is kept on the roof. Most sculptures in the temple are of Vishnu and his incarnation, Krishna. This shows that in the Middle Ages the *Shaivites* and *Vaishnavites* lived together in harmony.

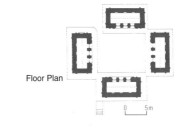

Floor Plan

0   5 m

❶ Temple's exterior and entrance to the courtyard. ❷ Terracotta panels depicting Gods. ❸ Temples around a central courtyard.

GHURISA ★   17

GOPALA LAKSHMI TEMPLE
19th C/ Hindu

The terracotta temple in Ghurisa 30 km from Shantiniketan, has a cubic shrine with many small towers on its upper portion. Such temples are called *Ratnas* (precious stones). A single-tower temple is an *Eka Ratna* while a five-tower temple is a *Panch Ratna* and a nine-tower temple is a *Nava Ratna*. The temple here is influenced by the European style.

Right: The straight eaves reflect the European influence. Left: The central pillars.

BARAKAR *

BARAKAR ★

18

BEGUNIA GROUP OF TEMPLES
Hindu
SIDDHESHWARA TEMPLE 9th C
GANESHA TEMPLE 16th C
DURGA TEMPLE 16th C
KALI TEMPLE 16th C

Most of the Middle Ages temples of Bengal do not exist any more. They were destroyed to construct mosques when Islam grew powerful after the 13th century. Yet a group of temples still stands in Begunia which is near the Bihar border. The style of temples in Orissa in the south, is different. The temples there are made of stone and have high *rega* (spires). Siddeshwara Temple belongs to this early style. In the 16th century when Bengal was under Emperor Akbar's rule and since his reign was peaceful and tolerant of other religions, three more temples were built here. All were built in the same style as the Siddheswara Temple, but the new temples' proportions are longer and sleeker. This style adopted by Bengal was later used in the *Ratna* temples made of bricks.

Kali Temple

Up: Siddheshwara Temple Down: Durga Temple and Ganesha Temple.

HADAL-NARAYANPUR ★

19

TERRACOTTA TEMPLES ★
19th C/ Hindu

This village, 50 km from Burdwan has six temples. Britain reigned supreme In the 19th century, a fact that was reflected in temples, too. Terracotta sculptures were replaced with plaster sculptures. This heralded the Mannerist phase and the strength of the structures and importance given to minute details, declined.

Right: Rasa Mancha / 1858
Left: Radha Damodara Temple.

BISHNUPUR (VISHNUPUR) ★ ★ ★

Bishnupur 150 km west of Kolkata (Calcutta), was the capital of the Mallabhumi dynasty. They ruled over a small region until the 8th century. In the 16th century they expanded and became powerful during the reign of King Birhan Bir. His fort is almost gone, but he developed the city with many lakes and ponds in true Bengali style. Simultaneously during the Hindu revival, Chaitanya preached his faith and many temples were built as a result. There are 30 temples (17th-18th century) in Bishnupur that are a treasure-trove of terracotta sculptures. Krishna, an incarnation of Vishnu and his love Radha, are deified in most of these temples. The Mallabhumi dynasty also had cordial relations with the *shaivites*. In the 17th century they fought the Marathas and in 1806, the East India Company took over, gave control to *zamindars* (local chieftains) and Vishnupur faded into oblivion.

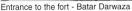
Entrance to the fort - Batar Darwaza

Terracotta panel in Shyama Raya Temple (*Rasa Mandala*)

MURALI MOHANA TEMPLE
1665/ Hindu

This temple with a small, *shikhara*-type tower called *eka ratna* is quite different from other temples, as walls surround the first floor and it has a pillared corridor on all four sides. This type of open pathway is rare in Bengali temples. The roof looks like the roof of ordinary houses.

❶ Distant view of Murali Mohan Temple.

MADANA MOHANA TEMPLE ★
1694/ Hindu

This temple is dedicated to the deity of the Mallabhumi dynasty, Madana Mohana or Krishna. The walls of the brick temple are decorated with legends of Krishna depicted in terracotta sculptures. The parapet on the roof and the arches reflect an Islamic influence.

❷ Main entrance. ❸ Terracotta murals. ❹ Porch interior.

RASA MANCHA ★
1600/ Hindu

This temple is quite unique in style. It has a cubic shrine, pillared corridors on three sides and a pyramidal roof. It was constructed by the most prominent ruler of the Mallabhumi dynasty, Birhan Bir. Every year during the Rasa festival, statues from other temples were brought here and lined up.

Full view of the temple.

RADHA SHYAMA TEMPLE
1758/ Hindu

This temple was built during the last days of the Mallabhumi dynasty and has large precincts close to the Kesta Raya Temple. Its *Eka Ratna* tower is not tiered but looks like an Islamic dome. It is a laterite structure, finished with stucco. The stucco has sculptures like those on terracotta panels.

Front view.

SHYAMA RAYA TEMPLE ★★
1643/ Hindu

Raghunath Singh who succeeded King Birhan Bir, built three temples. Of these, the Radha Shyama Temple along with the Keshta Raya Temple are the best examples of terracotta architecture. This temple is built of bricks. The exterior and interior are clad with high quality, densely sculpted, terracotta panels. It is a *Pancharatna* with a main tower and four small towers in the four corners. The temple has a square plan with porches on all four sides and a three-arch entrance, on each of the four sides. The ceiling is an Islamic dome with a terracotta finish that is not seen in any other temple. It reflects a strong Islamic influence, but it also reflects, the complex construction methodology followed in India for the different styled towers. This brings to mind the complex Armenian construction of the Middle Ages. Most of the sculptures are of Krishna. There are *Rasa mandalas* with Krishna, Radha and Krishna's *gopis* (cowherd girls).

Floor plan

❶ The temple inside the fort. ❷ Domed ceiling in the porch. ❸ An entrance with three arches. ❹ Terracotta panels on the wall.

KESHTA RAYA TEMPLE ★★
1655/ Hindu

The *jyoru bungalow* or *jor bangla* temple, has two traditional Bengali houses placed together and the sloping split roof is called the *Bangaldar* roof. The Mughals adopted this style when they reigned over Bengal and built this style of roof in Delhi and Agra, too. From there the Rajputs took these roofs to west India and incorporated this style of roof into their architectural repertoire.

It is interesting to see the façade of the two structures placed together. In the same way that wooden structures have been copied and transformed in Barabar Hills, here wooden structures and small roofs over load-bearing structures, have been copied using brick and terracotta as the building material.

Usually, in *Jyoru bungalows,* the front *bungalow*

is the porch and the one behind is the shrine. While the plan reflects two structures, in reality, it is a single centripetal, square structure. The reason for this difference is not known. This is the most fascinating building in Bishnupur.

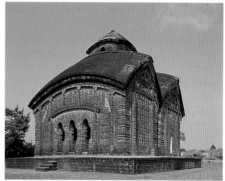

Full view, temple on top of a laterite platform.

Side view-There is a small square roof on top.

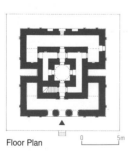

Floor Plan   0 ____ 5m

Right: The inside wall is finished off with plaster.
Left: Details of the capital of the pillar.

On the southern outskirts are seven temples made of laterite and not brick. Laterite, which is red clay, is also called red earth. Since it is a hard stone it can be used for construction. However, it is coarse in appearance and hence is usually finished with stucco. Since it is much cheaper than stones, it is used for foundations, platforms and even walls of buildings. The sculpting on stucco is generally of a very poor quality and it wears off after some time. The most popular *eka ratna* temples of Bishnupur are all made of laterite.

JORA MANDIR
1726/ Hindu

This is a group of three temples in the front and another temple at the back. All four temples have the same façade, on all four sides. Tales from the Ramayana are sculpted on the laterite walls of these temples.

KALA CHAND TEMPLE
1656/ Hindu

Raghunath Singh constructed this *Eka Ratna* temple of the early period. The *amalaka* is very large in proportion and it is possible to climb onto it. The eaves of the lower tier clearly show that wood has been used for its construction.

RADHA GOVINDA TEMPLE ★
1729/ Hindu

This large temple with a miniature *Eka Ratna* shrine has no sculptures. Stone wheels have been attached to the low platform. Perhaps, this is meant to be the chariot in which Krishna took Arjuna to battle in the *Mahabharatha*.

❶ Jora Temple group.
❷ Miniature shrine of the Radha Govinda Temple.
❸ The wall of the Kala Chand Temple.
❹ Kala Chand Temple.

Kalna was once a very prominent town on the shores of the Bhagirathi River, 60 km from Barddhaman. There are a number of terracotta temples here, especially near the palace. In contrast to Bishnupur this place has more Shiva temples, as there were many *shaivites,* or devotees of Shiva, concentrated in this area.

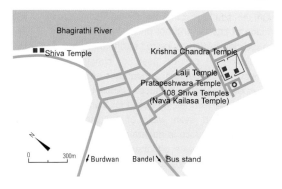

TERRACOTTA TEMPLES Hindu
KRISHNA CHANDRA TEMPLE ★★
1752

This temple is a *Pancha Vesyati, Ratna* temple with 25 *ratnas.* Small towers are added all around the main tower which makes it very decorative. *Ratnas* could be 1,5,9,13,17, 21 and so on, in number. This temple has a large tower at the centre, with four small towers on the sides. The next level has 8 towers, then 12 towers and so on, arriving at a total of 25 such towers. Even though the scale is small, there are two such temples in Kalna. Since a 25 tower temple construction is complex, it does not have many sculptures. It has a rare *Bangaldar,* hipped roof in front.

The second floor plan.

The pattern on the upper portion of the temple.

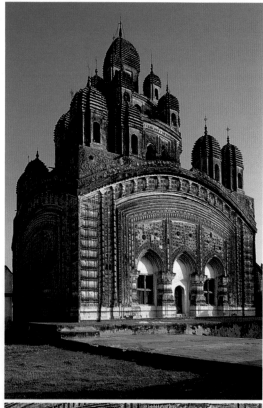

Up: Krishna Chandra Temple Down: Terracotta porch.

LALJI TEMPLE ★ 1739

This *Pancha Vesyati Ratna* temple is similar to the Krishan Chandra Temple. On the second floor are three tower groups and therefore the centre is octagonal in plan. That is where this temple differs from the Krishna Chandra Temple. The porch in front measures 3 spans x 4 spans.

SHIVA TEMPLE 1753

This pair of Shiva temples stand in a row on the banks of the river on the northern outskirts of town. The roof surface is called *chala* and since a square temple has four roof surfaces, it is called *Char Chala*. As the roof of the Shiva temple has eight surfaces in two stories, it is called *Aat Chala*. In the split Bangla roof, there are two surfaces and is called *Do Chala*.

PRATAPESHWARA TEMPLE 1849

A simple one-tower *shikhara* is called *rega* or *deul*. Both are styles from Orissa and so is the terminology. The temple is very simple, but has delicate and minute sculptures on terracotta. The daily life of everybody, from the king to the commoner, is depicted here.

❶ Top portion of the Lalji Temple. ❷ The twin Shiva Temples. ❸Pratapeshwara Temple. Krishna Chandra Temple seen afar.

108 CIRCULAR SHIVA TEMPLE ★
1809/ Hindu

These temples where the *Shivalinga* is deified are different in style from other temples. These shrines with *Aat Chala* are in two circles and are totally 108 in number. They are built of laterite and not terracotta. Inside-facing temples, with no decorations on the outside are very rare. The temple which most resembles this one is perhaps, the Chausatt Jogini Temple in Hirapur.

The shrines arranged in two circles.

BRINDABAN CHANDRA GROUP ⋆
17th~18th C/ Hindu

There is a group of temples in Guptipala 10 km from Kalna. The *aat chala,* Brindaban Chandra Temple is at the entrance. On the right is the *eka ratna,* Rama Chandra Temple and on the left is the *aat chala,* Krishna Chandra Temple. The bases of these three temples are connected. The oldest temple at the far end is Chaitanya Deva Temple. The Rama Chandra Temple is an octagonal *ratna* and has terracotta sculptures of a very high quality.

The upper portion of the Rama Chandra Temple.

The Brindaban Chandra Temple as seen from the entrance.

HINDU TEMPLES

Near Bansberia 50 km from Kolkata (Calcutta), are two temples close to a pond. Take the train out of Kolkata, alight at Bander Junction and then take a 30 minutes ride in an auto-rickshaw, to reach these temples.

ANANTA VASUDEVA TEMPLE ⋆
1679

This Armenian-style, small tower called *Eka Ratna,* is decorated with terracotta sculptures. Since Vasudeva is another name for Krishna, the sculptures on the walls also depict legends of Krishna. The designs on the pillars are noteworthy.

HANSESHWARI TEMPLE
1814

This temple, built a century after the neighbouring temples has prayers conducted in it everyday. Islamic and European influences are very strong in this temple. The entrance and the central hall, are not traditional. The temple has thirteen towers and is called *Traiyodashya Ratna.* It is reminiscent of a Russian monastery.

❶Ananta Vasudeva ❷ Pillars of Ananta Vasudeva ❸ Hanseshwari

RADHA GOVINDA TEMPLE ★
1768/ Hindu

Atpur is located by the side of a huge pond, 60 km northwest of Kolkata (Calcutta). It is a 15-minute road trip. In the open space is an *Aat Ratna* temple, an open *Dol mancha*, and a *Rasa mancha*. Precincts of the Radha Govinda Temple are surrounded by a fence and the entrance faces the square. This temple is very similar to the Brindaban Chandra Temple of Guptipala. It has a hipped roofed *mandapa* in front of the *Aat Chala*. These portions and the ceiling, shaped like the hull of a ship, are decorated with terracotta and have the legends of the *Mahabharata* and the *Ramayana*, sculpted on the front wall and the side walls, respectively.

Up: The façade from the entrance.
Down: Inside the *mandapa*.

Terracotta sculptures.

CHANDI MANDAPA
17th C/ Hindu

Opposite the Radha Govinda Temple is a rare, wooden *ek bangla* The structure was built with timber from jackfruit trees, 300 years ago. The sloping roofs are of wood and bamboo. This roof's method of construction is a technical marvel. Unlike houses, the pillars, beams and joints are all very delicately carved.

Left: Chandi *mandapa*.
Right: The joints in the small room.

Kolkata (Calcutta), the main city in east India, is on the banks of the Hoogly River. The city's population including that of the suburbs exceeds 10,000,000. It was a small village until the 17th century. In 1690, the British established the East India Company and built Fort William, which later became their stronghold and the seat of government. Over the next century until New Delhi was made capital, Calcutta continued to develop as the capital of the country, and during this time many European style structures were transplanted here. No traces of the traditional Indian style is seen in these structures which were damaged after 1947 and have not regained their formal glory. Over-population has also taken its toll. As Kolkata also stagnated economically, its building industry lags far behind Delhi and Mumbai.

Even so, India's first subway was started in Kolkata in 1984. The city is reinventing itself, to become a formidable force in Asia, once again.

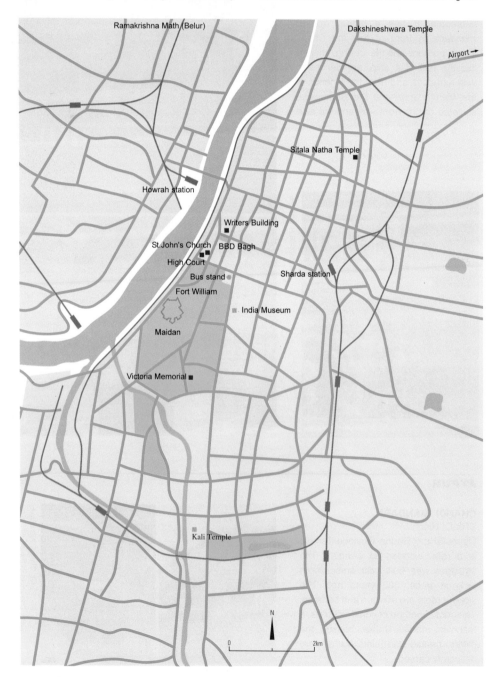

VICTORIA MEMORIAL HALL ★★
1921/ Colonial
Architect: William Emerson

After the death of Queen Victoria of Britain, who also took on the title of Empress of India, construction of a memorial to commemorate her, began in 1905 and was completed in 1921. The proposal for building the memorial was initiated by the Governor General of India, Lord Curzon. The inhibitions of Emerson's early days, gave way to this dignified building, which is a fusion of the classic doctrine of the Italian Renaissance and Mughal style. It bears a resembles to the Taj Mahal.

Indian style pavilion in the corner.

The memorial with its reflection in the lake.

ST. JOHNS CHURCH
1787/ Colonial
by James Agg

Most of the important buildings are centered around Dalhousie Square, with its large reservoir. This Cathedral was planned by architect Agg during his twenties and is modelled after London's, St Martin-in-the-Fields Church. The solid pillars on the ground floor, contrast sharply with the sleek steeple on top.

The pillared corridor was added in the year 1797.

WRITERS BUILDING ★
1780-1880/ Colonial
Writers building, with its long façade facing Dalhousie square, was designed by Thomas Lyon in 1780 as company quarters for the employees of the East India Company. A simple building, it was refaced in 1880 so that it presented a befitting Imperial image. It is now the state government Secretariat.

Up: The view of the left portion of the building from Dalhousie Square.
Down: The magnificent central block.

The corner of the building.

HIGH COURT ★
1872/ Colonial
By Walter Granville
This Gothic structure with its richly contrasting, red brick and white plaster, was built by Walter Granville. It is very similar to the Government building of Hamburg designed by Gilbert Scott. Fearing earthquakes, the tower was not built to its designed height, so the building appears squat.

There is a courtyard behind the façade.

SITALANANTHA TEMPLE
1867/ Jain
This temple of the Shwethambara Jains, built by a jeweller, is dedicated to Sitalanantha, the 10th *tirthankara* of Jainism. It is a blend of European and Islamic styles, with a traditional Indian *shikhara*, set in an Italian style garden. The interior is richly decorated with mirrors and Venetian glass mosaics.

Pavilions in the garden with a pond.

DAKSHINESHWARA TEMPLE ★
1855/ Hindu

On the banks of the river Hoogly, on the northern outskirts of Kolkata (Calcutta) is a large temple built by a devotee, Rani Rashmoni. Known locally as the Dakshineshwar Kali Temple, it is built in a very traditional Bengali style even though it is a new structure. The walls however, are not clad with terracotta panels but are plastered. In the *Nava Ratna* shrine, goddess Kali has been deified and in the *Aat Chala* shrine, Shiva has been enshrined. Open to all castes and creeds, it is said that the Hindu saint Ramakrishna himself, (1836-86) lived in this temple as a priest.

Up: View from the tank.
Down: Pilgrims stand in a row to enter on festival days.

RAMAKRISHNA MATH (AT BELUR) ★
1899/

Vivekananda, who was a disciple of Ramakrishna founded a social service organization, Ramakrishna Mission and made this the world headquarters. Ramakrishna preached unity in religion and the doctrine of one God, which is reflected in the temple structure that is a combination Hindu, Muslim and Christian architectural styles. The huge shrine is completely covered with ochre cladding stones, with Indian motifs as decorations. The design of this serene building resembles a Latin Church.

Small temple near the Hoogly River.

Down: Façade from the south Up: The minutely decorated main shrine.

BANGLADESH

In 1947, Bangladesh was made a part of Pakistan and was called East Pakistan. But even though they shared a common religion, the difference in language and the distance of 1600 km between them, made it quite impossible for East and West Pakistan to stay together as one nation. In 1971 East Pakistan separated from Pakistan and called itself Bangladesh or the land of Bengalis and made Bengali its official language. Since it is the eastern part of Bengal, they share the same culture, language and history. Even Bangladeshi architecture that features in this book is not much different from its West Bengal counterpart. Over 50 years have passed since Partition and each part of Bengal has developed its own identity. The special feature of Bangladesh is that the towns and villages are very clean.

When Tagore sang about the golden land, he meant the plains where the Ganges and the Brahmaputra joined the sea. It is indeed a land of water and greenery with a network of tributaries flowing through. The waterways also create a lot of problems by flooding during the rainy season every year. Bangladesh does not have much of an architectural culture. There are few tourists since there is little by way of sight-seeing. Puthia town a miniature of Bishnupur in India, with its group of terracotta temples is idyllic.

When referring to the more contemporary architecture of Bangladesh, Louis Kahn an American architect is worth mentioning. While India asked Le Corbusier to design the city of Chandigarh, Bangladesh commissioned Louis Kahn to design the National Assembly Hall of Bangladesh. Just as Le Corbusier's three-dimensional design blended with the Indian style of architecture, the geometrical design that Louis Kahn produced was very Islamic. If his Kimbel Museum is transferred just as it is, to a Muslim country, it will not look out of place.

Villagers in front of Kantaji Temple in Kantanagar.

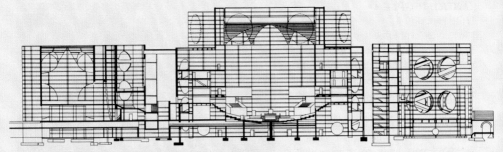

Cross-section of National Assembly Hall designed by Louis Kahn.

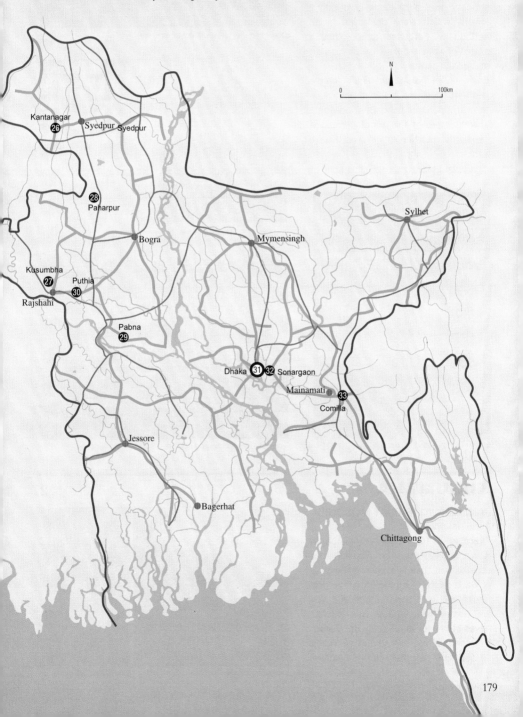

KANTAJI TEMPLE ★★
1752/ Hindu

The Kantaji Temple located 26 km north of Dinajipur is the most magnificent temple in Bangladesh. Since there are no taxis, a 40-minute bus ride followed by a 15-minute walk with a local guide gets you to the temple.

It is a huge precinct in the middle of a field. The magnificent temple located here is not the original one. The original structure was a *navratna* type with 9 towers, which were destroyed in an earthquake. Fergusson's book has a sketch of what it looked like at the start of the 20th century.

Each side of this *Pancha Ratna* temple is 15 m wide and is symmetrical in plan. The porch is used as a passage. The structure of this Hindu temple is geometrical and orderly like an Islamic structure.

Decorated with terracotta from end to end.

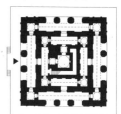
Floor Plan
0   5m

The temple as it looked at the start of the century.

Interior of the second floor porch

Terracotta panels showing soldiers.

JAMI MASJID (FRIDAY MOSQUE)
1558/ Islamic

There is a 16th century mosque in Kusumba 42 km from Rajshahi. Its construction style is similar to the style of Gaur, which is on the Indian border. It was built with basalt stone and has six domes. The façade has curved eaves but is not elaborately decorated. In contrast, the *mihrab* and the ladies section have delicately carved details.

View from outside

Small stone *Mihrab*.

SOMAPURI VIHARA
(MONASTERY) ★
8th~9th C/ Buddhist

Buddhism was widespread in the Bengal region from ancient times to the Middle Ages. It was so prominent that the largest monastery in the Indian subcontinent was built in Paharpur. Later Buddhism lost out to Hinduism and all Buddhists converted to Islam. If the Buddhists were to become Hindus, they would have been relegated to the lowest class in the Hindu religion and hence, they preferred to become Muslims, which is a classless religion.

King Dharmapala of the Pala dynasty built this monastery, which was 300 m long on one side. It had 170 monks' rooms and a cross-shaped central shrine with entrances on all four sides. The top of the monastery was destroyed but it might have been the five-shrine type. The whole structure is of brick with a decorative terracotta finish. The decorations carved on wet clay slabs and baked in the kiln, have a brush written effect. Images of Hindu gods prove that Buddhism was at the Tantrik Age during that time.

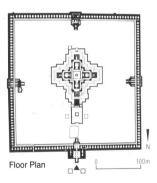

Floor Plan   0   100m   N

❶ 100 m foundation platform. ❷ The precincts. ❸ Terracotta sculptures.

GOPINATHA TEMPLE
1698/ Hindu

These thatched roof structures in the Bengal style have been built side by side. The style is called *jor bangla*. This style must have come from Vishnupur in West Bengal. Of the two, the *bungalow* in the front is the porch and the one at the back is the shrine. The entrance has three arches and the walls are decorated with intricately carved terracotta panels.

Side view of the *jor bangla*.

In Puthia, 30 km from Rajshahi, are ten small and large Hindu temples surrounded by tanks and trees. This temple is a small-scale reproduction of the temples in Vishnupur showing various types of brick construction. Most of them are made of terracotta and they belong to the 1st and the 2nd centuries. The view of their reflection in the pond, in between the coconut palms is very beautiful. A Shiva Temple and *dhol mancha* can be seen on the other side of the lake.

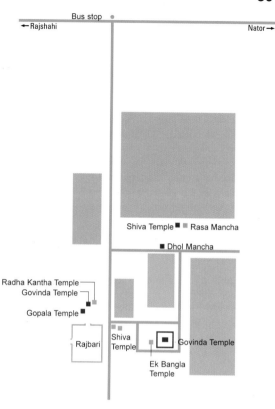

Bus stop

←Rajshahi
Nator→

Shiva Temple ■ ■ Rasa Mancha

■ Dhol Mancha

Radha Kantha Temple
Govinda Temple
Gopala Temple ■

Shiva
Temple
Rajbari

Shiva
Temple
Govinda Temple

Ek Bangla
Temple

Govinda Temple

GOVINDA TEMPLE ★
1895/ Hindu

This four-storeyed terracotta temple has the same façade on all four sides. It has rather bulky proportions. A unique feature is the central tower with four smaller towers in the corners, called the *char chala*. The terracotta walls are richly sculpted with delicate designs from end to end.

Up: The precinct is surrounded by walls.
Down: Terracotta panel which depicts the daily life of the villagers.

One of the small towers

GOPALA GROUP ★
Hindu

The Govinda temple is a *char chala* type and the Gopala temple is an *ek bangla* type with *char chala* attached on both sides. Both are small terracotta temples. Since *char chala* type temples were preferred, more than half the temples in Puthia are of this type.

Govinda and Gopala are two different names for Lord Krishna. The flat-roofed Radha Kantha Temple is nearby.

Up: Govinda temple and Gopala Temple
Down: The eaves in Govinda Temple.

Interior-Gopala Temple

SHIVA TEMPLE
1823/ Hindu

This magnificently built temple on a high platform is of the *Panchagruha* type, but not Bengali in style. *Ratnas* are north Indian style *shikharas* whose eaves are not curved. The design of the ground floor is very Islamic and the walls are not finished with terracotta but are plastered. There is an octagonal *Rasa Mancha* in the vicinity.

Shiva Temple

Pathway/ pillared corridor.

DHOL MANCHA
1895/ Hindu

A square structure with a pyramidal appearance, it appears to have been constructed without deliberations. It is open on all four sides and resembles the *Rasa Mancha* of Bishnupur. Located as it is, in an open space in the middle of the town, it was perhaps used to display statues of gods and goddesses during festivals. It is now used as a market place.

Dolmancha in an open space in town.

During the Mughal era in 1606, Islam Khan, shifted the capital from Sonargaon to Dhaka. From 1664, when the British started the East India Company, to 1704 when the Mughals shifted to Murshidabad, Dhaka was a business centre. It became the capital of East Pakistan after Partition and continues to remain so. Dhaka has not been left with a great architectural legacy and it is only the contemporary buildings that make Dhaka architecturally famous. Louis Kahn's National Assembly Hall requires special mention for its incredible design, on the edge of a water body.

Satogunbad (17th C)

Up: Curzon Hall(1905) Down: Independence Mosque (20th C)

AYUB NATIONAL HOSPITAL ★
1969/ After Independence
By Louis Kahn

When designing the National Assembly, Kahn also designed the National Hospital. A Medical College was also included but the requirement changed into an examination room and staff hostel and was completed in 1969. At the time he also designed the Indian Institute of Management, Ahmedabad, on a low budget using a repetitive, 'space and arch' module. One can feel the continuation of Islamic architecture in this modern building.

Out-patients room

Open courtyard in the hostel.

SHER-E-BANGLA NAGAR ★★
(National Assembly Hall)
1983/ After Independence
By Louis Kahn

Louis Kahn, the American architect, was asked to design an Assembly Hall at Dhaka, the capital of East Pakistan in 1962. Construction started in 1964, but stopped when the Independence struggle began in 1971, again restarted after Independence and was completed only in 1983. Kahn died in 1974, before completion of the building. In contrast to the hospital and hostel, which are of red brick, the Assembly Hall is of white concrete, with a marble border. The geometrical design that reminds one of the old Muslim style desert forts, is the symbol of a new nation. Since this concrete building has no eaves, maintenance requires great effort.

Red-bricked hostel block.

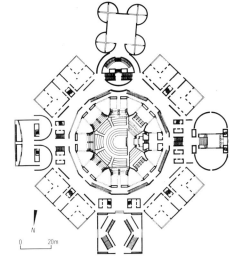
Floor plan

Red-bricked hostel and the National Assembly.

Assembly Hall appears to be floating on water.

LALBAGH FORT
17th C/ Islamic

The construction of this fort was started by the 3rd son of the Mughal Emperor Aurangzeb. The construction could not be completed and only a few buildings and the fort wall remain. This palace was the dwelling of Shaista Khan. It has a visitors' room and *Hammam* (bath house). This is a simple palace where a Bengali flavour has been added to the Mughal style.

Hamam and visitors' room in the fort.

SONARGAON ★

32

GOALDI MOSQUE
1519/ Islamic

Sonargaon is 25 km east of Dhaka. It was the local capital during the age of the Delhi Sultans. The Goaldi Mosque with its single dome is in the Gaur style. Built earlier than the Kusumba Mosque, this mosque was built with bricks and decorated with carved terracotta tiles. Only the *mihrab* inside is made of stone and it is richly sculpted.

Exterior, which looks like a *Ekaratna*.

SONARGAON

32

RAJBARI (PALACE)
19th C/ Colonial

Old Sonargaon is a ghost town. This place was not really prominent during the 16th-17th century, but the ruins of a town of the British times.

There are a number of abandoned *Rajbaris* (Royal family dwellings) in Bangladesh. They are all European in style. This one in Sonargaon is better preserved and is rich with Italian style decorations.

Around the courtyard

Up: Looking up at the second floor Down: The entrance.

JAGANNATHA TEMPLE ★
17th C/ Hindu

This rare Hindu temple on the eastern outskirts of Comilla, is an octogonal structure with a curved roof on every side. The roof has small towers making it the only *Saptadashiya ratna* (17-tower) temple in Bangladesh. The brick edifice does not have much terracotta decoration and hence looks better from afar than up close.

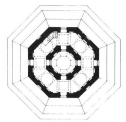

Plan of the 3rd floor.

Plan of the 5th floor

Detail of Jagannatha Temple.

Plan of the 1st floor

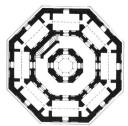

Plan of the 2nd floor

Temple in the middle of the field.

MAINAMATI MONASTERY
8th-12th C/ Buddhist

The old Buddhist monastery, on the western outskirts of Comilla has 20-odd structures, of which the *Salban Vihara* is the most prominent but smaller than the *Somapura Vihara* of Paharpur. A cross-shaped prayer room surrounded by 115 monks' rooms in the middle of the large precincts, has walls decorated with sculpted terracotta panels.

The central shrine of *Salban Vihara*

ORISSA

Orissa, the Kalinga kingdom of the past, is often called the Kalinga region. During the 3rd century BC, Emperor Ashoka unified most of India by conquering this region, killing over 150,000 people in the process. Recoiling from this extreme bloodshed Ashoka renounced violence and converted to Buddhism. He built *stupas* (stone monuments over earthen mounds) and *stambhas* (memorial pillars) at various sites. Buddhist ruins (7th-10th century) are scattered around the Khandagiri, Udaygiri and Lalitgiri hills. (*Giri* means mountain or hills). Jain rock-cave temples in Orissa are much older and date back to the 1st century, BC. These Middle Ages buildings are Orissa's only architectural legacy. Temples with *shikharas* that almost touch the sky and the abundant decorations are models of stone construction. These temples are all built around Bhubaneshwar. In terms of standard and quality, the temples in Bhubaneshwar easily measure up to those in Khajuraho. Bhubaneshwar is interesting because every milestone in architectural development from the 7th-13th century is seen here. Maturity in design and the scale of the Lingarajesvara Temple of Bhubaneshwar and the Jagannatha Temple in Puri, is equal to that of Gothic cathedrals. The Surya Temple in Konark is the zenith of Orissa's architecture. Hindu temples can be broadly divided into the north and the

south style. South temples have pronounced horizontal lines where the layers of the structure are stepped. In contrast, the north style of temple has enhanced vertical lines and is crowned with a bullet-like tower. The names of the various parts of the temple are also different. In the north, the whole tower is called *shikhara*, while in the south; only the topmost part of the tower is the *shikhara*. Temples of Orissa and Khajuraho are of the northern type and so are the temples of west India, except that they are larger. A further study of the Orissa temples reflects that they are built solidly and present an archaic style. Mukhalingam Temples in Andhra Pradesh, are clubbed with those of Orissa in this book, because they reflect the typical Orissa style.

Full view of the Brahmesvara Temple /1060/ Bhubaneshwar.

Surya Temple in Konark by Fergusson.

KHANDAGIRI and UDAYGIRI ★★

CAVE TEMPLES ★★
Around 1st C, BC/ Jain

The Kalinga kingdom lost its prominence after being defeated by Ashoka. In the 1st century BC, King Kharavela brought the area from the Gangetic plains to south India under his rule. The eastern part of present Bhubaneshwar, Sisupalgarh was his capital. Achievements of this king are written in an epitaph in Hathi Gumpha (Elephant Cave), the 14th Cave in Udaygiri. The epitaph points to his belief in Jainism and he dedicated rock-cut cave temples, 6 km from Bhubaneshwar, to Jainism. These are the earliest architectural traces in Jain history.

There are 18 caves left on Udaygiri hills and 15 caves on Khandagiri hills. First among these is the Rani Gumpha (Queen's Cave) which was in use from the 1st century, BC. It has corridors with a double row of pillars and a row of rectangular monks' rooms, and can be called a cave monastery. Above each entrance is an arch, resembling the *torana* sculptures of Sanchi, on which rules for people's daily life have been carved. There are ruins of wooden temples on the hill.

The Jain temple in Khandagiri belongs to the 19th century. In the caves around the temple, statues of *tirthankaras* (saints) from 11th-15th century have been sculpted. After this period, no more cave, or Jain temples, were built in Orissa.

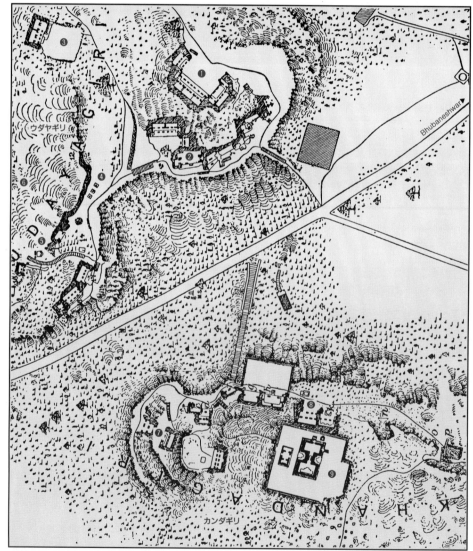

UDAYGIRI

❶ Cave 1, Rani Gumpha
❷ Cave 9
❸ Cave 10, Ganesha Gumpha
❹ Cave 14, Hathi Gumpha
❺ Cave 12, Bagh Gumpha
❻ Wooden temple ruins.

KANDAGIRI

❼ Second Cave
❽ Group of caves housing *tirthankara* statues.
❾ Jain temple built in the 19th century.

❶ Entrance to the monks' rooms, Rani Gumpha.
❷ The First Cave in Udaygiri, Rani Gumpha (1st C, BC)
❸ The Ninth Cave in Udaygiri (1st C, BC)
❹ Full view of Udaygiri
❺ The Ninth Cave in Khandagiri (1st C, BC)
❻ The Twelfth Cave in Udaygiri, Bagh Gumpha (1st C, BC)
❼ The Tenth Cave in Udaygiri, Ganesha Gumpha (1st C, BC)
❽ The Jain temple in Khandagiri (19th C)

STUPA AND MONASTERY
7th~9th C/ Buddhist

Located on three hills, Ratnagiri, Udaygiri and Lalitgiri, 90-100 km from Bhubaneshwar, are some Buddhist ruins. Ratnagiri, the centre of Buddhism during the Middle Ages was also a Buddhist university like Nalanda. On the peak of the hill, is the foundation of a *stupa* and around it are a number of small *stupas*. There is no temple but there is large monastery and a small one. The large monastery, built with bricks has Gupta dynasty style statues of Buddha carved around the entrance and on the doorway of the shrine.

Foundation of large *stupa* with smaller *stupas*

Up: Closed corridor around courtyard. Down: Monastery entrance.

STUPA AND MONASTERY
9th~10th C/ Buddhist

A large range of Buddhist buildings and statues from the Baumakara dynasty were excavated at Udaygiri. Half way up the hill is a restored stupa with a *chaumukha.* A Buddhist monastery on the hill has a larger-than-life statue of Buddha enshrined in the central courtyard. There are wonderful sculptures on the pillars at the shrine's entrance. At the foot of the hill is a 10th century stepwell, rare in east India.

❶ The entrance to the shrine of the monastery.
❷ The sculptures on the pillars of the entrance.
❸ The huge statue of Buddha, within the shrine.

One of the two *Bodhisattvas* inside the shrine.

Bhubaneshwar, the capital of Orissa is divided by a railway line into the old and new city in the south and north respectively. The new city was built by Otto H Koenigsberger, to replace Cuttack as the state capital in 1948. Bhubaneshwar is a medium-sized city with around 500,000 people. Visitors flock here to visit the many temples dating back to the Middle Ages in the old town which is built around the lake Bindu Sagar. There are over a hundred temples of the Nagara style that reflect the splendour of the temple town.

Most of the structures in the Orissa style are built in and around Bhubaneshwar. From the 8th-13th century more than 7000 temples were built of sandstone and thus high quality stone construction technology was developed. The stones have been so precisely cut that the joints between the stones cannot be seen at all. Instead of mortar, iron clamps have been used to attach one stone to another and thus towers have been raised up to heights of 50 m. A special feature of Orissa's architecture is the sculptures of deities and detailed carving. Orissa's architecture, renews one's fascination for classical Indian architecture.

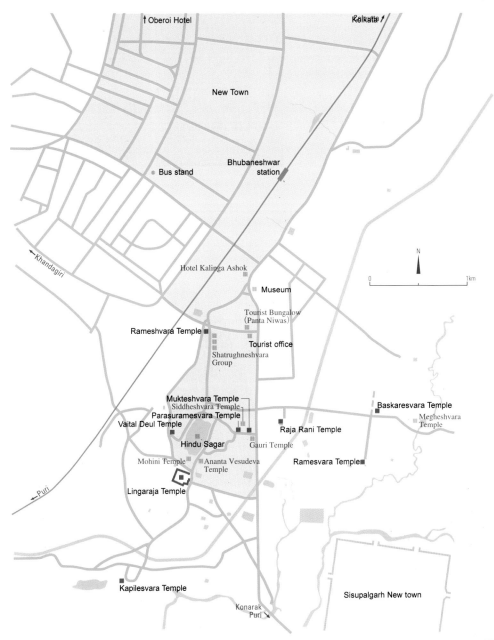

PARASURAMESVARA TEMPLE ★
7th C/ Hindu

This temple from medieval times reflects the emerging style of Hindu temples. The early style saw temples which were very basic with only the *garbhagriha* and the *shikhara* over it. Later the *mandapa* was added and the *mandapa* and shrine style evolved. The Parasuramesvara Temple also went through this process and the low *mandapa* was added later. Its rectangular *mandapa* has a 2-tiered hipped roof that lets in the sunlight and lets out the smoke. This roof style was also used for wooden houses. One can see that it is a copy of the wooden houses of that era. The curved surfaces of the *shikhara* too have their origins in wood framework roof style where curved bamboo rafters have been used.

❶ The temple has been designed without a base platform.
❷ Lattice work sculptures on the window.
❸ Interior of the *mandapa* (prayer room).

VAITAL DEUL (TEMPLE) ★
8th C/ Hindu

The tower atop the shrine is different from the usual *shikhara*. Its shape is semi-cylindrical and it is called *khakhara deul*. *Shikharas* have been placed in the four corners of the *mandapa* (bottom right of the picture.). This *khakhara* has its origins in rooftops of houses made with bamboo and wood. The *mandapa* is similar to the one in the Parasuramesvara Temple, with a two-tiered hipped roof.

Interior of the *mandapa*

Main shrine (*Khakhara Deul*). *Mandapa* is on the right.

BRAHMESVARA TEMPLE ★★
1060/ Hindu

In Orissa, the *garbhagriha*(*sanctum sanctorum*) is called *deul* and the *mandapa* (prayer room) is called *jagamohan*. Temple designs of north Orissa are complete when the tower called *rega deul* above the *deul* and the *pidha deul* above the *Jagamohan* are built. *Pidha* are flat layers, piled one over the other like a pyramid. *Pidha*

deul resembles the temple style of the south. The Brahmesvara Temple is a *pancharatna* (5 shrines), which includes small shrines with square *shikharas*. The height of the *shikhara* is 18 m. The precinct is surrounded by a fence. The temple reflects the orderly nature of Hindu temples. The complex details of the sculptures (full view on page 188) are also fascinating.

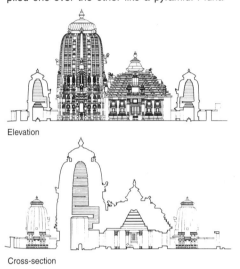

Elevation

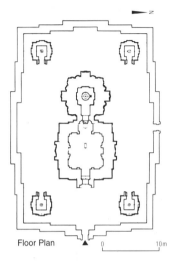

Cross-section

Floor Plan ▲ 0   10 m

❶ Five towers at dusk. ❷ Interior of the *Jagamohan*. ❸ Base of *Rega Deul* & a small shrine. ❹ *Jagamohan* & a small shrine.

MUKTESHVARA TEMPLE ★★★
10th C/ Hindu

Mukteshvara Temple is the dividing line between the earlier and the later styles of Orissa architecture. This jewel of a temple, which is built on a small scale, has an excellent finish. There are a number of small shrines inside the precincts. A low wall surrounds the base, which is densely sculpted. The pillars of the arch-like *torana* in front of the temple are moderately sculpted, but the actual arch has dense carvings that make the *torana* quite spectacular. At the back is a rectangular tank for ablution.

This *deul and jagamohan* style temple has a pyramidal roof. The sculptures on the walls and on the *shikhara* are perfectly proportioned. The structure was completed and then sculpted on and it is here that the fine skill of the craftsman is visible. The ceiling is elaborate. The roof was constructed by placing beams on all four sides one on top of another, the gap was narrowed down and a thick plank was placed on top, to cover the gap.

Excellent sculptures on the *torana*.

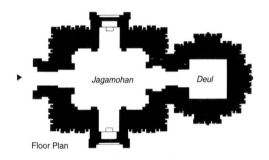
Jagamohan   Deul

Floor Plan

The *torana* and the temple surrounded by a low wall.

❶ Temple & tank. Siddeshvara Temple-far right. ❷ Sculptures on *Rega Deul.* ❸ *Torana* & small shrines. ❹ *Jagamohan.*

BHASKARESVARA TEMPLE
12th C/ Hindu

It appears that this differently styled temple was built on a Buddhist *stupa* ruin. There is a shrine but no *jagamohan (mandapa* in front of the shrine), the building looks more like a *Pidha Deul* (a prayer hall with a pyramidical roof), but the roof is too prominently curved to be pyramidal and there are few sculptures on the wall. One assumes that this different style was brought here during the rule of the Ganga dynasty from the south.

Southern façade of the temple.   View from a distance.

LINGARAJA TEMPLE ★★★
11th C/ Hindu

The Lingaraja Temple 37.5 m in height, has the tallest tower in Bhubaneshwar. It can be seen from anywhere in the old town. During Orissa's golden age of construction, right in front of the *deul* and *jagamohan*, a *nata mandir* and a *bhoga mandapa* were also built, thus enhancing the temple's overall spiritual ambience. *Jagamohans* styled like *pidha deuls* over both the shrines is quite normal. There are many small shrines in the precincts and the whole place bustles with pilgrims. As it is a temple that is in use, people of the lower caste are not allowed in.

Like this "King of Linga" Temple, most temples in Bhubaneshwar belong to the *shaivaites*. *Vaishnavism* spread in the 13th century. The *shikhara,* the symbol of a giant phallus, emphasizes the temple's strong vertical lines, but there are few sculptures. The circular disc on top is called *amalaka* and over this is placed, an inverted water jug shaped flower (*shikhara*).

Up: Precincts from the west. Down: Small shrines inside the precinct.

198

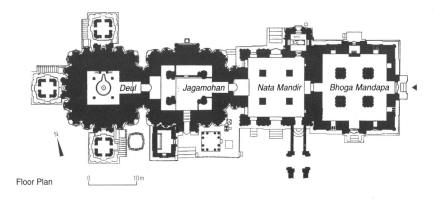

Deul   Jagamohan   Nata Mandir   Bhoga Mandapa

Floor Plan   0   10 m

Rega deul (tall tower) that is over 45 m high and the pyramid shaped *pidha deul*.

RAJARANI TEMPLE ★★
11th C/ Hindu

This temple has the most brilliantly constructed *shikhara* in Bhubaneshwar. When looking at the plan, it looks like the *shikhara* is tilted at 45 degrees. It is not actually so, but the surface has been partitioned and built on different levels which have been repeated regularly thus making the entire surface parallel to the central axis. Also, the partitioned surfaces look as if they are standing independent of each other, because a series of small *shikharas* have been put together to form a collective whole. The excellent carving on the base is beyond compare. In contrast the *jagamohan* looks simple and the sculptures are also moderate. Round pillars at the entrance on which entwined snake goddesses are carved are very impressive.

❶ The *Rega Deul* which is a collection of small *shikharas*.
❷ The deity no longer inside the niche.
❸ Statues of *Apsaras* (heavenly damsels) are on every surface.
❹ A full view of the temple.

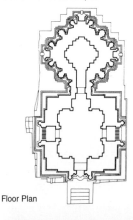

Floor Plan

A Nagin or snake goddess statue on the *Jagamohan*.

RAMESVARA TEMPLE ★
13th C/ Hindu

One of the four temples still standing in the old town, is the Ramesvara Temple that belongs to a later age. Its *jagamohan* is separated from the *deul* and the roof is not a *pidha deul* but the earlier style of three-tiered hipped roof. The walls have almost no sculptures and reflect the end of artistic excellence in Orissa.

Full view of Ramesvara temple.

KAPILESVARA MAHADEVA TEMPLE
17th C/ Hindu

The very large Kapilesvara Temple on the southern outskirts of the city is not open to people of other religions. The large temple tank reflects the bond between temple and water. Around this period of time, architectural activity stopped in Orissa and began developing in Bengal.

Various shrines seen along the *ghats*

OBEROI HOTEL ★
1983/
by Satish Grover

The Oberoi Hotel is located to the north of the city. It was designed by Satish Grover, who is an architect and also an architectural historian. It is designed like a monastery or *caravan sarai* with square rooms and enclosed corridors, surrounding a pool. The architect is deeply interested in traditional Indian architecture. Other than planning this hotel, he has had no contact with the traditional construction of Orissa.

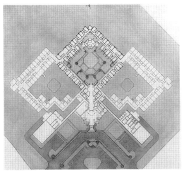

Floor Plan

Up: Pool with surrounding corridors. Down: Second floor corridor.

DHAULI ☆

38

SHANTI STUPA
1970/ Buddhist
Dhauli on the Kalinga plains, is the site of the battle of Kalinga in which more than 150,000 people were supposedly killed. It is said that the repentant Ashoka converted to Buddhism. His imperial edicts still exist. As it is a sacred place, the Myohouji temple of Japan built a *stupa* here. This Peace Pagoda is a concrete structure modelled after the Amravati stupa.

The *stupa* on top of the hill.

HARIPUR ☆

39

CHAUSATT YOGINI TEMPLE
11th C/ Hindu
This unusual temple in Haripur village 10 km from Dhauli, has no roof and is only a small shrine, surrounded by a circular wall. The outside of the wall has nine niches and the inside is lined with niches which have black statues of *yoginis*. These 64 *yoginis* are attendants of gods and are referred to by their number, *Chausatt*.

Yoginis in a row on the circular wall.

PURI ☆

40

JAGANNATHA TEMPLE ★★
12th C/ Hindu
Jagannatha (emperor of the world) is another name for Krishna. This temple in Puri facing the Bay of Bengal, is the largest and one of the most sacred temples in India. Every year during the Chariot Festival more than 200,000 pilgrims flock to this 40,000 sq m temple. Non-believers are barred from this temple. Like the Lingaraja Temple, this one has four shrines in a row and a 55 m high *shikhara*. This temple heralds the decline of architecture in Orissa. The details and richness of the walls of the Konark and Bhubaneshwar temples, is absent.

The *Rega Deul* and the *Pidha Deul*, painted white.

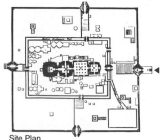

Site Plan

SURYA TEMPLE ★★★
13th C/ Hindu

Konark Temple, located in a coastal village, 65 km from Bhubaneshwar and dedicated to the Sun God, *Surya*, is the ultimate in the architectural legacy of Orissa. Construction of the temple started when Narasimha Deva I was a prince and finished 20 years later when he became King. Most of the 180 m x 220 m complex is built in the centre and has many shrines and statues surrounding it. (Diagram of the restored building on pg 189)

Since the *pidha deul* is 39 m, the *rega deul* must have been at least 60 m. The reason for the *shikhara* to have broken is not known, nor does one know if the *shikhara* ever existed. Fergusson wrote that a part of the *shikhara* was built in 1839. Since the *jagamohan* was also in danger of collapsing, stones were piled inside during the British period. Despite this crude style of protection, the temple stands majestically and impresses people as the best construction of Indian architecture.

According to Veda mythology, *Surya* goes around heaven in a chariot drawn by seven horses. The chariot-shaped temple in Konark, has 24 huge wheels carved on the plinth or foundation platform, and horses sculpted in front of it. The pyramid roof of *jagamohan* is three-tiered and the *amalaka* on top is excellent. The roof of the *nata mandir* (dance hall) is destroyed, but the walls are richly carved. The temple is famous for the sculptures of male and female coitus on the walls.

The Surya temple is spectacular even at night.

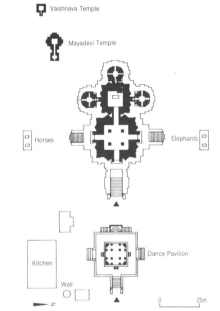

Floor Plan

There are 24 wheels sculpted on the stone. Each wheel is 3 m in diameter.

❶ The peak of the
pidha-deul.
❷ Foundation platform.
❸ The sculptures on the
foundation platform.
❹ The *shikhara* was
constructed to the left of
the *jagamohan.*
❺ Sun God.
❻ Sculpture depicting
the war front.
❼ *Nata mandir* (shrine).
❽ The walls of the *Nata
mandir.*

VARAHI TEMPLE ★★
10th C/ Hindu

This small gem of a temple which receives few visitors, is 25 km from Konark, and from the same period as the Mukhtesvara Temple in Bhubaneshwar. It is built on a platform devoid of decorations, but the temple itself is elaborately decorated with carving of high quality from corner to corner. The shrine is not the usual square but a rectangle, the *shikhara* is not centripetal and there is no *amalaka*. This is a form in the evolution of the *kharkhara deul* where a semi-cylindrical ridge crowns it. Seen collectively, it is a set of small *shikharas* in a group. The west side of the *deul* is actually the rear area, but it has been so richly sculpted that one could mistake it to be the front. A beautiful statue of *Surya* is installed in the niche. Instead of the *pidha deul*, it has a two-tiered hipped roof. This temple which was in disrepair, has been restored.

The walls of the *jagamohan* with latticed windows.

View from the west.

The niche where *Surya* is placed.

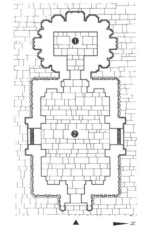

Floor Plan
❶ *Deul* (shrine) ❷ *Jagamohan* (Prayer room)

MADHUKESVARA TEMPLE ★
8th C/ Hindu

Madhukesvara or Mukhalingesvara Temple located in Mukhalingam, the old capital of the east Ganga dynasty, is older than temples in Puri and Konark. The best preserved temple of the Orissa style, it has many shrines but the style is *panchanata* (five main shrines). It has a simple *shikhara* and on the walls are *shikharas* sculpted in a row, under which are statues of gods. Sculptures on pillars near the entrance, show the temple's link with the Buddhist era.

To go to Mukhalingam one should take the six-hour train journey to Chennai from Bhubaneshwar, get off at Srikakulam and then take a taxi.

❶ Full view of the temple.
❷ The small shrine.
❸ Sculptures on the pillars near the entrance.
❹ *Shikhara* style reliefs, in a row on the wall.

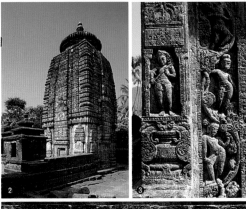

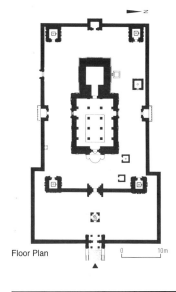

Floor Plan   0   10m

BHIMESVARA TEMPLE
8th C/ Hindu

Bhimesvara Temple is a small temple that was built at the same time as the Madhukesvara Temple. It resembles the Madhukesvara Temple in its style of architecture. The *deul* walls are plain, with niches. The simple *shikhara* has pronounced horizontal layers like a *pidha deul*. Another single-shrine type temple in the region is the Somesvara Temple.

Right: Niche on the wall
Left: *Shikhara* on the shrine

Pakistan

JAISALMER 14

KIRADU 12

59 BHUJ

58 KUTCH

GUJARAT

47 MORVI

WADHWA

49 WANKANER

DWARKA 57

56 GOP

SEJAKPUR 48

GHUMLI 55

JUNAGADH 51 52 GIRNAR

SATRUNJAYA

SOMNATH 54

53

DIU

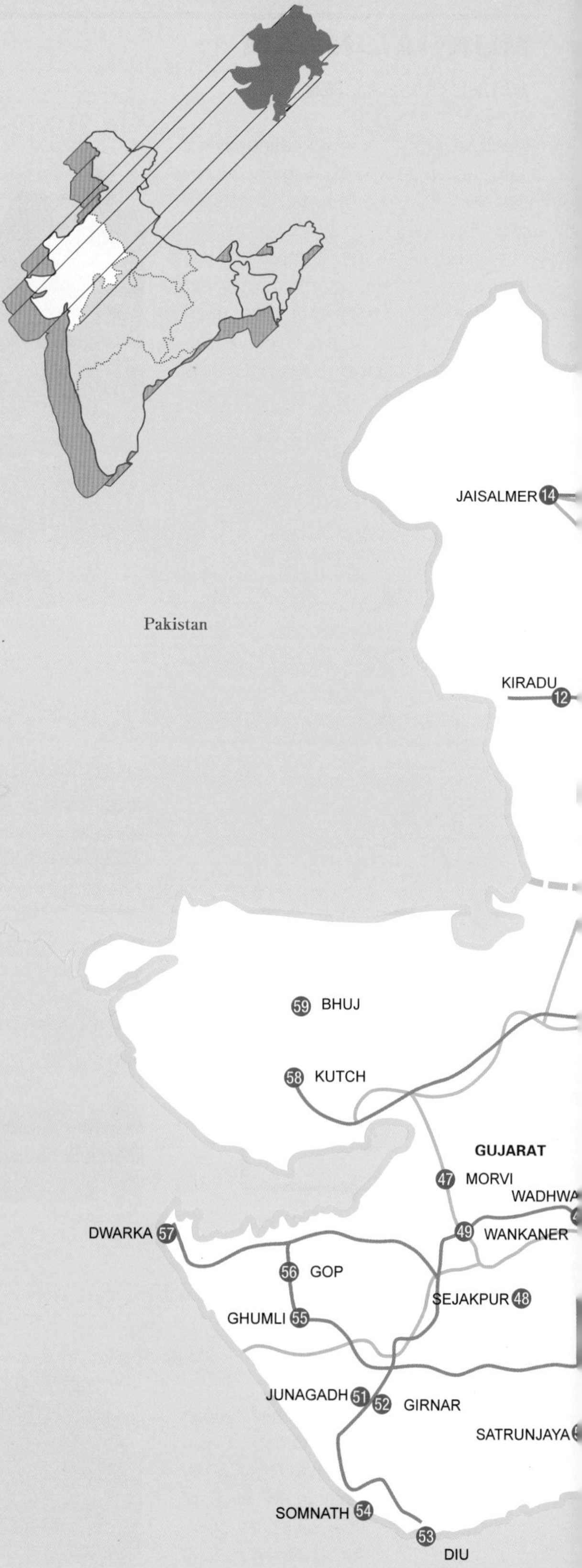

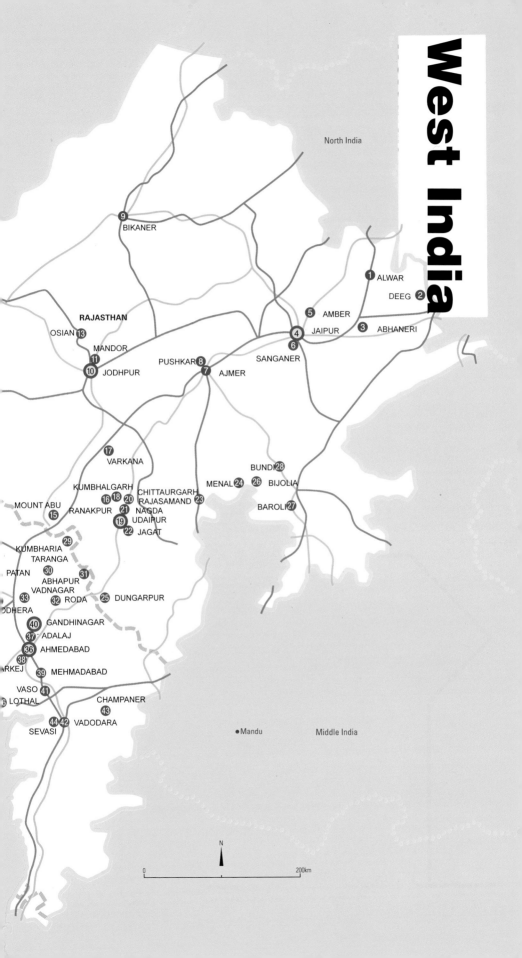

West India

North India

9 BIKANER

RAJASTHAN

1 ALWAR
DEEG 2
5 AMBER
OSIAN 13
MANDOR
11
4 JAIPUR
3 ABHANERI
PUSHKAR 8
10 JODHPUR
7 AJMER
6 SANGANER

17 VARKANA

BUNDI 28
KUMBHALGARH
MENAL 24 26 BIJOLIA
CHITTAURGARH
16 18 20 RAJASAMAND 23
MOUNT ABU
RANAKPUR 21 NAGDA
BAROLI 27
15
19 UDAIPUR
22 JAGAT

KUMBHARIA 29
TARANGA
PATAN 30
ABHAPUR 31
VADNAGAR
33
RODA
32
25 DUNGARPUR
DHERA
40 GANDHINAGAR
37 ADALAJ
36 AHMEDABAD
38
RKEJ
39 MEHMADABAD
VASO 41
LOTHAL
CHAMPANER
43
44 42 VADODARA
SEVASI

• Mandu   Middle India

N

0   200km

TRAVEL INFORMATION (West India)

AROUND JAIPUR

Jaipur, the capital of Rajasthan, along with Delhi and Agra, form a famous triangle. A bus trip covering all three places is possible, as they are approximately within six hours of each other. They are well connected by air and rail, too. Alwar or Deeg, en route, can be accessed by bus or taxi. Phool Bagh Palace is a medium range palace hotel. There are a number of hotels in Jaipur, of which the Deluxe Hotel at Khalsa Koti is reasonably good. Rambagh is a former palace converted into a luxury hotel. Abaneri is approximately two hours by taxi, while Ajmer is a two-and-a-half-hour bus ride from Jaipur, and four hours from Jodhpur. Here, Mansingh Hotel is recommended. One of the pleasures of touring Rajasthan is being able to stay in former palaces or guesthouses of Maharajas (kings) that have been converted into hotels.

DESERT CAPITAL

Jodhpur is connected to Udaipur and Jaipur by road and rail. Express buses take five hours from Jaipur and nine hours from Udaipur. Ajit Bhawan Hotel is a good place to stay, while Umaid Bhawan is a luxury hotel. Balsamand, Mandor and Osian can be seen in a day-trip, by taking a taxi. Bikaner is 5 hours by bus or train (from Jaipur it is 7 hours) and Jaisalmer is 8 hours. Avoid night buses but the night train from Delhi is a good option. Dhola Meru tourist bungalow is a good place as the Lalgarh Palace Hotel is further away. Jodhpur to Jaisalmer by the night train is a good option. The day train takes 9 hours and fast buses take 5 hours. Small planes now fly from Jaisalmer to Jodhpur and Delhi. Mosmal Tourist Bungalow is an ordinary hotel, but inside the fort one can find Hotel Jaisal Castle and other medium range hotels.

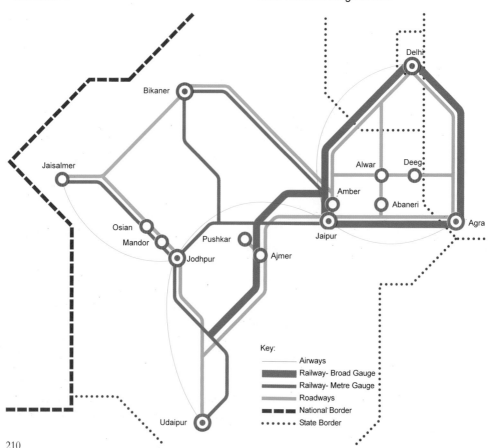

Key:
- ———— Airways
- ▬▬▬▬ Railway- Broad Gauge
- ▬▬▬▬ Railway- Metre Gauge
- ———— Roadways
- ▬ ▬ ▬ National Border
- •••••• State Border

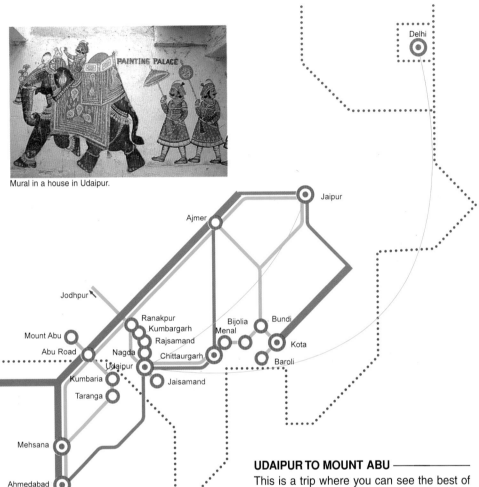

Mural in a house in Udaipur.

UDAIPUR TO BUNDI

Udaipur is well connected to most places by air, but the night train from Ahmedabad is very convenient. Udaipur has many hotels. Lake Palace Hotel needs prior reservation and the Laxmi Vilas Palace Hotel is very convenient. Nagda or Rajasamand in the north, are accessible by bus or taxi. Jaisamand and Jagat in the south can be covered in one trip. It is three hours to Chittaurgarh, where one can stay at Panna Tourist Bungalow. From there, take a taxi to Menal, Bijolia and Bundi. Reservations are needed for Brijraj Bhawan Palace Hotel. It takes five and a half hours to travel from Kota to Ajmer or Jaipur. Both Bundi and Baroli can be covered in a single trip.

UDAIPUR TO MOUNT ABU

This is a trip where you can see the best of Rajasthani architecture. It is practical to take the first bus from Udaipur to Ranakpur (four and a half hours), check into Shilpi Tourist Bungalow and visit the temples in the afternoon. The hotel is simple and the food is vegetarian. To see Kumbhalghar, hire a jeep and then go to Ranakpur. From Ranakpur take the bus to Mount Abu or Jodhpur. You can go by train, alight at the Farna station, take another train to Abu Road station and then take a bus or taxi to Mount Abu. There are direct buses from Udaipur and Ajmer, too. Of the many hotels, Hotel Hillstone is very conveniently located. There are palace hotels, too. Kumbharia is an hour's journey by taxi from Abu Road. Since there is no accommodation here, it is better to cover it and go further from there to Mehsana, after visiting Taranga (1 hour).

TRAVEL INFORMATION (West India)

KATHIAWAD PENINSULA ——————

Bhavnagar, the entrance to the Kathiawad peninsula can be reached from Mumbai by air or by bus from Ahmedabad (four hours). Palitana is an hour and a half by road from Bhavnagar. Stay at Hotel Sumeru and take a tonga (horsecart) at dawn to Shatrunjaya Mountain. It takes an hour and a half to climb to the top or a *doli* (simple palanquin) can be hired. Get permission for photography at the entrance to Vimala Vasi Doug. To get from Palitana to Diu, a five-hour bus journey to Una, then take an auto-rickshaw to Diu. Simple hotels are available here. From Una to Junagadh by bus is four hours. Stay in the Hotel Girnar and take a rickshaw early in the morning to the base of Girnar mountains, from where it is a painful two-hour climb, on uneven steps. From Junagadh to Rajkot, is two hours by bus, while it takes an hour to reach Wankaner. Stay in the guesthouse, near the palace and dine at the palace with the royal family. Go by bus to Porbunder and Dwarka and visit Rajkot. From Porbunder, take a taxi to Bileshwar, Ghumli and Gop.

The entrance gate to Porbunder town.

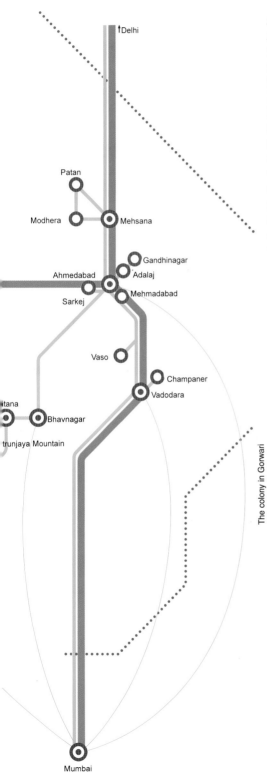

Delhi

Patan

Modhera   Mehsana

Gandhinagar

Ahmedabad   Adalaj

Sarkej   Mehmadabad

Vaso

Champaner

Vadodara

itana   Bhavnagar

trunjaya Mountain

Mumbai

AROUND AHMEDABAD ———

Ahmedabad, Gujarat's main city can be reached by fast trains and by air from Delhi and Mumbai (nine-hour trip on the night train from Mumbai.) Hotel Mascot is comfortable. It takes 3 days to see the city. Visit Calico Museum, designed by Le Corbusier, in the same complex as the Sarabhai family home and the art museum in the LD Research Centre, designed by Doshi. Rickshaws are very convenient within Ahmedabad and charge by meter. Sarkhej in the west is 30 minutes away and so are Adalaj in the north and Gandhinagar, which can be covered in one trip. Go by taxi to Isanpur, Vadodara and Mehmedabad in the south. To get to Modhera and Patan, take the day train to Mehsana. From there, Modera is 30 minutes and Patan is 45 minutes by taxi. Return to Ahmedabad by the night train. Ahmedabad to Vadodara is two and a half hours by bus or train. Stay at the Express Hotel. Champaner is two hours by road from Vadodara. Return to Mumbai by air or train.

BHUJ, KUTCH ———

The colony in Gorwari

To visit Kutch, you have to go to Bhuj, by air from Mumbai or by bus from Ahmedabad (7 hours by overnight buses). There are buses from Rajkot through Wankaner and Morvi, too. Hotel Prince is a good place to stay in. On reaching Kutch, get a permit from the District Collector's office or the police station to visit the villages. The settlements in Banni can be visited by taxi, in a day. Visit four to six such villages but in Muslim villages, take care not to focus the camera on women.

RAJASTHAN

In this book, West India is made up of the states of Rajasthan and Gujarat, a dry, fascinating landscape where rivers are scarce. Its unique blend of cultures transports one into a 'Thousand and One Nights' ambience.

Before Independence, Rajasthan, meaning "Land of Kings", was called *Rajputana* the land of the Rajputs. The land of the Rajputs which spreads over a large area, includes the Thar Desert and touches Pakistan. Around the 5th century, tribes from Central Asia mixed with the local populace to form the present tribe. This tribe that also advanced into northern and central India is called Rajput. The Rajputs could never establish a unified nation, as they were always fighting for supremacy among themselves. When the Muslims swept into India from the west, they had to fight against them too.

When the Mughals established their rule in Delhi and began extending their empire, Rajput chieftains came under Mughal rule and became their vassals. A new blend of Hindu and Islamic culture came into being.

All Mughal forts, palaces and tombs reflect this culture and even Hindu temples show a strong Islamic influence. Jaisalmer, an important town in Rajasthan effectively depicts the blend of Indo-Islamic culture.

Rajasthan was attacked from the west and the strife did not end until the Middle Ages. As a result, there is not much left of its ancient architecture. The temples built during the Middle Ages have been destroyed. Muslims needed to build mosques in the land they conquered, so they pulled down the temples and used the material to construct mosques. To avoid this Jains started building their temples deep in the mountains. The temples in Mount Abu and Ranakpur are some such examples. These temples, with their excellent architectural style and exquisite stone carvings are beyond compare. The temple of Ranakpur, built in the traditional style, with its unconventional interior, is an architectural masterpiece.

After colonization British influences crept into Rajput architecture. Jaipur has many buildings designed by British architects.

Left: The mural inside the palace in Jaipur (Rang Mahal of Jaisalmer). Right: Kirti Sthamba in Chittaurgarh (Jain).

PALACE QUARTER
Rajput
CITY PALACE ★
18th C
TOMB OF BAKHTAWAR SINGH
19th C
SAGAR (ARTIFICIAL LAKE)
Alwar, built by the Rajput Rao Pratap Singhji in 1771, was the capital of the kingdom. A wall surrounds the city at the top of which, is the fortified palace with various facilities that reflect the high standard of living the royalty enjoyed during the Middle Ages. The five-storeyed palace that was begun in 1793 by King Bakhtawar Singh has a wide courtyard, pavilions and cantilevered windows that give a unique appearance to the west-Indian style palace. The roofs are the *bangaldar* style that was prevalent in the Bengal area in east India. There is a *sagar* (man-made lake) behind the palace, which has a tank where the royal women and children could bathe. *Chhatris* have been built surrounding the rectangular *sagar*, thus creating a magnificent watering place.

The biggest *chhatri* is the tomb of Bakhtawar Singh, which is a five-domed marble structure, built on top of a red sandstone base. Inside is a hall open on all four sides from where the palace or the waterfront is visible. For the royalty, this place must have been heaven on earth.

❶ The courtyard and pavilion of the City Palace.
❷ View of the Bakhtawar Singh Tomb.
❸ Ceiling of the Bakhtawar Singh Tomb.

❹ Bakhtawar Singh Tomb facing the *sagar*.
❺ The palace facing the *sagar*.
❻ The palace and *sagar* surrounded by rugged mountains.
❼ *Chhatris* extending into the *sagar*. The fort can be seen on the mountain.

DEEG (DIG) ★   2

PALACE COMPLEX ★
18th~19th C/ Rajput

Deeg was the capital of the Jat Rajputs and Deeg Palace is surrounded by wide gardens. Palace buildings set amidst gardens and the lakes on either side make a fantastic picture. Structures face each other on the central axis of the Muslim-style *char bagh,* while the palaces on the east and west, face the lakes on the east and west, respectively. The entire scene is very different and visually, very appealing.

Up: Keshav Bhavan pavilion facing Roop Sagar.
Down: The cloister in the courtyard of the Suraj Bhavan Palace.

Main palace, Gopal Bhavan facing Gopal Sagar.

ABHANERI ★ ★

KUND (STEPPED CISTERN) ★★★
9th C/ Hindu

These Kunds (step-wells) where steps lead down to the water, were not just wells but were also used for religious ceremonies, and hence had a deep connection with temples. They developed into an art form. The most impressive of the step-wells is this one in Abhaneri. The foundations of the Harshamata temple found nearby show that there must have been a religious connection with the step-well.

The Kund is 35 m on each side with steps leading down from each side and water can be drawn from any level. On one side are multi-storeyed rooms and at the rear is the shaft of the well. The well must have been in use even during the Mughal era, as it was accessible even after the temple was destroyed. From ground level looking down into the kund which is as deep as a seven-storeyed building is a very impressive sight.

Hiring a taxi from Jaipur or Alwar is better as getting to Abhaneri may be a problem.

❶ Cloisters surrounding the well. (18th century)
❷ Rooms with an arched entrance. (Mughal era)
❸ Two Hindu shrines on the lower half.
❹ Steps on the opposite side visible from the cool rest rooms.
❺ A plant-pot design has been sculpted on the pillars of the rooms constructed earlier.

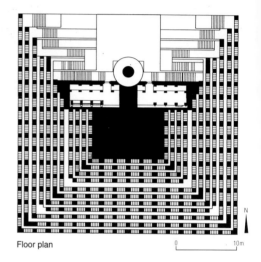

Floor plan

0 ⊢⊣ 10m

N

Tank with seven floors underground and a depth of more than 20 m in Abhaneri.

JAIPUR ★ ★ ★

Jaipur, the capital of Rajasthan, was designed by Maharaja Sawai Jai Singh II. In 1727 he developed his new city, 11 km south of Amber and called it Jaipur, after himself. The city was divided into 9 squares of 800 m with the palace quarter and the Jantar Mantar in the centre. It has earned the name *Pink City*, because most of the buildings are painted pink. Another characteristic of Jaipur is its grid of well-planned roads.

Recently, in the southern part, a new city has been developed, where the Government offices are located. Jaipur, with its gardens, palaces and tombs with their spectacular gardens is a popular tourist spot.

Vidhyadhar Gardens is named after Vidhyadhar Bhattacharya, the architect who helped Sawai Jai Singh II design the city.

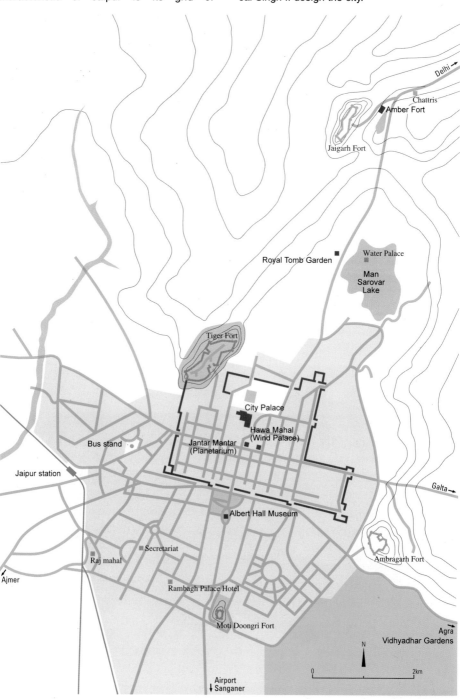

CITY AND PALACE QUARTER
18th C/ Rajput
Sawai Jai Singh II advanced into the plains and his buildings reflect a heavy influence of Islamic-Mughal architecture. The palace is designed in the Islamic style and different areas of the Palace Quarter have been given Islamic names.

CITY GATES
The city is surrounded by a 6 m high wall flanked by a 10 km road which is 34 m wide. The wall has eight city gates painted in the *bangla* colour. The most magnificent of them all is Ajmeri Gate, with three entrances and *chhatris*.

CITY PALACE ★
Sawai Jai Singh moved into the palace in 1733 and the royal family still lives there. This group of palaces, with connecting courtyards is Islamic in style and its excellent design is very appealing. Mubarak Mahal Palace was designed in 1890 by the British architect, Samuel Swinton Jacob as a guest house for the Maharaja.

HAWA MAHAL ★
It is a very arresting building constructed by Sawai Jai Singh in 1799. Its pink façade, with stone *jalis* (lattice screens) and *jharokhas* (windows) face the main street, from where the royal ladies could watch processions below without showing themselves.

❶ City Gate (Ajmeri Gate)
❷ The broad road in the Pink City.
❸ Hawa Mahal (Palace of Winds).
❹ Diwan-i-Khas (Private audience palace)

The layout of Jaipur City.

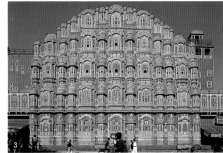

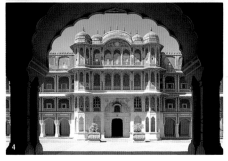

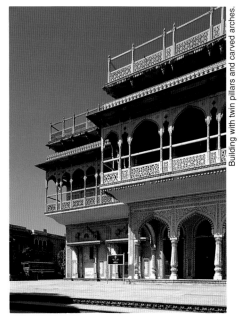

Building with twin pillars and carved arches.

JANTAR MANTAR
(OBSERVATORY) ★★
1734/ Rajput

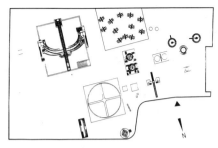

Layout

Sawai Jai Singh II, was an enlightened monarch. He could understand Sanskrit and Persian well and also had a great passion for the natural sciences. He had a keen interest in astronomy and had a large collection of books on the subject, from Persia and Europe. To improve the astronomical calendar, he built Jantar Mantar, which has a giant sundial, constellation observatory, astronomical observatory, meridian observatory, all outdoors. He built an observatory in Delhi and later, one each in Ujjain, Varanasi and Mathura. In Jaipur, the observatory is in the Palace Quarters. It was inspired by Mirza Ulugh Beg's observatory built in Samarkand, three centuries earlier.

Even though the Rajput chieftain took his idea from Islamic traditional natural sciences, his observatory is not built in the traditional style. It has been built on the basis of the requirements of natural sciences and as a result has given us a unique architectural marvel that is still relevant today. Some of the instruments are still used for weather and crop forecasts.

❶ Samrat Yantra (height 27 m)
❷ The wings of the 12-piece Rashivalaya Yantra.
❸ Rashivalaya Yantra (12 in number).

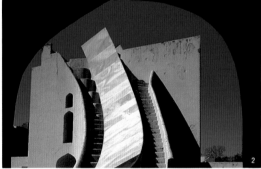

ALBERT HALL MUSEUM
1887/ Colonial
by Samuel Swinton Jacob

Jacob, the Executive Engineer of the Rajput Kingdom and master of the Indo-Saracenic style, built the Albert Hall now known as the Central Museum. It is built in tiers and the centre is crowned with a dome. The lowest level has fascinating courtyards, surrounded by a corridor. Jacob also built Rambagh Palace, which is now a luxury hotel.

View of the *chhatri* from the corridor.

Up: Full view. Down: The courtyard with the surrounding corridor.

ROYAL CHHATRIS (AT GAITORE)
★

18th C/ Rajput

On the northern outskirts of Jaipur are the marble cenotaphs including that of Sawai Jai Singh II and other royalty. Because of the Islamic influence, various Rajputs started building tombs, but since they were Hindus, they are all empty cenotaphs. These open *chhatri*-type tombs are of white marble, with the domes supported on pillars.

Chhatri means umbrella in Sanskrit. These domes standing on four or more pillars, came to be called *chhatris* and later, even the tombs were called *chhatris*. Decorative pavilions on top of buildings are also called *chhatris*.

❶ The dome-type tomb of Sawai Jai Singh.
❷ The platform and base of a pillar.
❸ Madho Singh I's Tomb.

AMBER ★★

5

FORT AND PALACE ★★
17th~18th C/ Rajput

This fort of the Doundar kingdom with the palace within, is in the mountains, 11 km from Jaipur. The town spreads out below. This was the capital of the Kachhawaha Rajputs until Sawai Jai Singh II shifted his base to Jaipur in 1727. This vast complex is a blend of Rajput and Islamic styles. To the north are four courtyards in a row and the third courtyard continues right up to Ganesha Gate.   The palace is similar to the Alhambra palace, set in an Islamic paradise garden. Jai Mandir Palace is King Jai Singh's Palace (1639), the interior of which reflects the rich and lavish lifestyle of royalty.

❶ Glimpse of the fort palace from the highway.
❷ Ganesha Gate.
❸ Pillars in the Jai Mandir Palace.
❹ The courtyard in Jai Mandir Palace.

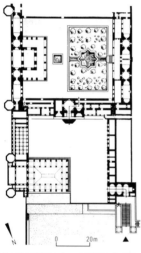

Courtyard and floor plan of Jai Mandir Palace

SANGANER ★

6

DIGAMBARA TEMPLE ★
15th C/ Jain

There is a 15th century Jain temple in the small town of Sanganer, 11 km south of Jaipur. This Digambara temple has an unusual design. The front courtyard is surrounded by a cloister. The courtyard has an open marble shrine in which six *tirthankaras* (Jain saints) have been deified.

The open marble shrine.

Ajmer town, by the side of Ana Sagar Lake, was a land of dispute among various Rajput kingdoms until the year 1556, when Akbar brought it under the control of the Mughals. This is a holy city in the Muslim world. To the west of the city is the *dargah* of the Muslim saint, Khwaja Mu'inuddin Chishti, which is always crowded with pilgrims. Khwaja Mu'inuddin Chisthi came to India from Afghanistan at the end of the 12th century, and began propagating the Chishti religious group in India. Ajmer is surrounded by a stone wall with five gateways.

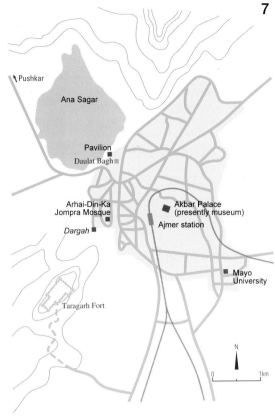

Dargah.

AJMER   7

ADHAI-DIN-KA-JOMPRA MOSQUE ★
13th C/ Islamic

It is one of the earliest mosques built along with the Quwwat-ul-Islam mosque in Delhi. As in the case of the complex in Delhi, Qutbuddin Aibak of the Slave Dynasty designed the mosque in 1210 and in 1230, Iltutmish continued the construction. Jain and Hindu temples were demolished and the materials were used to build the mosque. Its most impressive feature is the magnificent façade of seven arches. These along with the dome ceiling have been built using traditional methods.

Façade, built by piling stones, one over another.

Pillars have been erected after removing the images sculpted on them.

AKBAR'S PALACE
1572/ Islamic

A simple palace built by Emperor Akbar in the middle of a fortified area. The double-storeyed square building with its pillars, beams and broad eaves is in an architectural style propagated by Akbar. This yellow sandstone palace is presently used as the Government museum.

Facade of Akbar's Palace.

PAVILIONS BY ANA SAGAR
17th C/ Mughal

This man-made lake was constructed in 1135. It was not only the water source for the city, but also a place of recreation for the citizens. The shore of the lake towards town has beautiful gardens and terraces and many marble pavilions built by the Mughal Emperor, Shahjahan.

View of the pavilions by Ana Sagar.

MAYO COLLEGE ★
1875/ Colonial
by de Fabeck

The English architect who designed the College for Rajput princes used a traditional Indian style. Modelled after an English University, it has arches and *chhatris* on the central roof ridge in the Mughal architectural style. There is a statue of the then viceroy, Lord Mayo in front of the building.

PUSHKAR ★   8

GHATS AND TEMPLES
Hindu

Pushkar, 11 km west of Ajmer, is a sacred Hindu place. The *ghats* (stepped terraces) surrounding Pushkar Lake along with the temples and houses form a unique vista. The temples around 400 in all, with their touches of the Islamic architectural style, are richly different.

Bikaner, a dry city to the north of the Thar Desert, was built in 1488 by Rao Bhikaji of the Rathore Rajput family. Rathore, a branch of the Jodhpur royal family, continued as chieftains, even during the British era. Bikaner, once prominent as the nodal point for east-west trade, is surrounded by city walls and has some very interesting houses, *havelis* (residences)

and old Jain temples. To the northeast of the former city, divided by the railway track, stands Junagarh fort and palace and the new city developed around it. On the outskirts, are the Royal Tomb Gardens and Lalgarh Palace designed by Samuel Swinton Jacob, which has been converted into a palace hotel. Buildings in this desert city are of red sandstone.

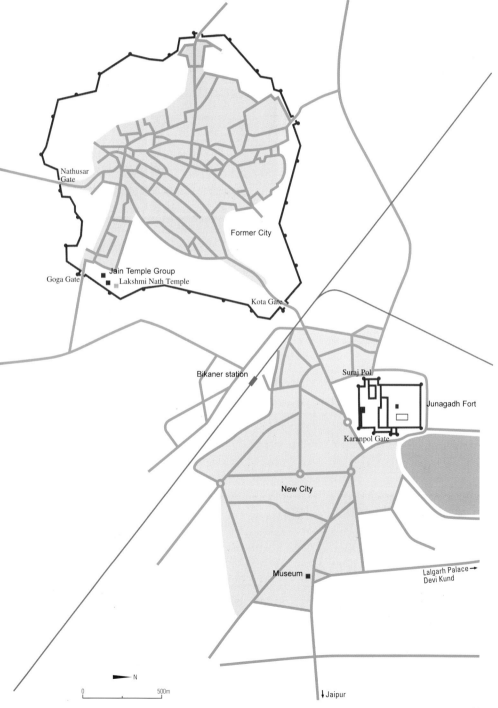

JUNAGADH FORT ★★
16th C/ Rajput

A century after the city of Bikaner was designed, a new palace was built outside the palace walls as the existing one was too small. Construction was completed in 1593, but additions to the palace continued and what finally resulted was an imposing, five-storeyed structure. The surrounding wall is more than 1 km in length. The only entrance Suraj Pol or Entrance of the Sun, faces east as in Jaisalmer and other places. At the entrance is a large courtyard, which leads to more entrances and courtyards.

This design feature serves a dual purpose: defense against invasion, as well as preserving the privacy of the residents. All palaces have delicately carved *jalis* (stone lattice screens) and *jharokhas* (extended windows); important features in the palace architectural style of western India. The oldest building is the Lal Nivas.

The flower pattern on the walls and ceilings of this palace bears eloquent testimony to the skill of the artisans of those times. The red and gold interior of the colourful Jewel Throne Room in Anup Mahal, inspires awe.

❶ *Jharokha* (the stone lattice windows).
❷ The second courtyard.
❸ The golden interior of Anup Mahal.
❹ Interior of Lal Niwas Palace.
❺ Suraj Pol of Junagarh Fort.

OLD TOWN AND JAIN TEMPLES
16th~17th C

Since Bikaner was formerly a walled city, it could not spread horizontally. This resulted in tall buildings being constructed within the city. In the old red-brown residences four or five storeys high, the first floor is partially sunken with a door facing the road. These luxurious dwellings are called *havelis*, some of which, like the Rampuria Haveli are decorated as magnificently as palaces.

Although murals in Jain temples are very rare. there is an old group of colourfully painted Jain temples, clustered together like a temple town. The Parshavanatha Temple has a *chaumukha* (statue facing all four directions), though the building is not open on all four sides.

❶ The view of the old city. ❷ The old city gate. ❸ Rampuria Haveli. ❹ Interior of the Parshavanatha Temple.

ROYAL CHHATRIS (AT DEVI KUND)
Rajput

Amidst bleak landscape, 8 km east of the city, are the Royal Tomb Gardens, surrounding a tank. They are divided into two groups and fenced. The main group has twelve geometric shaped, white marble *chhatris*, each supported on twelve pillars, which remind one of the Mughal Tomb Gardens.

Jodhpur, a fortified town, was the capital of the Marwar kingdom until the 13th century when the Rathore clan conquered it. In 1459, the present city was developed by Rao Jodha. A branch of this family built Bikaner, Pokhran and Jaisalmer.

Jodhpur was a prominent nodal city for trade between the east and the west and is now the second largest city of Rajasthan. The palace and fort are built on a hill while the city spreads below.

The new city is built on the other side of the railway line, to the south-east. The new Umaid Bhavan Palace houses the royal family in one section, while the remaining section has been converted into a luxury hotel.

MEHERANGARH FORT ★★
17th~19th C/ Rajput

Meherangarh Fort perched on a rocky mountain, at a height of 120 m, looks majestically down on the city below. Among the many forts found in west India, this fort is one of the most impressive. Previously this fort could only be accessed on foot, but now it has a motorable road. The fort wall has seven entrances and a number of palaces within, all connected with courtyards. The structures with their *bangaldar* roofs resemble the Bikaner Palace and are clearly influenced by Islamic architecture. The only difference is that while Islamic palaces stand independently, all the buildings here, stand in one continuous row. Moti Mahal (House of Pearls, 18th century) and Takhat Vilas (19th century) are other buildings worth seeing.

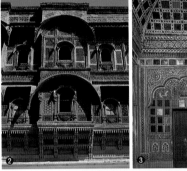

❶ The courtyard of Moti Mahal.
❷ *Jharokha* of Janaki Mahal
❸ The interior of Sheesh Mahal (Glass palace).
❹ Interior of Janaki Mahal.
❺ The Fort Palace rising above the city.

UMAID BHAWAN PALACE ★
1943/ Rajput
by Henry V Lanchester

Umaid Bhawan was designed by the British architect, Henry Lanchester, as the new palace of the Maharaja. Building commenced in 1929 as a famine relief exercise when the monsoons failed for a third consecutive year. 3000 workers took 14 years to build this 347-room palace of brown sandstone and marble. After 70 years, it still looks new. The royal family reside in a portion of the palace while the rest of the structure has been converted into a hotel.

Interior of the central hall.

Up: The concrete roof topped with a dome. Down: Front view.

JASWANT THADA ★
1899/ Rajput

This white marble palace, built half-way up the hill, has sculptures in the traditional style. Inside is a large hall with a steel frame, built as a mausoleum for Jaswant Singh II. The exterior with its open platform and flowing water is especially noteworthy. The white palace half-way up the hill, the fort at the top, and the city below contribute to a magnificent sight.

BALSAMAND LAKE PALACE
19th C/ Rajput

Due west on the road from Jodhpur to Mandor, is a small, summer palace built in the European style, with a garden in the Mughal style, facing a man-made lake. The lake was created in 1159 and later widened, while the gardens were designed in 1936. Water for the garden is drawn from this lake.

ROYAL CHHATRIS
17th~18th C/ Rajput

Mandor 8 km north of Jodhpur, is an old city that was the capital of the Marwar kingdom before it shifted to Jodhpur. There are no architectural traces of that era, but there is a group of red sandstone buildings that belong to a later era. The structures look like temples but are actually tombs of the royal family of Jodhpur, with Islamic touches to the traditional Hindu temple style. The largest is the mausoleum of Ajit Singh.

❶ The group of *chhatris* that look like temples.
❷ Ajit Singh's Tomb, 1724.
❸ The pillars with Islamic-style carving them.

HINDU TEMPLES
10th~11th C/ Hindu

There are five temples in the desert 25 km from Parmeet. The place is very desolate with just the skeletons of the temples remaining. The oldest is the Vishnu Temple while the best preserved is the Someshwara Temple. All of them have rich sculptures carved on the pillars, walls and over the entrance.

Up: Vishnu Temple and the three Shiva Temples behind.
Down: The *mandapa* of the Someshwara Temple, whose ceiling is broken.

Osian, 65 km from Jodhpur, has a group of twelve temples depicting the early northern style. The Sachiya Mata Temple on the hill and the Mahavira Temple of the Jains are the larger temples. Vertical *shikharas* depict the architectural style of the northwest. Towards the south is a *kund* (stepwell), belonging to the same age which could have been used for religious purposes.

HINDU TEMPLES
8th~9th C/ Hindu

The Osian temples are built on high platforms which are artistically carved. The small temples are half-temples, each with a porch in the front. They were the *pancharatna* type, with small shrines in the four corners. The *shikhara* of the shrine was styled like a cannon with a circular *amalaka* crowning it. The largest temple, the Sachiya Mata Temple on the hilltop has various shrines. *Toranas* which are similar to the *tori yane* of Japanese temples, flank the steps leading to the shrine .

MAHAVIRA TEMPLE ★
8th~11th C/ Jain

The 8th century Jain temple in Osian had its *shikhara* added during the 11th century. Besides the main shrines there are many small shrines within the complex which is encircled by a wall. Excellent sculptures reflect the style of the early Pratihara dynasty and the later Solanki dynasty.

❶ Surya Temple 2 (8th C)
❷ Harihar Temple 1 (8th C)
❸ Row of *toranas* in the Sachia Mata Temple (11th-12th C)
❹ Mahavira Temple

Step-well (8th C), and Sachiya Mata Temple.

Jaisalmer, the capital of the Rajputs since the Middle Ages, is in the Thar Desert. The buildings with skillfully carved façades are made of honey-coloured sandstone. When sunlight falls on the city, the buildings glow golden in the light, which is why Jaisalmer is referred to as the Golden City.

Maharawal Jaisal of the Bhatti Rajput family, built this fort city on a hill in 1156. Jaisalmer became a prominent centre in the trade route across the Thar Desert between India and the West. Though it was under Hindu rule, it was the Jain traders who made Jaisalmer prosperous with trade activities.

However with the advent of the British, the growth of maritime trade between India and the West, ended the overland trade route and consequently, Jaisalmer's prosperity. When the border with Pakistan was sealed after 1947, this city was forgotten.

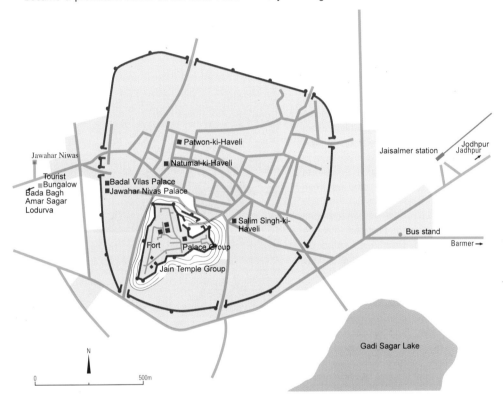

The Gadi Sagar Lake looks like an oasis in the middle of the desert.

FORT AND PALACES ★★
17th C / Rajput

This fort built 80 m above Trikuta Hills, was a citadel within which most of the population lived. It has two outer walls running parallel to each other, one high and one low and more than a hundred semi-circular bastions, which make it look very impressive. Most of the bastions were built in the 17th century with rooms in the interior for sentries and stores for weapons.

After you enter through Suraj Pol, you enter Hawa Pol on an incline which opens on to a vast area surrounded by palace buildings. There are five palaces in a row from Zenana Mahal (ladies quarters), of the 16th century to the Gaj Vilas, of the 19th century, which reflect the highly developed architectural style of their times. Jaisalmer was a prosperous city, being a prominent trade centre for the east and the west. The palace complex does not show any Islamic touches like square gardens etc, since it was not designed all at one time, but had structures added on through the years. After the palace became too small for the family and since the royal family adopted the western way of living, two new palaces where constructed in the plains, called Jawahar Vilas and Badal Vilas. At present, the royal family lives in Badal Vilas, while Jawahar Vilas has been converted into a hotel. Architecturally, these buildings are very traditional with very little European influence.

❶ The city spreads below the citadel.
❷ The view of city from the fort.
❸ Space between the high and the low walls are used as pathways.
❹ Badal Vilas Palace.
❺ Jawahar Vilas Palace (end 19th C).
❻ A close-up of a common balcony.
❼ Guj Vilas Palace towering over the open space (19th C).
❽ Interior of Rang Mahal Palace (end 18th C).

Suraj Pol (Sun Gate) entrance to the citadel.

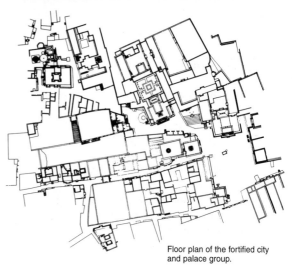

Floor plan of the fortified city and palace group.

ROYAL CHHATRIS
Rajput

Situated on a hill in the desert, 5 km from Jaisalmer, are the Royal Tombs facing a garden called Bada Bagh. Ten magnificent *chhatris* made of yellow sandstone, stand in a row. As in the palace, the roofs with eaves are in the *bangaldar* style, the domes and arches are Islamic but otherwise, the pillar and beam method of construction has been adopted.

TOWN AND HAVELIS ★★★

Buildings and roads have been built surrounding Trikuta hills, where the fort is located. In the 18th century, this unplanned city was extended to the plains below. The city has spread naturally, without a formal layout. In 1750 the city walls were built.

Until 1750, it was contained within the walls of the fort, but as the population increased, the buildings inside the fort became multi-storeyed structures. The façades of the *havelis* were richly decorated and carved. Rich Jain merchants built *havelis* that competed with the palaces.

Outside the city walls, is a large man-made lake, Gadi Sagar, which is the water source for the city. The yellow sandstone pavilion in the middle of the lake, looks like it is floating on water.

PATWON HAVELI ★★ 1805/ Jain

This beautiful five-storeyed *haveli* was built by a Jain, Patwa, for his five sons. A part of this 5-storeyed building also stretches over the road with a gate-type opening and the facade facing the road is completely made up of *jharokhas.*

NATHUMAL HAVELI★ 1885/Hindu

Nathumal was minister to the King. This four-storeyed haveli has courtyards at the front and back and 40 rooms. The front courtyard is a salon and the back courtyard was the work place with an entrance for camels. It now houses a family of 24.

SALIM SINGH HAVELI 1815/ Hindu

It is said the tyrant Salim Singh, was assassinated after building this *haveli.* This architecturally-rich building, called Jahaj (ship) Mahal is designed such that the top seems to be floating.

❶ The Gadi Sagar Tank and pavilion.
❷ Row of houses in the castle town.
❸ A curving flagstoned pathway with open drains.
❹ Looking up from the courtyard of Patwon-ki-Haveli.

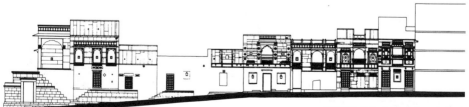

Elevation of the fortified city and street.

Patwon-ki-Haveli

Cross-section of a *haveli*.

❶ Salim Singh-ki-Haveli. ❷ Patwon-ki-Haveli that crosses over the road and acts as a gate. ❸ Town shops. ❹ Sculpture on the wall of an ordinary house. ❺ The second floor of Nathumal-ki-Haveli.

JAIN TEMPLE ★★
15th C/ Jain

The royalty of Jaisalmer were Hindus, but the powerful business community who had trade relations with the west, were Jains. Since they had economic power, their temples were more magnificent than Hindu temples. There is a group of seven temples in the inner part of the city. The basement of the Sambhavanatha temple was used for storage of ancient documents. The *gyan bhandar* has a collection of 11th century documents. The oldest, the Parshvanatha Temple(1417) and the last, the Shantinatha Temple (1547), reflect the architectural style of that era. Shantinatha temple encompasses the pathway and the temples on both sides have entrances through this temple. Walking around them gives one a curious feeling of space. This style of architecture developed in Gujarat between the 10th and 13th centuries.

Up: Chandra Prabha Temple.
Middle: The ceiling of the *mandapa* of the
Chandra Prabha Temple.
Down: The *mandapa* of the Parshvanatha temple.

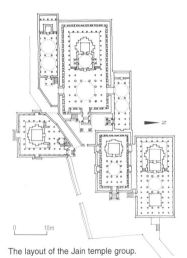

0   10m

The layout of the Jain temple group.

A distant view of the Jain group of temples.

JAIN TEMPLE AT AMAR SAGAR ★
19th~20th C/ Jain

In Rajasthan, lakes or tanks that are man-made by collecting rainwater are called *sagars*. Amar Sagar, 5 km from Jaisalmer, has a Jain temple that has been under renovation for the past 20 years.

The exterior is a blend of the traditional *shikhara* and the Rajput palace style. The hall in the interior has been exquisitely carved and reminds one of the Alhambra in Spain. To its right is a square garden and a palace built by Amar Singh.

❶ Entrance to Adheshwara Temple. ❷ *Rang Mandapa*. ❸ Jain temple and sagar, with very little water even during monsoons.

JAIN TEMPLE AT LODRUVA ★
17th C/ Jain

Lodruva, 15 km from Jaisalmer was the capital city, before the Jaisalmer citadel was built. This city was destroyed twice and not even its ruins exist today. Only one magnificent Jain temple that was restored recently is still standing. The walls of the *mandapa* have lattice screens of stone and the tall *torana* on the front façade is extremely eye-catching.

DILWARA (DELWARA) TEMPLES

11th~15th C/ Jain

Most Jain shrines are built on mountains. Mount Abu 1200 m above sea level, was originally a sacred place for both the Hindu Shaivite group and the Jains, but after the Dilwara Temples were established here, it became the most sacred site of the Jains after Satrunjaya Mountains.

There are 5 temples here. But they do not have a master plan or axis line that are common to each other. They were built one after another from the 11th to the 15th centuries. Although each temple was designed along a main axis, it does not have a comprehensive plan.

Mahavira is the 24th and last *tirthankara*. Every Jain temples deifies one *tirthankara* whose statue becomes the main idol in the temple which will also bear its name. The Dilwara temples are similar to Hindu temples except that the main shrine is surrounded by small shrines called *devagruha*. Even though there was only one main idol, the desire was to enshrine other *tirthankaras* too. Hence small shrines were built with cloisters around each which also acted as an ambulatory around the main shrine. All temples except the Chaumukha temple, are open on all four sides.

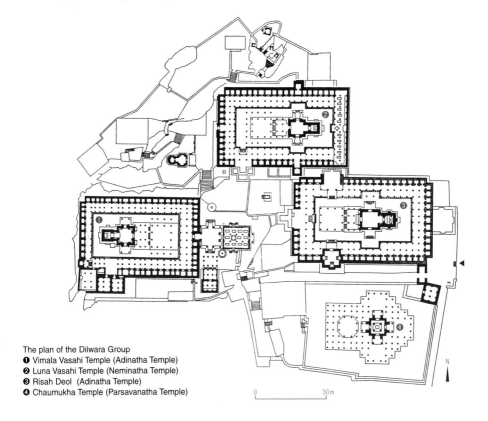

The plan of the Dilwara Group
❶ Vimala Vasahi Temple (Adinatha Temple)
❷ Luna Vasahi Temple (Neminatha Temple)
❸ Risah Deol (Adinatha Temple)
❹ Chaumukha Temple (Parsavanatha Temple)

0   30 m

Pittarhara Temple that is incomplete without the *ranga mandapa*.   Kaladhara Temple with a new plan.

VIMALA VASAHI (ADINATHA TEMPLE) ★★★
Around 1032/ Jain

One of the ministers, Vimala Sah, committed many political murders, so to atone for his sins, he constructed the Adinatha Temple and hence the temple is called Vimala Vasahi. (Vasahi is *Vasati* in Sanskrit, which means temple). Originally, it was in the usual temple style, with a *garbhagriha* (sanctum sanctorum), *gudhamandapa* (prayer hall) and the *Trika mandapa* (front hall). One more hall, *ranga mandapa* was added in the front, in 1150 A D and the whole structure was surrounded by a three-sided ambulatory. The interior of the whole temple was redone and looked quite fantastic. The entire structure, is made of pure white marble. While the exterior is unremarkable, the interior with the pillars, beams, ceilings, etc are so exquisitely carved that one is left speechless with amazement. It must have been constructed before the land was riddled with strife.

❶ Top view of the temple.
❷ The west corridor can be seen from the south corridor.
❸ Sculptures on the ceiling.
❹ The corridor can be seen in the *Rang mandapa* (front hall).
❺ Entrance to a small shrine from the corridor.
❻ The capital of the two-step pillar. The *torana* is suspended from the bottom step.
❼ Sixteen Vidyadevi (Goddess of Wisdom) figures have been sculpted on the ceiling of the *Ranga mandapa*.

LUNA VASAHI (NEMINATHA TEMPLE) ★★★
1230/ Jain

In the 13th century, Vastupala and Tejapala of the Pragvata family, became patrons of a large number of Jain temples, just like the Medici family in Italy. They were ministers in the Vaghela princedom and were also said to be merchants. The Neminatha temple that they built, though similar in style to the Vimala Vasahi, is more exquisite. The artistically carved patterns on the pillars, *toranas*, arches and the minute, delicately carved decorations on the ceiling are unequalled. Since the dome is not a true dome, the span is small. The diameter of the largest dome is only 7.5 m and cannot be compared with truly large Islamic domes.

❶ The central domed ceiling in the front hall.
❷ The decorative *torana* arch.
❸ The decoration on one section of the ceiling.
❹ The courtyard surrounding the shrine.
❺ The very imaginative sculptures on the ceiling.
❻ Enclosed corridor with the *tirthankara* statue at the end.

The front hall seen from the entrance.

RANAKPUR ★ ★ ★

ADINATHA TEMPLE ★★★
1439/ Jain

After a four-and-a-half-hour road trip uphill from Udaipur, in a secluded wooded valley of the Aravalli Hills is the Adinatha temple. It reflects the high quality of Indian architecture of that period. Formerly, there was a township here, called Ranpur. The temple is dedicated to the first *tirthankara*, Adinatha.

Surrounding the temple are smaller shrines and *dharmashalas* (pilgrim resthouses). The temple stands on a 60 m x 62 m foundation. Since the site slopes down to the main entrance in the west, the temple with its high plinth looks like a citadel. Up the flight of stairs, is another flight of stairs and a stairwell that goes up three storeys. The resulting space when especially when bright with sunlight is very dramatic. As if to symbolize this, the interior is elegantly different. Every available space other than the floor is richly carved. The temple is square in plan and the entire structure made of white marble is quite incomparable.

The style of the interior, first developed in Mount Abu, has been repeated in this temple but is on a much larger scale. Large and small domes are at different heights. Sunlight enters through the space in between the domes and through the corridors lighting up the rich sculptures on the pillars and ceilings.

Jain temples use space in a style that is not seen in Hindu temples. As Hindu temples are "Houses of God" they focus on the "shrine and the *mandapa*". Jain temples on the other hand believe in a godless doctrine and their temples are places where the preaching of the *tirthankaras* are explained to the world. Therefore, the shrines have four statues facing four sides, with entrances on all four sides. On all sides of the *garbhagriha* (shrine) there is a *ranga mandapa,* in front of which is the *meghanada mandapa*. They are all accessible from the outside and are also inter-connected. The temple is in the *panchayatana* style with five shrines, surrounded by smaller shrines and a corridor. Unlike the temples in Mount Abu, the exterior of this temple is very impressive. It is the blend of a high quality exterior and interior that makes this temple so unique.

According to the stone inscription, the name of the architect is Depaka, who was obviously a genius.

❶ The front view of the temple that looks like a fort.
❷ *Chaumukha* shrine is seen as you enter the courtyard.
❸ The samprana roof of the west *meghanada mandapa.*
❹ Statues are carved in the corners of the roof.

RANAKPUR

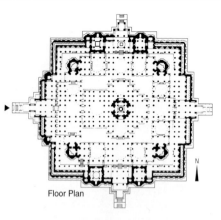

Floor Plan

❺ The *garbhagriha* (shrine) where Adinatha is enshrined.
❻ Ceiling of the west *meghanada mandapa.* (high hall)
❼ The shrine can be seen from the west *meghanada mandapa.*
❽ The ceiling sits on a pillar and beam structural system.
❾ Northwest courtyard.
❿ The west *ranga mandapa* with the shrine in the front.

PARSHAVANATHA TEMPLE ★
15th C/ Jain

The exemplary feature of Indian temple architecture is the *shikhara*. Sculptures on the foundation platform and walls at mid-level are also quite exquisite.

The foundation platform of this temple, dedicated to the 23rd *tirthankara,* Parshavanatha is simple. It has been divided into units and then further divided into horizontal panels. Intricate designs have been carved on these panels, all around the temple.

Left: Full view of the temple.
Right: The foundation stone and the wall above, filled with exquisite sculptures.

SURYA NARAYANA TEMPLE
15th C/ Hindu

There is just one Hindu temple dedicated to the Sun God (Surya), among the Jain group of temples. Up front, it looks like any ordinary temple, but the hall in front of the shrine is octagonal. Other than the front and the back entrance, the six other sides have windows with projecting balconies that are unique. The whole structure stands on a foundation platform and the *shikhara* is vertical in design.

VARKANA ★   17

PARSHAVANATHA TEMPLE ★
15th C/ Jaina

At a distance of 8 km from Ranee Station, 35 km from Ranakpur, is a Jain temple made of marble. Perhaps enough land was not available in this small town and given the irregular site, the temple too is irregular. This temple with a shrine, *mandapa* and many connecting halls from where you can also climb on to the roof is a miniature version of the Ranakpur Temple.

KUMBHALGARH ★★

HILL FORT★★
15th C/ Rajput

The Kumbhalgarh fort walls are the most impressive walls of all the mountain forts in Rajput country. The fort is on a mountain, more than 1000 m above sea level and the fort wall covers a great distance on this mountain. The 4 m wide fort wall has semi-circular bastions that also doubled as cannon stands. It was the capital city of the Mewar kingdom and the second most important citadel, after Chittaurgarh. The main buildings are destroyed and now there is just a group of 365 Hindu and Jain temples left. The breathtaking Badal Mahal (Palace of Clouds), sits on the highest hill. Many gates which were constructed as a defense measure, lead to the palace. In the 2nd century, it was a Jain fort but after the Rajput king, Rana Kumbha built the grand fort walls in the 15th century, the palace is called Kumbhalgarh after him.

❶ The fort walls that are difficult to attack.
❷ There are temples and mausoleums at the foot of the palace.
❸ The palace can be seen from the approach road.
❹ The courtyard of the simple, new palace.

Chittaurgarh, the capital of the Sisodia Rajput family of the Mewar kingdom, was conquered by Emperor Akbar in the 16th century and Uday Singh built a new capital 100 km away in Udaipur. He created Fatif and Pichola lakes, by constructing a dam. The lakes provide water to the city, as well as defend the city. Since a water body creates the "floating upon water" image, the city came to be called "water city". The palace at the centre of Pichola Lake was later converted into the luxury, Lake Palace Hotel. Since there are so many places to marvel at, Udaipur is an architectural delight.

Lake Palace Hotel in the centre of Pichola Lake.

UDAIPUR 19

CITY PALACE ★★
16th~19th C/ Rajput

The City Palace, facing the lake, is the symbol of Udaipur. It was built in the 16th century by Uday Singh II. Additions and embellishments which were added later to this palace reflect the artistry of the Rajputs. Access to the palace is through the *tripolia* (3 arched gate). The palace stands five-storeys high in the huge courtyard. Irregular in plan, the palace has many courtyards and rooms that have beautiful designs etched on them. Balconies and *chhatris* detract from the magnitude of the building.

Courtyard on the topmost floor, with wall murals.

Up: *Mardana* in City Palace. Down: Decorations in the courtyard

ROYAL CHHATRIS (AT AHAR) ★★
17th C/ Rajput

There is a large Royal Tomb Garden in Ahar, outside Udaipur. Designed in the usual style, these *chhatris* of various sizes are interspersed with streams and ponds, which make them beautifully different. Among them, King Amar Singh's *chhatri* is very different and stands on a high foundation platform with 36 pillars. It has a dome on top and a clerestory, that lets in air and sunshine.

Up: King Amar Singh's *chhatri* made of white marble
Down: Open roof of Amar Singh's *chhatri*.

The group of *chhatris* by the stream.

RAJSAMAND ★ 20

SAGAR AND GHATS ★★
1660/ Rajput

In west India, building dams across rivers and creating man-made lakes was an ancient practice. The best examples can be seen in Jaisamand and in Rajsamand where *ghats* have been built on the banks of the water body. There are also docks for boating. The *toranas* indicate that this was a religious place, too. The pillars and ceilings of the pavilion have detailed carvings on them.

Carved capital on the column of a *torana*.

Up: Ghats at the edge of the water. Down: *Toranas* in good condition.

SAAS BAHU TEMPLES ★★
10th C/ Hindu

There is a group of temples in the mountains, 24 km from Udaipur and a few near Bagra Lake. Nagda town is a ghost town today, but the Saas-Bahu Temples, facing the lake reflect the prominence this town once enjoyed. These west-India style temples have very fine sculptures and embellishments. Bahu Temple has a rare, three-way entrance.

❶ The *torana* in front of the Bahu Temple.
❷ Saas Bahu and a group of small temples.
❸ Interior of the Sas (mother-in-law) Temple.
❹ Sculpture on Bahu (daughter-in-law) Temple.

AMBIKA MATA TEMPLE ★★
961/ Hindu

The squat Ambika Mata Temple is located 60 km southeast of Udaipur. Built in 961 AD, it is quite well preserved and has exquisite sculptures of a very high quality. The Ambika Temple belongs to the Pratihara dynasty. The walls are completely covered with statues of various gods or goddesses which along with the architectural design of the temple, is remarkably like the Kajuraho group of temples which came much later.

Shikhara of the shrine, *mandapa* and porch

Entrance to the *sanctum sanctorum* can be seen from the *mandapa*.

On the plains of Chittaurghar is a long ridge, 180 m high, 1 km wide and 5 km long. On this ridge, is Mewar Fort, which fell to the 3rd attack of the Khilji army in the 14th century. In 1567, after a vigorous battle between Emperor Akbar and Rana Kumba, the fort was captured by the Mughals and over a thousand women immolated themselves rather than be captured by the enemy. Later, the capital of the Mewar kingdom shifted to Udaipur and the fort was abandoned. As you pass through the many gates and reach the top, the hills surrounding the plains are visible as far as the eye can see. The fort is large and accommodates palaces, Hindu temples and Jain temples.

Tower architecture, very rare in India, is perfectly preserved in these two structures in Chittaurghar. Before Islam with its minarets came into India, there must have been many towers in the country. Today, other than the *shikharas* crowning temples, independent towers are found only in Chittaurghar.

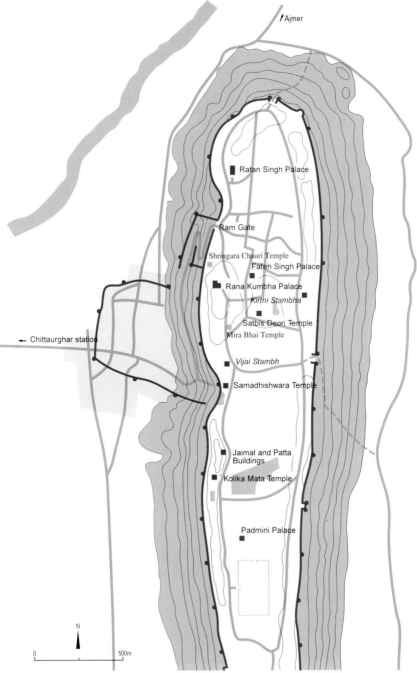

/ Ajmer

Ratan Singh Palace

Ram Gate

Shringara Chauri Temple

Fateh Singh Palace

Rana Kumbha Palace

Kirthi Stambha

Satbis Deori Temple

Mira Bhai Temple

← Chittaurghar station

Vijai Stambh

Samadhishwara Temple

Jaimal and Patta Buildings

Kolika Mata Temple

Padmini Palace

N

0   500m

CHITTAURGARH

FORT ** AND PALACES *
8th~15th C/ Rajput

There are seven gates on the way up to the fort, of which the last gate, *Ram Pol* (gate) leads you into the fort. Inside the walls were residences, towers, temples and palaces.

The oldest is a large, L-shaped palace constructed by Emperor Rana Kumba in the 15th century. This magnificent, completely plaster-finished palace is a deviation from the usual constructions. A fascinating sight towards the north of the fort is the Rana Ratan Singh Palace with a tank built in the 16th century. It is said that Uday Singh who built Udaipur was born here.

Padmini Palace was erected in the middle of the tank in the 19th century, with pretty gardens around it. In 1930 the present King, Fateh Singh erected Fateh Prakash Palace in the central area of the fort. This palace is now a museum housing royal artifacts.

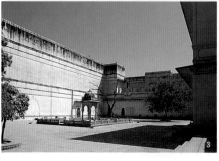

❶ Rana Ratan Singh Palace at the northern end of the fort.
❷ *Ram Pol* (1459), the last gate before entering the fort.
❸ The courtyard of Fateh Prakash Palace.
❹ Chittaurgarh Fort & the *Jayastamba* on the right.
❺ Rana Kumba Palace seen from *Suraj Pol*.
❻ Rana Kumba Palace, 1433-1468.
❼ Jaimaru and Patta buildings.

KIRTI STAMBHA ★★★ (TOWER OF FAME) AND JAIN TEMPLES ★
13th-15th C/Jain

The rulers of Mewar were Hindus, but they tolerated other religions as is clear from the many Jain temples inside the fort. The Tower of Fame, called *Kirti stambha*, is a Jain memorial tower (13th century). Statues of *tirthankaras* have been sculpted on the tower. This seven-storey high, 24 m tall tower stands on a foundation platform. A staircase inside the tower enables the visitor to climb to the top and enjoy the scenery. *Stambha* means pillar and Emperor Ashoka built memorial pillars in every area of his kingdom. This practice was then followed by Jain temples in south India.

The Sat Bees temple, built in the style of the Mount Abu Temples, is excellent. These temples are built of sandstone and not marble.

❶ The other half of the surrounding ambulatory in the Sat Bees Temple is incomplete.
❷ Interior of the Sat Bees Deori Temple.
❸ Exquisite workmanship of the *Kirti Stambha*.
❹ The view from the top of the *Kirti Stambha*. The Tower of Victory can be seen in the distance.
❺ *Tirthankaras* carved on the *Kirti Stambha*.

VIJAY STAMBHA (TOWER OF VICTORY) ★★★ HINDU TEMPLES ★
15th~16th C/ Hindu

Vijay stambha or the Tower of Victory, built in 1458-1468, is yet another tower built by Rana Kumba after his victory in the battle against the Muslim army. This 9-storey, 36 m high tower looks very slender from the outside. It has a unique spiral staircase that weaves in and out of the structure, all the way to the top. This design is not seen anywhere else in the world.

❶ Interior of the *Jaya Stambha* where the staircase interchanges.
❷ The *Jaya Stambha* is dedicated to Lord Vishnu.
❸ Samiddhesvara Temple (originally temple of Jina Aristanemi) (13th-15th C)
❹ Kalika Mata Temple (8th C, renovated in 1556).

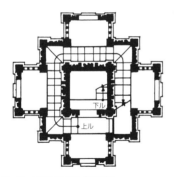

The floor plan of *Jaya Stambha*.

MENAL ★★

24

MAHANALESHVARA TEMPLE ★★
Late 11th C/ Hindu

En route to Bundi, from Chittaurgarh, are two temples in Menal and Bijoria that are worth seeing. The temple in Menal is encircled by a wall and has a magnificent entrance. The Mahanaleshwara Temple is rather well preserved and it reminds one of the Udayeshwara Temple of Udaipur. The strong vertical *shikhara* is made of small *shikharas* carved on all four sides, which gives it a unique appearance. Surrounded by groups of small shrines scattered in the precincts, this large temple also boasts of a very rare Hindu monastery. There is a small temple and monastery on the other side of Menal River that belonged to the Pashupata group. The monks' rooms are wide with four pillars in each room.

❶ Interior of the monastery.
❷ The rear of the *shikhara*.
❸ Full view of the Mahanaleshwara Temple.

DUNGARPUR ★

25

UDAI VILAS PALACE
18th~19th C/ Rajput

There are two palaces in the kingdom of Dungarpur, which was a part of the Mewar kingdom. The new palace, Udai Vilas was constructed after the old palace Juna Mahal, was destroyed 200 years ago. The courtyard of the new compact palace facing the lake has a pavilion that doubles as a prayer hall. The palace is a unique blend of Hindu, Islamic and European styles.

HINDU TEMPLES ★★ AND KUND
11th~13th C/ Hindu

Bijolia, 16 km from Menal, has a step-well Mandakini Kund, around which are four temples. The Vedanatha Temple of the 11th century, is in the style of west Indian temples. Quite different is the Videsvara Temple (13th century), which is topped with three *chhatris*, giving it a dynamic appearance. Perhaps, the *chhatris* were added later. The floor of the shrine is lower than that of the *mandapa* and water from the *kund* enters the shrine and flows around the *linga* which is the main idol.

Hindu temples-Vedanatha Temple in the centre.

Up: The *kund* and the temple. Down: Vedesvara Temple with *chhatris*.

GHATESVARA TEMPLE
927 A D/ Hindu

There is a group of early temples including a small shrine in the middle of the tank, south-west of Kota which are in the style of temples in west India in appearance. The Ghatesvara Temple is a five-shrine temple, with an independent, exquisitely sculpted open *mandapa* in front of it that must have been added a century later.

❶ The small shrine in the middle of the tank.
❷ Full view of the Ghatesvara Temple.
❸ The temple can be seen through the open *mandapa*.

Bundi, 37 km from Kota, has no proper roads or hotels and has not become a popular tourist spot and therefore still retains its appeal. Originally built by Rao Deva of the Hara Chauhan Rajput clan in the 14th century, it became a vassal of the Mughals. The city is surrounded by mountains and the palace is half-way up the mountains built in a stepped formation. At the top of the mountain is Taragarh Fort. The most interesting features in the city are the step-wells and the step-tanks.

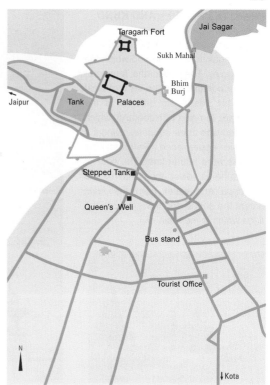

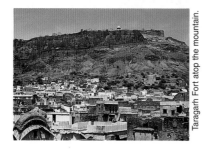

Taragarh Fort atop the mountain.

BUNDI

28

TARAGARH FORT AND PALACE ★
14th~17th C/ Rajput

Balwant Singh started building this palace, below Taragarh Fort, in 1580. Chattar Mahal is just beyond *Hathi Pol* while the more luxurious Chitra Mahal is at the top. The courtyard is filled with trees and tanks. The rooms facing the courtyard have very artistically and tastefully painted wall murals, in the true Rajput style.

❶ *Hathi Pol* of Chattar Mahal.
❷ The courtyard of Chattar Mahal.
❸ The wonderful murals in Chitra Mahal.

RANI-KI-BAOLI (STEP-WELL) ★★
1700/ Rajput

Rani-ki-baoli (Queen's step-well) is the most beautiful step-well in Rajasthan. It is said that after the death of King Aniruddha, his second wife handed over the prince to the first wife and devoted her time to charitable work. She constructed this step-well as a memorial to the king. The stairs go straight down to the lowest level and meet each other in the middle at right angles. Pillars and beams have been exquisitely decorated with *torana* arches and elephants.

❶ The beautiful arched entrance in front of the well shaft, where there is a two-tiered flight of stairs.
❷ *Chhatris* have been placed facing each other, over the entrance to the staircase.
❸ There are two step-wells in the city.
❹ The stairs seen from the well shaft.
❺ The well shaft can be seen through the pillars and beams.

GUJARAT

Gujarat, positioned at the extreme west of India faces the Arabian Sea. The centre of the state juts out into the sea and is called the Kathiawar or Kathiawad peninsula, or Saurashtra. The northern part of Gujarat is Katchch or Kutch, with the Rann or the marshy land extending up to the border of Pakistan. This area is just a few metres above mean sea level. It becomes a swamp during the rainy season and during the dry season it turns into a desert. The area is dotted with sparsely populated villages. The houses and the people, who live in this land which is afflicted by very severe weather, are quite unique.

Since it has a long coastline open to the sea, Gujarat has had trade relations with the West since time immemorial. It also had overseas trade links with Mesopotamia. Most of the ruins of the Indus Valley Civilization are now in Pakistan, but there are some sites scattered in Lothal. There is a famous story that the temple of Somnath looked like a mountain of treasure and Muhammed of Gazni (Afghanistan) attacked this place and plundered it.

Most of the people here speak Gujarati. The main religion in Gujarat was, and is, Jainism. Jainism, which took birth in eastern India, spread to the south and the west. Today the maximum numbers of believers live in Gujarat. Even so, they are just a small religious group comprising 0.5 per cent of the Indian population. Nonetheless, there are a large number of Jain temples in India. This is because the Jains believe in *ahimsa* or non-violence. This is why they are neither agriculturists nor military personnel. Most of them are business people and therefore economically well off and in a position to build a large number of temples. What is unique, is the creation of temple towns in the deep mountains where there is no human habitation. The actual experience of visiting and seeing this spectacle is breathtaking.

Another feature worth talking about, are the water bodies starting with the step-wells. In western India, where rainfall is scanty, water sources are sacred. Tanks and wells were constructed on a magnificent scale and in large numbers. One cannot but be amazed at the sight of underground structures that can be mistaken for palaces of feudal chieftains.

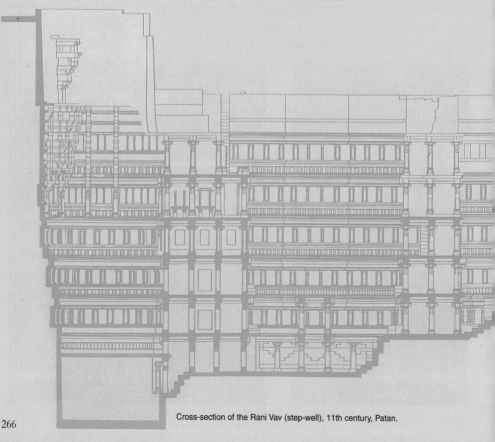

Cross-section of the Rani Vav (step-well), 11th century, Patan.

Muslims praying in a small mosque in Sarkhej.

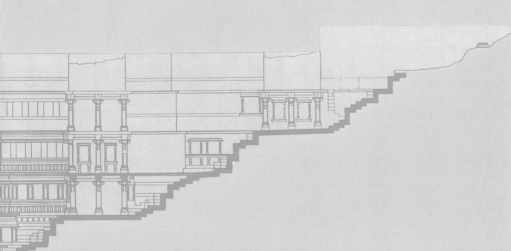

EDITOR'S NOTE:
On 26 January 2001 an earthquake rocked Gujarat and in one fell
swoop, either destroyed or damaged monuments of Gujarat's rich past.
The *toranas* of temples in Vadnagar. Rani Vav and Sahasra Linga in
Patan, Surya Temple in Modhera, the Jami Masjid in Ahmedabad and
Ruda baoli in Adalaj were all slightly damaged. Ranjit Vilas Palace in
Wankaner and the Royal Tombs in Junagadh suffered a slightly worse
fate, while Aina Mahal and Prag Mahal of the Palace Quarters in Bhuj
were very badly damaged. The Royal Chhatris in Bhuj, have collapsed.

KUMBHARIA ★★

KUMBHARIA ★★
Jain Temples
11th-12th C/ Jain

During the Middle Ages, Kumbharia, once known as Arasana, was a Jain religious centre of the Solanki dynasty, just like Mount Abu. At present there is nothing left of the city, except for five well-preserved temples where pilgrims come to pray in large numbers. The Jain temples in Kumbharia, are all made with rich, white marble. It is said that the Delwara group of temples were built in Mount Abu, with marble taken up 1200 m from a place near Kumbharia. The Delwara Temples and the Kumbharia Temples, both have the same style of construction and a similar style of sculpture. The Delwara Temples were built in stages between the 11th and 14th centuries, while the Kumbharia Temples were built at a stretch, in a span of 100 years, starting from the middle of the 11th century. All five temples in Kumbharia face the northeast. As in the case of Mount Abu, there is no preconceived design or pattern that has been followed.

MAHAVIRA TEMPLE ★★ 1062
SHANTINATHA TEMPLE ★ 1082

The first temple is dedicated to the 24th *tirthankara,* Mahavira, and the 2nd temple is dedicated to the 16th *tirthankara,* Shantinatha. Both are constructed in the 'shrine with *mandapa*' style, surrounded by smaller shrines. Since there is a roof between the *mandapa* and the smaller shrines, sunlight enters only from the rear and the space is not well illuminated. The eaves of the small shrines jut out from the ceiling, leading one to believe that the small shrines must have once been independent structures.

Neminatha Temple

Sambhavanatha Temple

Mahavira Temple

Parshvanatha Temple

Shantinatha Temple

Temple Office

River

Abu Road

Location Map

❶ The ceiling of the Mahavira Temple.
❷ *Mandapa* of the Mahavira Temple.
❸ Small shrines and the corridor of the Mahavira Temple.

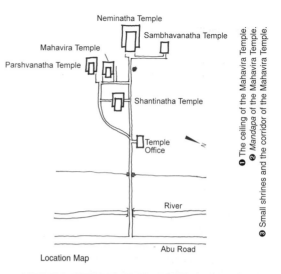

Exterior of the Shantinatha Temple.

PARSHVANATHA TEMPLE
1105

This temple is dedicated to the 23rd *tirthankara*, Parshvanatha. As one climbs up to the hall above the staircase, it can be seen that the *mandapa* is lit by sunlight entering through the door of the hall. The eaves of the corridor around the temple are missing.

NEMINATHA TEMPLE ★
1134

This is a large temple dedicated to the 22nd *tirthankara*, Neminatha. The entrance is three-dimensional and the dome of the *mandapa* is elevated flooding the *mandapa* with sunlight. This spatial architectural style is similar to the Adinatha temple in Ranakpur.

❹ The ceiling of the entrance to the Parshvanatha Temple.
❺ Entrance to a small shrine in the Parshvanatha Temple.
❻ Exterior of the Neminatha Temple.
❼ The *mandapa* can be seen from the entrance of the Neminatha Temple.
❽ The ceiling of the *paranaka* (entrance) of the Neminatha Temple.

AJITANATHA TEMPLE
1166/ Jain

King Kumarapara who reigned from 1143-1172, listened to the teachings of the Jain preacher, Hemachandra and converted to Jainism. He dedicated the temple to the 2nd *tirthankara*, Ajitanatha, which reflects the next era in the construction style of temples. During that time Jain literature and crafts developed greatly.

There is a large *shikhara* at the top of the shrine. The base and the shrine are abundantly carved and it appears to be a complete temple. The dome rests on eight pillars. The decorations on the exterior, the sturdy circular pillars within and the height of the ceiling, makes this temple different from the temples of Mount Abu and Kumbharia. It is however, not very different from Hindu temples. If there were no corridors around the temple and the open dome was in place, this could easily be mistaken for a Hindu temple.

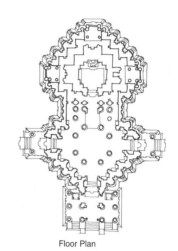

Floor Plan

❶ Full view of the temple with the lake in the foreground.
❷ The magnificent *shikhara* made of red sandstone.
❸ The murals on the wall were improved in 1585.
❹ The robust circular pillars inside the *mandapa*.

ABHAPUR *

31

LAKHENA TEMPLE
16th C/ Jain

Deep in the mountains, 40 km from Idal, is Abhapur, now an abandoned town. The construction using the slope of the land is fascinating. As you enter and climb the stairs, there is an open *mandapa*, 3-storeys high. Unfortunately the ceiling is destroyed. That apart, this extremely beautiful building gives one a feeling of visiting Romanesque shrines in the Pyrenees Alps.

❶ A big open *mandapa* where the dome is broken.
❷ Two circular pillars have been added to reinforce the beam.
❸ A small room made of stone lattice screens.

A view of the Lakhena Temple.

RODA *

32

HINDU TEMPLES AND KUNDA
8th C/ Hindu

Situated 15 km from Himanagar in Roda, are five early Hindu temples of the Maitraka Dynasty era. These temples have a *paranaka* or shallow porch, in front of the shrine. A step-well near temples 2 and 3, must have been connected to the temples. One side of the step-well has caved in. It is best to engage a guide from Himanagar to visit the temples.

Small shrines at the four corners.

VADNAGAR *

33

TORANAS OF TEMPLE *
12th C/ Hindu

The temple that once stood here has completely vanished, but two *toranas* still stand to tell the tale. The arch spanning two pillars is called a *torana*. This style of *torana* originated in Sanchi and was built at the entrance of every religious institution. These are in a typical west-Indian style and very decorative.

RANI VAV (QUEEN'S STEP-WELL) ★★
11th C/ Rajput

There must be at least a hundred step-wells in Gujarat. The largest of them all, Rani Vav, is in the capital of the old Gujarat kingdom, Anhilwada or present day Patan. Rani Vav, was built by the queen after the death of her husband, King Bhimdeva I of the Solanki dynasty. It is 65 m long, 17 m wide and 28 m deep. A seven span multi-layered line of pillars in three rows, supports the earth pressure on both sides. There is nothing above ground but underground Rani Vav is a massive structure of seven storeys. The lower you go, the cooler it gets. There are not many pillars or beams, but the walls are replete with sculptures of gods and goddesses. The step-well was buried under earth, until 1986, when the Indian government cleared and restored it.

❶ Full view of the step-well. The top most portion of the structure has fallen apart.
❷ Statues of gods covering the wall surface.
❸ At the far end is the main well where a bucket can be lowered.
❹ Even the pillars used for the structure are well sculpted.

SAHASRA LINGA TANK
1137 A D/ Rajput

Near Rani Vav a canal was dug to the river Saraswati and a water sluice was also built. Many tanks were built in this way as reservoirs for irrigation. The structures built in the 12th century for water supply and irrigation evokes deep interest. There must have been a thousand small Shiva shrines around here for the tank to get the name Sahasra Linga. The upper portion of the tank has collapsed.

SURYA TEMPLE AND KUNDA ★★★
1022-1027/ Hindu

The Surya temple is a masterpiece of the Solanki dynasty. *Surya* (Sun God) has been venerated from *Rig Vedic* times. Just three Surya temples exist today. One is in Konark, the other in Martand and the third here in Modhera. This east-facing temple is the third largest. At dusk, during autumn and spring, sunlight enters through the door into the *garbagriha* and lights up the main statue. The *samprana* roof of the temple is broken but the lower portion of the structure is filled with sculptures which are quite impressive.

There is an open *mandapa* in front of the *garbagriha* and *nritya mandapa*, which is more like a giant *chhatri*, with only pillars and no walls. The whole design is along a central axis. The huge tank in front of the temple measures 35 m x 55 m and is surrounded by steps on all four sides. At every side, on the steps are small shrines and at the centre of each side is a group of shrines. At dawn, when the sunrays light up the whole ensemble, the effect is exceptionally wonderful.

The water level rises depending on the amount of rainfall.

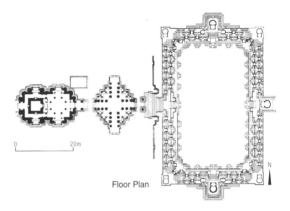
Floor Plan

The Surya Temple stands on the longer side of the tank facing it.

❶Tank where restoration work is complete. ❷ Shrine on the smaller side of the tank. ❸ Small shrines on the steps.

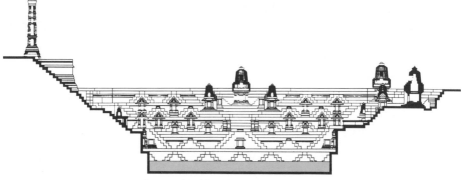

Cross-section of the tank.

❹ The upper portion of the *torana* in front of the open *mandapa* is broken.
❺ Full view of the Surya Temple.
❻ Domed ceiling of the *rangmandir*.
❼ Details of the sculptures on the wall.
❽ The row of pillars inside the *mandapa*..

Ahmedabad was built in 1411 by Sultan Ahmad Shah. Humayun of the Mughals took over Gujarat in 1534 but soon lost it. It was reclaimed by Akbar in 1572 and hence has a legacy of Indo-Islamic architecture. The city was surrounded by walls that still exist. It gained prominence due to its cotton textile production and a new city developed on the other side of the Sabarmati River. At present, it is the largest city in Gujarat, but the capital is the new city, Gandhinagar, located 30 km from Ahmedabad. When Mughal rule waned in the18th century, the Solanki style of architecture revived and many Hindu and Jain temples were built, but Islamic architecture in Gujarat itself had adopted the traditional west-Indian style of architecture.

Mahatma Gandhi, opened his *ashram* and started his Independence movement from Ahmedabad. After Independence a disciple of Le Corbusier, B V Doshi, started his architectural practice here. His work, along with that of Le Corbusier and Louis Kahn make Ahmedabad, India's Mecca of modern design.

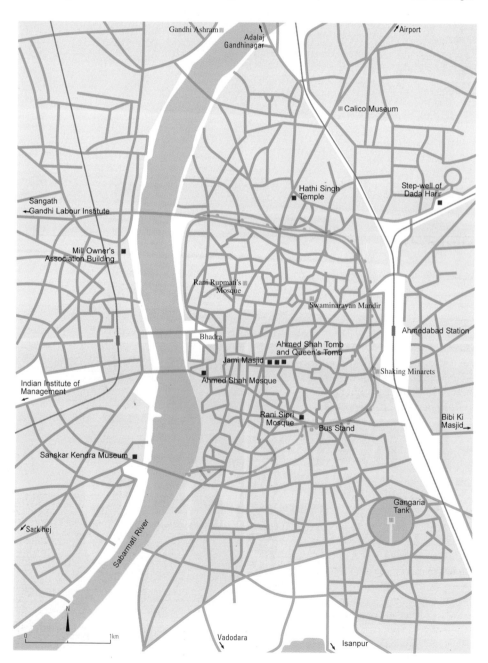

AHMAD SHAH'S MOSQUE ★
1414/ Islamic
When Ahmad Shah built the first mosque, he destroyed Hindu and Jain temples and used the materials for construction of the mosque. Figures from the pillars and beams were removed, but the post and beam system and the use of domes were retained. The façade has a large arch with two minarets on either side, thus paving the way for a new style of mosque, called the Gujarati style.

Carved pillars originally from Hindu temples.

The upper portion of the minaret fell off in an earthquake.

TOMB OF AHMED SHAH
15th C/ Islamic
The mausoleum of Ahmed Shah is near the Jami Masjid. Across the pathway is the mausoleum of the Queens. The former has a dome and the latter is open with a courtyard around and thus both have contrasting styles. The cenotaph again shows the skill and dexterity of the craftsmen.

Cenotaph of Bibi Mughali.

BIBI KI MASJID ★
1454/ Islamic
This small mosque, in Rajpur district, was constructed by Ahmed Shah II, for his mother. The upper portion of one of the two minarets is broken. They could be connected at the foundation. It is very interesting that when one minaret is shaken, the other one begins shaking too, hence they are called the Shaking Minarets. Ahmedabad has many examples of this type of minaret.

Shaking minaret.

Upper portion of the minaret.

277

JAMI MASJID (FRIDAY MOSQUE) ★★
1424/ Islamic

The old Jami Masjid is the largest in Ahmedabad. The prayer room measures 27 spans x 15 spans and has15 domes supported on 260 columns. The courtyard is surrounded by an enclosed corridor and enables the faithful to assemble for Friday prayers. In the centre of the façade is the three-arch *iwan*. The minaret has broken but the shaft is exquisitely carved. Inside the arch the post and beam structural system appears a misfit, but on entering, one finds a certain charm in the space created by the row of columns and dome sequence. A row of columns in the hall within the mosque, is an Arabic style. Sculptures on the dome and *jalis* are evidence that traditional Indian craftsmen and architects built it. Other than the fact that there are arches and no statues, one gets the feeling that this building is no different from a temple. Gujarat displays a blend of Islamic and Hindu architecture.

❶ The façade of the prayer room facing the courtyard.
❷ The dome supported by columns.
❸ The row of columns in the hall inside the mosque.

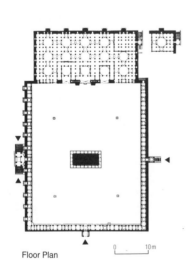

Floor Plan

0   10m

TOMB OF RANI SIPRI (SAPRAI) AND MOSQUE ★★
1514/ Islamic

A large number of mosques and mausoleums were constructed in Ahmedabad. The most impressive of them is the ensemble of Rani Sipri. The depth of the mosque is 2 spans smaller than the length and it connects with the mausoleum along the central axis. Both the mausoleum and the mosque do not have Islamic arches, but is a post and beam system, crowned with domes. It is embellished with Islamic parapets, stone eaves, carved ceilings and *jalis* (lattice stone screens) crafted in traditional Hindu style. This blend of Hindu and Islamic architecture was incorporated here even before Akbar's Fatehpur Sikri.

❶ The tomb was fenced due to the increase in the amount of traffic.
❷ Rani Sipri's mausoleum walls are made entirely of latticed screens.
❸ The minaret of the mosque is geometric and very intricately carved.
❹ The beautiful *mihrab* is typical of Gujarat.
❺ The tomb has a dome with a clerestory.

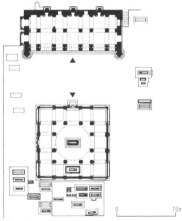

Floor Plan

An elevation of the mausoleum.

DADA HARIR VAV (STEP-WELL) ★★
1499/ Islamic

The oldest step-well in the city is the Mata Bhavani step-well (11th century). Now it is being used as an underground temple. The Muslims used this as an example and built a splendid ensemble of a step-well with a mosque and mausoleum of the Queen Dada Harir (also called Bai Harir Sultani). The step-well is 6 m x 70 m and 20 m deep. There are intermittent columns to control the earth's pressure, which produce a marvellous effect. Since it is an Islamic structure, there are no statues. It has a hall with a water cistern in front of the shaft of the last well where people could draw water. The framework of this stairwell has been richly sculpted. Both sides of the hall have spiral staircases, as a shortcut to the ground above.

❶ Void above the hall.
❷ Interior seen from the second floor landing.
❸ One of three pavilions over a flight of stairs.
❹ Main stairway seen from balcony surrounding the hall.

ISANPUR STEPWELL ★
19th C/ Hindu

South of Ahmedabad there is a group of mosques and mausoleums that is worth seeing. A step-well now completely dry, which dates back to the 19th century, lies outside the city limits. The post and beam construction technology of old has been used to build this magnificent structure. A pavilion has been built at the landing of the big stairway and only this is visible above the ground.

The pavilion above the big stairway

KEJARSINGH HATHEESINGH SHAH TEMPLE
1848/ Jain

Of the large number of Jain temples in Ahmedabad, the biggest is the one built by Hatheesingh, dedicated to the 15th *tirthankara*, Dharmanatha. The Islamic effect is seen in the generous use of arches, but the Solanki era style of the Middle Ages has been revived with its traditional stone carvings. Recently a new *stambha* was erected inside the precincts, but it cannot be compared with the Chittaurgarh *stambha* that was used as its model.

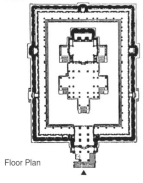

Floor Plan

Up: Façade of the decorative entrance. Down: Open *mandapa*.

HAVELIS
19th-20th C

Since wood was scarce in Gujarat, it was imported from elsewhere for the building of temples and houses. Intricate carving techniques have been perfected in the wooden architecture of Gujarat. These wooden houses are still found in the old residential areas of Ahmedabad. The more opulent houses are called *havelis*. The brackets, window frames, columns, etc that face the road are exquisitely carved. Most of them have a *chowk* (courtyard) that in addition to providing ventilation and sunlight, also acts as the salon. It is unfortunate that today these *havelis* are falling apart. The *havelis* in Vadodhara and Vaso are in better condition.

❶ *Haveli* that is still in residential use.
❷ *Haveli* being preserved as a cultural asset.
❸ The kitchen faces the courtyard in the *haveli*.

MILL OWNER'S ASSOCIATION BUILDING ★
1956/ Post Independence
By Le Corbusier

Le Corbusier who was already commissioned to design Chandigarh, designed the museum and this Association Building in Ahmedabad along with the Sarabhai and Shodan residences. The concrete framework on both sides of the 3-storeyed domino box-like building adds considerable shade. Its geometric design with light and shadow, goes well with traditional Indian architecture.

Up: The long pathway and the stairway break the long façade.
Down: Conference room on the third floor.

Third floor plan

SANSKAR KENDRA MUSEUM
1957/ Post Independence
By Le Corbusier

The concept of a spiral Art Museum that originated in 1931 was incorporated here and later in Tokyo and Chandigarh too. The emphasis is on geometrical composition and analogical thinking in terms of a natural spiral (snail) shell. The whole structure stands on pillars surrounding a courtyard, which gives a floating effect as if it is separated from the land.

Up: The whole building floats in space with the roof too, floating above it.
Down: Ramp leading to the second floor.

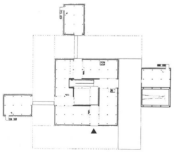

Floor Plan

INDIAN INSTITUTE OF MANAGEMENT ★★

1962-74 / Post Independence
By Louis Kahn

Like Le Corbusier, Louis Kahn of America (1901-74), greatly influenced Indian architecture. His main project was the National Assembly Hall in Bangladesh. If Le Corbusier's three-dimensional style blended with traditional Indian architecture, then Louis Kahn's pure geometric shapes blended well with traditional Islamic architecture. This university building was not out of place in Ahmedabad where Islamic flavour is strong. Originally Balakrishna Doshi was supposed to have designed this building, but he believed that a creation of Kahn's would be better in the Indian architectural scene and hence invited him to design it and co-operated with him. Kahn rose to the occasion, using less expensive materials like concrete and bricks and using unskilled labour, he created an architectural piece of high quality. He died the year he completed this building.

Floor plan

An effective mix of brick & concrete.

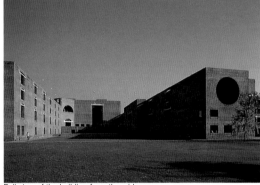
Full view of the building from the wide open square.

One of the dormitories that looks like a fortress.

SANGATH (DOSHI ATELIER) ⋆
1980/ Post Independence
By Balakrishna Doshi

Doshi (1927~) who was trained in the atelier of Le Corbusier, helped in architectural design activities in Chandigarh and Ahmedabad. He chose to settle down in Ahmedabad where he started his own architectural practice. His office-cum-residence called *Sangath*, is also a training centre for young architects. It has a vaulted roof with mosaic tiles which was influenced by the temples of Girnar. This fascinating building is richly different in its exterior design and in its usage of interior space.

View of the building from the garden.

Terrace on the roof.

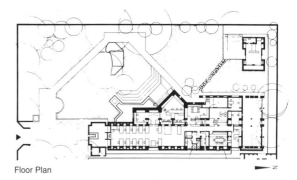
Floor Plan

GANDHI LABOUR INSTITUTE ⋆⋆
1984/ Post Independence
by Balakrishna Doshi

Doshi seems to have followed in the footsteps of Japanese architect, Kunio Maekawa, who was also a disciple of Le Corbusier. At first he designed buildings with rough concrete exteriors and later in the second phase of his career, he paid more attention to interiors, using traditional materials. An intimate space unfolds by enclosing the courtyard; this is reminiscent of Rajput palaces. This is one of Doshi's finest works, creating a rich environment for people.

Floor Plan

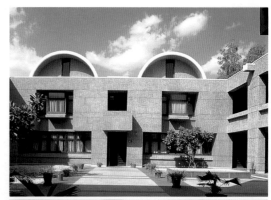

Up: Courtyard. Down: The corridor below the vaulted roof.

RUDA BAOLI (STEP-WELL)
1502/ Hindu

The intricately sculpted step-well in Adalaj, 17 km from Ahmedabad, is well preserved. It is also one of the best underground structures. The trabeated structure which controls the internal earth pressure as one descends, gives the impression of a forest. The quality and quantity of the carvings are exceptional.

This small village was a large town 500 years ago. Queen Ruda of the Hindu Waghra dynasty built this well for her subjects, around the same time as the Dada Harir Vav in Ahmedabad, hence they are similar. The one difference is that Dada Harir Vav is vertical, while Ruda Vav has stairways from three sides meeting on a wide landing from where it continues down to the water level. This space is surrounded by eight pillars with a large flat ceiling in the middle of which, is an octagonal space open to the sky. There must have been a domed pavilion here originally. Entrances of this style can be seen in the step-wells of Isanpur and Wikia. The octagonal pavilion in the Jami Masjid of Champaner must have been influenced by this structure. A step-well was not only used for practical purposes, it must have been used for religious ceremonies as well. Hence this hall with seats for spectators must have been an important stage, too.

❶ The step-well continues from the landing where the three stairways meet.
❷ The glimpse of the stairway from the octagonal landing.
❸ Rows of trabeated construction style visible from the hall.

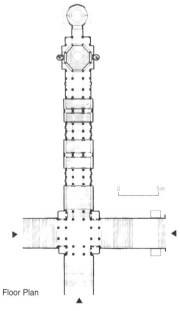

Floor Plan

❹ An octagonal stairwell on top of the water tank, in front of the well shaft in Adalaj.
❺ Sculptures on the pillars and beams are Islamic in style; some figurines are carved here.
❻ Small niches are carved in various levels on the wall of the shaft.
❼ Small Hindu shrines are designed in the four corners of the octagonal hall.
❽ Carved *jharokha*.

SARKHEJ (SURKHEJ) ★ ★

TANK, MOSQUE, MAUSOLEUM AND PALACE COMPLEX ★★
15th-16th C/ Islamic

In the dry west of India where water was important, Muhammed Begadha constructed a large tank in Sarkhej, 8 km from Ahmedabad. This tank is 200 m x 250 m and has a separate palace and health resort near it. There was a mosque and the Rauza (sacred tomb) of the Sufi Saint Sheikh Ahmed Khattu, which people came to visit. Later, the tomb of Muhammed Begadha was also constructed here. Since then it has become a shrine-cum-bathing place. The domes are supported by a post-and-beam structure, not by arches. The pavilion standing by itself in the middle of the courtyard presents a strange but fantastic appearance.

❶ The tank where people bathe and wash their clothes.
❷ Palace of Muhammed Begadha
❸ Tombs of Muhammed Begadha and Bibi Rajbhai.
❹ Interior of the tomb of Muhammed Begadha.
❺ Tomb of Sheikh Ahmed Khattu seen from the pavilion.
❻ Pavilion surrounded by tombs and mosques.

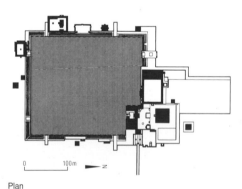

Plan

TOMB OF MUBARAK SAYYID
1484/ Islamic

Earlier, it was known as Mehamudabad because Mehamud I built the city. Now it is called Mehmedabad. The Mubarak Sayyid Tomb lies in fields 3 km from here. This building is unique in that unlike Sarkhej, the whole structure is made of arches and domes with *chhatris* on top and Rajput-style stone slab eaves. Possibly it was designed by an architect in Persia and then built by Indian artisans. Since the central tomb is surrounded by two rows of pillared corridors and has an elongated porch in the entrance, when viewed from the outside, the whole edifice looks as if it is entirely constructed with pillars.

❶ Full view of the structure.
❷ Porch at the main entrance.
❸ The capital of a pillar.
❹ *Jali* (lattice screen) made of stone.

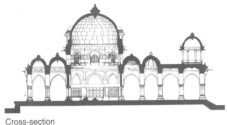

Cross-section

Plan

0   10m

NEW TOWN AND SECRETARIAT
1965-1970/ Post Independence

When Bombay state was divided into Maharashtra and Gujarat in 1960, Gujarat needed a new capital. Since Gandhi was born in Gujarat, Gandhinagar was named after him. It was designed as a garden city like Chandigarh and was similarly divided into sectors. The business district is linear.

The Secretariat is the core of the town.

WOODEN HAVELIS

Even though Gujarat lacked wood resources they imported teak to build their houses as they wished to surround themselves with wood. They could do this because they were rich, thanks to a vigorous overseas trade. These wooden houses are called *havelis*. A large number of wooden houses can be seen in Vaso, 50 km south of Ahmedabad.

MAHENDRA DESAI'S HAVELI ★★
19th-20th C

The most magnificent of Vaso's *havelis* is the one belonging to the politician Mahendra Desai. It has a large courtyard and pillared corridors that are noteworthy, as is the miniature chowk which is very similar to a courtyard in Nepal. Surrounding all three floors are corridors with exquisite wood carving.

❶ The *haveli* painted white
❷ Carved capitals of pillars in Amin Haveli
❸ Corridor facing the courtyard in Mahendra Desai's Haveli.
❹ Chowk (courtyard) with a step-well, Mahendra Desai's Haveli.
❺ Fountain on the 3rd floor, Mahendra Desai's Haveli.

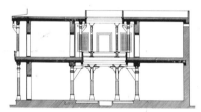

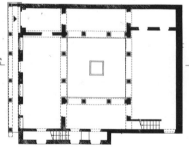

Cross section and floor plan of Amin Haveli.

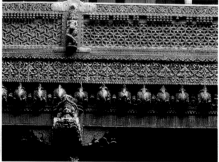

Details of wooden carving on the wall facing the courtyard.

WOODEN TEMPLES AND HAVELIS
19th-20th C/ Hindu

Baroda was developed in the 18th century by the Gaekwad family who were allies of the Marathas. Some wooden temples and *havelis* in the old city are dilapidated and in danger of collapsing. The wooden temples or *haveli mandirs* do not have *shikharas*. They are constructed in the same style as the dwellings but they are colourfully painted.

❶ Courtyard of Shreshawar Desai Haveli.
❷ Shreshawar Desai Haveli facing the pathway.
❸ Colourful *mandapa* of the Mairal temple.

Façade of the Narasimha Temple.

SENATE HOUSE OF VADODARA COLLEGE ★
1880/ Colonial
By Robert Fellows Chisholm

Robert Fellows Chisholm, an English architect designed three buildings in Baroda, the Senate House of Vadodara College, Lakshmi Devi Vilas Palace and the Museum. Each building is designed differently. Here he has built a large dome over a brick structure and decorated it with earthen artifacts. It exudes a Byzantine flavour.

Chisholm's designs were extremely versatile.

An exotic blend of Muslim, Hindu, Byzantine and English details.

JAMI MASJID FRIDAY MOSQUE ★★
1523/ Islamic

There are four forts inside the fort of Champaner, 40 km north-east of Vadodara. It was originally a Rajput fort. In 1484 Muhammed Begadha captured it, built a new city and made this place his capital. This mosque is built in the same style as the Jami Masjid in Ahmedabad. But the prayer room here is small and the number of large domes is fewer compared with the 15 in Ahmedabad. The central dome is three-storeyed with an atrium through the opening of which light pours in. This is similar to that of the Jain temples in Ranakpur. Small domes are built around the central dome and other large domes are built on a lower level around the central dome. Two tall minarets rise from the centre of the third floor on the side that faces the courtyard. These are more three dimensional than the one in Ahmedabad. The magnificent entrance pavilion in the courtyard is also quite unique.

❶ View from the top of the city gate. ❷ Entrance pavilion where the dome is broken. ❸ Central dome resting on eight pillars.

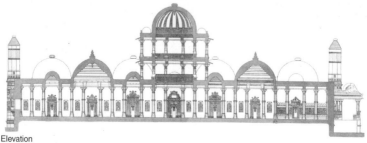

Elevation

BORAH MASJID ★
16th C/ Islamic

This mosque, within the city walls is called Sahar ki Masjid. It is a simple horizontal structure, with a visual contrast of two slender vertical Turkish minarets. There are various openings to the mosque and the base of each minaret is engraved with exquisite sculptures.

Up: Full view of the mosque with the fort atop a hill in the background.
Down: The centre of the façade.

The hall lined with pillars.

NAGINA MASJID ★
16th C/ Islamic

Access to this mosque is by foot through undergrowth as the road is not motorable. The mosque is built in a wide area facing the tomb. It is designed in the Jami Masjid style with a touch of the Champaner or Gujarati effect. It is not very long but the detailing on the three dimensional spatial architecture is exquisite. Even small areas are excellently designed. The dome unfortunately no longer exists, but because of that the interior is bright and the sculptures on the pillars and the *mihrab* can be easily observed in minute detail.

❶ Mosque seen between the pillars of the grave.
❷ The well-decorated central *mihrab*.
❸ Pillar designs in light moulding

SEVASI *

44

STEP-WELL *
1485/ Rajput

This step-well lies in Sevasi village, 3 km from Vadodara. The width of the access is narrow but it is so long that it goes to the bottom of the well. The width of the sculptures cannot be compared with those in Adalaj, but the post-and-beam structure is very impressive. There are pavilions on the top at both ends and a three-way entrance.

Left: A view deep inside from the entrance. Right: The solid structure of stone.

WADHWAN (VADVAN) *

45

MADHA STEP-WELL
1294/ Rajput

Ganga Vav and Madha Vav are two step-wells which were built in the village of Wadhwan, 8 km from Sundernagar. Both are unique in that each has a pyramidal roof on top of the post-and-beam structure, instead of domes. There are six paths in the 55 m deep Madha Vav while Ganga Vav has a magnificent gate.

The water level below the earth is high, and has risen well above the top of the steps.

LOTHAL *

46

SITE OF INDUS CIVILIZATION
2500-1700 BC

While the main ruins of the Indus Valley Civilization lie in Pakistan, some ruins are found in India too. Among them Lothal is prominent as the Walled City and as the port from where overseas trade was conducted. The dwellings were constructed with baked bricks and had underground drains as in Mohenjodaro.

The dwellings and the paved drains underground.

The dwellings and pathway.

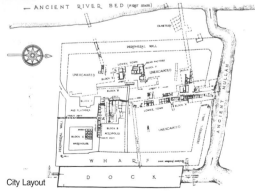

City Layout

GOVERNMENT HOUSE, HIGH COURT, TEMPLE COMPLEX ★
20th C

This large, traditional Rajput building, called Willingdon Secretariat, has a courtyard in the middle and houses government offices. A large temple sits in the courtyard. Apart from the shrine with its *shikhara,* there is also a breathtaking *mandapa* at the front which looks like the visitor's room in a palace.

NAVALAKHA TEMPLE
12th C/ Hindu

Sejakpur,10 km east of Wankaner, has an abandoned temple built during the Solanki dynasty. Made of yellow sandstone the sculptures on the wall are rich and of a very high quality. Since the outer walls are chamfered or stepped, the whole structure looks circular, but the inside shrine is square in plan.

RANJIT VILAS PALACE
1914/ Rajput

The Maharaja (feudal lord) of Wankaner designed this symmetrical palace in a blend of Hindu and Western styles. The structure facing a courtyard has fountains in the centre, reminiscent of the Italian style. The watch tower on the top has a Mughal-style dome while the interior is English. This palace is still inhabited by the royal family while a part of it is a hotel. An interesting west style vertical step-well, lies at the foot of the hill near the guest house.

Up: Full view of the palace above the hill.
Down: Dining Hall.

The western style step-well.

SATRUNJAYA ★★★

TEMPLE CITY ★★★
12th-20th C/ Jain

Satrunjaya (Shatrunjaya) Mountain, 2 km from Palitana, is the most sacred place for Jains. The first *tirthankara* of Jainism, Adinatha, used to visit this place very often and his disciple Pundalika, attained *nirvana* (spiritual enlightenment) here. It is not known when the temples were constructed, but each of the 863 temples here is dedicated to one of the 24 *tirthankaras*.

Monks and pilgrims start climbing at dawn and return at dusk. A large *dharamsala* (pilgrim rest house) has now been built at the foot of the mountain in Paranad.

Jains built temples on mountain-tops, because of their belief that mountains were holy. Another reason was that in the Middle Ages, Muslim invaders destroyed the temples in the regions they conquered. This could be the reason why Jains started building their temples in almost accessible places.

A cluster of temples occupy two peaks and the valley in between. They are referred to as *tuk and* are encircled by a high wall. To the north are 6 *tuks* starting with the Khataravasi *tuk*. Motisah *tuk* and Vallabhai *tuk* are found in the valley. Spreading over the entire southern peak is the Vimalavasi *tuk*.

The temples were all built at different points in time but there is not much difference in their styles. All of them are designed in the north-west Indian style with *shikharas*. But they are different from Hindu temples in that they have *chaumukha* shrines, open on all four sides.

This temple town with no houses or shops becomes a ghost town during the four months of the rainy season when the steps become too slippery and dangerous to climb.

❶ It takes two hours to climb up to the top. ❷ The temple town spread on the other side of the mountain in the light of dawn.

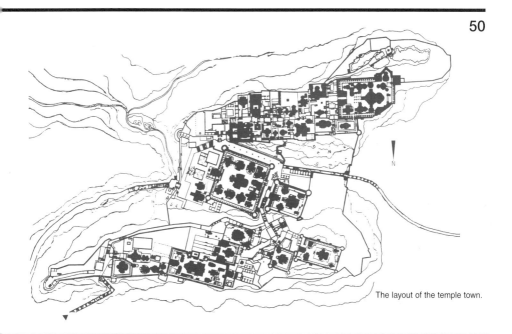

The layout of the temple town.

❸ The temples look imperiously down at the plains. ❹ The fortress-like Moti Shah *Tuk* and Vimalavasi *Tuk* in the south.

MOTISAH TEMPLE 1836

The huge Moti Sah *Tuk* is made up of many temples in a row. In the middle is Moti Sah Temple built by a Jain businessman from Bombay. The *mandapa* is rectangular and has a pyramidal *samvarana* roof from which small bell-like structures are located in a row at an angle of 45 degrees. The shrine is open on four sides.

VIMALA SAH TEMPLE ★ 1320 AD

This temple at the entrance of the Vimalavasi *tuk,* is also called Bhulavani (labyrinth) Temple. It has a complex design. The shrine is 3-storeyed, open on all four sides with the *chaumukha* statue enshrined on all three floors.

❶ Khartaravasi *tuk* on the northern peak.
❷ Fortified Vallabhai *tuk* deep in the valley.
❸ Motisah *tuk* group of temples in the valley.
❹ Hathiapol (Elephant Gate) of Vimalavasi *tuk.*
❺ Main street of Vimalavasi *tuk.*
❻ Four-sided open shrine with the statue of a *Tirthankara* facing all four sides.
❼ Open three-storeyed shrine of Vimala Sah

ADISHVARA TEMPLE
1155, 1315 and 16th C

Proceeding further into the Vimalavasi *Tuk,* one can see the Adishvara Temple. It has been renovated and it is always crowded with pilgrims. This temple blends both Islamic and Hindu styles. The tall *shikhara* is actually a collection of a number of small *shikharas* at various levels that clearly reflect the north Indian construction style. The *mandapa* has two floors and is built according to the Islamic style. The second floor gallery with its varied space and design is unflaggingly interesting.

❶ Adisvara Temple and the surrounding small shrines.
❷ The upper portion of the entrance as seen from the temple's 2nd floor.
❸ *Chaumukha* (four-faced statue) has been enshrined on the 2nd floor too.
❹ The design on the wall of the temple. There are *chaumukhas* all over the surrounding area.
❺The Islamic effect can be seen in the *mandapa* of the temple.

The history of this city goes back to ancient times. Sculpted edicts of Emperor Ashoka from the 3rd century BC still exist. It was the capital of the Kshattrapa dynasty. 2nd century Buddhist and Jain rock-cut monasteries of the time are scattered all over the area. In the 15th century, Muhammed Begadha reconstructed the fort and made it a Muslim city. In 1880, the city was developed and the gates, etc, constructed during that time, still exist. It is the main city of this region and it is also the base for pilgrims visiting Girnar Mountains 3 km away.

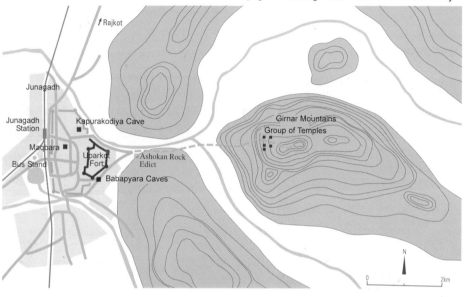

JUNAGADH   51

CAVE TEMPLES
2nd-4th C/ Buddhist, Jain

There are 3 main caves. The oldest Babapyara cave (2nd century) is Jain, while the cave in Uparkot Fort and the Kapurakodiya caves (3rd-4th century) are Buddhist. Since they were mostly used as living quarters for monks they are simple with very few carvings. Only the Uparkot cave has ancient carvings on its walls and pillars. Another interesting feature is that there are five water tanks inside the Kapurakodiya caves.

UP: Kapurakodiya caves.
Down: Interior of Buddhist cave of Uparkot fort.

Row of simple pillars inside the cave.

UPARKOT FORT AND JAMI MASJID
15th C/ Islamic

The fort has been in existence since B C years. It was neglected for a long time and was invaded from time to time. In the 15th century, it was established as an Islamic fort. There are step-wells, water tanks and caves inside the fort. The largest building, the Jami Masjid was formerly a palace but was converted into a mosque by Muhammed Begadha. The interior is Gujarati in style.

❶ The fort with Girnar Mountains as a backdrop. ❷ Exterior view of Jami Masjid. ❸ Interior of the Jami Masjid.

MAQBARA (ROYAL TOMBS) ★
19th C/ Islamic

It is a fantastic *maqbara* with a fusion of Indo, Islamic, and Venetian Gothic style. It is similar to the strange buildings which were designed in Japan with a fusion of Japanese-Western style during the Meiji period by artisans who had never visited the West. The Nawab (Islamic protector) of the small state in the region and other important people must have had strong Western leanings.

Up: Tomb of Mahabat Khan (1892).
Down: Tracery on the wall of the tomb.

The tomb of Bahar-ud-din Bhar (1896).

GIRNAR ★★

TEMPLE CITY
12th-19th C/ Jain

Girnar Mountains 6 km east of Junagadh, is a mountain temple city like the Satrunjaya mountains. Here 3500 steps have been carved on the cliff face; to reach the top one needs to climb another 1000 steps. It is said that the 23rd *tirthankara*, Neminadha attained *nirvana* here. Pilgrims start climbing the steps at dawn when it is cool and pray at each of the 10 temples built here. The temples are all in the west-Indian style. In front of the *samvarana mandapa* is the *trika mandapa*. The mosaic finished domes of these *mandapas* have colourful designs on a white base. The rough sandstone has weathered and become discoloured. The mosaic technique which came into use much later in the beginning of the 20th century, was used to restore the badly damaged domes.

NEMINATHA TEMPLE ★1128

Neminatha Temple, the oldest and largest temple built on a cliff, has an ambulatory surrounding the precincts which leads to the group of temples to the north. The interior is very bright. Photography is prohibited.

PARSHVANATHA TEMPLE ★★1231

The unique feature of this temple is that there are 2 halls with domed ceilings on the right and left of the *mandapa*. Inside, Astapada and Sammeta shikhara are enshrined on platforms and pilgrims consider this place sacred.

SAMPRATI RAJA TEMPLE 1453

The *trika mandapa* is big and the entire shrine is made of *jalis* (lattice screens made of stone). Each of the lattice work panels is different; and each shows the dedication of the craftsman towards his work.

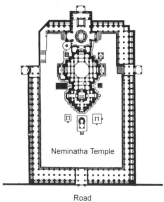

Neminatha Temple

Road

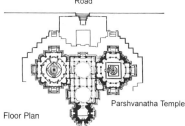

Parshvanatha Temple

Floor Plan

❶ It takes 2-3 hours to climb the precipice.
❷ The entrance gate to the group of temples.
❸ Around ten temples look down majestically from the top of a cliff, 900 m high.
❹ Parshvanatha Temple and Neminatha Temple.
❺ *Mandapa* of the Parshvanatha Temple.
❻ The platform symbolizing Meru Mountain inside the same temple.
❼ Group of temples in the northern end.
❽ Double dome of the temple decorated with mosaic.
❾ *Jali* of the Samprati Raja Temple.
❿ The *shikhara* of the temple painted white.
⓫ The *mandapa* of the Samprati Raja Temple.

DIU *

FORT AND CHURCHES
16th-19th C/ Colonial

Diu, a small island off the Kathiawad peninsula became a Portuguese colony. Western style churches and forts were built here in the 15th century. This region was taken back from the Portuguese with military force in 1961. As a result most of the buildings were bombed and destroyed. Even so Portuguese style buildings still stand in many places.

❶ Entrance to the fort.
❷ Cloister in Saint Paul's Cathedral.
❸ Saint Paul's Cathedral built in 1610.

City Gate

SOMNATH *

54

SOMANATH TEMPLE
Reconstructed in the 20th C/ Hindu

Also called Prabhas Patan, this sacred place looked like a mountain of treasure to the Muhammed of Gazni dynasty who attacked this famous temple in the 11th century and destroyed it. The project for restoring this temple was started in the 20th century and it was reconstructed in the Solanki style. The sculptures on the wall are still being done.

GHUMLI *

VIKIA VAV (STEPWELL)
12th C/Rajput

On the way to Banwad, 35 km from Porbunder, is a ruined step-well in the wilderness. It is a huge and fascinating step-well, 60 m long and 4.5 m wide. The entrance pavilions still stand in three places.

GOP ★

VISHNU TEMPLE ★
6th C/ Hindu

This type of temple on a high platform is in Jinawari village, near Gop station, north-east of Ghumli. It belongs to the Maitraka dynasty that ruled this place after the Guptas. Since the surrounding walls and roof have collapsed, the existing central portion looks like a tower. A row of horse-shoe shaped, arched *chaitya* windows were purely decorative, not functional.

Up: The holes on the wall look like they held the rafters for the ceiling.
Down: The *chaitya* window decorations.

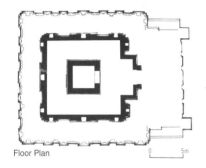

Floor Plan   0   5m

DWARKA ★

DWARAKADHISHA TEMPLE ★
12th-16th C/ Hindu

Situated at the west end of the Kathiawar peninsula is a large temple on top of the hill, which has an unusual five-storeyed tower. It has an atrium and is crowned with a dome. The legend is that Lord Krishna built his empire here, which was later swallowed up by the sea with only the temple remaining untouched.

Right: Balcony around the *mandapa*.
Left: View of the shrine.

DWARKA

RUKMINI TEMPLE ★
12th C/ Hindu

Built on the rocky coast, this temple is the shrine and *mandapa* design with a porch in the front. Originally the dome of the building must have been a *samprana* roof. Along with its detailed carving, the *shikhara* is noteworthy. Photography is prohibited as devotees worship at this temple even now. The weather here is cool due to sea breeze.

PALACE QUARTER ★
18th-19th C/ Rajput

The Palace Quarter was in the centre of the complex. Parag Mahal, the new palace, at the entrance has a majestic, Romanesque shrine-like appearance. Small pavilions had been constructed in the Armenian style on top of the *campanile*. This exquisite structure was designed by Henri Wilkins in the second half of the 19th century. He used sandstone and marble. The large hall on the second floor brings to mind the Rajput palaces of the past. At the other end of the courtyard was Aina Mahal, the former palace, which is now a museum. Here the rooms and artifacts displayed give the viewer a fair idea of palace life.

❶ Another building seen from the 2nd floor corridor.
❷ The main entrance of the new palace as seen from the gate.
❸ *Darbar* hall on the 2nd floor.

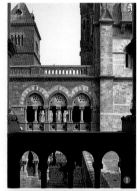

ROYAL CHHATRIS ★
17th-19th C/ Rajput

There is a big lake in Bhuj which is the main water source for the city. It becomes completely dry during the dry summer months. Near the lake on the other side of the city, the *Maharao* (king) has another palace and not far from the royal *chhatris* made of brown sandstone which are now destroyed by the earthquake. It is said that the oldest one dated back to 300 years. They were richly sculpted.

❶ The tomb of *Maharao*.
❷ Details on the inside of the tomb.
❸ Sculptures on the wall of the tomb.

Rich and detailed sculpture on yellow sandstone.

To the north of the Kathiavad peninsula, surrounded by Pakistan and Kutch bay is Kutch. Half of it is low marshy ground called Rann that gets flooded for five months during the rainy season which begins in May.

This whole area is salt encrusted barren land. It is a desert when you travel north from Bhuj to Banni. But even here there are some small villages. Most of the villagers belong to the Sunni Muslim group, but there are also Hindu villages belonging to the lowest caste, the Harijans. Their dwellings are similar but their life style is entirely different. Permits available in Bhuj are required for visiting these villages. The dwellings built in very severe climatic conditions, have wooden rafters on circular earthen walls, thatched on top. This is the living room called *Bhunga*. To this a rectangular room called *chouki* is attached and used as a kitchen, etc. This whole edifice is built on a low platform that protects it from floods and also demarcates the boundary of the family. These houses are very clean and only recently has the area been electrified.

Mosque in the Muslim village of Dhordo.   A woman in the Hindu Ludia village.

VILLAGES IN BANNI ★★
VILLAGES OF LUDIA, BHIRENDIARA
Harijan

The village of Ludia, 45 km north of Bhuj, is bleak terrain. Bhirendiara is 60 km east. Both are Hindu villages where the lower castes reside. Their occupation is handicraft items. The walls of their houses are painted with murals and the brightly costumed women of the village are very friendly.

VILLAGES OF GOREWALI, DHORDO ★
Islamic

40 km to the west of Bhirendiara, after Hadka are the villages of Gorewali and Dhordo. This is 80 km from Bhuj. Since the residents are Muslims, the womenfolk are not seen much, though the men act as guides. The mosque is not very different from the houses but is colourfully decorated.

❶ Mural on the wall of a house in Ludia.
❷ *Bhunga* designed on top of a platform in Bhirendiara.
❸ *Bhunga* in Dhordo village. Shoes are removed at the entrance.
❹ Ceiling in a house in Bhirendiara. Sometimes a central pillar is also used.
❺ Interior of the *Bhunga* in Bhirendiara village.
❻ Interior of the *Bhunga* in Ludia village. Food items are displayed, decoratively.
❼ A cradle in Gorewali village.

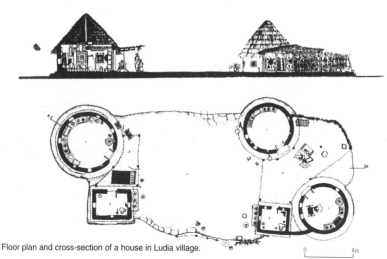

Floor plan and cross-section of a house in Ludia village.

0   4m

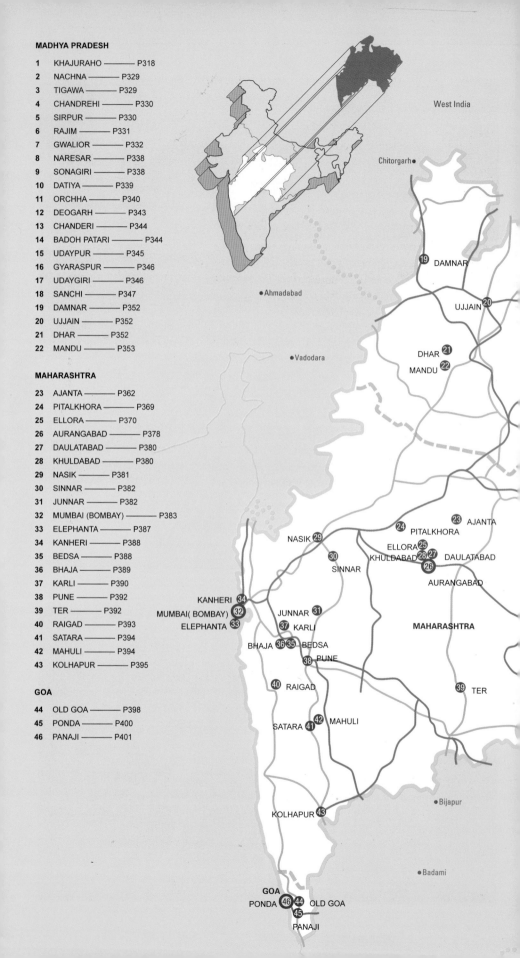

West India
Chitorgarh
Ahmadabad
Vadodara
19 DAMNAR
UJJAIN 20
DHAR 21
MANDU 22
23 AJANTA
24 PITALKHORA
NASIK 29
ELLORA 25
30 SINNAR
KHULDABAD 28 27 DAULATABAD
26 AURANGABAD
KANHERI 34
MUMBAI(BOMBAY) 32
ELEPHANTA 33
JUNNAR 31
37 KARLI
BHAJA 36 35 BEDSA
38 PUNE
MAHARASHTRA
40 RAIGAD
39 TER
SATARA 41
42 MAHULI
Bijapur
KOLHAPUR 43
Badami
GOA
PONDA 46 44 OLD GOA
45
PANAJI

Central India

NARESAR
GWALIOR
North India

SONAGIR
DATIYA
ORCHHA
●Allahabad

CHANDERI
KHAJURAHO
DEOGARH
NACHNA
CHANDREHI
ADOH PATARI
UDAYPUR
GYARASPUR
TIGAWA
DAYGIR
SANCHI
OPAL

MADHYA PRADESH

SIRPUR

RAJIM

East India

●Warangal

●Hyderabad

South India

N

0   200km

TRAVEL INFORMATION (Central India)

AROUND KHAJURAHO

It is easier to fly in to Khajuraho from Agra or Varanasi (Benares). Jhansi to Khajuraho is is four and a half to six hours by train. There is a bus service too. If you go by train, alight at Mahoba and take the bus to Khajuraho. Buses from Agra and Gwalior to Khajuraho take 12 hours and 9 hours respectively. You can also travel by train from Allahabad to Satna (4 hours) and from there take a bus (4 hours) to Khajuraho. Khajuraho has hotels to suit every budget. Hotel Khajuraho Ashok is very comfortable. The Tourist Bungalow is economical while Hotel Payal is a medium-budget hotel. To go to Nachna or Tigawa hire a taxi and stay overnight in Katni. You can go to Kundarpur and return too. Tigawa is 35 km northwest of Sihora by road. The name of the village is Tigma.

Temple city of Kundarpur.

The sculptures in Khajuraho Vishwanatha Temple.

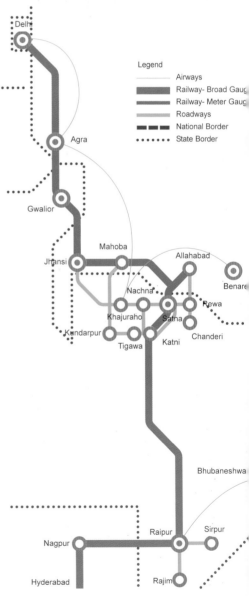

Legend

	Airways
	Railway- Broad Gaug
	Railway- Meter Gaug
	Roadways
	National Border
	State Border

Delhi · Agra · Gwalior · Jhansi · Mahoba · Allahabad · Benare · Nachna · Rewa · Khajuraho · Satna · Kundarpur · Tigawa · Katni · Chanderi · Bhubaneshwa · Raipur · Sirpur · Nagpur · Hyderabad · Rajim

ALLAHABAD TO RAIPUR

From Allahabad, travel to Rewa (3 hours) visit Chandrehi by jeep and take the night train to Raipur. It is better to buy the tickets from Allahabad. After visiting Nachna and Tigawa by taxi from Satna, catch the train at Katni. Stay at Hotel Sharda, hire a taxi and make a round trip to Sirpur and Rajim. Since the total distance is 260 km, returning on the same day may not be possible. You can consult the tourist office at the station too. From Raipur you can fly east to Bhubaneshwar or take the train to Nagpur (6 hours) and enter south India. Usually, researchers and not tourists take this route.

GWALIOR TO MANDU

Those who want to visit the Buddhist ruins, usually go straight to Sanchi from Agra. There are many places one could visit on the way. One should not miss Gwalior that is 3 hours by bus or 2 hours by train, from Agra. Hotel Tansen or Usha Kiran palace, which is a palace hotel, are good places to stay at. From Gwalior to Jhansi is the same distance by bus or taxi and Hotel Jhansi is a decent hotel. Datiya, to the north seen from the train as you travel past, takes one hour by bus. Orchha, in the south is a 30-minute ride away. Hire a taxi to visit Datiya (one hour). In Orchha stay in the old palace, Sheesh Mahal. From Jhansi to Lalitpur by train is one-and-a-half hours; take a taxi to Deogarh. Through a different route you can reach Chanderi in one-and-a-half hours. The roads to Udaypur are bad. It is better to go to Sanchi and go to Udaygiri and Udaypur by jeep (from the hotel) the following day.

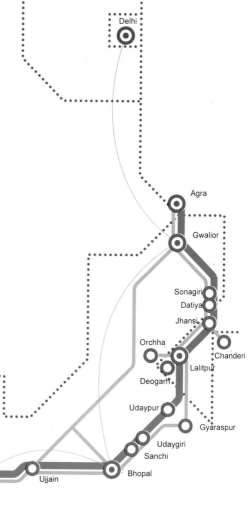

Stay at the tourist bungalow and climb the hill early in the morning to visit the *stupa*.

For travelling from Sanchi to Mandu, go to Bhopal airport by jeep (1 hour, 20 minutes) and fly to Indore; take a bus or taxi via Dhar (4 hours). If not in a hurry, go to Bhopal by bus (direct bus - an hour-and-a-half), then take the bus to Indore (5 hours) and stay at the Hotel President. There are frequent buses to Ujjain (an hour-and-a-half). In Mandu, it's best to hire a bicycle and visit the ruins. Stay at the tourist cottage. Return to Indore and go to Maharashtra (Ajanta and Ellora) by bus (12-15 hours). Stay in Jalgaon for a day and then proceed to Fardapur. Flying to Bombay is the easiest.

TRAVEL INFORMATION (Central India)

AROUND MUMBAI (BOMBAY) ————

Mumbai is a convenient point to end the tour. Since most tourists stay in the Colaba area, at times it is difficult to get a room here. There is the luxury Taj Intercontinental. Medium budget, Grand Hotel is near CST station. Visit Nalanda bookshop inside the Taj Hotel and the Strand Book Stall near the Tokyo Mitsubishi Bank. Elephanta Islands are an hour by boat from the Gateway of India. To get to Kanheri caves, take the suburban train from Churchgate to Borivli (40 min) and from there take a taxi or auto-rickshaw (10 min). To see the Buddhist caves, take the train to Lonavla (3 hours) and from there hire an auto-rickshaw and visit, Karli, Bhaja and Bedosa. It takes 20 minutes to Karli and another 20 minutes to climb the mountain. Bedosa is 30 minutes away. You can take the train from here to Pune, if you are in a hurry (1 hour, 20 minutes). If not, stay in Lonavla for a day in a hotel near the station. A simple holiday camp is also available near the caves. Pune, a big city, has many hotels. Hotel Aurora Towers is comfortable. To see Maratha culture, you have to go further south from here.

Gateway of India and Taj Hotel.

Stone cave temple group in Ajanta.

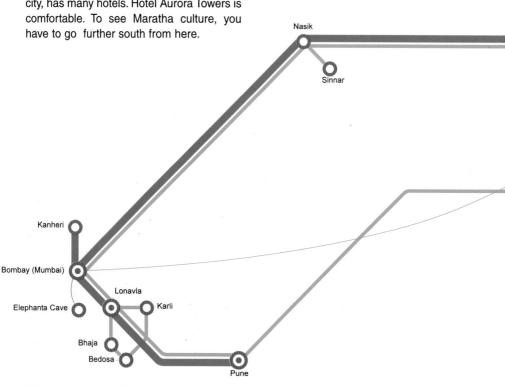

ROCK CAVE TEMPLE GROUP —

The best rock-cave temples are at Aurangabad. Fly from Bombay or take the night train. Nasik, *en route* to Aurangabad is 4 hours from Bombay. Stay overnight at Nasik and continue to Aurangabad (three and a half hours by train). In Nasik, Shalini Palace Hotel (5 km) is a good place to stay at. To get to Pandor, take an auto-rickshaw. It takes 1 hour by bus to get to Sinnar. Aurang Ashok in Aurangabad is a convenient halt. Explore the city and the caves, in an auto-rickshaw. Ajanta is two and a half hours from here. Go to Wardhapur which is 5 km away from Ajanta, and visit the

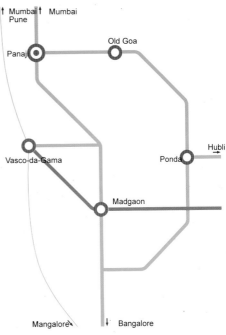

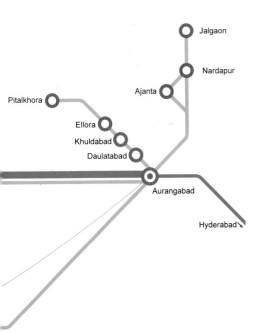

GOA —

The airport and railway station are both in Vasco-da-Gama, which is a 45-minute bus or taxi ride to Panaji, the capital of Goa. There are flights from Bombay, Pune and Bangalore and overnight trains and buses to Bombay. There are many hotels in Panaji (Panjim). Cidade-de-Goa, is a 10-minute ride out of Panaji. Old Goa and the temples around Ponda can be visited in a day trip by auto-rickshaw. Cross over Karnataka by bus to Hubli, or take a bus to Mangalore (10 hours). The Konkan railway runs through Goa, from Bombay to Trivandrum in Kerala.

Cidade de Goa Hotel

ruins at a relaxed pace. Stay in the holiday resort. Ellora is an hour by bus from Aurangabad. Visit the temple and tank in Belur village. On the way to Ellora, Daulatabad and Khuldabad can be visited by bus. Take a taxi to Pitalkhora caves (2 hours). Since taxi charges are exorbitant from Aurangabad to Pitalkhora, and the roads are bad, hire a jeep. Aurangabad to Pune is 6 hours by bus. To go to the south, take the train to Hyderabad (14 hours).

MADHYA PRADESH

Madhya Pradesh, India's largest state is located at the centre of the country, with more than half the state on the Deccan plateau which forms the central portion of the Indian peninsula, bordered on either side by the hills of the Eastern and Western Ghats. The people here speak Hindi and culturally too, it is not very different from the rest of north India. Noteworthy structures are all concentrated to the northwest of the state, near Delhi and Agra. The reason is that the Vindhya Mountains, running from east to west, did not allow much movement between north India and the southeast. Sanchi, which is near the capital, Bhopal, has some important Buddhist ruins. Ruins of temples, monasteries and three *stupas* of various sizes, are strewn on hilltops giving a serene ambience to the area. To the west of the *stupas* are *toranas* (memorial arches), whose exquisite sculpture belongs to the period between the 1st century BC and the 1st century AD. This Buddhist art was the inspiration for Asian Buddhist art.

The most famous group of Hindu temples belonging to the Middle Ages is also located at Khajuraho in Madhya Pradesh. The architectural style of these temples, the Khajuraho style, is a sub-classification of the Orissa type and the west-Indian type, which again is a sub-classification of the overall

Cross-section of the Lakshmana Temple , 954, Khajuraho.

north-Indian type. Many temples were built shaped like mountains, because of a belief in mountain worship. The *ardhamandapa* (porch), *mandapa, mahamandapa, vimana* and *shikhara,* built by the next generation resemble a mountain, while the inside of the temple reminds one of cave temples. The statues of males and females based on tantrism, carved in great detail on the wallls, are a feast for the eyes. This standard of temples can be seen all the way, from Agra to Sanchi.

Mandu, in west India, is spread over 20 sq km on a plateau, deep in the mountains. It is located in an isolated area, 634 m above sea level. Inside the fort wall is a palace, mosque, tombs, *caravan sarai,* etc dating back to the 15th century. In contrast to the ornamentation adorning Hindu structures, these buildings are austere. Before Mandu was abandoned in the 17th century, it was a self-sufficient city.

Detailed sculptures of males and females on the walls.

Two Rajput families from west India advanced into the northern and central parts of India and established their kingdoms there. The first was the Pratihara dynasty (8th-11th century) and the next was the Chandela dynasty (10th-13th century). Khajuraho, later called Bundelkhand, was the capital of the Chandela Dynasty. It is now a small village, with only 4,500 people. Once, there were 85 architecturally beautiful temples but now there are only 25. These abandoned temples are restored by the Archaeological Survey of India and the area has been designated an archaeological museum open to the public. The scale of the temples and the quality of construction is spectacular. There are three types of temples, the north Indian type depicted in Khajuraho, the east-Indian type found around Bhubaneshwar and the west Indian type. The Bhubaneshwar temples were built from the 7th-13th century, while those in Khajuraho were built between 10th-12th centuries and hence have many similarities. *Shikharas* of the Khajuraho temples are straight and majestic.

The temples can be broadly classified into three groups, the West, East and South Group. There is a wall around the main temple groups. The garden around the temples is looked after by the Archaeological Survey of India. The West Group is the largest and is close to the hotels, museum and markets. The Matangeshwara Temple, where prayers are still conducted, is outside the wall and the unique Chausatt Yogini Temple stands on a hill, a little away from the other temples. Four temples of the East Group, are about 1-2 km away scattered in the village. In the east, amidst fields, are Jain temples, which are the main temples in the East Group. Recently, a Jain exhibition hall has been opened there. South of here are two temples of the South Group.

Chausatt Yogini Temple (middle 9th century)

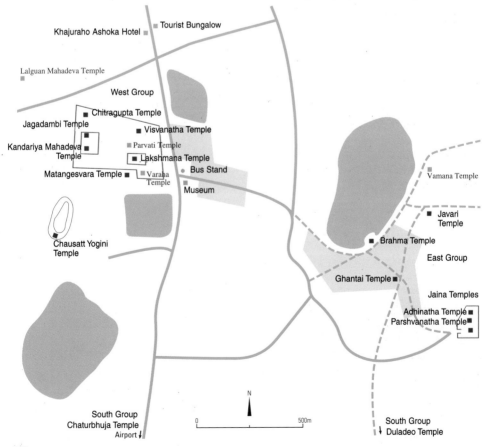

Khajuraho Ashoka Hotel ▪   ▪ Tourist Bungalow

Lalguan Mahadeva Temple
▪

West Group

▪ Chitragupta Temple

Jagadambi Temple ▪

▪ Visvanatha Temple

Kandariya Mahadeva ▪   ▪ Parvati Temple
Temple

▪ Lakshmana Temple

Matangesvara Temple ▪   ▪ Varaha   ● Bus Stand
  Temple

▪ Museum

Chausatt Yogini
Temple

Vamana Temple ▪

▪ Javari
Temple

▪ Brahma Temple

East Group

Ghantai Temple ▪

Jaina Temples

Adhinatha Temple ▪
Parshvanatha Temple ▪
▪

N

0   500m

South Group
Chaturbhuja Temple
Airport ↓

South Group
↓ Duladeo Temple

MATANGESHWARA TEMPLE *
10th C/ Hindu

This is the only temple in the North Group where prayers are still offered everyday. It has its own unique style since it was built much before the Khajuraho style was established. It is a simple temple with a *ardhamandapa* in front. The circular hall inside has a domed ceiling and a giant *linga* under the dome, which makes it a really unique temple.

Linga, the symbol of Shiva is deified in this temple

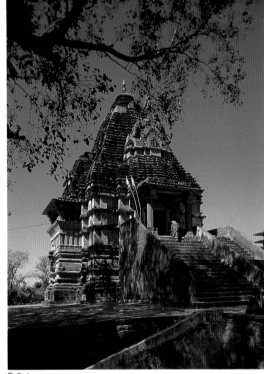

Full view

CHITRAGUPTA TEMPLE *
11th C/ Hindu

This large temple has no ambulatory, nor does it have a balcony, but the *mandapa* is very large and lets in bright sunlight. It has a classic interior where the *mahamandapa* has four pillars, on which a beam has been placed and the dome rests on this beam. Inside the *garbhagriha,* is a statue of a three-sided *Surya* (Sun God).

Full view of Chitragupta temple.

Entrance to the shrine is visible from the *mandapa*.

KHAJURAHO

LAKSHMANA TEMPLE ★★
950 AD/ Hindu

This is a large temple of the early days, with all the qualities of the Khajuraho style of temples. There are actually four interconnected *mandapas* in a row. The *shikhara* over each hall becomes larger with each consecutive hall. *Shikharas* of Hindu temples resemble mountains. Perhaps, this temple was conceived as the mountain range of the Himalayas. The meaning of *shikhara* is mountain peak. As seen from the cross section, the *shikharas* are very tall, but the rooms inside, especially the shrine under the tallest *shikhara*, is small.

This temple is constructed in the centre of a high platform, with four small shrines at the four corners, which make it a *Pancharatna* temple or a five-shrine temple. Jain temples are built with the *tirthankara* facing all four sides called *Chaumukha* and they are extended on all four sides too. As Hindu temples are "Houses of God", they cannot be extended on all four sides. The shrine has to be a room, closed on all sides except for the main door. Hence, even if it is a large temple, it can only extend in the front. That is why the four shrines are established separately in each of the four corners.

❶ Main entrance can be seen from the staircase to the platform.
❷ The small shrines of the *Panchratna* are on either side. The Matangeshwara Temple can be seen at the rear left corner.
❸ The platform is built in different layers. In various places, statues of Gods have been deified in each of the niches.

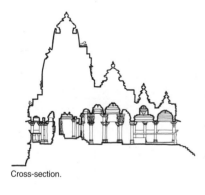

Cross-section.

❹ The sides of the platforms are sculpted with images of musicians, battle scenes, elephants, horses, etc.
❺ The shrine seen from the *mandapa*.
❻ The ornamental details of the wall made of sandstone.

Elevation of the balcony.

KHAJURAHO

JAGADAMBI TEMPLE ⋆
11th C/ Hindu

This temple was either built at the same time as the Chitragupta Temple or precedes it. It is even the same size. The temple has no circumbulatory around it but has one open *arthamandapa* (porch). The whole roof structure is therefore built in three steps. There is less ornamental decoration on the walls than that of the Chitragupta Temple, but the sculptures of various gods on the outer walls are excellent. Though Parvati is the main deity, like other temples, originally this one was also dedicated to Vishnu.

Up: Jagadambi Temple and the Shiva shrine in front are built on a high platform as is the Kandariya Mahadeva Temple. Down; Sculptures on the wall.

VISVANATHA TEMPLE ★★
998 A D/ Hindu

Like the Lakshmana Temple, this is also a *Panchayatana* temple. Two of the four small shrines no longer exist. A large platform extends to the front and a Nandi shrine has been installed facing the main shrine. The steps leading to the platform are between the main shrine and the Nandi shrine. *Nandi* (bull) is the *vahana* (mode of transport) for Shiva. In case of large temples, a separate shrine is built for *Nandi.* In this temple, the Nandi shrine too, has a pyramidal *shikhara* along with the main shrine and the dome ceiling is quite exceptional. Benches surround the statue of *Nandi* and sitting here one can enjoy the view of the temple and the landscape around.

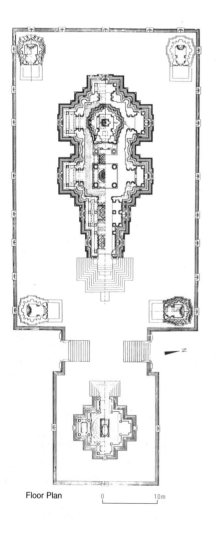

Floor Plan   0   10 m

❶ The temple looks like a mountain range with small shrines on all four sides.
❷ The pathway around the shrine. Lights from the balcony.
❸ The Nandi shrine in front of the main shrine.
❹ *Nandi* sitting in the middle of the open hall.

KANDARIYA MAHADEVA TEMPLE ★★★
11th C/ Hindu

Construction activity in Khajuraho was at its zenith after the Lakshmana Temple and the Vishwanatha Temple were built. These temples were dedicated not to Vishnu, but to Shiva.

The Kandariya Mahadeva Temple is one of the most beautiful temples, towering to a height of over 30 m (including its foundation platform). The temple consists of an *ardhamandapa*, *mandapa, mahamandapa, garbhagriha* and *pradakshina* or cirumbulatory which is the corridor around the shrine. The grandeur, scale and proportion of this temple, make it one of the best examples of the north Indian type.

Granite has been used for the construction of the Chausatt Yogini Temple, the Lalguan Mahadeva Temple and the Brahma Temple. The other temples are all made of sandstone. The walls are exquisitely carved with statues of gods, humans, animals, and other mythological beings. There is a wonderful statue of *mithuna* (man and woman lovingly embracing) inside the temple. These erotic groupings can be seen in Hindu temples all over this region, especially in Khajuraho and Konark. The exact reason for the presence of such statues is not known. Perhaps, it was a good luck symbol for the people of the Middle Ages.

The *shikhara* of this temple is exceptional.

Eighty-four small *shikharas* have been sculpted on the surface of the main *shikhara* and each small *shikhara* is crowned with an *amalaka* and an inverted pot shaped finial called *kalasha*. This style of a *shikhara* from central India was later adopted as the model for *shikharas* in most west Indian temples.

Sculptures on the walls, showing sexual postures.

The Kandariya Mahadeva Temple and JagadambiTemple share a foundation platform. There is a small Shiva temple in between.

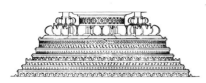

Elevation and plan of the ceiling of the *mandapa*.

Up: Ceiling of the porch. Down: Ceiling of the *mandapa*.

❶ Sculptures on wall surfaces. ❷ Entrance to the *sanctum sanctorum* where Shiva is deified. ❸ The large *shikhara*.

PARSVANATHA TEMPLE ★★
10th C/ Jain

The Eastern Group of temples, made up of mainly Jain temples, reflects the broad outlook of the Hindu Chandela Kings as far as religion was concerned. Seeing temples of different religions standing together, is not a rare sight in India and can be seen in Ellora and Chittaurgarh too.

A wall encircles the group of Jain temples and shrines here. The most prominent is the Parshvanatha Temple, which was built before the West Group of Khajuraho Temples was built. This temple does not have any balconies on the surface of its walls and hence its outer view is not very spectacular. The quality of the sculptures on the walls of this rectangular temple is very good (the woman applying eye shadow on page 317 is especially very famous). The style of the statues is not different from the Hindu style and it is the *tirthankara* statues in various places that tell us this is a Jain temple. Besides, both the Jain and the Hindu temples were designed by the same architects and perhaps, built by the same artisans. The only difference that can be pointed out is that the back of the temple has a niche that has been carved and a statue of Parsvanatha has been installed there.

❶ Parsvanatha Temple can be seen in the far left-hand corner of the temple group.
❷ There is no balcony on the outer walls, but they are covered profusely with sculptures.
❸ *Tirthankara* statue on the wall of the *mandapa*.
❹ *Pradakshina* (path) going around the shrine.

Ceiling of the porch.

ADINATHA TEMPLE ★
11th C/ Jain
Adinatha, the first *tirthankara* has been deified here. It is a simple temple with one simple room, to which a porch was later added. Since there is no balcony, the tall *shikhara* looks thin and delicate. This temple does not have the customary collection of small *shikharas* but has simple straight lines, which points to the fact that it might have been built during the 10th century.

The base and the sculptures on the wall.

The rear view of the *shikhara*.

GHANTAI TEMPLE
10th C/ Jain
Only the *ardhamandapa* and pillars of the *mandapa* of this temple stand in the middle of Khajuraho village, today. The temple was perhaps, much larger in scale than the Parshvanatha Temple. The bell and chain carving on the round pillar is a unique motif and the temple is called *Ghantai* after this bell.

BRAHMA TEMPLE
10th C/ Hindu
This temple belongs to the Early Ages and was very different from more mature temples. Originally it was a Vishnu temple. It is an early phase of the Matangeshwara temple style, but instead of the balcony on each side, it has lattice windows. It now has a four-faced *Linga* deified within. The *ardhamandapa* in front is missing.

JAVARI TEMPLE ★
11th C/ Hindu
This temple stands majestically on a high foundation platform in the middle of a field. It is a medium sized temple with no *mahamandapa* or *pradakshina* (cirumbulatory) around the shrine. The entrance facing the bright *ardhamandapa* is very beautiful. It has the most elaborate carving in the temple. At the entrance is another wooden door, which is closed at night, so that God can rest. There is a headless statue in the *sanctum sanctorum.*

Full view of Javari Temple   Beautifully carved entrance of Javari temple

DULADEO TEMPLE
12th C/ Hindu
The Chaturbhuja Temple and the Duladeo Temple belong to the Southern Group of Temples. They were both constructed at the start of the 12th century. Details of these structures are quite complicated and the *mahamandapa* is wide and fascinating. Unfortunately some portions of the temple have started collapsing.

CHATURBHUJA TEMPLE ★
12th C/ Hindu
This beautiful temple, far from the riverside, is dedicated to Vishnu and resembles the Javari Temple. The scale of this temple reflects the economical thinking of the Chandela dynasty. The floor plan may be small but the *shikhara* is straight and tall.

NACHNA ★★

PARVATI TEMPLE
5th C/ Hindu

Construction of stone temples began in the 5th century during the Gupta dynasty. Parvati Temple, built at the same time as Tigawa Temple, is 100 km from Khajuraho. This five sq m shrine, on a foundation platform, has a circumbulatory around it. Goddess Ganga and other deities are sculpted on its entrance walls.

Left: Entrance
Right: Sculptures on the wall.

NACHNA

CHAUMUKHA MAHADEVA TEMPLE ★
9th C/ Hindu

This is an old temple, very close to the Parvati Temple, built during the Pratihara dynasty. The *ardhamandapa* in front was built later. The shrine has a simple *shikhara*. In most Shiva temples, a *linga*, the symbol of Shiva, is deified. Here, heads have been sculpted on the *linga,* on four sides. Hence, it is called *Chaumukha Linga*.

Left: Full view
Right: Four-faced or *chaturmukha* Linga

TIGAWA ★

KANKALI DEVI TEMPLE
5th C/ Hindu

This square temple was the forerunner of stone temples of the Gupta dynasty. It is very well preserved and is similar to Buddhist Temple 17 of Sanchi. It does not have a circumbulatory, but it does have an *ardhamandapa*, which was originally just a pathway. The walls on both sides of the *ardhamandapa* were attached later. The roof is flat and there is no *shikhara*. As in Sanchi, lions are sculpted on top of the pillars. Though getting to Sanchi 200 km south of Khajuraho, is difficult, it is worth a visit.

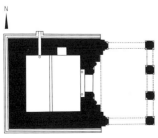

Floor Plan

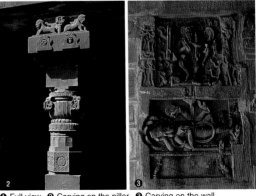

❶ Full view. ❷ Carving on the pillar. ❸ Carving on the wall.

CHANDREHI ★★

SHIVA TEMPLE ★
10th C/ Hindu
The circular plan of this unique temple, continues upwards as a *shikhara.* The walls divided into 16 parts, have no sculptures on them. From the *pradakshina* (open ambulatory of 27 spans), the domed ceiling of this early construction style is visible. Reaching the temples involves a 2-hour jeep ride, a boat-ride across the river and a 15-minute walk, with a village guide.

The circular *shikhara.*

Up: Full view from the roof. Down: The ceiling of the shrine.

CHANDREHI

HINDU MATHA *
972/ Hindu
This a rare Hindu monastery, which is very similar in plan, to that of Buddhist monasteries. As opposed to Buddhism, in Hinduism the caste of a person is decided by birth and there was no need for monasteries. There are two floors of monks' rooms and common rooms with a circumbulatory surrounding a courtyard. The sculptures at the entrance of this structure are excellent.

Courtyard viewed from the 2nd floor.

SIRPUR ★★

BUDDHIST MONASTERIES
7th C/ Buddhist
Two Buddhist monasteries located just 3 km away from the Lakshmana Temple have a typical layout of a monastery, where monks' rooms are around a courtyard. Hinduism and Buddhism thrived together in this place. The rooms are of brick and the pillars of stone. A statue of Buddha is deified here.

LAKSHMANA TEMPLE ★
7th C/ Hindu

This is the best-preserved temple among the brick temples of the early ages. While more than half the *mandapa* is destroyed, the shrine and the *shikhara* are intact. The horseshoe shaped *chaitya* windows, adopted from Buddhist architecture are merely decorative and not functional and the small entrances on the sides of the walls have some wonderful carving.

❶ The top of the *shikhara* is broken
❷ The *shikhara* has been constructed by placing horse-shoe shaped arches, one on top of another.
❸ Details of the murals on the brick walls.

RAJIVALOCHANA TEMPLE ★
8th C/ Hindu

On the banks of the River Mahanadi, 50 km southeast of Raipur, is Rajim village with many temples belonging to the 8th century. Since all of them are painted white, the minute carvings are lost. All of them are simple temples with more or less the same designs. They have the *chaitya* arch window motif as the main design. The main temple is the Rajivalochana Temple, belonging to the Vishnu group. Prayers are still being offered in this temple. The sculptures of *nagins* (snake goddesses), on the framework of the entrance to the shrine, are wonderful.

❶ The temple in the middle of the huge precincts.
❷ The *shikhara* painted white.
❸ Brahmins at the entrance of the temple, in charge of the offerings.

Gwalior, 120 km from Agra, to the north of the state, has a thousand-year history. It was originally a Hindu kingdom until Il-tutmish occupied it and brought in Islamic rule in 1232. Man Singh of the Tomar family of Rajputs, recaptured it and built the present fort. In 1516, it was taken over by the Lodhi dynasty and then by the Mughals. In 1754, Marathas occupied it, until 1804, when the British East India Company took over. During British rule, the chieftain of Gwalior continued to be in charge.

With such a checkered history, it is not surprising that architectural styles also intermingled. Every religion and age has left behind its special legacy.

Gwalior has a 100 m high, 3 km long hill, which forms a natural fort. Some Hindu temples and Man Singh fort occupy the top of the hill and there are Jain cave temples and *trithankara* statues at the foothills. Islamic buildings are in the northeast, starting with Jami Masjid. To the south is the new palace, new market place, etc.

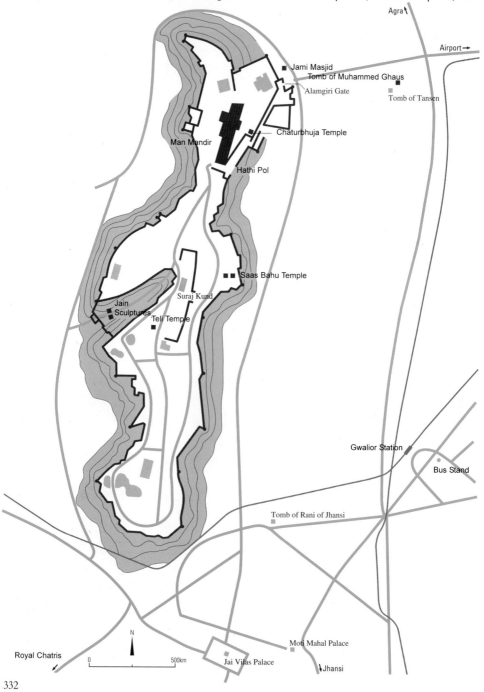

TOMB OF MUHAMMAD GHAUS ★
16th C/ Islamic

This structure, built during the reign of the Mughal Emperor Akbar, is a tomb of a Sufi saint. A square building where each side measures 30 m, it has in the corner and the middle of each side, *chhatris* on top of extended areas, which gives the impression of a very complex structure. The outer part looks like walls, but are actually *jalis* (stone lattice screens)which present an astounding sight from within. The tomb has thick walls and a large dome with blue tile cladding, surmounting it.

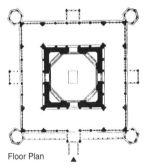

Floor Plan ▲

❶ Full view ❷ *Jali*, as seen from the inside. ❸ The *jali* from the outside.

ROYAL CHHATRIS ★
19th C/ Rajput

To the south of the city, is an area called Chhatri bazaar, which has some royal tombs, within a wide garden which were built in the 19th century. The largest, the tomb of Sayyaji Rao, is at the far end of a rectangular hall and has vertical *shikharas* crowning the roof. The tomb of Jiwaji Rao, who died earlier, is small, but of high quality. The interiors have beautiful murals.

❶ Sayaji Rao's tomb.
❷ The interior of Jiwaji Rao's tomb.
❸ The murals on the walls of Jiwaji Rao's tomb.

Jiwaji Rao's Tomb.

MAN MANDIR (PALACE) ★★
15th~16th C/ Rajput

Man Mandir, built by Man Singh is the most beautiful fort palace, in India. *Mandir* means temple, but the term is also used for large palaces. One should enter the Hindola gate, at the foot of the hill and travel up a curving road, looking down at the city nestling below. At 120 m the fort sits with its bastions that also double as buttresses at regular intervals. At the end of the road is Hathi Pol, the entrance to the palace. To the left of Hathi Pol is a group of temples and to the right is the palace complex. The first structure is the palace of Man Singh and then, the area for officials. At the far end is Vikramaditya palace. Man Mandir, made of yellow sandstone, has green and yellow tiles on its walls, with blue tiles as the main colour. The palace rooms open on to two courtyards. Islamic influence here is minimal and the delicate stone carving, though quite fantastic in appearance, differs from west Indian palaces.

❶ Hathi pol (gate) on the far left of the fort.
❷ The murals on the wall.
❸ The bastions have arches in the Hindu style and are embellished with tiles.
❹ The area of the court officials.
❺ The first courtyard can be seen from the entrance hall.
❻ The hall and rows of pillars facing the first courtyard.
❼ The hall on the far side of the 2nd courtyard.
❽ The elephant brackets facing the 2nd courtyard.

Floor Plan
❶ Hathi Pol
❷ 1st Courtyard
❸ 2nd Courtyard
❹ Officials' quarters
❺ Vikram Palace

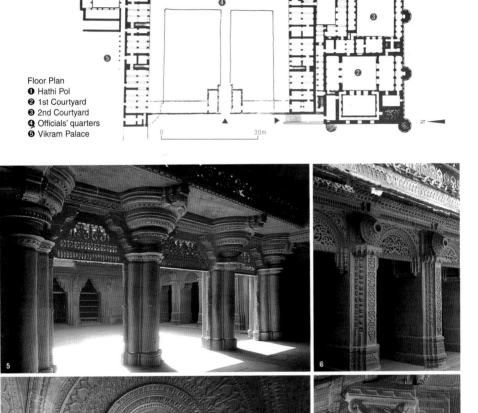

TELI KA MANDIR ★★
8th C/ Hindu

During the 8th century, Man Mandir was not just a palace; it was a citadel. Teli Temple inside the fort that rises up 25 m, is awe-inspiring. It is a tall vertical structure with a semi-cylindrical tower on top, similar to the one found on the Vaital Deul in Bhubaneshwar. It is called the *khakhara deol* in Orissa. The front *mandapa* is smaller than the *garbhagriha* and the roof is attached to the main building. The carvings on the exterior of the temple are more dense and of a higher quality than those in the interior. The design looks like a variation of the *chaitya* caves.

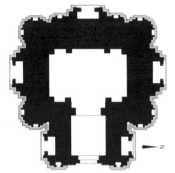

Floor Plan

An elaborately carved archway.   Up: South façade. Down: The murals at the entrance.

CHATURBHUJA TEMPLE
875 / Hindu

This is a rare stone temple on the way up to the fort. Carved out of sandstone this small temple reflects the style of the 9th century Pratihara dynasty, like the temples inside the fort. The *shikhara* is broken and simple repairs have been carried out. The base of the temple is a little weathered, but the sculptures have been preserved.

Up: Full view
Down: Porch

SAAS BAHU TEMPLES ★★
1093/ Hindu

In Nagda in west India, there is a pair of temples, one big and the other small, called Saas and Bahu (mother-in-law and daughter-in-law) Temple. The style, entirely different from that of the Teli Temple, is perhaps the style of the Kachhawaha dynasty, which came to power after the Pratihara dynasty weakened. The *shikhara* of the three-storeyed Saas temple, with a large *mandapa* is broken. The Bahu Temple though badly destroyed, has beautiful sculptures that are worth seeing on the entrance facing the *mandapa*.

❶ Saas Temple
❷ Bahu Temple
❸ Interior of the Bahu Temple.

The porch and stairwell in the Saas Temple.

ROCK CUT JAINA IMAGES
7th~15th C/ Jain

In this area, Hindus and Jains lived together in harmony. Though the original temple no longer exists, images of *tirthankaras* carved in various places on the rocky surface are still visible. The highest statue is 19 m high. Most of the temples are in groups and have pillars, beams and a canopy frame.

JAMI MASJID (FRIDAY MOSQUE)
1661/ Islamic

Mohammed Khan constructed the Jami Masjid near the entrance to the fort. Like the mosques in Delhi or Agra, it was constructed during the Mughal rule and is in the Mughal architectural style. This red sandstone structure has two minarets on either side of the *iwan* and is topped by a dome of white marble.

NARESAR ★

8

HINDU TEMPLES
8th~9th C/ Hindu

A group of Hindu temples older than the Teli Temple, nestle on the slope of a hill, 20 km from Gwalior. The temples are approached by climbing the hill for 30 m, a distance of 2 km down the highway. All ten small temples, reflect the style of the early Pratihara era. Among them is also a *Kharkhara Deul* type temple similar to the Teli temple.

SONAGIRI ★

9

JAINA TEMPLE CITY*
16th~17th C/ Jain

The Shatrunjaya Hill temple city has been reproduced in many places. There are 84 temples In Sonagiri, 60 km from Gwalior. Most of them were built recently and the influence of the Islamic style is apparent. Every single temple is white and the effect is spectacular.

A temple that resembles a Russian church

Up: Temples in the lower half of the city. Down: The temples at dusk.

GOVIND MANDIR (PALACE) ★★
1620/ Rajput

Govind Mandir, a fort palace built by Bir Singh Deo in Orchha is in the same style as Jahangir Mahal. It is a symmetrical square structure, heavily influenced by the Islamic style. The unique feature here is the high building at the centre of the square inner courtyard that is connected to the roofs of the surrounding buildings with bridges. This creates a vista and space that is entirely unique. A new palace in the city, a little further, is being used as the District offices. Inside the complex, encircled by a wall, are traditional temples and palaces in the western style, standing side by side.

❶ Southern façade.
❷ The high building in the middle of the courtyard.
❸ Bridges are suspended from all four sides of the high building in the centre of the courtyard.
❹ The uppermost rooms were the king's bedchambers.

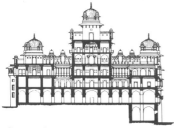

Cross-section

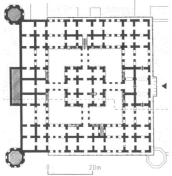

Floor plan

0   20m

New Palace

In the 16th century the capital of Bundelkhand, which was under the Rajput Bundela family, shifted to Orchha, 20 km south of Jhansi. Today, it has many ruins on the banks of the Betwa River. King Rudra Pratap Singh (1501-31) chose this place and his palace Ram Pal Mandir, is converted into a temple. Bir Singh Deo, the royal designer (1605-26) built Chaturbhuja Temple, Jahangir Palace and Govind Mandir, in Datiya, 30 km from Sanchi. On the southern side of the city are the four-storeyed royal tombs. Because of their friendship with the Mughals this was a very important kingdom. In the 18th century, it was attacked by the Marathas followed by the Jats and was finally forfeited in 1788.

Palace group seen from Chaturbhuja Temple.

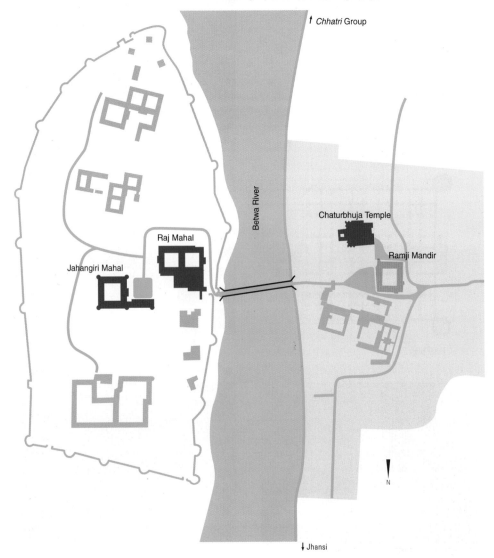

↑ *Chhatri* Group

Betwa River

Chaturbhuja Temple

Raj Mahal

Ramji Mandir

Jahangiri Mahal

N

↓ Jhansi

JAHANGIRI MAHAL AND RAJ MAHAL ★★
16th~17th C/ Rajput

Raj Mahal and Jahanagiri Mahal are two palaces, on an island surrounded by the Betwa River. A bridge connects the island to the main land. Construction of the Raj Mahal began in 1554 and was completed in 1591. This very large palace was built in the Rajput style.

Bir Singh Deo built Jahangiri Mahal to welcome the Mughal Emperor Jahangir. It is very Islamic in style with a symmetrical building surrounding a courtyard. The style reminds one of *madrassas* (schools). The whole structure is five storeys high and has nine domes crowning it. The palace in Datiya is designed in the same style but there, the building is in the centre of the courtyard.

Up: The hall facing the courtyard in Raj Mahal palace.
Middle: The room with murals in Raj Mahal palace.
Down: Jahangir Mahal palace with many *chhatris*.

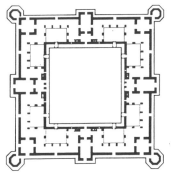

Floor plan

The symmetrical structure of Jahangir Mahal.

CHATURBHUJA TEMPLE ★
Beginning 17th C/ Hindu

This is a large building on the far side of the river, built by Bir Singh for the *Vaishnavites*. It stands much taller than the Ram Mandir palace nearby. The *mandapa* (prayer hall) is shaped like a cross and has a dome on top of an arched entrance structure and is very Islamic in style, with no sculptures of deities. This may be due to the effect of the temples of Brindavan which is a sacred place for believers of Krishna.

❶ Temple can be seen from the fort.
❷ The *mandapa* that appears very Islamic in style.
❸ The rear side of the temple.

Ceiling of the *mandapa*.

ROYAL CHHATRIS ★
17th C/ Rajput

The royal tombs are situated at the south of the city along with small *chhatris*. Most of them are uniformly five storeys high and are in a style similar to that of the Chaturbhuja Temple, even though the purpose of the two buildings differs. It is a *pancharatna* structure, but only the central structure has a *shikhara* and the other four have Islamic domes.

Right: The domes on four sides of the *shikhara*, which has *chhatris* on each of its four corners.
Left: Similar looking *chhatris*.

DASAVATARA TEMPLE ★

Circa late 5th C/ Hindu

Deogarh, 32 km from Lalitpur railway station, belongs to Madhya Pradesh, but is intricately linked with Uttar Pradesh.The ancient temple at the foot of the mountain, like the temple in Nachna, has a circumbulatory around the shrine but the roof is broken. Murals and sculptures on the doorway belong to the Gupta dynasty.

❶ Originally a *pancharatna* temple on a foundation platform.
❷ Gods protecting the doorway of the temple.
❸ The reclining Vishnu on the south wall.

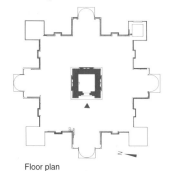

Floor plan

JAIN TEMPLES

9th~10th C/ Jain

All that remains of Deogarh fort on the hill, is a cluster of small Jain temples. The Pratihara dynasty and later the Chandela dynasty built temples and created statues. This city boasts of many statues of *tirthankaras*. The largest temple, Temple 12, built in 862, has a typical Pratihara-style *shikhara*.

❶ Temple group. Temple 12 can be seen on the far right.
❷ The sculpture on the wall of Temple 13.
❸ *Tirthankara* statues attached to the walls.

Site layout.

343

CHANDERI ★   13

BADAL MAHAL DARWAZA (DOOR)
1460/ Islamic

Chanderi, 40 km from Lalitpur, was the northern capital of Malwa. The fort on the hill has a unique entrance, Badal Mahal Darwaza that was built as a memorial after Independence. There are two arches suspended, one on top of another, on two vertical pillars. The arch on top has been carved through very delicately to create a *jali*.

CHANDERI   13

KOSHAK MAHAL (PALACE) ★
1445/ Islamic

Ruins of a beautiful palace can be seen in Fatabad, four km from Chanderi. Of the original 7-storeyed structure, only 4 storeys remain. The symmetrical cross plan has a hall that is open at the top and rooms surround it on all sides. The staircase is very rare for such an old structure. Arches where the halls cross each other, were also used as bridges.

Right: The rooms on the first floor.
Left: The central hall.

BADOH PATHARI ★   14

GADARMAL TEMPLE ★
9th C/ Hindu

Badoh and Pathari, two villages 20 km from Udaypur, have both Hindu and Jain temples. The largest temple called Gadarmal Temple, now abandoned, has the unique distinction of being an eight-shrine temple where three more shrines have been added to a *panchayatana* temple. A monumental temple, it had a very decorative *torana* on the extended foundation platform in front of the main temple. The surfaces around the doorway and pillars in the front are beautifully carved.

Part of the *torana*, in front of the temple.

The entrance doorway seen from the *mandapa*.

UDAYESVARA TEMPLE ⋆⋆
1080/ Hindu

Udayesvara Temple in Udaypur, 85 km to the northeast of Vidisha was built by King Udaydita of the Paramara dynasty. The sculptures in this red sandstone temple are comparable to those of the Khajuraho Temples. The temple is well preserved except for the *sabhamandapa* and the eaves that are broken. The plan has a *sabhamandapa* with a *garbhagriha* but has no *circumbulatory* around it. The *mandapa* has been extended in three directions and benches have been added. The *shikhara* is a collection of small vertical *shikharas*. A thick straight line accentuates the centre of each side. A small shrine facing the temple was perhaps a dancing hall or a *Nandi* shrine.

❶ Full view of the temple. The precincts are surrounded by a low fence.
❷ The mural on the *shikhara*.
❸ The interior of the small shrine in front of the temple.
❹ Entrance doorway of the shine as seen from the *mandapa*.

A row of small *shikharas*, one on top of another.

GYARASPUR ★★

16

AATA KHAMBA (EIGHT COLUMNS) AND MALADEVI TEMPLE ★
9th C/ Hindu

The *aata khamba* (eight columns) is the only remains of a large temple built by a Chandela prince Krishna in 983 A D. The engravings on the pillars and entrance doorway are of a very high quality. The Maladevi Temple is in the southeast of the village, near the mountain. One part of the temple is cut out of the rock. A circumbulatory goes around the shrine and the *mandapa* has two small balconies on both sides.

Aata khamba

Southern façade of the Maladevi Temple.

UDAYGIRI ★

17

CAVE TEMPLES
5th C/ Hindu

There is a group of very old Hindu cave temples, built during the Gupta reign, 4 km from Vidisha, on the rocky mountains. There are more than 20 small caves at this location. The beginning of Hindu art and architecture can be traced to these caves. Cave 5, has a 4 m high statue of *Varaha* (one of the reincarnations of Vishnu) while Cave 4, has a *linga* with a face carved on it. There is a Jain cave temple in the hills that looks like a natural cave.

The cave temples on a rocky hillside.

❶ Cave 6. ❷ *Varaha* statue in Cave 5. ❸ Entrance to Cave 19.

Before Buddha images were made, only symbols of Buddha like the *stupa, Bodhi*, Buddha wheels, etc, were worshipped. A *stupa* is a simple tomblike structure, little better than a burial tomb, which was used not only by Buddhists but also by Jains. When Buddha left for his heavenly abode, his ashes were buried in eight different *stupas*. It is said that Ashoka further divided and placed them in 84 *stupas*. Most of these *stupas* vanished as Buddhism weakened. There are *stupas* of various sizes in the Sanchi hills that belong to the period between BC-AD times. Sanchi was a large Buddhist centre with many temples and monasteries. While the remnants of the buildings are important sources of architectural history, the carvings on the *toranas* in front of the *stupas* are even more valuable. Very pastoral in nature, they depict cities, forts, the customs and lifestyles of the times, thereby acting as a historical resource. Sanchi, a village 95 km from Vidisha, is near the railway station, has many simple hotels and is a comfortable place to visit.

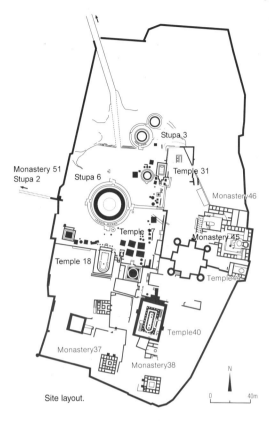

Site layout.

Stupa 1 on the left, part of Stupa 3 on the right and a *torana*.

STUPA 1 AND TORANA ★★★
3rd C BC - 2nd C AD/ Buddhist

The largest *stupa*, (36 m dia x 16m ht) was only half its present size when it was built in brick in the 3rd century BC, during the reign of Ashoka. The present *stupa* built in stone, in the 2nd century AD, during the reign of the Junga dynasty has at the apex a square stone with an umbrella-like canopy over it. The *stupa* stands on a high platform and has two levels. The chicken-coop design of the stone fence around the whole structure is adopted from a primitive style of wood fencing. All four entrances have magnificent *toranas* belonging to the 1st century, that stand on two pillars on which are suspended three long and thin flat stones.

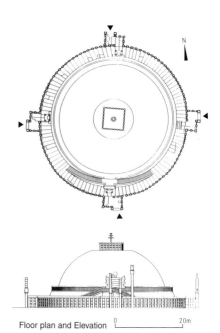

❶ *Toranas* with pillar capitals depicting Buddhist figures.
❷ Excellent sculpture of an *apsara* on the north *torana*.
❸ The centre of the north *torana* (half the wheel is broken).
❹ Pillar capital of the north *torana* with elephant heads facing in different directions.
❺ Relief on the west *torana*.

Floor plan and Elevation   0   20m

The south *torana* with the pillar capital of lions and the *stupa*.

STUPA 2, 3 AND TORANA ★
2nd C BC - 1st C AD/ Buddhist

Stupa 3 on a hill is modelled after Stupa 1 and has a foundation platform and *toranas*. Stupa 2, at the foot of the hill, has a wall around it but no *toranas*. The diameter of the *stupa* is 15 m and has the remains of the disciples of Buddha. Stupa 1 has a three-tiered umbrella-shaped canopy, but in contrast Stupa 3 has a very simple canopy and the one on Stupa 2 is broken. There are many small *stupas*, which indicate that *stupas* were venerated even before the advent of the Buddha. These scenes can be seen in the relief work on the *torana*.

❶ New temple can be seen behind Stupa 3.
❷ Top part of the *torana* depicting the worship of *stupas*.
❸ View at dusk of Stupa 3 and the *torana*.
❹ Stupa 2 at the foot of the hill.
❺ Fence of Stupa 2 with a medallion design.

TEMPLES 17, 18, 31
5th C/ Buddhist

Temple 17, the most important temple on the hill has influences of the Gupta dynasty (5th century). Temple 18 (7th century), of which a number of pillars still stand, has the *chaitya* style design of a circular rear and a straight front façade. The *stupa* at the far end of the temple is broken. Temple 31, which was built much later, has a statue of Buddha that was worshipped by many.

Interior of Temple 31.

Up: Temple 17 and 18.   Down: Temple 17.

MONASTERIES 45 AND 51
7th C/ Buddhist

Monastery 51 is the most orderly among the seven in Sanchi. It measures 33 m on all sides. There are various rooms surrounding a courtyard and the monks' rooms are in a row, separated by a corridor. The shrine was straight across the entrance.

Monastery 45 had a tower-like room on top of the shrine. Corridors, with three rooms on each side are extended on either side of the shrine.

Up: Ruins of monastery 51 on the hill.
Down: Buddha statue in the ruins of monastery 45.

A view of monastery 45.

DHAMNAR *

19

CAVE TEMPLES
4th-5th C/ Buddhist
DHARMANATHA TEMPLE *
8th~9th C/ Hindu

There are more than 50 small Buddhist caves and many small *stupas* on a laterite plateau, 20 km west of Shyamghar. Working from the top, a large rock-cut 8-shrined temple was carved out of the rocky mass. Unfortunately once the plaster peeled off the rough surface, the minute detailing of the sculpture was lost.

❶ Rock-cut temple of Dharmanatha.
❷ A sculpture of Buddha carved in laterite stone.
❸ Cave 12 is a group of small caves surrounding the *chaitya* cave.

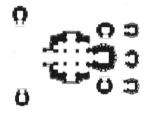

Floor plan of the rock-cut Dharmanatha Temple.

UJJAIN *

20

JANTAR MANTAR (OBSERVATORY)
1725/ Rajput

Samrat Yantra is one of the five observatories built in different places by Sawai Jai Singh II of Jaipur. As in the other places, the Samrat Yantra with its spread wings, sun clock etc, has been wonderfully executed. The instruments are all made of stone, plastered over and then painted white.

Narivaraya and Samrat Yantra

DHAR *

MOSQUES
15th C/ Islamic

Dhar, *en route* from Indore to Mandu, was the capital of the Dhar kingdom. The town has a fort, two Arab style mosques called Bhojshala Mosque and Lat Masjid, and the tomb of Saint Kamal Maula. The mosques built in the Gujarat style, have interconnecting prayer rooms, and a pillared circumbulatory around the courtyard.

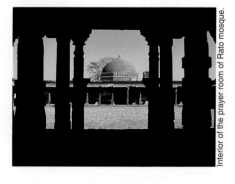

Interior of the prayer room of Rato mosque.

Ruins of Mandu, lie on a plateau, 40 km south of Dhar. The fort stretches along 40 km, 630 m above sea level and is protected by deep ravines. The original fort (10th century) was built by a Hindu king. In 1304, it was controlled by the Delhi Sultanate. When the Pathans invaded India, in 1401, the Malwa kingdom was freed from the rulers of Delhi through the Afghan leader, Dilawar Khan Ghauri. During his son, Hoshang Shah's reign, the capital shifted from Dhar to Mandu and thence started the golden age of Mandu, which continued for over a century and an architectural legacy we see today, was left behind. Finally in 1534, when the Mughals invaded Delhi, Mandu came under the control of the Mughals and construction activities declined. When the Mughal dynasty weakened and the kingdom went to the Marathas, the capital shifted back to Dhar and Mandu became a ghost town. Compared with the splendid architecture of India the Islamic architecture of Mandu is simple and practical. The rough-hewn and robust undecorated look is typical of the functional style of the 15th century.

Up: Delhi Gate that is the entrance into Mandu.
Down: View of Bhangi Darwaza

JAHAZ MAHAL PALACE ★★
15th C/ Islamic

Towards the left, on the main street of the fort, is the palace complex and immediately through the gate is Jahaz Mahal, the most delicately designed building in Mandu. It has no *jalis* or *jharokhas* and the glazed tiles are non-existent today.

Water has a close association with this palace, which is 120 m in length and faces a *talao* (man-made lake). It has pavilions extending onto the lakefront. The first and second floors have flower-shaped tanks through which water from the *talao* enters the garden. The water then passes through a water-channel with fountains and *chaddars* into another garden pond. The palace looks like a ship floating on the water and is therefore named Jahaz Mahal.

Jahaz Mahal sitting at the edge of a man-made lake.

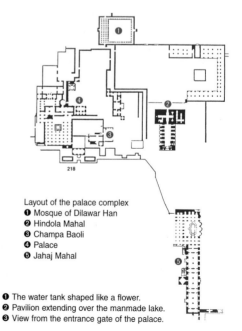

Layout of the palace complex
❶ Mosque of Dilawar Han
❷ Hindola Mahal
❸ Champa Baoli
❹ Palace
❺ Jahaj Mahal

❶ The water tank shaped like a flower.
❷ Pavilion extending over the manmade lake.
❸ View from the entrance gate of the palace.

HINDOLA MAHAL (PALACE) ★
1425 / Islamic

This T-shaped palace has small rooms and a staircase in the horizontal axis. The vertical axis is a single huge space. The strong pillars, which curve inwards and the double arches that are in a straight row, have no decorations at all and are purely functional in nature. The vaulted ceilings between the arches have completely collapsed because although the Hindu dynasty was destroyed, the technology of Islamic architecture had not been perfected yet.

The southern façade.

The interior of the large hall where the roof has collapsed.

CHAMPA BAOLI
(UNDER GROUND WELL) ★
Islamic

A large hole has been dug in the living area for a reservoir. This square tank is surrounded by 8 arches that give it a uniformly circular appearance. A grand staircase has been very skillfully incorporated into the walls, which leads to a big basement hall and connects to a gallery facing the *talao*. This space was used by the royal ladies to stay cool during summer and indulge in water sports.

The circular portion in the centre is the *baoli*.

The underground reservoir.

JAMI MASJID ★★
1454/ Islamic

The Jami Masjid is one of the many large structures in the village. This Arab-style mosque, the largest in Mandu, is very simple. Like other mosques in Mandu, this mosque too does not sport a minaret. Around the *mihrab* are some embellishments and the *mimbar* (preaching platform) is extremely lavish. The brackets are in the Hindu architectural style. Another feature of the mosque is the cubical entrance hall on the eastern side. It has a flight of stairs leading up to the entrance and a magnificent dome crowning it.

❶ Prayer hall facing the courtyard. Corridor in the north has collapsed.
❷ The main entrance hall in the east.
❸ Arched construction in the prayer room.
❹ *Mihrab* and *mimbar* in the prayer room.

TOMB OF HOSHANG SHAH *
1440/ Islamic
The tomb of Hoshang Shah is on the west side of the precincts of the Friday Mosque. When believers pray facing the *Quibla* wall in the west, it will also mean that they are praying to Hoshang Shah. When Hoshang Shah designed the mosque, he began the building of his own tomb at the same time. In Mughal constructions *chhatris* were built on the four corners of the big domes, but here instead of *chhatris,* small domes have been built.

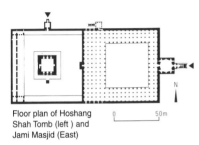

Floor plan of Hoshang Shah Tomb (left) and Jami Masjid (East)

Up: South view of the marble tomb. Down: Interior of the 15 m long tomb

ASHRAFI MAHAL (MADRASSA)
15th C/ Islamic
Muhammed I built the *madrassa* (school) facing the mosque, which is now abandoned. Muhammed Harji had also extended his tomb here in 1443, though nothing is left of that now. It had a 'victory tower' that was seven stories high. If it were standing it would have been on par with the *Vijaya Stambha* in Chittaurgarh.

The gate facing the Friday mosque

TOMB OF DARYA KHAN
1526/ Islamic
Of the many buildings constructed in the area, a small rectangular tomb remains, casting its reflection in the tank. Murals on the walls were decorated with enamelled tiles that are now lost. There are four similar small domes constructed on the four sides of the dome which is shaped like an arch.

MOSQUE OF MALIK MUGHITH ★
1432/ Islamic
This is one of the old mosques in Mandu. As with Dilawar Khan's Mosque, this one was also constructed with materials taken from a destroyed temple. All the decorations have been completely erased and it is difficult to say that the materials are from a temple. The pillars and beams are definitely Hindu. The whole edifice is built on a high plinth, below which are arcades and rooms. There is a large *caravan sarai* in front of the mosque.

❶ The interior of the prayer room. ❷ Entrance from the right. ❸ Domed ceiling.

DAI-KI-CHHOTI-BEHAN-KA MAHAL
Islamic
The beautiful tomb south of the *caravan sarai* has four entrance arches while the other four arches are just decorative. At that time, the whole octagonal tomb was decorated with blue tiles of which only the tiles on the lower edge still remain. The eaves have broken and only the brackets remain proving that it is difficult to build stone eaves with the construction technique normally used for wooden eaves.

PALACE OF BAZ BAHADUR ★
1509/ Islamic

Rewa Kund, a reservoir, is located 3 km south of the village. Near it is a small palace built by Baz Bahadur, who later became the king. Of the two courtyards within, the larger one has a water tank. This tank was filled with water, from Rewa Kund with the help of a water-drawing device. Two pavilions face each other on the terrace.

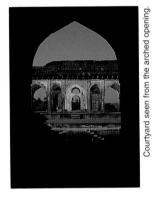

Courtyard seen from the arched opening.

Up: View from Roopmati Palace. Down: Courtyard with the tank.

ROOPMATI'S PAVILIONS (PALACE) ★
15th C/ Islamic

To to the south of Baz Bahadur Palace on a hilltop, within the fort, is Roopmati Palace. The double-storeyed edifice has two pavilions on the terrace, facing each other. Each pavilion has 12 pillars with arches and a dome on top. Such pavilions are called *bharaha dhari,* which means 12 doorways.

Northern end of the palace.

Up: Pavilion on the terrace. Down: The view from Baz Bahadur Palace.

Maharashtra means Maratha kingdom and the spoken language is Marathi. During the 2nd half of the 14th century, the Mughals conquered the Deccan plateau. Shivaji fought against them and established the Maratha kingdom, which was mainly Hindu. His base of operations being the mountains, Shivaji built forts in Raigad and other places and used guerrilla warfare. When the Mughals weakened, this area was taken over by the British. The Maratha alliance then made Pune their base and fought 3 battles against the British. Shivaji, is the first national hero, who fought against the British for India's Independence. Even now Maratha temples can be seen in Pune and Mahuli.

Portugal gifted Mumbadevi (Bombay) as Catherine de Braganza's dowry when she married Charles II in the 17th century. Now called Mumbai, it was made up of seven islands connected with reclaimed land. It was developed as a metropolis under British rule. Mumbai, the commercial capital of India has many colonial buildings, but more famous in Maharashtra are its rock-cut cave temples. There were also many man-made caves. These caves, where the monks renounced the world and lived together, came to be called *viharas* and the caves

where *stupas* were built and prayers offered, were called *chaitya* caves. *Chaitya* caves had high ceilings and were monumental. The oldest Buddhist monasteries in Gandhara are made of brick. Hence the cave monasteries in the Deccan plateau are second in the hierarchy of monasteries. Rock caves are found all over India, but the greatest number is in the Deccan plateau.

The most interesting aspect of the cave temples, with their pillars and beams is that they were built according to wooden structures. Wooden structures built using this technology have long since broken, but these rock caves are a historical resource. When Hinduism adopted the idea of cave temples, the caves were transformed dynamically and became rich and bright. Hindus went one step further and started carving on the rocks from the top, thus creating the "rock-cut temples" that are 3-dimensional and look exactly like the temples built in masonry. The Kailasanatha Temple in Ellora is the largest of these rock-cut temples. Evolving from cave temples to rock cut temples was like evolving from the Stone Age to the Middle Ages.

Up: The statue of *Nataraja*(dancing Shiva).
Down: Fort of the Maratha kingdom built by Shivaji, 17th century, Pratapgarh.

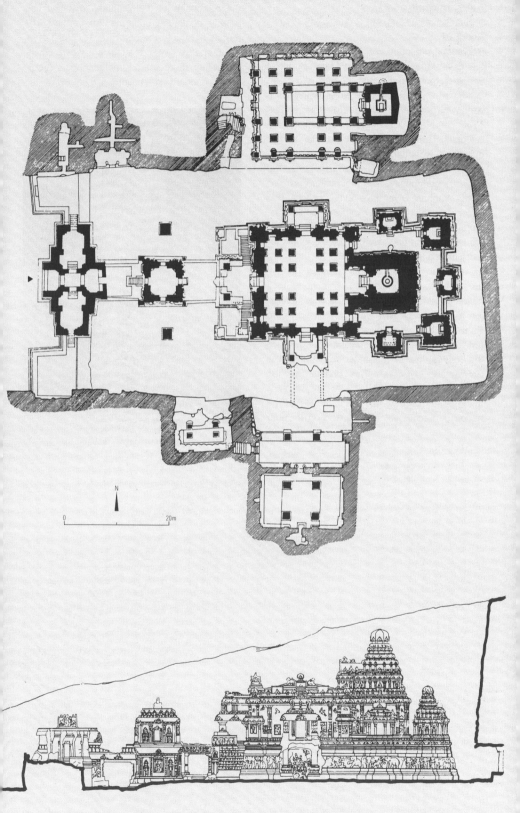

Plan and elevation of Kailasanatha rock-cut Temple.

AJANTA ★ ★ ★

CAVE TEMPLES ★★★
2nd C BC-1st C BC, 5th C AD to 6th C AD/
Buddhist

Buddhist art is found in Sanchi, Bodhgaya and the cave temples of Ajanta. Many Buddhist temples, monasteries and *stupas* had been destroyed, but in contrast, cave temples are very well preserved. There are around 1200 cave temples, 75 percent of which are Buddhist. The caves at Ajanta, display a high quality of workmanship helped no doubt by royal patronage and support from the business community. The mountains encircled by the Waghora River have 30 such caves. This major Buddhist centre exhibiting sculptures, murals and decorations was abandoned in the 7th century and was overrun by the jungle for more than a thousand years.

In 1819, an English hunter chanced upon it during a hunting expedition. The world took notice and started surveying and documenting the murals. The caves were developed in the Early and the Later Phases. The Early Phase (2nd-1st C BC) is the Hinayana period where the caves were monasteries during the Satavahana dynasty. This phase saw the development of Caves 8 -13, except Cave 11. In the 5th-6th century AD, during the Mahayana period, magnificent *viharas* were built under the patronage of the Vakataka dynasty. This activity continued until the 7th century. The murals belong to the Later Phase. While there are 5 *chaitya* caves, the rest are *vihara* caves. Altogether there are 11 monasteries. Ajanta village once a trading centre is 8 km away.

Sculpture on the walls of the caves.

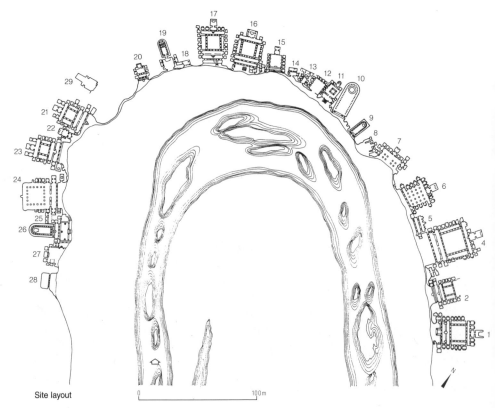

Site layout

0   100m

❶ Full view of the rock cave temples seen from the hill opposite. Following the rainy season, the hills are a lush green.
❷ A view of Caves 24, 25, 26 and 27. Cave 26 is the *chaitya* cave.
❸ Cave groups seen from the terrace of Cave 1.
❹ Murals on the veranda of Cave 2.
❺ Mithuna statues sculpted on the capital of a pillar of Cave 24.
❻ The unfinished interior of Cave 24.

CAVE 1 ★★
5th C/ Buddhist

Viharas are cave temples where monks who renounced the world, lived. Monks' rooms are located around an open courtyard. Since the courtyard in a cave is not open to the sky, rooms surround it on three sides and the courtyard extends into a veranda on the fourth side, for ventilation and light. In Ajanta, the walls have decorative murals of a very high quality, belonging to the 6th century, depicting the Jataka tales.

❶ The front looks like a pillared corridor. The porch in the centre is broken.
❷ Walls and ceiling inside is fully painted.
❸ Capitals of a pillar on the veranda.

CAVE 2 ★★
5th C/ Buddhist

Cave 2 is similar to Cave 1 except that it is smaller. It has 12 pillars around the central space as against 20 in Cave 1. Once the object of worship changed from *stupas* to images of Buddha, monasteries also designed shrines where a statue of Buddha would be installed at the back and images of Buddha were painted on walls, giving the impression of a Buddha temple.

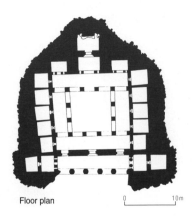

Floor plan   0   10m

Up: Shrine at the far end of the front room Down: Room with murals.

CAVE 7 ★
5th C/ Buddhist
This cave is not a normal *vihara* cave but is wide and deep. The 2nd porch from the veranda has been extended and is supported on 4 pillars. Since there is no central hall behind this, the statue on the altar gets a lot of light. It has very few monks' rooms and has an image of Buddha with his hand raised in blessing. This cave has many images of Buddha in the cells and in the antechamber. The images were also plastered like the pillars and painted.

Pillared porch in the front.

Statue of Buddha with his hand raised in blessing.

CAVE 9 ★
1st C, BC/ Buddhist
In the early days, since images of Buddha were not worshipped, *stupas* were treated as objects of worship. These sacred caves were called *chaitya* caves. There are two such caves from the early days, Cave 9 and Cave 10. The overall appearance is similar but a distinct style called the *chaitya*-cave style was established. The roof is high and vaulted and the top of the façade had a horse-shoe shaped window, called the *chaitya* window, which let in a lot of light. A row of pillars meets behind the *stupa* where the rear of the hall is semi-circular. As in Sanchi, the *stupa* here is shaped like an earthen mound. On top of the *stupa,* the square *harmika* gets larger as it goes up. The umbrella like canopy is broken. The Buddha paintings found on the walls were painted later.

Up: Row of small decorative *chaitya* windows below the large *chaitya* window.
Down: The *chaitya* cave is 14 m deep.

CAVE 12 ★
2nd C, BC/ Buddhist

Cave 12, the largest among the older *vihara* caves was mainly used as living quarters and hence is very simple. The roof is flat and the central hall does not have pillars like in the Later Phase There are 12 rooms facing a connecting hall. On the wall above the doorways are a row of horse-shoe shaped decorations in relief.

CAVE 16 ★
5th C/ Buddhist

Inscriptions written by Varahadeva (minister of Vakataka dynasty), and those found in Cave 17, shed light on the era of these cave temples. Cave 16 and Cave 17 each has 20 pillars surrounding a central hall. Caves 16 and 17 have 14 and 16 monks' rooms, respectively. This large shrine has so much space; one can walk around the Buddha statue.

CAVE 19 ★★
5th C/ Buddhist

There are three *chaitya* caves of the Later Period. Cave 19 is small in scale and similar to cave 9 of the Early Phase. The style, however is different, but it has a very refined appearance. It is perhaps the only cave temple in Ajanta that has a high quality finish. On the façade, just below the high *chaitya* window is a porch and it has many images of Buddha with carving of a very high quality. The row of pillars, and the frieze on top also exhibit very high quality carving. What is different from the Early Phase is that a statue of Buddha has been sculpted on the *stupa*. This is because the Buddhist priests here worshipped the statue of Buddha more than they worshipped the *stupa*.

The rock-cut beams on the ceiling shows that a wooden temple was the inspiration for this temple. None of the wooden temples of that time exist today. These rock cave temples give an idea of what they must have looked like.

Façade surrounding the front courtyard.

The umbrella-like canopy above the stupa in Cave 19 almost touches the ceiling.

CAVE 26 ★★
5th C/ Buddhist

Cave 26, a large *chaitya* cave was built before Buddhism declined. At the apex of Buddhist architectural evolution, in comparison with Cave 19, its entire surface is covered with excellent carving. Unfortunately the pillars and roof are broken. The ceiling has carved wooden beams which make it appear like a wooden temple.

This cave, with 28 pillars, has a depth of 20 m. The elongated *stupa* has statues of Buddha carved on the sides. In the front is an intriguing statue of Buddha, carved to look as if it were inside a shrine. The top of the shrine reminds one of south Indian styles, like the Ganesha Ratha - Mahabalipuram.

❶ Frieze sculptures on top of a row of pillars.
❷ Canopy on top of the *stupa* is broken.
❸ The magnificent façade with no veranda.
❹ The 7 m high reclining Buddha in the left corridor.

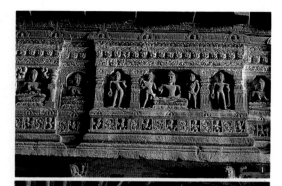

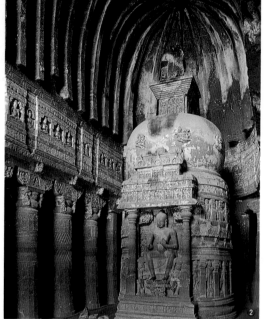

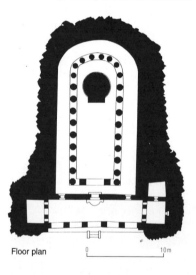

Floor plan   0 |————————————| 10 m

PITALKHORA ★★

CAVE TEMPLES ★
2nd C, BC to the 1st C, AD/ Buddhist

The Pitalkhora group of caves is about 11 km on a side road, about 70 km down the Aurangabad-Ellora road. There are 13 caves in all. They were built by the Satavahana dynasty at roughly the same time as the early Ajanta caves. The quality of the rock of the hill is such that with most of the facade broken, they look like natural caves. Cave 3, one of the 2 main caves, is a *chaitya* cave, with a broken *stupa* but the murals are still intact. Cave 4, the other main cave is also a *chaitya* cave with a wide terrace in the front. There is a staircase from below to the first floor and the many Buddhist figures to the right look as if they are supporting the entrance. What is most interesting in the monks' room is that apart from the reclining platforms and shelves carved out of the rock, even the ribs on the ceiling, usually found in wooden constructions, have been carved out.

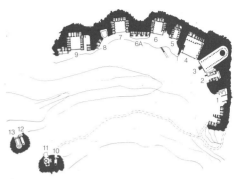

Site Plan

❶ Group of caves lined up in the valley.
❷ The top portion of Cave 4 is broken.
❸ Buddhist figures are painted on the pillars of Cave 3.
❹ A monks' room in Cave 2. Reclining platforms and shelves have been cut out from the rock.
❺ Rafters on the ceiling of the monks' rooms in Cave 4.

ELLORA ★ ★ ★

Ellora caves, located 30 km northwest of Aurangabad, make up one of the major cave temple groups in India. They belong to a much later period, than the Ajanta caves. In Ellora there are Buddhist, Hindu as well as Jain cave temples, spread over a stretch of 2 km. These are not just cave temples but also temples sculpted out of rock and are much richer in style and detail.

Caves 1-12 are Buddhist, 13-29 are Hindu and 30-34 are Jain, excavated in that order.

Some believe that the Hindu temples were constructed before the Buddhist temples, but since there are no inscriptions to that effect, it is difficult to determine exactly when they were built. Perhaps, all religions thrived peacefully at that time because the dynasty in power was tolerant of different religions.

The first caves were excavated during the rule of the Chalukyan dynasty. The rock cut Kailasanatha Temple, in the centre of the group, is a fine example of the south Indian architectural style promoted by the Rashtrakutas.

The circular carving, not seen in Buddhist architecture till date, can be seen in the front hall, in the Nandi shrine and all over the large Kailasanatha Temple. Jain temples that were built later, also adopted this design. There are three unfinished, half-cut temples in the vicinity.

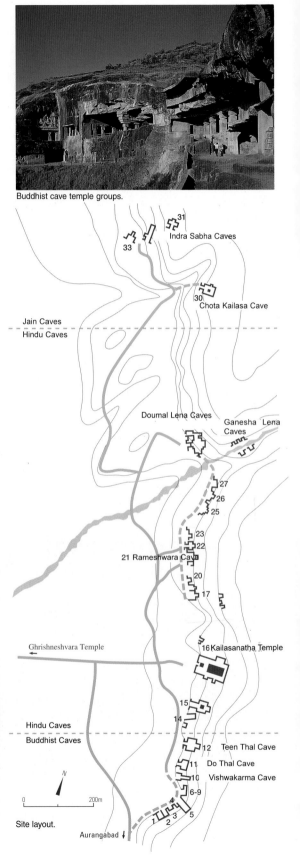

Buddhist cave temple groups.

Beautiful sculpture of an *apsara* in Cave 21.

BUDDHIST CAVE TEMPLES
7th~8th C/ Buddhist

The first thing that catches one's eye in Ellora, are the twelve Buddhist cave temples. Since they belong to the later stage in the evolution of Buddhist architecture, they differ greatly from the Buddhist cave temples in Ajanta.

The layout ranges from *viharas* surrounding courtyards as in Caves 2 and 3, to *viharas* without courtyards, but with a Buddhist hall as in Caves 11 and 12. The only *chaitya* cave is Cave 10. It has a picturesque but monotonous façade on the far end of the porch instead of the horseshoe - shaped *chaitya* window. In front of the large *stupa*, Buddhist statues have been erected that detract from the 'larger than life' look of the *stupa*. In Caves 11 and 12, pillared porches have been added on all four sides. Pillars placed very close together makes the interior a little claustrophobic.

The influence of the Hindu architectural style is strong with graven images of amorous couples. A far cry from the early days of Buddhist asceticism. One could say that the decline of Buddhism is reflected in its architecture.

❶ There must have been an auditorium at the far end of the deep Cave 5.
❷ The façade of the three storeyed construction in Cave 11 (Do Taru cave).
❸ View of the interior from the balcony of Cave 10.
❹ Façade of Cave 10, Vishwakarma Cave Temple.

HINDU CAVE TEMPLES ★★
6th~9th C/ Hindu

There are 17 Hindu caves in Ellora. They start with the Buddhist caves and change to Hindu temples half-way down the line. Besides these, above the waterfall is a large group of small caves, Ganesha Lena.

Hindu temples do not have monasteries, but every cave enshrines deities. This may be the reason why Hindu cave temples are more dynamic than Buddhist caves. The statues in the caves are rich in quality and large in number. This may also be because Hinduism is a more worldly and active religion as compared with Buddhism, which stresses on meditation as the means to salvation. Hinduism which adopted the idea of cave temples from Buddhism, felt dissatisfied with the limited space available and improvised on it to suit their ideology. Having more than one central axis was one of these innovations. Materialization of the grand temple in Cave 16 marks the end of the age-old cave temple architecture.

Up: Sculptures, Cave 14 (7th C). Down: Pillars, Cave 17 (8th C).

CAVE 21 ★
6th C/ Hindu

The style of Cave 21 is the basic Hindu temple style with a *mandapa* (hall), *garbagriha* (shrine), a *pradakshina path* (circumbulatory) around the shrine and small shrines on either side of the *mandapa*. Though a small temple, the carvings are exquisite. The *apsaras* on the pillars outside and the Mother goddess on the right side of the small shrine are examples of exquisite carving. Since it is a Shiva temple, the *linga*, is enshrined here.

Apsaras and the Mother goddess statues.

Up: *Nandi* in front of Cave 21. Down: Shrine in the *mandapa*.

GANESHA LENA GROUP
9th C/ Hindu
There are twenty small caves on the mountain, above Cave 28. They surround the flowing river, making it look like a pond. These are Hindu caves belonging to a later era. Other than the murals, there is nothing else of merit. The atmosphere of the place though, is wonderful, with the sound of flowing water and a view that is out of this world. Upstream, is another group of caves called the Jogeshwari group.

Small caves surround the river, making it look like a pond.

CAVE 29 (DHUMAR LENA CAVE) ★★
6th C / Hindu
Barring Kailasa Temple, this is the largest rock cave temple. The shrine of Shiva is at the end of a pillar lined *mandapa*. There is one more axis, which is perpendicular to the main axis. As in Elephanta caves, the space looks cavernous and dynamic. The height of the ceiling is 5.3 m. The sculptures are similar to those in Cave 21.

The simplicity of the southwest façade.

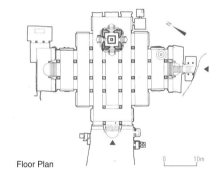

Floor Plan

0   10m

Large statues of gods are sculpted around the shrine.

KAILASANATHA TEMPLE ★★★
8th C/ Hindu

This temple is built using different styles of construction. Visitors stand in awe and gaze fixedly at this architectural feat. The 47 m high and 85 m deep temple has been carved out of a basalt hill. The result is a 32 m high temple, with shrines, *stambhas* (memorial pillars) and elephants. Inside the temple, the *mandapa* and the shrine have carved pillars and beams. There is a turret in the front, followed by a Nandi shrine, *mandapa* and *vimana* (shrine). Around the *vimana* are five small shrines. The surrounding rocky walls, closed corridors and additional cave temples were built in two stages.

This project was started by Krishna I (757- 773) of the Rashtrakuta dynasty. His rule had also spread to southern India, hence this temple was excavated in the prevailing style. Its builders modelled it on the lines of the Virupaksha Temple in Pattadakal.

Being a south Indian style temple, it does not have a *shikhara* common to north Indian temples. Instead, the shrine extends to the top, over which is a circular stone, resembling a mountain peak. Kailasa is the holy mountain in the Himalayas and the abode of Lord Shiva. Since Shiva is the temple deity, the whole temple is an analogy of the holy mountain.

(Floor plan & cross-section-page 361)

❶ Full view. The palace is inside the tower gate.
❷ The *stambhas* on either side of Nandi are 17 m high.
❸ *Vimana*, *mandapa* and the *Nandi* shrine.
❹ Porch on the north of the 2nd floor of the *mandapa*.
❺ There are many shrine shapes carved on the outer walls.
❻ The pillar-beam style of stone temples is seen inside the *mandapa*.

ELLORA

JAIN CAVE TEMPLES ★★
9th C/ Jain

Amoghavarsha I of the Rashtrakuta dynasty (814-878) embraced Jainism and was a generous patron of Jain art. There are five Jain cave temples at the northern end of Ellora that lack the superior construction techniques of Hindu or Buddhist temples. The interior however is of a high quality. A unique feature is the number of statues of *tirthankaras* that are carved everywhere. Cave 30 is a miniature of Cave 16 and is called *Chota* (small) Kailasa.

CAVE 32 ★★
9th C/ Jain

This is a very interesting cave. IT has a court- yard in front, which has a rock-cut shrine and a *stambha*. The *chaumukha* shrine is in the unique Jain style, with the four-faced statue of a *tirthankara* facing all four directions. This is the forerunner of the style that was popularized in western India many centuries later. On the first floor of the cave is a regular temple, while the 2nd floor is a hall with richly carved pillars.

CAVE 33 ★ AND CAVE 34 ★
9th C/ Jain

Cave 33 and Cave 34 have a common second floor, which is so spacious that it belies the fact that these are two separate caves. Though the cave is small, the sculptures are superb.

❶ Cave 30 -*Chota* Kailasa Temple.
❷ The *stambha* and main shrine behind the gate of Cave 32.
❸ Sculpture on the *chaumukha* shrine.
❹ Interior of the second floor of Cave 32.
❺ Interior of Cave 34.
❻ Façade of Cave 33.
❼ Kubera statue in Cave 33.
❽ *Tirthankara* statue in Cave 33.

The courtyard of Cave 32

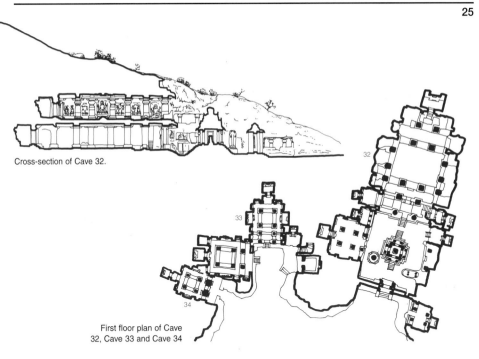

Cross-section of Cave 32.

First floor plan of Cave
32, Cave 33 and Cave 34

AURANGABAD ★★

Aurangabad has temple groups that date back to the period between 1st and 7th century A.D. With Aurangabad as a base, it is possible to visit Ajanta and Ellora. Emperor Aurangzeb, made Aurangabad his headquarters during his attempt to conquer south India. The new city with the railway station is in the south, while the old Mughal city is in the north. Aurangzeb's wife's tomb is the most magnificent monument there, while, his own tomb, located 26 km northwest of the city, in Khuldabad, is very simple. After Aurangzeb's death, the Nizam of Hyderabad ruled until Independence.

To cave Temples ↑
Ajanta ↗
Bibi ka Maqbara ■
■ Jami Masjid
Pan Chakki ■
← Ellora
● Bus stand
Airport →
Aurangabad station
N
0   2km

Jami Masjid (1612)

AURANGABAD

CAVE TEMPLES ★
1st~7th C/ Buddhist

There are two groups of five temples each, 1.3 km away from Aurangabad. Cave 4 is the *chaitya* cave (1st century BC/AD). The others are all *viharas* (5th -7th century AD), belonging to the Vakataka dynasty and the Kalachuri dynasty. Cave 6 and 7 have verandas with a rear courtyard-type hall. The Buddhist shrine reflects the days when monasteries became palaces, during the period of Buddhism's decline.

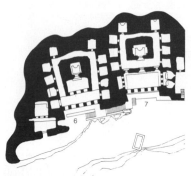

Floor plan of the Caves 6 & 7.

Up: Cave 4 -*Chaitya* shrine. Down: Verandah of Cave 7.

BIBI-KA-MAQBARA ★★
1678/ Islamic

When Emperor Aurangzeb's Queen, Rabia Daurani died, the crown prince engaged architect Ata Ullah to construct her tomb. The white marble tomb is centered in a 274 x 457 m garden, resembling the Taj Mahal in Agra. It has four minarets along the central axis. The building does not have the Taj Mahal's grace. The minute details on the structure are also not of the same standard as those in the Taj Mahal, perhaps, because the Mughal dynasty had started weakening militarily and culturally.

❶ The water channel with a row of fountains facing the tomb.
❷ The interior of the tomb.
❸ Embellishment on the walls of the side wing.

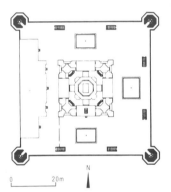

0   20m

N

Floor plan

The view of the tomb from the garden is fantastic.

DAULATABAD ★★

27

CITADEL (FORTRESS) ★★
14th C/ Islamic

Daulatabad, 13 km from Aurangabad was formerly a Hindu stronghold called Deogiri. In 1326, Mohammed-bin-Tuglaq, shifted his capital here, from Delhi and it was renamed Daulatabad (city of riches). The citadel is located on a 180 m high hill, which itself acts as a fortress.

Mohammed-bin-Tuglaq, built a fort city below the fort, where all the residents of Delhi migrated, but the city was later abandoned and everybody had to return to Delhi. From the fort walls, palace, mosque etc. that are left behind, it is easy to imagine an Islamic town of the Middle Ages. Chand Minar that can be seen from a great distance is 60 m high. It was a victory tower built by Alaud-din of the Bahmani dynasty, in 1435. After the Qutb Minar, it is the 2nd tallest minaret in India.

Up: Distant view of the Daulatabad Fort.
Middle: The city as seen from the fort.
Down: Seen on the other side of the strong walls is the citadel where the palace is situated.

Chandminar on the main street.

KHULDABAD (RAUZA) ★

28

TOMB OF AURANGZEB
1707/ Islamic

Situated 13 km from Daulatabad is Khuladabad, which is so full of tombs that it is also called *Rauza*. The main tomb is that of the Mughal Emperor, Aurangzeb. Since he was a devout Muslim who frowned upon rich grandeur, respecting his beliefs, his tomb is simple, but elegant, with only a stone *jali* (lattice wall) surrounding it.

PANDU LENA CAVE TEMPLES ★★
1st C, BC-2nd C, AD/ Buddhist

Nasik has some important Buddhist caves (1st century BC-5th century AD), on the mountain side, 8 km, southwest of the city. There are 24 caves of which, Cave 18 is the *chaitya* cave and the rest are monasteries or *viharas*.

The cave temples belong to the same era as Karli in the west. The capitals of pillars have *stupa*-like designs, over which are carved statues of human beings, sitting on different animals. The same design is repeated on the entrance of Cave 18, below the *chaitya* window, which is rare. It is also rare that there are symmetrical staircases going up to the caves on either side. Inside Cave 3, on the wall of the central hall, a giant *stupa* has been carved that is worth seeing. This was perhaps, the first step towards the designing of the latter day Buddhist shrines.

Up: Façade of Cave 18.(1st century BC)
Middle: Capital of a pillar head in Cave 10. (2nd century AD)
Down: Façade of Cave 3. (2nd century AD)

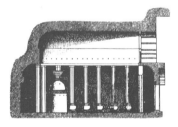

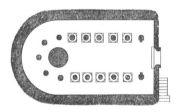

Cross section and floor plan of Cave 18

Central hall in Cave 3

GONDESHWARA TEMPLE ★★
11th C/ Hindu

Gondeshwara Temple is a *panchayatana* (five shrine) temple built by the Yadava dynasty. It consists of a shrine and a *mandapa*. There are porches on three sides of the *mandapa* that act as the entrance. There are four shrines with porches in the four corners. Surya, Vishnu, Parvathi and Ganesha are enshrined in them respectively. All the shrines have a porch and face each other, giving these temples a certain sense of harmony.

❶ Full view. The top of the *shikhara* is broken.
❷ The temple, with a broken roof seen from the eastern entrance.
❸ Capital of a pillar inside the temple.

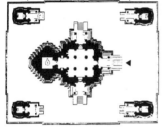

Floor Plan

CAVE TEMPLES ★
2nd BC~2nd C AD/ Buddhist

Situated in Junnar, 80 km from Pune, is a 300 m high hill fort looking down majestically at the countryside, where the Maratha chieftain Shivaji, was born. In the surroundings are some Buddhist temples divided into three groups. On the eastern side is the Buta Lena group, on the western side is the Tulja Lena group and on the other side of the river, up the mountainside is the Ganesha Lena Group. There are more than 100 caves, most of them are small and were all dwellings of monks who had renounced the world. Since the Ganesha Lena group belongs to the later days, the capitals of the pillars here have decorations resembling the Nasik style. The *chaitya* cave is cave 6 and cave 7 is the biggest *vihara* cave.

❶ Buta Lena Group. On top of the cave 45, the *chaitya* window design and the *stupa* design are carved.
❷ Ganesha Lena Group. On cave 6 has a *chaitya* design carved.
❸ The row of pillars and the stupa inside cave 6.

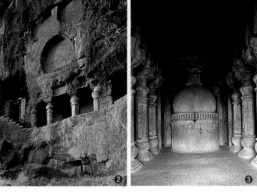

Bombay, now called Mumbai, is the commercial capital of India. It was originally seven islands, when the Muslim Sultan, Bahadur Shah ceded the town to the Portugal Emperor Hoas III. In 1661, it was given as dowry to the British king, Charles II, when he married the Portuguese princess Catherine. It thus came under the control of the British East India Company. In the 19th century, the trading harbour and many colonial buildings were constructed here. Fort, on the southern side of VT, has many colonial buildings. Other than Hindus, many other communities like the Parsis (Zoroastrians), Christians and Jains made a living by doing business here. Mumbai has very few religious buildings. Post-independence, has seen high-rise buildings come up on the seafront, which are noteworthy. Population:1,50,00,000 people.

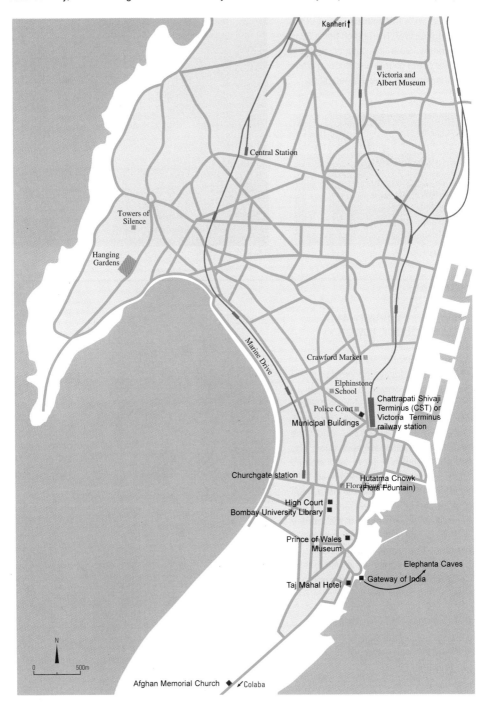

Kanheri↑

Victoria and
Albert Museum

Central Station

Towers of
Silence

Hanging
Gardens

Marine Drive

Crawford Market

Elphinstone
School

Police Court

Municipal Buildings

Chattrapati Shivaji
Terminus (CST) or
Victoria Terminus
railway station

Churchgate station

Hutatma Chowk
Flora (Floral Fountain)

High Court
Bombay University Library

Prince of Wales
Museum

Elephanta Caves

Taj Mahal Hotel

Gateway of India

N

0   500m

Afghan Memorial Church ◆ ⁄ Colaba

AFGHAN MEMORIAL CHURCH OF ST. JOHN THE BAPTIST ★★
1858/ Colonial
by Henry Conybeare

The British Church Architects Association designed this church in order to introduce into India, the British Gothic style prevalent in London, in 1848. This style was incorporated into the church in south Bombay, built to commemorate the soldiers killed in the First Afghan War. The church has a 58 m high belfry. Both the interior and the exterior of the church are made of stone and the windows have stained glass.

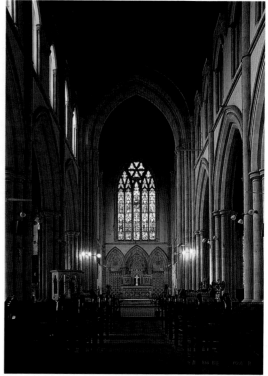

The entrance porch.

The main hall that has just been restored.

UNIVERSITY LIBRARY AND RAJABAI CLOCK TOWER ★★
1878 / Colonial
by George Gilbert Scott

The university facing the *maidan* (open ground) has a library building with an impressive clock tower. George Gilbert, who was a Gothic revival architect, designed this structure and the church-like auditorium next door. The second floor has a room with stained glass windows. The clock tower, now called the Rajabai Tower, is 80 m high and below it is the entrance to the library. The workmanship of the tracery and the small white marble towers, is excellent. This masterpiece of Scott's, is a well-known landmark. It is said that he designed the building without coming to India.

❶ The entrance below the tower with the auditorium on the far right.
❷ The top of the Rajabai Tower.
❸ Reading room of the library.

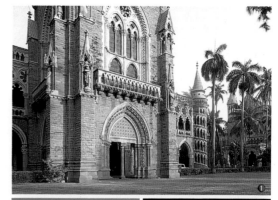

VICTORIA TERMINUS ★★
1888/ Colonial
by Frederick William Stevens
The two main railway stations in Mumbai, were projects where the British Empire could show their prestigious standing in India. Frederick William Stevens designed both of them. Victoria Terminus now Chattrapati Shivaji Terminus (CST) has a European flavour mixed with Indian traditional styles. The architect was 30 years old when he started this structure. In the 10 years that it took to complete the structure, it became the most majestic Victorian-Gothic building in India.

The central dome.

Up: Southern façade. Down: The Municipal offices across the terminus.

MUNICIPAL BUILDINGS ★
1893/ Colonial
by Frederick William Stevens
Stevens (late 19th century), studied in Bath and came to India at the age of 19 where he excelled in his profession. Besides designing two major railway stations, he designed the Municipal Offices that stand in front of Victoria Terminus. The symmetrical structure is on a triangular piece of land, with roads on both sides. The monumental structure competes with Victoria Terminus in grandeur. Churchgate station, is in the Indo-Saracenic style, with domes on either side.

Churchgate Terminus

The Municipal Building, 78 m high.

HIGH COURT ★
1879/ Colonial
by James A. Fuller
Compared with the work of Scott and Stevens, the work of Fuller at the age of 50 is quaint, rustic but magnificent. Fuller came to India at the age of 20 and restored many buildings, including the University Library and the High Court (Old Army Quarters) next to Bombay University.

TAJ MAHAL HOTEL ★
1903/ Colonial
by W Chambers
The founder of the Tata Empire, J.N.Tata, built the Taj Mahal Hotel. It was one of the better hotels in British India. The central dome is Italian in style but the domes at the four corners are Indian. At present, there is an annexe built at the rear which cannot compare with the old structure.

The main building is a mix of styles.

GATEWAY OF INDIA
1927/ Colonial
by George Wittet
Gateway of India, the entrance to the port town of Bombay, was built in 1911, to commemorate the arrival of the British monarchs, King George V and Queen Mary. The most prominent architect in Bombay at the time, George Wittet, designed it blending the Hindu and Muslim architectural style of Gujarat.

Boats ply from here to Elephanta.

PRINCE OF WALES MUSEUM ★
1937/ Colonial
by George Wittet
The foundation stone of the Prince of Wales Museum was laid when King George V was still the Prince of Wales. The centre of the building was finished in 1914 and the wings were completed in 1937. It is in the Indo-Saracenic style and has a concrete dome.

SHIVA CAVE TEMPLE ★★
6th C/ Hindu

Elephanta is an hour by boat from the Gateway of India. It was originally called Karapulli islands until the 16th century, when the Portuguese intrigued by the elephant carved on the rock, called it Elephanta caves. There are the 6 caves on a 200 m high hill, said to date back to the 6th and 7th centuries. They greatly resemble Jogeshwari Temple in north Mumbai and Cave 28 of Ellora, hence they may be from the era of the Konkan Maurya dynasty. The Shiva Temple in Cave 1 is exceptional. There is a massive statue of Shiva with three faces, on the front wall of the pillared hall. Shiva is enshrined on the axis of a shrine. This cave temple does not have a single-axis space like the Buddhist temples; it has a multiple-axis space, which gives one an overpowering feeling.

❶ The interior of the verandah of the shrine in the east.
❷ The pillared hall with 3 open sides.
❸ The height of the three-faced Shiva is seven metres.
❹ Shrine, open on four sides and walls with sculptures.

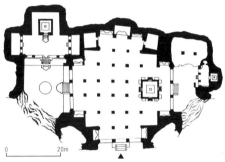

Floor Plan

CAVE TEMPLES ★
2nd~9th C/ Buddhist

There are 109 caves on a mountain in the Sanjay Gandhi National park, 42 km from Bombay. Monks lived in this Buddhist pilgrimage place for many centuries. They are mostly *vihara* caves and many are just natural caverns. The largest, Cave 13, has a compound wall, with sculptures in the front and a *stupa*. It looks like the Karli *chaitya* cave. The traditional-style *stupa* is simple and the carvings were added later.

❶ The caves lining the uneven rocky mountains. ❷ Façade of Cave 3 (end of 2nd century) ❸ Sculptures on the walls of Cave 67.

CAVE TEMPLES ★
1st C/ Buddhist

With Lonavla, 130 km from Mumbai as base, one can visit these early Buddhist temples. Bedsa Cave in the far east, 20 km from Lonavla, is a mix of the Bhaja caves style and that of the Karli caves. The temple itself has four pillars and the wall is well sculpted, but the pillars inside the temple are plain, without a base or a capital. The *vihara* caves are more decorative and have no pillars in the hall while the back portion of the cave is semi-circular in shape. There is a compound wall in front of the temple.

There are 11 monks' rooms in the *vihara*. (Cave 11)

Decorative pillars and wall sculptures on the *chaitya* cave (cave 7).

CAVE TEMPLES ★★
2nd C, BC~1st C, AD / Buddhist

The Karli mountains and the Bhaja mountains are both near Lonavla. The cave temples of Bhaja are some of the earliest. The Jain cave temples on Khandagiri and Udaygiri hills and this temple in Bhaja belong to the same genre. In Jain cave temples, rooms for disciples staying away from their homes and the *chaitya* cave where the *stupa* is deified, were clearly defined. But as a style Jain cave temples were still undeveloped. The *chaitya* caves did not have a wall in the front. They were open and may have been enclosed by a wooden fence. The wood construction of the time has been copied on the ceiling. The 20-odd, *vihara* caves did not follow the usual pattern and were much smaller. Cave 19 is the oldest and has deities sculpted on the front veranda.

❶ Other caves centered around 12th century, *Chaitya* cave.
❷ Façade of Cave 19 (*Vihara*).
❸ Sculptures on the veranda of Cave 19 (Surya and Indra).

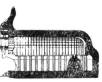

Cross section of Cave 12

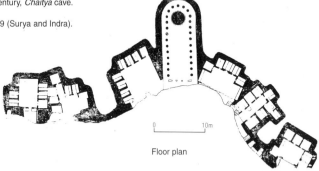

Floor plan

KARLI (KARLE) ★★

CAVE TEMPLE ★★★
1st C BC/ Buddhist

The *chaitya* cave temple of Karli is the epitome of cave architecture in India. It has a high ceiling and a deep interior, which is curved at the back and straight in front. A *stupa* has been carved out at the centre of the circular portion. Enough sunlight enters the cave. This perspective effect and the proportions of the interior is the ultimate in Buddhist architecture in India. There are two rows of pillars that join behind the *stupa*. They have the inverted pot motif on their base and capital. On top is a sculpture with two pairs of men and women sitting on an elephant. This repetition of a man-woman design brings rhythm and life to the highly mysterious interior.

There are around 10 cave temples in Karli, one of which is a *chaitya* cave temple. In front of these is a modern Hindu temple, the facade of which does not blend with the ancient temples. On the left is a *stambha* of which half the inside screens have been destroyed. The front room is replete with sculptures. The walls are filled with the same man, woman and elephant motif. The statues of Buddha are an addition from the later Gupta dynasty. Most of the temples in the Deccan plateau belong to the Satvahana dynasty, but this temple was built during the Kushaharada dynasty.

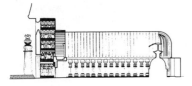

Cross-section

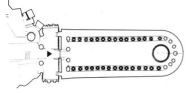

Floor Plan

❶ Teak ribs are still left on the ceiling of the hall (34 m depth, 14 m height) with rows of pillars.
❷ On top of the pillars are statues of two man and two woman on elephants.
❸ Sculptures on the walls of the room in front.
❹ The walls of the front room have laminated arches above the elephant.
❺ The *stupa* on the left has a four-faced lion.
❻ The ribbed ceiling above the *stupa* looks like an umbrella.

PUNE (POONA) ★★

SHANIWAR WADA
1736/ Maratha
Pune, the main bastion of the Marathas allies who opposed the British, is today a big city with a population of 2,800,000 people. When the Marathas weakened, the Peshwar (Prime Minister)took control and ruled the allies. All that is left of the palace built by the 2nd Peshwar, Baji Rao is the Delhi Gate, surrounding walls and the wide courtyard within.

Wide open space near Delhi Gate.

PUNE

RAMA TEMPLE
18th C/ Maratha
This is a small temple inside the city, surrounded by houses and shops. The *shikhara* is conical in the Maratha style with *Bangaldar* roof-like niches on the surface, where various gods have been deified. There is an open *mandapa* made of wood, in front of the shrine.

Right: The conical *shikhara*.
Left: Small shrines within the precincts.

PUNE

PARVATI TEMPLE
1758/ Maratha
Parvati Temple sits at the top of Parvati hill, south of the city. This colourful temple in the Maratha style was built by Peshwar Baji Rao. The *shikhara* of the temple is an onion-shaped dome which makes it look like a Russian Byzantine church. Instead of the *mandapa* there is a *pradakshina path* (cirumbulatory) around the shrine.

TER ★

TRIVIKRAMA TEMPLE
3rd C/ Buddhist
There is a small brick Buddhist temple in Ter a small village, 90 km from Sholapur. When Buddhism declined, it was converted into a Hindu temple with a *mandapa* in the front. In cave temples, the *chaitya* hall was inside, but since this is not a cave temple it can be seen from the outside too.

HILL FORT OF MARATHAS ★★
Circa 17th C/ Maratha

When Mughal rule spread to south India, Shivaji led the movement to re-establish the Hindu kingdom. He built forts and engaged in guerrilla warfare with the Mughals. In 1664, the capital of the Marathas was established at Raigad, 870 m above sea level, 60 km north of Mahableshwar.

Visiting Raigad is not easy. The mountain has 1500 steps leading to its peak. At approximately two thirds of the way, is a magnificent gate, *Maha Darwaza*, with 20 m tall turrets on either side. On the plateau right on top, the remnants of this town; the fort palace, water tanks and market place tell the tale of the self-sufficient lifestyle led by the people who lived here. At the northeastern end of town is Jagadishwara Temple and Shivaji's Samadhi. He died here, in 1680.

❶ The fort gate can be seen on the mountain.
❷ The two turrets of the palace.
❸ The solemn Jagadishwara Temple devoid of decorations.
❹ Beyond the palace walls is a sheer precipice.
❺ Entrance to the palace area, *Naggar Hana*.
❻ Fort entrance, *Maha Darwaza*.

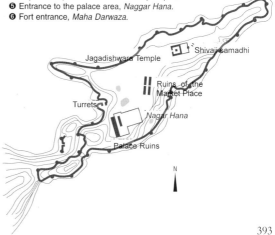

Jagadishwara Temple
Shivaji Samadhi
Ruins of the Market Place
Turrets
Nagar Hana
Palace Ruins
N

NEW PALACE (WADA)
1844/ Maratha

Satara is associated with Shivaji and many of his relics are still found here. Satara's new *wada (*Maratha palace) is a large wooden structure built around a courtyard, with three sides of the central hall facing the courtyard. Today, this palace is being used as government offices.

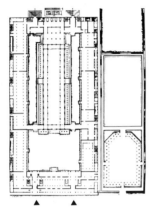

Floor Plan

Up: Façade facing the square. Down: Northern courtyard.

VISHVESHWARA MAHADEVA TEMPLE ⋆
1735/ Maratha

In Mahuli, 5 km from Satara, is a hill fort of the Maratha regime. Many temples were built at the foot of the hills in the recent past. The view of the temples with the mountains and forests as a backdrop and the river flowing nearby, is very picturesque indeed. In the stone *deepamala* (lamp tower), thousands of lamps are lit during festivals.

Shikhara of the temple.

Vishveshwara Mahadeva Temple and the lamp tower.

OLD TOWN HALL ★
1873/ Colonial
by Charles Mant

Kolhapur is an old town with temples dating back to the 10th century. It was also an important town of the Marathas and is now a business town with 4,17,300 people. There are a number of colonial buildings here, which include the designs of the English architect, Charles Mant. One of the best examples of the work of Charles Mant, who came to India at the age of 19 and blended European and traditional Indian architecture, is the District Government's office buildings. It does not conform to the Indo-Saracenic style but reminds one of the bold eclectic styles of the American architect Richardson, who was a contemporary of Charles Mant.

Up: Eastern façade with a Gothic touch. Down: Southern wing.

NEW PALACE ★
1881/
by Charles Mant

In 1810, during colonial rule, there was a huge fire in the former palace of the chieftain of Kolhapur. Since the British wanted to make Kolhapur a model city under British rule, they requested Martin to be the architect of the new palace, located on the northern outskirts of the city. Charles Mant designed a European style palace with a dome, *bangaldar* roofs and details from Hindu and Jain temple architecture, thus creating a palace, Indo-Saracenic in style. This blend can be clearly seen in the lookout tower that dominates the structure. Even now, the royal family lives in one part while the other portion has been converted into a museum.

Up: View of the palace. Down: Wall surface, a blend of different styles.

GOA

Goa, Daman and Diu were colonies of Portugal until 1961, nearly 42 years ago. Goa is now the smallest state in India, with a population of 1,300,000 people.

The Portuguese army took over the area from the Muslims in 1510 and made it their base for trade between Asia and Portugal. Christian missionaries travelled to southeast Asia to preach their religion. One of them, Francis Xavier, even reached Japan. After he died on the high seas, his body was embalmed, and is now kept in the Basilica do Bom Jesus, in Goa. The body of this saint is brought out for public veneration once every 10 years. At that time, people not just from India, but from all over the world come to Goa.

This city called 'Golden Goa' fell prey to bubonic plague, around the time the new capital was being formed at Panaji. The city of Goa was subsequently abandoned. Now, the old European city on the banks of the Mandovi River is being preserved by protecting the churches and monasteries, as they are. The former city of Goa, now called "Old Goa", attracts a large number of tourists, as does Panjim and many resort villages.

At the time Goa was under Christian rule, temples were built in the hinterland. Those recently constructed temples around Ponda, are in a style of temple architecture, so unique, that it cannot be seen anywhere else in India. The architects and artisans of the time, were building Christian churches and they excelled at this art. When they built Hindu temples, they incorporated this art into the temples, which gave rise to a unique blend of styles, the Indo-Christian style of architecture. The *campaniles* (bell towers) in front of the Latin cross-shaped temples are actually lamp towers and can be seen only in Goa and nowhere else in India.

The wooden altar of St. Cajetan church.

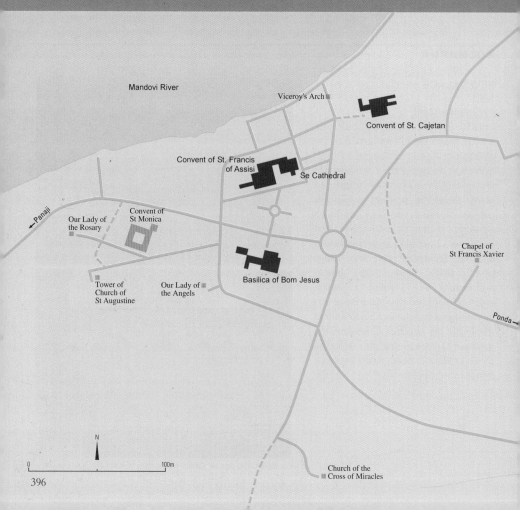

Mandovi River

Viceroy's Arch

Convent of St. Cajetan

Convent of St. Francis of Assisi

Se Cathedral

Panaji

Our Lady of the Rosary

Convent of St Monica

Chapel of St Francis Xavier

Tower of Church of St Augustine

Our Lady of the Angels

Basilica of Bom Jesus

Ponda

N

0   100m

396

Church of the Cross of Miracles

SE CATHEDRAL
17th C/ Colonial

Old Goa, 8 km from Panaji, could be called an open-air heritage museum. Known as Golden Goa in ancient times, it has many churches and convents. The largest, Se Cathedral, was begun in 1562 and completed in 1619. The altar was completed in 1652. Built in the orthodox Renaissance style, with Tuscan exteriors and Corinthian interiors, it has a serene appearance. One of the two belfries on either side of the cathedral, collapsed. The other still stands.

Up: The main entrance of the church, facing east, modelled after Italian Tuscany churches.
Down: The long, pillared nave, 76 m long.

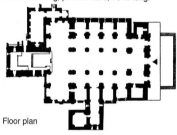

Floor plan

CHURCH OF SAINT CAJETAN ★
17th C/ Colonial
by Francesco M Milazzo & others

This church was built in 1649 by the Theatines, Italian friars sent by the Pope to propagate the Catholic religion in Asia. Modelled after St. Peter's Cathedral, it was completed in two years. Since good quality stones are not easily available in Goa, laterite has been used. The façade has been plastered and painted white. Basalt was brought from elsewhere to accentuate some parts of the façade. The wooden altar is a spectacular Baroque masterpiece.

Full view of the solemn monastery.

A dome over the intersection of the Latin cross-plan.

BASILICA DO BOM JESUS ★
17th~18th C/ Colonial

The construction of Bom Jesus basilica started in 1594 and finished in 1605. The style is a blend of the Renaissance and Baroque styles. Unlike other churches, the plaster on the façade of this church was removed at some point in time. The exterior is a rich Baroque, while the interior is comparatively plain and simple. In 1663, a fire destroyed the Professore House, which was restored in 1783. The body of St. Francis Xavier is preserved in a chapel in the Basilica.

The cloister painted white.

Up: The west façade, facing an open space. Down: Nave of the church.

CONVENT OF ST. FRANCIS OF ASSISI ★
16th~17th C/ Colonial

To the left of the cathedral is an Episcopal building belonging to the convent of St. Francis of Assisi. This building, presently a museum, was built by the friars in 1517 and completed in 1520. The church was reconstructed in 1661. When Muslims invaded India, they destroyed Hindu temples and used the materials to build a mosque in its place. The Portuguese however, completely destroyed Hindu temples and built entirely new, European style buildings in their place. As a result, there is no blending of Hindu and Christian architecture in Goa. Even then though the architects were Portuguese, the artisans were Indians, a fact that is reflected in the altar of this church that has woodwork in the south Indian style. The interior of this church, with a deep nave and side aisles is very interesting. It is completely sculpted and frescoed and reflects an austere beauty.

Up: White, Tuscan exterior. Down: Frescoed and coloured interior.

SHANTA DURGA TEMPLE ★
1738/ Hindu

Since the Portuguese were intolerant of Hindu temples and made no effort to protect them, Hindus fled with their gods and deities and built new temples in villages, in the hinterland. One of Goa's cities, Ponda, 35 km southeast of Panaji, has a number of temples in its vicinity. Shanta Durga Temple was built by a Maratha minister Shahu, grandson of Shivaji, by taking over an existing building in the complex. The roofs are tiled and over the *garbhagriha*, is a 4-storeyed, domed tower, instead of the usual *shikhara*. In front of the temple, is a lamp tower, which looks like the Italian *campanile*. In its details, the building appears western. Artisans living in Goa, started building Hindu temples, in the same style being used for Christian churches, at that time.

❶ The steep, sloping tiled roof of the building.
❷ A chariot used at the time of festivals, in front of the lamp tower is also non-Hindu in appearance.
❸ The domed tower on top of the shrine.

MANGUESHI TEMPLE ★
18th C/ Hindu.

No other temple reflects the style used for Christian churches, as much as the Mangueshi Temple in Mardol, located 7 km from Ponda. It has a lamp tower at the entrance and some convent-like structures around. The main shrine has a porch in front and a prayer room shaped like a Latin cross. The corridors have two rows of pillars giving the appearance of three corridors. A dome has been erected over the intersection of the cross plan. There are absolutely no sculptures on the outer walls, which is the case in most temples in Goa.

The base of the traditional wooden chariot.

Up: Colourfully painted building. Down: Main building and lamp tower.

NAGUESHI TEMPLE
18th C/ Hindu

Nagueshi Temple located in Bandora village 4 km from Ponda, like the other temples has a tank near the precincts where people bathe. It resembles the Shantadurga Temple. The lamp tower is not in the front but at the back. The plan is the Latin cross and the tower is not at the intersection of the cross, but is independent and the corridor in the wings also boasts of a tower, making it appear very Islamic.

Interior of the prayer room.

Up: Full view of the temple. Down: Tank. in front of the temple.

CIDADE DE GOA HOTEL *
1982/ After Independence
By Charles Correa

This is a resort hotel, south of Panaji, on the rocky coast. The slope has been levelled and the various buildings make it look like an independent city. It is richly different from the traditional Goan architecture. Since it was built on a low budget, the walls have been painted, but the effect is still picturesque.

Lounge facing the small courtyard.

Up: Pool in front of the open restaurant. Down: Staircase and corridor.

Middle India

BIDAR

GULBAR

Panaji

18 GULBAR

20 BIJAPUR

24 AIHOLE

22 PATTADAKAL

BADAMI 21 23 MAHAKUTA

25 DEGAMVE

ITTAGI 28 27 KUKKANUR

DAMBAL 26 29 31 HAMPI

LAKKUNDI

KURUVATTI

HAVERI 32 30

KARNATAKA

33 KELADI

34 IKKERI

35 BHATKAL

PENUKONDA 16

17

LEPAKSHI

NANDI 5

KARKALA 37 SRINGERI

38

39 BELAVADI 41 HARNAHALLI

MUDABIDRI 42 40 44

MANGALORE 36 BELUR 43 HALEBID 50 ARALAGUPPE

DODDA GADDAVALLI

SHRAVANABELGOLA 46 45 BANGALORE 52

KAMBADAHALLI

48 SRIRANGAPATNAM

MYSORE 47 49

SOMNATHPUR

PAYYANNUR 79

CALICUT 80

TRICHUR 81

PERUVANAM 83

COCHIN 82 KERALA

VAIKOM 85 84 ETTUMANUR MADURAI

86 THIRUVALLA

87 KAVIYUR

KALUGUM

77

KAZAKUTTAM 88

TRIVANDRUM 89

PADMANABHAPU

78

N

0 200km

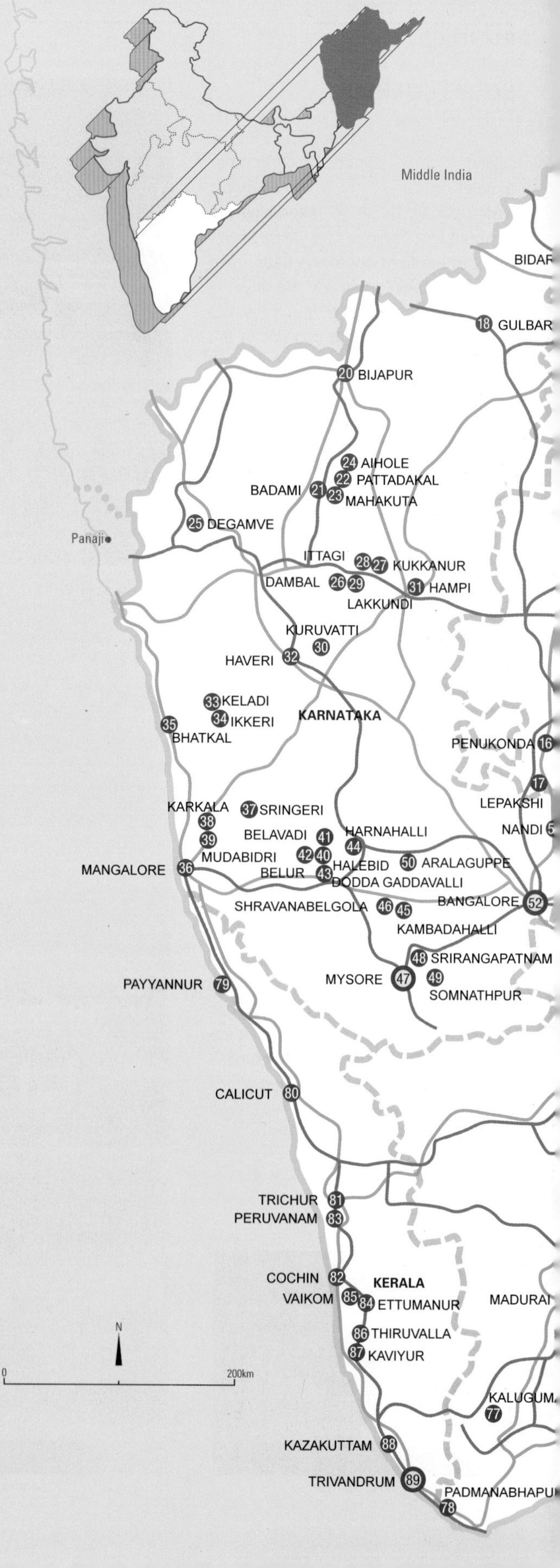

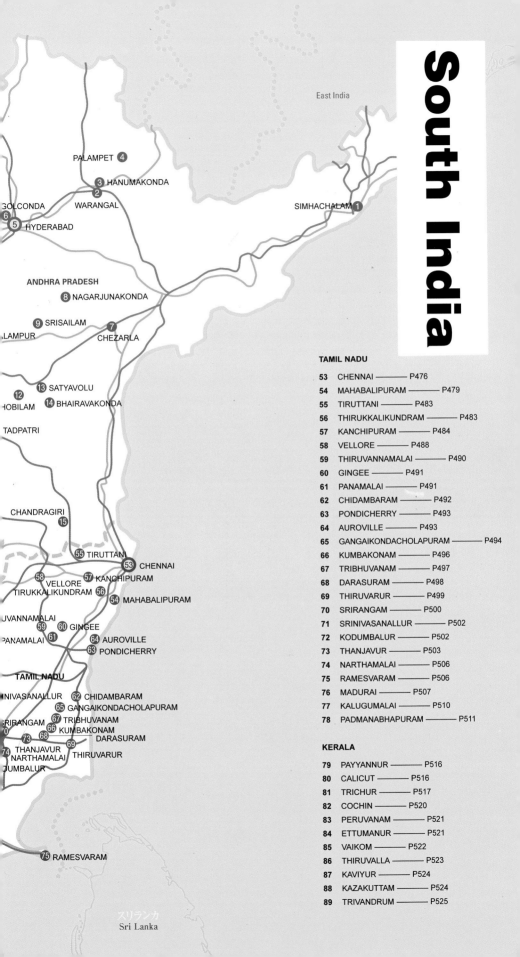

South India

East India

PALAMPET ④

③ HANUMAKONDA
②
GOLCONDA
⑥ WARANGAL
⑤ HYDERABAD

SIMHACHALAM ①

ANDHRA PRADESH

⑧ NAGARJUNAKONDA

⑨ SRISAILAM
⑦
LAMPUR
CHEZARLA

⑫
⑬ SATYAVOLU
HOBILAM
⑭ BHAIRAVAKONDA

TADPATRI

CHANDRAGIRI
⑮

⑤⑤ TIRUTTANI
⑤③ CHENNAI
⑤⑧ ⑤⑦ KANCHIPURAM
VELLORE
TIRUKKALIKUNDRAM ⑤⑥
⑤④ MAHABALIPURAM

JUVANNAMALAI
⑤⑨ ⑥⓪ GINGEE
PANAMALAI ⑥①
⑥④ AUROVILLE
⑥③ PONDICHERRY

TAMIL NADU

NIVASANALLUR ⑥② CHIDAMBARAM
⑥⑤ GANGAIKONDACHOLAPURAM
⑥⑦ TRIBHUVANAM
SRIRANGAM ⑥⑥ KUMBAKONAM
⓪ ⑦③ ⑥⑧ DARASURAM
⑦④ THANJAVUR ⑥⑨ THIRUVARUR
NARTHAMALAI
JUMBALUR

⑦⑤ RAMESVARAM

スリランカ
Sri Lanka

TRAVEL INFORMATION (South India)

ISLAMIC ARCHITECTURE - SOUTH INDIA

Bijapur the treasurehouse of south India is three and a half hours by bus or train from Sholapur to the south. Even with such a legacy Bijapur only has simple hotels like Hotel Mayura. From Bijapur to Gulbarga is four-and-a-half hours by road where Hotel Pariwar is not too bad. Hiring a rickshaw for the day is advisable in Gulbarga and Bijapur. Bidar is 3 hours away by bus. Hyderabad is a metropolitan city and hence has a range of hotels from luxury to budget. Go to Palampet and back by taxi (1 hour 20 minutes.) Here Hotel Kandhari is a good place to stay at. Hire an auto-rickshaw and visit the tombs nearby. It is a four-hour road journey, to Hyderabad. Take a rickshaw to Golconda.

ANDHRA PRADESH

Hyderabad to Warangal is 3 hours by bus or train. Stay at Hotel Chalukya near Kazipet station; visit Warangal and Hanumakonda by auto-rickshaw. Go to Palampet by taxi (1 hour, 20 minutes). Warangal to Vijayawada is 4 hours by train. Hotel Kaveri International is a good place to stay at. Transport here is not up to the mark so hire a taxi for four days.

Visit Undavali, Amaravati and Chezarla, but stay in Nagarjunasagar. Travel to Nagarjunakonda by boat, then visit Srisailam and stay at Nandyal. Hire a taxi for 4 days. After going through Satyavolu and Bhairavakonda stay in Allagudda. Ahobilam and back and then on to Tadpatri by taxi a total of 1100 km. Better take the train from Hyderabad to Kurnool (6 hours) and stay in Hotel Raja Vihar. Visit Alampur by taxi from here (40 minutes). Take a bus to Tadpatri and the train to Hospet via Guntakal.

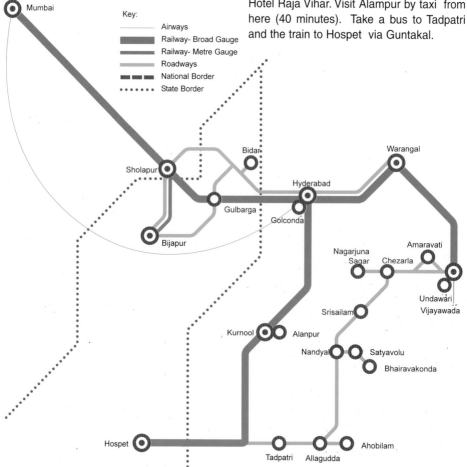

Key:
- Airways
- Railway- Broad Gauge
- Railway- Metre Gauge
- Roadways
- National Border
- State Border

Mumbai

Bidar
Warangal
Sholapur
Hyderabad
Gulbarga
Golconda
Bijapur
Amaravati
Nagarjuna Sagar
Chezarla
Undawari
Vijayawada
Srisailam
Kurnool
Alanpur
Nandyal
Satyavolu
Bhairavakonda
Hospet
Tadpatri
Allagudda
Ahobilam

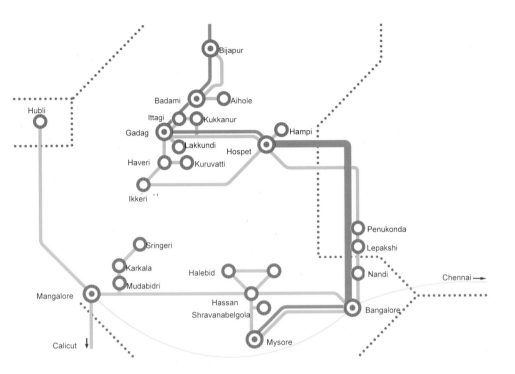

KARNATAKA ───────────

Badami is three hours south of Bijapur by rail or road. Stay at Badami Court and take a taxi to Mahakuta, Pattadakal and Aihole, on a day's trip. Then take the train to Gadag and stay in Hotel Durga Vihar. Visit Kukkanur, Ittagi, Lakkundi, and Dambal by taxi. It takes two-and-a-half hours to get from Gadag to Hospet. Here, try the Malligi Tourist Home. Hampi is half an hour away, but it is a vast place and it will take at least two days to cover it adequately. It is better to take an auto-rickshaw or bicycle and walk when you get to the riverbank. Instead of going from Gadag to Hospet you can go via Haveri, Ikkeri and Kuruvatti. Since a day's trip is tedious, stay the night in Sagar or Harihar.

Go to Bangalore by train and take a vacation in this large and cool city. Seeing Nandi, Lepakshi and Penukonda at a stretch, may be a bit of a strain as it is a distance of 350 km, but an overnight journey by taxi is possible. Mysore is 3 hours by bus or train. Here, Metropole Hotel is recommended or alternatively there is the high budget Lalitha Mahal Palace Hotel. Srirangapatnam is 30 minutes from Mysore by bus or taxi.

Somnathpur is 1 hour by taxi. Hassan, the base for the Hoysala Temples is three hours away. Medium class, Hassan Ashok Hotel is good. Shravanabelgola is one-and-a-half hours by bus, while Kambadahalli is 30 minutes away. Belur and Halebid can be reached by bus, but covering Kaddavalli and Berawadi too, by taxi (110 km) is more enjoyable. Hassan to Mangalore by train is four hours. Buses are convenient and Hotel Moti Mahal is recommended, but there are many hotels here. Visit Mudabidri and Karkala. Sringeri is 2 hours away. Cover all these places in two trips. Mangalore to Batkal is three-and-half hours. Further down south, begins the tour of Kerala.

The road to Badami.

TRAVEL INFORMATION (South India)

KERALA

Since Kerala is a long state, sandwiched by the Arabian Sea in the west and the Western Ghats in the east, a tour of the state is a straight route. Calicut is five hours by train from Mangalore with Hotel Malabar Palace a good place to stay at. Thrissur is three hours away you can stay at the palatial Ramanilayam government guest house or at the medium budget Hotel Yatri Nivas. When visiting the Vadakkunathan Temple enter from the south gate, before noon. Take a taxi and visit Peruvanam. It is two hours to Cochin and Ernakulam by bus or train. Here, Hotel Presidency is recommended or Palace Hotel in Bolgatti islands, reservations for which can be made at the tourist reception centre in Ernakulam. Vaikom is one hour, away, Kaviyur is thirty minutes, Quilon by bus or train from Thiruvalla is two hours. Most Kerala temples are closed from 11 am. to 5 pm, so go as early as possible.

Take the bus from Thiruvalla to Alleppey, stay overnight and take the backwater trip to Quilon. Here, Alleppey Prince Hotel is good. In Quilon, you can stay at the tourist bungalow. Both are a short distance away from the city. Trivandrum is an hour and a half by train and has many good hotels like the Mascot Hotel near the Art Gallery. Kazakuttam can be visited by taxi. Padmanabhapuram is in Tamil Nadu, but can be visited from Trivandrum (45 minutes).

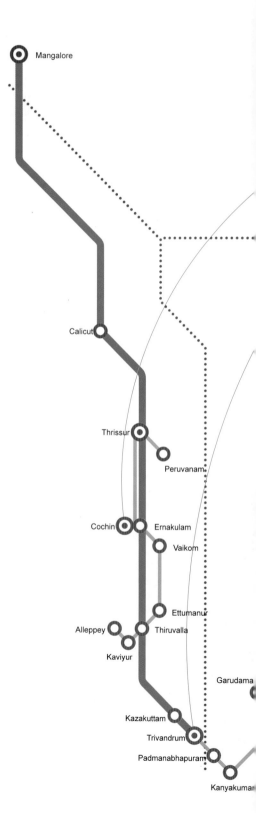

Back waters in Alleppey.

TAMIL NADU ———————————

Chennai, the capital of Tamil Nadu is one of the four metropolitan cities in India. It has an International Airport. There are many flights from Bombay and Delhi. Start the trip from Mahabalipuram, which is 2 hours from Chennai. There are many seaside cottages, and the ruins can be visited on a bicycle. Tirukkalikundram is en route. Stay in Baboo Surya Hotel in Kanchipuram. Note that all the temples here are closed from 12 noon to 4:30 pm. Vellore is 2½ hours by bus. Stay in the River View Hotel. Thiruvannamalai is 2 hours south by bus. Hotels here are a problem but try Hotel Trishul. Take a taxi to Pondicherry and visit Gingee and Panamalai on the way. The total distance is 120 km. Stay at Hotel Mass in Pondicherry. Take an auto-rickshaw to Auroville, where there is a visitor's centre.

Pondicherry to Chidambaram is 2 hours by

Mural in the temple in Thanjavur.

bus. Stay in the simple Hotel Tamil Nadu. Kumbakonam is 2 hours by bus or train, while Tanjore is 3 hours. Stay in Hotel Parisutham. Visit Gangaikondacholapuram from Kumbakonam by taxi,(1 hour). There are buses to Trichy and Kumbakonam from Thanjavur. Madurai is 3½ hours by bus from Trichy. There are three good hotels on the other side of the river and hence a little inconvenient. The simple Hotel Tamil Nadu is closer to the temples and hence convenient. Rameswaram is an overnight trip, which takes 4 hours by bus and 5½ hours by train. Madurai to Trivandrum is 7 hours. To visit Garudamalai go to Kovilpatti and take a taxi there and back (40 minutes).

ANDHRA PRADESH

South India comprises four states that speak the Dravida language. Telugu is spoken in Andhra Pradesh, Kannada in Karnataka, Tamil in Tamil Nadu and Malayalam in Kerala. It is entirely different from the Aryan language and script of the North and they comprise 25 percent of the population of India. It is said that the Dravidas developed the ancient Indus Valley Civilization. They moved south due to constant north-south strife and for the need to free themselves from the control of Aryan people and the Hindi language.

The heart of Andhra Pradesh is the former feudal kingdom of Hyderabad. Even during British rule this kingdom was independent and after Indian Independence it joined the Indian Democratic Republic rather than continue independent. At present the capital of Andhra Pradesh, along with Secunderabad in the north has a population of 4,500,000. It is the sixth largest city in India. Charminar, the symbol of this city, is an Islamic memorial tower that is also the name of a popular brand of cigarettes and easily recognized.

Golconda, much older than Hyderabad, some kilometres to the west, was a prominent Islamic capital in the 16th and 17th centuries. Today only the citadel and the Qutb Shahi royal tombs remain to tell the tale. As in Karnataka the northern half of the state became a stronghold of Islam and the southern states continued predominantly Hindu till the end. The Dravidian temples start from here. The state is blessed with many good quality structures, but not as classic as the ones in Tamil Nadu.

Buddhism spread here from the north and ruins can be seen in Amravati and Nagarjunasagar. Unfortunately the top portions of the structures have collapsed and one cannot get a clear idea of how the building may have looked.

In South India more than secular architecture, Hindu temples linked to history and Hindu mythology are more famous and are major pilgrim centres even today. It is said that one such temple in Tirumalai has more than 10,000 pilgrims visiting every day. This photograph is the temple town of Kalahasti 40km from Tirupati as seen from the large temple on top of the hill. The pathway in front of the *gopura* leads to the temple and on this path the chariot which is used for temple festivals can be seen. The Swarnam river flows through the plains on the left of the opposite hill only during the rainy season. The riverbed is dry in this picture.

Floor plan of Vijaya Mahal (palace) belonging to the Vijayanagar Dynasty in Chandragiri (17th century)

SIMHACHALAM ⋆

1

VARAHA NARASIMHA TEMPLE ⋆
rebuilt 13th C/ Hindu

This temple is built on a mountain 16 km from Vishakapatnam, fairly near to Orissa. It was built during the East Ganga Dynasty at the same time that the temples in Puri and Konark were built. A South Indian style *gopura* is built at the entrance of the temple, thus effecting an East-Indian and South-Indian blend of styles. A high double wall surrounds the temple. Inside the precincts is a small shrine resembling the Konark temple with the horse and wheels on the north-eastern side. The *shikara* on top of the shrine has the step design of the South while the walls and the plinth have high quality sculptures of humans and fantasy creatures.

Up: Full view of the temple. Down: The North Eastern type Chariot shrine.

WARANGAL ⋆

2

4 TORANAS (TEMPLE DOORWAYS) ⋆
12th C/ Hindu

South-east of today's Warangal city, lie the ruins of the capital of the Kakatiya dynasty which was also known as Warangal. The town had three concentric rings of walls protecting it. Ruins of temples stand on the crossroads of main roads that traverse the town. Only four gates of this abandoned Syayambhu Temple, are left standing at the four cardinal points. They are similar to the *toranas* of Sanchi; two pairs of pillars with a beam across the tops.

Few sculptures are seen on the *torana*

The temple is in ruins today

SHIVA (1000 PILLARED TEMPLE)*
1163/ Hindu

A 12th century temple between Warangal and Kazipet, was built by King Rudradeva of the Kakatiya dynasty. The temple, constructed with dark green basalt, has three shrines with Shiva, Vishnu and Surya deified respectively. All three shrines share a common *mandapa*. Facing this is another *mandapa* with a large number of pillars. Together they are called the thousand-pillared *mandapa*. The actual number is around 100 pillars.

The shrine of the 1000-pillared *mandapa*

Entrance, doorway and pillars of the 1000-pillared temple

RAMAPPA TEMPLE *
1234/ Hindu

Ramappa Temple in Palampet village, 70 km from Warangal, was also built during the Kakatiya dynasty. The style is the same as that of the temple in Hanumakonda. This temple also sports broad eaves that are carved even on the underside. The angled struts supporting the eaves have sculptures of *apsaras*, musicians and animals. Since there is only one shrine, the *mandapa* is open on three sides and is very bright. The brick built tower is plastered. Ramappa temple is one of the finest medieval Deccan temples.

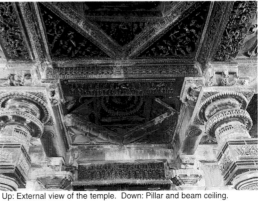

Details of decorative eaves surrounding the shrine

Up: External view of the temple. Down: Pillar and beam ceiling.

HYDERABAD ★★

CHARMINAR
(FOUR MINARETS) ★
1591/ Islamic

Muhammed Quli Qutb Shah of Golconda built this city, which later became the capital of the Hyderabad fiefdom. Today, it is the state capital. Muhammed Quli Qutb Shah erected the Charminar (four minarets) as a memorial after an epidemic ravaged the city. Now Charminar has become the symbol of Hyderabad. The height of the entrance gate is 56 m and it has the latticework prevalent during the time. The tomb of Qutb Shah lies nearby but it was damaged during the Mughal rule. The city can be seen from the minarets but now unfortunately, no one is allowed to climb up into the minarets.

❶ Charminar rising up in the heart of the former city
❷ The main entrance of the Charminar.
❸ Details on the walls of the arch, with a line of small arches.

GOLCONDA ★★

CITADEL (BALA HISAR) ★
16th~17th C/ Islamic

The ruins of the Golconda fort which was the capital of the Qutb Shahi dynasty, lie 8 km from Hyderabad. It was destroyed by Emperor Aurangzeb and was abandoned. The Bala Hisar Complex is the inner citadel. It was encircled by a wall of 11 km. Now an orderly fort wall surrounds the citadel where palaces and mosques stand even now.

❶ The mosque can be seen at the top of the citadel.
❷ The royal tombs can be seen on the far side of the fort wall.
❸ Fateh gate - entrance to the city.

The interior of the mosque.

ROYAL TOMBS ★★
16th~17th C/ Islamic

More than 12 tombs of Qutb Shahi emperors lie outside the city walls. These reflect the early Islamic style of the Deccan. A cubic tomb room has been built on a foundation platform and an onion-dome roof has been placed on the top. There were different styles like the octagonal Jamshed tomb too. Most magnificent is the tomb of Muhammed Quli Qutb Shahi, who built Hyderabad city. It has a height of 42.5 m. The royal flower pattern has been exquisitely sculpted. Enamelled tiles were inlaid on the tombs, but not many remain today.

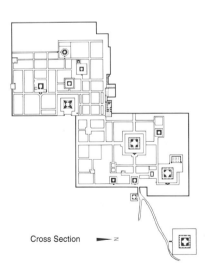

Cross Section

❶ Tomb of Abdullah Qutb Shah (1530)
❷ Tomb area. Muhammed Quli Qutb Shah tomb is seen in the distance.
❸ Tomb of Muhammed Quli Qutb Shah (1612)
❹ Tomb of Jamshed Quli Qutb Shah (1550)
❺ Badshahi Hammam (royal bathhouse)
❻ Inside the Hayat Baksh Begum (1667)

KAPOTESHWARA TEMPLE
3th C/ Buddhist

Chezarla is a small village which has Buddhist temples dating back to the 3th century. These temples belong to the same period as those in Ter. It has the same design as that of the temple in Ter with its straight front and rounded rear pattern. After it was converted into a Hindu temple a *mandapa* was constructed at the front. The temple has a *chaitya* shrine with a sealed *chaitya* window which has Hindu sculptures carved on it. Reaching this village is difficult. One has to travel from Vijayawada west to Nurzrapet, then to Nukarikart village in the north, then west again along a curving road to finally reach the village.

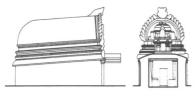

Side elevation and front elevation of the temple

Up: The closed *chaitya* window. Down: The shrine is lower at the rear.

BUDDHIST REMAINS
3rd ~ 4th C/ Buddhist

The waters of the Nagarjuna dam would have inundated these vast Buddhist ruins, so they were relocated to the island in the middle of the lake. Buddhism thrived during the 3rd to 4th centuries. During the Ikshraku dynasty, a large number of stupas, riverside ghats and Buddhist temples were constructed. Artefacts even more ancient have also been excavated here.

The ruins of Simha Vihara monastery.

MALLIKARJUNA TEMPLE ★
14th ~ 16th C/ Hindu

This temple built on a mountain draws a large number of pilgrims. It is enclosed by a high wall, which has relief sculpture and *gopuras*. There are many shrines within. The main Mallikarjuna temple has the 14 century pyramidal style with no embellishments. It has a pillar lined *mandapa* at the front which was built in 1405.

Temple lit up at night   Sculptures on the walls.

HINDU TEMPLES ★★
7th ~ 8th C/ Hindu

The Chalukya dynasty which began its rule in the 6th century, contributed greatly to Hindu architecture of the Early Middle Ages. Badami in Karnataka state was the capital of the Chalukya dynasty. Later they spread east to Alampur area during the 7th century, where they built an important group of Hindu temples that still exist today. Alampur, 45 km from Kurnool on the banks of the river Tungabhadra, has nine small temples belonging to this era.

All the temples are dedicated to Shiva but every temple is named after Brahma. All have the basic style of *garbhagriha* and *mandapa* which is encircled by a low wall and cirumbulatory on which devotees can walk around the shrine. The shrine is crowned with a northern style shikara and the outer walls have ornamental niches, where various deities are placed. Above them, the *chaitya* window style motif has been sculpted with dancing *apsaras* on both sides.

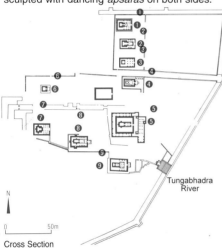

Cross Section
❶ Vishwa Brahma Temple ❷ Veera Brahma Temple
❸ Aloka Brahma Temple ❹ Kumara Brahma Temple
❺ Bala Brahma Temple ❻ Taraka Brahma Temple
❼ Padma Brahma Temple ❽ Swarga Brahma Temple
❾ Garuda Brahma Temple

❶ Swarga Brahma Temple (Year 689)
❷ Walls of the Vishwa Brahma Temple (8th C)
❸ Shikara of the Bala Brahma Temple (7th C)
❹ Lattice work window in the oldest Kumara Brahma Temple (year 640)
❺ Inside Swarga Brahma Temple.

RAMALINGESVARA TEMPLE ★
16th C/ Hindu

The rule of Krishna Devaraya was the golden age of the Vijayanagara Empire and many temples were built during his time. Tadpatri has two interesting temples, in the Vijayanagara style. Ramalinga Naidu, who was the vassal of the Vijayanagara Empire controlling Tadpatri, built Ramalingesvara, a temple near the Pennar River north of the city. The huge rectangular *mandapa* has large and small shrines, (*vimanas*) with *mandapas* in front, and an unfinished *gopura* on the northern side. The plinth is 8 m high. The high quality stone and the skill and intricacy of the carvings encrusted with friezes of jewels and petal scrollwork, are better than the work on the shrine itself. James Fergusson has put it in a class of its own, incomparable to anything else.

Up: The main shrine with its pyramid shaped tower that is South Indian in style.
Down: The foundation of the *gopura* that is richly engraved.

VENKATRAMANA TEMPLE ★★
16th C/ Hindu

It is a large temple built 10 years later by Timma Naidu, son of Ramalinga Naidu. It dates back to the same era as the Vittala Temple of Vijayanagara (Hampi). It belongs to the later era of South Indian style and hence the decorations and carving are more stylistic. The pillars in the *mandapa* gives a fantastic illusion of space and has created an elegant Indian rococo pattern.

The chariot and flag-pole in front of the *mandapa*

The line of pillars and eaves in the open *mandapa*

UPPER NARASIMHA TEMPLE ★
15th~16th C/ Hindu

From Tadpatri to Alagudda to Ahobilam, an important Hindu pilgrimmage place. Ahobilam has a temple dedicated to Narasimha (man-lion), one of the 10 incarnations of Vishnu. The *gopura* is painted white and is impressive. The shrine is a natural cavern and very small, but the appearance of many towers among the green mountains creates a very serene ambience.

Left: The sculptures and pillars in the *mandapa*.
Right: The *gopura* against the green mountains.

LOWER NARASIMHA TEMPLE ★★
16th C/ Hindu

This temple is much larger than the one up in the mountains. It is also more orderly and decorative since it was built much later. Surrounded by green mountains, it exudes a special serenity. There are a number of shrines, on the way to the gate. The walls hold a statue of Krishna Dewaraya. A double fence encloses the rectangular precincts with *gopuras* and the temple in the middle. The sculpture on the pillars of the *mandapa* is more wonderful to behold than the pillars in Tadpatri; they exude an energy of their own.

An exterior view

The pillar groups in the *mandapa*

SATYAVOLU ★ 13

RAMALINGESHWARA TEMPLE ★
8th C / Hindu

This temple in the village of Satyavolu 70 km from Nandyal dates back to the East Chalukya dynasty. It was built at the same time as the temples in Alampur. It has a north style *shikara*, an open *mandapa* in the front and pillars with relief sculptures on them. Bhimalingeshwara temple built in the 7th century, which has a closed porch, is in the vicinity.

Temple in a serene setting.

BHAIRAVAKONDA ★ 14

CAVE TEMPLES ★
7th~ 8th C/ Hindu

Bhairavakonda is 100 km from Satyavolu. The journey is rough, but the location is beautiful. There are eight cave temples deep in the mountains, by a flowing mountain stream. The *linga* is deified here. There are lion sculptures on the pillars of cave No. 5, which are very similar to those in the cave temples of Mahabalipuram, built during the Pallava reign.

The porch of cave 5, wet with recent rains

CHANDRAGIRI ★ 15

VIJAYANAGARA PALACES ★
17th C/ Hindu

When Islamic forces advanced and strengthened their positions in South India in 1565, the Vijayanagara capital was transferred to Penukonda and later to Chandragiri. The weakened kingdom continued up to 1646. Below the citadel, palaces, temples, buildings, gates and fort walls belonging to that period can be seen. Raja Mahal (King's palace) is 45 m long, three storeys high and has a *shikhara* style lookout tower crowning it. The Rani Mahal (Queen's palace) is a blend of Hindu and Islamic construction. (Elevation on page 408)

The construction style of the walls in Rani Mahal

Up: Tower of Raja Mahal (King's Palace). Down: Rani Mahal

PENUKONDA *

PENUKONDA *

PENUKONDA ✶ 16

OLD TOWN OF VIJAYANAGARA
15th ~16th C/ Hindu

Penukonda was the capital of the Vijayanagara Empire for some time. As in Chandragiri, there is a fort on the hill, and the former city is surrounded by fort walls. There are some abandoned temples and palaces in this place. The 16th century Gagan Mahal is markedly Islamic with a large hall and private rooms above. It is topped with a lookout tower.

Lookout tower attached to the structure

LEPAKSHI ✶ 17

VEER BHADRA TEMPLE ★★
16th C/ Hindu

When Achyuta Deva Raya was the king of the Vijayanagara Empire in the 16th century, Lepakshi was the southern heartland of his empire. Governors of Penukonda, brothers Viranna and Virupanna, built the magnificent temple, which was originally a small rock temple called Kurumasheela. Double walls surround the whole precinct and the building is a complex structure built according to the terrain. There are three small shrines inside: Veerabhadra, Maheshwara and Vishnu. The *mandapa* has more than 100 pillars and colourful ceilings. Lepakshi is 55 km from Penukonda.

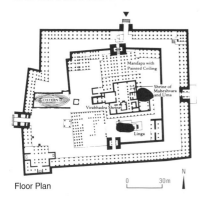

Floor Plan

Design on the ceiling of the *mandapa*

Up: The closed corridor. Down: Veerabhadra seen from the *mandapa*.

419

KARNATAKA

Karnataka stretches from the western coast on to the Deccan plateau and the language spoken here is Kannada. It used to be called Mysore state with Mysore city being the cultural heart of the state. Now the state capital is Bangalore.

Karnataka has rich and varied architecture. The three cities of Gulbarga, Bijapur and Bidar in the north have many structures reflecting South Indian Islamic architecture. Among them Bijapur is worth an intensive visit; not for nothing is it called the 'Agra of South India'.

Much further south (except for Srirangapatnam, or as the British called it, Seringapatam) was the Hindu cultural centre of the 18th century. Aihole, Badami and Mahakuta in the north, were the hub of construction activities during the Middle Ages. The Nagari style of the North in the later period and the Dravidian style of the south (early period) co-existed here. These were built by the early Chalukyas in the 6th~8th centuries. The later Chalukyas built temples that were a blend of the north and south styles with a star-shaped plan. James Fergusson, the first historian to chronicle Indian architecture, called it a "Chalukya style which is a blend of Aryan and Dravidian styles. It later came to be called the 'in-between style'". Generally however, even now it is referred to as the Chalukya style.

This in-between style was developed by the Hoysala dynasty further south and was called the Hoysala style. The three temples in Belur, Halebid and Somnathpur, adopt the star plan and have highly decorated walls with exquisite carving. In Vijayanagar (Hampi), the capital of the last Hindu empire in South India there are many ruins. The

effect of Islamic architecture is heavy in the fort and palaces. The temples in the capital look traditional except for the Vitthala temple which is different from the Hoysala style and could be called the Indian rococo style with its fantastically decorated interiors. The kingdom extended from Tamil Nadu to Orissa and in every area a Vijayanagar style temple was constructed.

Jain temples were built on the west coast. Buddhism and Jainism spread to South India from Bihar. It is a wonder that on the east coast one finds largely, ruins, while on the west coast there are numerous shrines and many temple towns. The west coast separated from the interior by the Western Ghats receives a lot of rains and hence the wooden constructions have steep roofs like that of the temple in Muda Bidri. The same style continues in Kerala too, which has a similar terrain.

Cross section of Jod Gumbaz (tomb of 2 siblings) (Bijapur)

Bhutanatha temple (7th C. Badami) looks as if it is floating on the man-made lake surrounded by the red sandstone mountain

The first to establish Islamic rule in the Deccan plateau was the Bahmani dynasty. Gulbarga was its capital in 1347 but later shifted to Bidar. Many structures other than the fort still exist. There are tombs and mosques but the palace has been destroyed. On the east side of the city is the *dargah* of the saint of the Chisthi group, belonging to the 15th - 17th century. Even today a large number of pilgrims visit daily.

The 17th century, arch facing the *dargah*

HAFT GUMBAZ (SEVEN TOMBS)
★

14th-15th Century/ Islamic

A group of seven tombs called Haft Gumbaz (seven tombs) lies in the east of the city. The group is designed on the lines of the South Indian tomb style of the Early Ages. They have emulated the tomb style of the Tughlaq dynasty in Delhi. It is a very archaic construction. The entrance is small, thick walls surround the interior and there is a half circular tomb crowning the top. The Firuz Shah Bahmani tomb built in the 15th century, sports two floors with many arches and has been decorated with latticework.

Up: Gumbaz Group (tombs). Down: Firuz Shah Bahmani tomb.

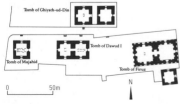

Cross Section

JAMI MASJID (FRIDAY MOSQUE) ★★
1367/ Islamic

This is in front of the Bala Hisar, inside the fort city, with gates on the east and west of the fort. It is said that the construction of this mosque was completed in the 15th century. It has a distinctly Persian design using a row of pillars. Unlike other mosques this one does not have a courtyard. The plan is geometric. In front of the central *mihrab* it has a large dome and medium sized domes in the four corners. It is encircled on the outer ring by a hull shaped vaulted roof. 75 small domes cover the rest of the space.

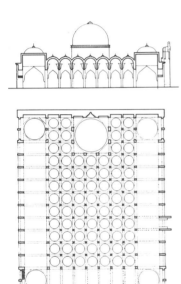

Cross-section and floor plan

❶ The fort and the Jami Masjid, facing the lake.
❷ Full view of the Jami Masjid.
❸ The line or arches that form the outer ring.
❹ In front of the *mihrab* is the biggest dome.
❺ The unique design around the central dome

BIDAR ★★★

FORT HH

15th~16th Century/ Islamic

In 1424 the capital of the Bahmani dynasty shifted 111 km away, to Bidar. Four other Muslim kingdoms of Bijapur, Golconda, Berar and Ahmednagar broke away from the Bahmani kingdom. Though they called themselves the Five Kingdoms they attacked each other.

The Bidar Fort reinforced over a period of 200 years is an impressive one. The fort is located north of the city. The exceedingly thick walls and bastions bend many times and should be more than 10 km in actual length. The fort is built with bricks and basalt, and decorated with Faience tiles.

The Rangin Mahal and Solah Khamba Mosque (1327) are in good condition, but most of the many palaces and mosques inside are destroyed. A Hindu style wooden structure is seen inside the Rangin Mahal, while the walls have Persian tiles. Solah Khamba mosque was originally designed as the Jami Masjid. After another Friday mosque was constructed in the city, this one was used as the prayer room of the royals.

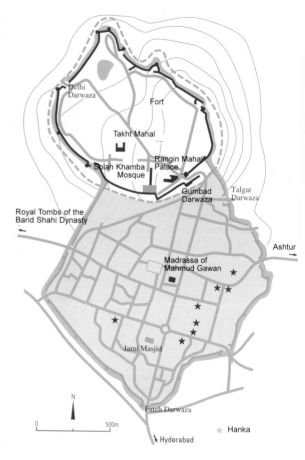

Gumbaz Darwaza (Dome Gate), The third entrance to the city made of bricks

❶ The fort wall and bastion chain reminds one of the expressionist group.
❷ Takht Mahal palace where the throne was located.
❸ Solah Khamba Mosque facing the Lal Bagh gardens
❹ The thick circular pillars remind one of the early Persian style.
❺ Rangin Mahal has a wooden interior with Faience tiles on the walls.
❻ One of the many *Hankas*. (Sufi prayer place)

BIDAR

MADRASSA OF KHWAJA MAHMUD GAWAN ⋆

1472/ Islamic

A half-open space with a huge entrance arch is called an *ivan*. Four *ivans* faced each other around a courtyard which is the entrance, classroom and the prayer room. The surrounding three-storeyed buildings were dormitories and lecture halls. This scale of *madrassa*, shows the cultural emancipation Bidar then enjoyed.

❶ Part of the structure surrounding the courtyard.
❷ Small mosque inside the *madrassa*.
❸ *Ivan* facing Mecca.

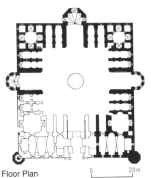

Floor Plan

0   20m

TOMBS OF ASHTUR ★
15th Century/ Islamic

The royal tombs of the Bahmani rulers are in Ashtur, 3 km north of Bidar. They are 2 to 3 storeys high and have no enclosing wall. The domes are high and large and the walls were inlaid with Faience tiles in intricate patterns. The Khalil Allah tomb in Chaukhandi is different. It is a four-sided building but from the outside it looks like an eight-sided building.

❶ Outer view of Ahmad Shah Bahmani
❷ Inside Allauddin Ahmad II tomb (1458)
❸ Tile inlay on the outer walls of Allauddin Bahmani's tomb

Khalil Allah's tomb in Chaukhandi

TOMBS OF BARIDI DYNASTY ★★
15th~16th Century/Islamic

The tombs of Baridi dynasty are 1.5 km away from the city. While the small tombs resemble the older tombs, those of subsequent generations were built higher, with more storeys and huge arch entrances spanning half the height of the tombs. The tomb of Ali Baridi Shah belongs to this generation and has been built on a foundation platform in the middle of a square garden. The tomb architecture of the Deccan after this time can be seen in the Royal tombs of Golconda.

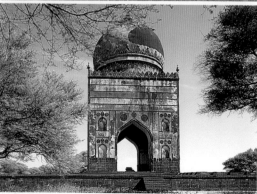

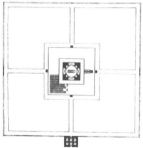

Floor plan of Ali Baridi Shah Tomb

Up: Small Tomb group. Down: Ali Baridi Shah Tomb.

Bijapur was the capital of the Adil Shahi dynasty (1490 - 1686) that suppressed the Bahmani dynasty. Bijapur, means the city of victory and has the largest number of Islamic ruins in South India. It was revived by the Belgaum head of the Bahmani dynasty and flourished during the times of Ibrahim II (1580-1626). A 10 km long wall surrounds the city and the fort is in the middle of the circular town. The fort has 96 bastions and five main

entrances. This dynasty had a deep understanding of architecture. Later it was attacked and in 1636 they accepted Mughal supremacy. In 1686 Aurangzeb attacked the city, fortunately most of the buildings still exist. The design that is most different from the North Indian design is the ball shaped dome that also resembles a lotus flower. It is a good place to study ruins. Unfortunately there are no good hotels in Bijapur, so few tourists visit here.

MEHTAR MAHAL ★★
1620/ Islamic

This is not a palace even though it is called a *mahal*. It is a turret with the Mehtar mosque behind it on the south east of the citadel. This small structure, with its exquisite entrance is one of the beautiful sights of Bijapur.

It is a two-storeyed structure where the first floor is an ambulatory. The ceiling is a stone lattice and there are latticework beam suspensions in the central hall on the way to the second floor. The roof has two delicate minarets standing straight and tall. The mosque behind does not have a dome roof. This is fundamentally a Hindu style wood construction. The window and the carving on it is very interesting.

❶ Mehtar Mahal facing the pathway.
❷ The window and eaves on the second floor.
❸ The central ceiling on the first floor.
❹ The small Mehtar Mosque behind.
❺ The roof has been covered by walls.

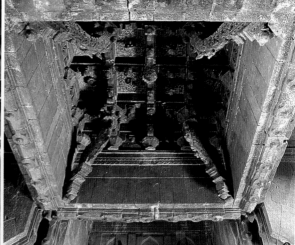

ASAR MAHAL
1646/ Islamic
Built as the court in a wide area behind the citadel, it was later converted into a sacred relinquary to house two hairs of the Prophet Muhammed. It faces a rectangular tank where, a Persian style half-hall has been created with four teak pillars in the front. On the second floor is a veranda with various rooms opening on to it. There are beautiful murals on some of the walls.

Dalal type big hall on the first floor

JAL MANZIL (WATER PAVILION) ★
Islamic
It is a miniature pavilion inside the fort, facing Sat Manzil, originally a seven storeyed pleasure palace. Originally built in the middle of the lake, it is now in a small area by the pathway. It is constructed in the wood construction style with broad eaves and very small minarets on the top with a huge dome in the middle. This is a unique building.

The wall surface had inlaid tiles originally

JAMI MASJID (FRIDAY MOSQUE) ★
16th~17th Century/ Islamic
This is a geometrical building with a prayer hall and ornamental pools to the left and right of the courtyard. The simple arches and pillars are in harmony with the surroundings. One side of the court is open and the gate is a short distance away. The entrance that is used is on the north side and has a small pillared ambulatory and pavilion. The combination of an orderly style and the unexpected break in this order gives this mosque a singular appearance.

Up: The geometrical prayer room with little ornamentation. Down: The dome of the prayer room seen from the courtyard.

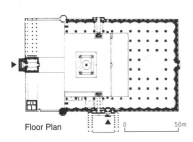

Floor Plan   0   50m

IBRAHIM RAUZA (TOMB AND MOSQUE) ★★
1626/ Islamic

Ibrahim Adil Shah II took Bijapur kingdom to great heights. His tomb and the mosque complex are situated about 700 km west of Zohrapur gate. It is just 30 m from the road. Walking up the path, with the tomb on the left and the mosque to the right of the entrance gate, the structures with their numerous minarets and the onion dome, make a fantastic sight.

The largest dome is on the tomb of Ibrahim with a diameter of 13 m. Below this is the tomb room with two rows of enclosed ambulatories.

The wall and doorway facing the closed corridor has wonderfully intricate decoration. The mosque and tomb face each other in a 130 m x 140 m area, encircled by a low wall on a common foundation platform with a tank in the centre. The mosque faces Mecca in the west and the east side is open with five arches. Persian architect Malik Sandal designed this geometrical arch type construction. Only the eaves supported by brackets look Indian.

❶ Ibrahim tomb in the right and mosque on the left face each other. ❷ The entrance facing the central platform. ❸ The façade of the mosque with five arches. ❹ Details of the complicated roof on Ibrahim's tomb.

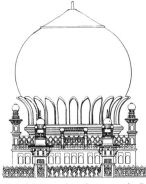

Elevation of the part where the mosque is situated

⑤ Wooden doorway has been attached to the windows of the tomb room facing the corridor.
⑥ Pillared ambulatory from where the tomb room surroundings can be seen.

BIJAPUR

TAJ BAOLI (TANK)

1620/ Islamic

It is the biggest reservoir in the city, different from the step-wells and tanks of West India. It is rectangular with steps going down, right and left from the centre. The rear portion has a terrace. On the other side buildings face the road. In the middle is an *ivan* with an onion dome on its left and right and on both sides of this are rest-rooms.

The central part of the building.

BIJAPUR

JOD GUMBAZ (TWO TOMBS) ★

Islamic

It is called Two Tombs but there are 4 tombs in the garden. The octagonal structure is the tomb of Khan Mohammed, who it is said, was killed by treachery. The carving around the eaves is beautiful. Eight small domes, in true Bijapur style, encircle the main dome. Each small dome is in turn encircled by eight smaller domes.

The detailing on the eaves of the dome.

GOL GUMBAZ ★★
1659/ Islamic

Muhammed Adil Shah II, who succeeded Ibrahim II, designed a tomb for himself, that was very different from any tomb in the past. He selected a large tract of land on the east side of the fort far away from the street and designed a square garden inside the gate. Here he built a tomb having a diameter of 44 m. On the four corners a seven-storeyed minaret was built and a dome 36 m in diameter was suspended on top. There is no buttress taking the pressure of this the largest dome in India. It just stands on the four sturdy walls. The height of the ceiling is 50 m. The space inside has no pillars and is devoid of decorations. At the base of the dome are balconies from where important personalities could look into the tomb.

❶ Small pavillions and the stairway to the roof. ❷ The large tomb seen from the gate. ❸ The vaulted ceiling seen from the balcony. ❹ The gate with the unfinished minaret

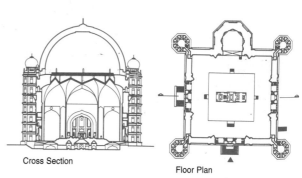

Cross Section

Floor Plan

BADAMI ★ ★ ★

It is one of the especially fascinating places in the South, unspoiled by tourism due to bad roads and poor accommodation. Pattadakal and Aihole nearby are also worth seeing. One should take a train to Sholapur then change to a local train via Bijapur. Hire a *tonga* from the station into the city to enjoy the beautiful tree-lined roads.

This is a small town of 20,000 people. In the 6th-7th centuries it was the capital of the Chalukya dynasty and was called Vatapi. Along with Aihole this is the place where South Indian architecture originated. A large manmade lake has red sandstone cliffs on three sides. The town is spread over plains on the fourth side while there is a fort on the mountains. Ancient stone temples blend with the northern and southern mountains they are built on. Bhutanatha Temple on the other side of the lake looks like it is floating on the water. The evening view is unforgettable. It looks like a painting of India in the Middle Ages.

❶ The city in the plains and the temples on the mountain.
❷ The Shivalaya temple (7th century) above. There is a stone temple on the other side.
❸ Bhutanatha temple on the other side of the tank.

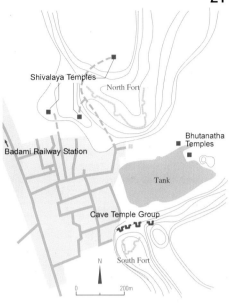

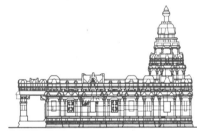

Elevation of Bhutanatha temple

Cross section of the Bhutanatha temple

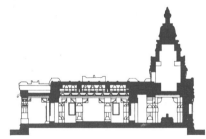

Floor plan of Bhutanatha temple

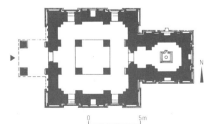

MALLEGITTI SHIVALAYA TEMPLE ★
7th Century/ Hindu

The three Shiva temples in this area are the Upper, Lower and Mallegitti Shiva temples. It is one of the temple groups of the Early Ages built with stones from the caves and is influenced by the Pallava style of the same age. It is very proportionate with *mandapa* and *garbhagriha* design with a small porch in front. Mallegitti temple is comparatively well preserved.

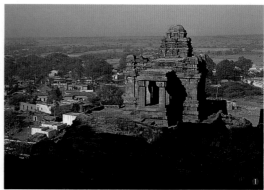

❶ The temple on the red sandstone mountain
❷ The sculpture in the horseshoe shaped arch
❸ Sculpture on the wall (Shiva)

BHUTANATHA GROUP ★
7th, 11th Century/ Hindu

The Bhutanatha group of temples at the far end of the lake vary in vintage and style. Temple No.1 with a verandah extending to the water surface is similar to the Mallegitti temple. The *shikara* could be North Indian or early South Indian as in the Mahabalipuram shore temples, built very close to the water. Temple No. 2 has a *vimana* made up of very small steps reflecting the early Chalukya style.

Up: View of Bhutanatha temple. These temples are prominent in South India too.
Down: Bhutanatha temple 2.

Inside Bhutanatha temple 2

CAVE TEMPLES ★★
6th Century/ Hindu, Jain

There are four cave temples on the mountains in the south, three Hindu which are the oldest Hindu temples in the south, while the fourth is Jain. Cave Temple 1 is dedicated to Shiva and 2 to Vishnu. Lively sculptures cover the walls. There are pillared *mandapas* with the *garbhagriha* at the far end. All three cave temples are different. The beams in No 1 are parallel to the façade. In cave No. 2, vertical and in cave No. 3, they takes the shape of the cave and thus all three caves are different. The Jain temple is the smallest and has statues of *Tirthankaras*.

Mithuna statues in cave No.3

Up: Cave 3 is 20 m wide (Hindu). Down: Inside Cave 4 (Jain)

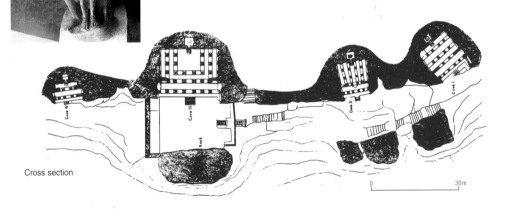

Cross section

0   30 m

BANASHANKARI TEMPLE
Hindu

Banashankari village is 9 km from Badami on the way to Gadag. There is a tank with a circumbulatory and a devi temple with black goddesses deified in it. Near the tank stands a rare sentinel tower that reflects the Vijayanagara blend of Hindu and Islamic style. The entire structure is called the 'victory tower'. It may belong to the Maratha age.

Sentinel tower   The corridor surrounding the tank

About 30 km from Badami on the way to Aihole is a group of well-preserved temples. The small village of Pattadakal was once the second largest city of the Chalukyas. It is said that the coronation of the king was always held here. There are 9 large temples, which reflect the maturity of architectural style in the Badami and Aihole region. One can see a blend of the north style and south style of the Middle Ages in these temples. The larger Virupaksha, Mallikarjuna and Sangamesvara temples have the southern style and are similar to the Pallava dynasty architecture of Kanchipuram. The Rashtrakutas adopted this style in the Kailasa temple in Ellora. The smaller temples of Papanatha, Galaganatha, Kashi Visvanatha and Jambulinga have north style *shikharas* on the *garbhagriha* which was the forerunner for the towering north and west Indian type *shikharas*. As you explore this place it is easy to imagine the large numbers of people who lived here at that time.

South type Sangamesvara temple (middle), far right is the Galaganatha temple, the north type Kashi Visvanatha temple.

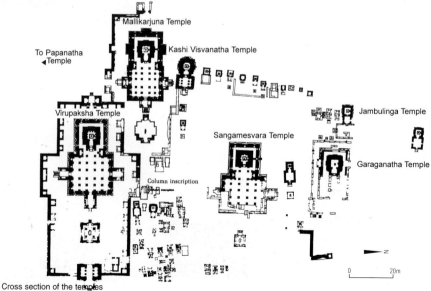

Mallikarjuna Temple

To Papanatha Temple

Kashi Visvanatha Temple

Virupaksha Temple

Jambulinga Temple

Sangamesvara Temple

Garaganatha Temple

Column inscription

Cross section of the temples

VIRUPAKSHA ★★ AND MALLIKARJUNA ★ TEMPLES
745 AD/ Hindu

These temples dedicated to Shiva, were a memorial built by the two queens of Vikramaditya II of the Chalukya dynasty, after he conquered the Pallavas. The king brought back one of the chief Pallava architects to Pattadakal. The strong Pallava style is similar to the Kailasanatha temple of Kanchipuram. The Mallikarjuna temple built behind the Virupaksha temple, is smaller. Both temples have a *pradakshina path* or cirumbulatory around the shrine and a *mandapa* with porches on three sides. In front is the Nandi shrine. A low wall encloses the entrance and the precincts. The style of the large Virupaksha temple is a forerunner of the Chalukya style. The queen who built this temple was Trilokaya Mahadevi.

❶ Sculptures on the wall of Virupaksha temple. A figure peeps perpetually from a south window. ❷ Nandi shrine in the same temple. ❸ The tower of Virupaksha temple. ❹ The north east side of the same temple. ❺ Inside the *mandapa* of Virupaksha temple. ❻ The south view of the Mallikarjuna temple.

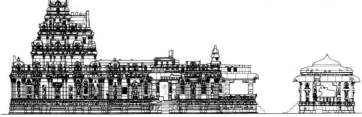

Elevation of Virupaksha temple

JAMBULINGA TEMPLE
8th C/ Hindu
This small temple is the *mandapa* and porch type. Earlier it had a large *mandapa* at the front and an *amalaka* which has gone. The shrine is 5 m long on one side and crowned with a northern type *shikhara*. An *amalaka* shape is sculpted at the corners of the 2nd step of the *shikhara*. Nataraja (dancing god) is carved on the front.

South East view of the temple

PAPANATHA TEMPLE ★
8th C/ Hindu
This temple, a little away from the others, is built in a horizontal style. In front of the *mandapa,* is another large *mandapa* with a Nandi in the centre. There is no pillar beam suspension inside and it looks very medieval. It has a northern-style *shikhara* and the style of the walls remind one of the Alampur temple.

Inside the large *mandapa*

JAINA TEMPLE
9th Century/ Jain
500 m from the temple area is a Jain temple which dates back to the 9th century of the Rashtrakuta dynasty. As in Ajanta, king Amoghavarsha or his son Krishna II, who patronized the Jain religion, built it. Unfortunately the wall of the circumbulatory round the shrine is in ruins.

Shrine and *mandapa* not very decorative

MAHAKUTA ★ 23

HINDU TEMPLES ★
7th C/ Hindu
In the forest at Mahakuta,13 km from Badami on the way to Pattadakal, there are a group of temples which reflect the development of the north-south style. There are two temples, Mahakutesvara and Mallikarjuna with a natural tank in the centre and a number of temples around. Even now there is a long line of devotees offering prayers.

Mahakutesvara temple is painted white

AIHOLE ★ ★ ★

19 km from Pattadakal village in Aihole, there are many small temples from 6th to 11th centuries belonging to early Chalukya, Rashtrakuta and later Chalukya dynasties. From half-broken temples to small shrines, there ' are around 140 temples in this once prominent trading city of the Chalukyas. It has one Jain cave temple and one Buddhist cave temple. All the other Jain and Buddhist temples are built with stone and resemble Hindu temples. Another interesting fact is that these temples were built during the Middle Ages before any style was established and hence there is a mixture of styles.

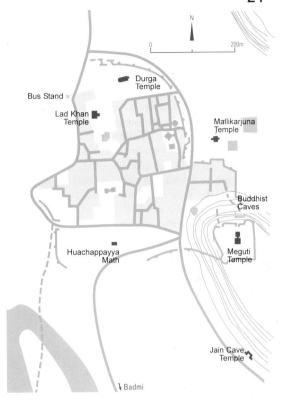

2nd floor verandah of the Buddhist cave (6th C).

JAIN CAVE TEMPLE
6th C/Jain

Temple constructions started with wood and when stone caves were built, the next step was stone constructions. Jain cave temples can be seen at the foot of the mountains in the south of the city. The *mandapa* is at the end of the verandah and there are shrines on three sides. There are two pillars at both entrances and the main shrine has a Parshavanatha statue.

MEGUTI TEMPLE
634 AD/Jain

This is a very old stone temple built by Pulakesin II of the Chalukya dynasty on a hill overlooking the town. It is a square plan with a *pradakshina path* around the shrine. The pillars on the outer walls, the base foundation and the parapet in this temple, are all hallmarks of the southern style of the Later Ages. The first floor was added on later.

LAD KHAN TEMPLE ★
700 AD/Hindu

The special feature of the Aihole temple is that it starts with the rectangular Gaudar Gudi temple and then continues on to the square Rashtrakuta temple style. Based on a wooden construction design, the square and rectangular plan has a steep roof, which is an adaptation of wooden styles in stone. The Nandi has been placed in the middle of the *mandapa* and in the far corner the *linga* has been deified. This reflects the trial and error method of building in the early days.

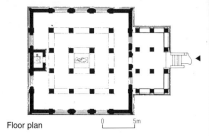

Floor plan

❶ South View ❷ *Mandapa* with Nandi ❸ Sculpture on the porch pillar.

HUACCHAPAYYA MATHA TEMPLE
7th C/Hindu

This temple can be seen on the route to Badami. It is a small square temple which stands majestically on wide precincts. The whole platform rests on a simple base and on the pillars, deities and Mithuna sculptures are carved. Inside there are very minute and detailed carvings. The carved panel on the ceiling is a special feature of Aihole.

MALLIKARJUNA TEMPLE ★
8th C/Hindu

Aihole has many temples with North Indian type *shikharas*. The temple on the edge of the tank is one of them. It has a *garbhagriha*, a *mandapa* and a four-pillared porch. The shrine has a north Indian type *shikhara* with an *amalaka* on the top. Instead of the vertical line, the *shikhara* has a south styled seven stepped horizontal design.

DURGA TEMPLE ★★
7th C/Hindu

Early Hindu constructions were based on Buddhist temple design. The Durga temple in Aihole has the straight front, and rounded apse of a Buddhist *chaitya* temple. Instead of a *stupa*, there is a circumbulatory around the shrine that continues on to the *mandapa* in the front. Usually there would be a porch in the front of the temple, but the unique element of this temple is the circumbulatory with its early Chalukya sculpture that surrounds the entire structure. The *garbhagriha* has a north Indian type *shikhara* and every layer has a horseshoe shaped arch. This unique design was not continued by later generations. Instead distinct north and south styles developed. The circular back, straight front can be seen in some temples in South India and the wooden temples of Kerala, but they have no *shikharas*.

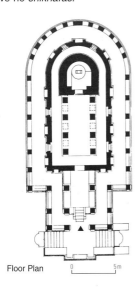

Floor Plan   0 ____ 5m

Inside the *mandapa*

❶ South view ❷ Front entrance ❸ Porch ceiling ❹ Corridors

441

DEGAMVE ⋆

25

KAMALA NARAYANA TEMPLE ⋆
12th C/ Hindu

It is a temple of Kadamba dynasty that ruled western Deccan. The peak is broken, so it is not much to look at from the outside. The interior has a lot to marvel at however. The temple has a long *mandapa* connecting three temples and the pillars with their exceptional work, are heavenly.

Pillars inside the *mandapa*

DAMBAL ⋆

DODDA BASAPPA TEMPLE ⋆
12th C/ Hindu

As you come down from Solapur by rail to Bijapur and Badami, the next stop will be Gadag, where one can explore Later Chalukya architecture of 10th to 12th century. There are three temples in the city of Dambal which is 20 km south east of here.

The Later Chalukya architecture has a star-shaped plan for the *vimana*. The Dodda Basappa temple in Dambal has so many star points that it almost looks circular.

One right angle is divided into four angles of 22.5 degrees. 48 such angles are further sub divided and decorated with minute carvings.

This style was common in the Hoysala dynasty(12th-14th centuries) too. The *shikhara* is neither north nor south style. Since it has incorporated both styles it can be called an "in-between style."

Dodda Basappa has so many star points it looks almost circular

KUKNUR ⋆

27

NAVALINGA TEMPLE ⋆
9th C/Hindu

Kuknur which is 40 km from Gadag, has a Navalinga temple complex built during the Rashtrakuta dynasty and a Kallesvara temple built during the Later Chalukya dynasty. Navalinga means nine *lingas* and accordingly nine *linga* temples are lined up. All of them have the south-Indian style in the upper portion of the *shikharas*.

Nine *linga* temples in a row.

MAHADEVA TEMPLE ★★
1112/ Hindu

There is a huge tank 7 km from Kuknur in Ittagi village. Facing this tank is a number of small temples and the Mahadeva temple which has a classic later-Chalukya plan, with a *garbhagriha* and a front hall (*antarala*) leading to the *mandapa*. The porch has been extended on all three sides with a doorway on each side. There is an open *mandapa* in the front hall, which has 26 circular pillars with sculptures worth seeing. The *vimana* and the tower also have minute carving. Most of these are decorative designs with very few images of deities. These carvings have been done on green schist which technique was adopted by the Hoysalas too.

STEPPED TANK

Temples in the Chalukya period always had a tank close to the complex. Only the main entrance of the tank has steps and the other three sides have sloping walls. This sculpture-less geometric design is very arresting and is seen in Aihole and Gadag too.

❶ The tower of the *vimana* is a later addition. ❷ Inside the *mandapa*. ❸ The details of the *vimana* tower.

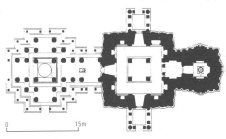

Floor Plan

There are steps leading above from left and right of the landing

LAKKUNDI ★★

The Chalukyas who wrested power from the Rashtrakutas (9th-10th centuries), made Kalyani their capital. Nothing remains of this city now. Most of the later-Chalukya temples are preserved in Lakkundi, 11 km from Gadag in the east. It is 24 km from Dambal and around 50 km from Kuknur. There are more than 15 Hindu and Jain temples in this town which was a prominent city a thousand years back. All the temples are made of green schist and the outer walls and entrances are very richly decorated. The *shikhara* is an in-between-style type and the parapet and the artistic division of the wall with pilasters is typical of the south-Indian style.

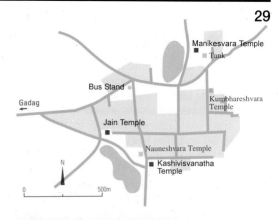

Naneshvara temple is a smaller replica of Kashi Visvanatha temple

---

LAKKUNDI

BRAHMA-JINALAYA BASTI ★
11th C/ Jain

This Jain temple is the largest and oldest temple in Lakkundi. That there are three other Jain temples here, shows that the later-Chalukyas were religiously tolerant. This temple has a *garbhagriha* shrine and *mandapa* style with deep beams on the *mandapa* from where the eaves are cantilevered. It resembles the Muda Bidri Jain temple.

Inside the open *mandapa*

Up: Full view. Down: *Tirthankara* statues on the south style parapet

KASHIVISVANATHA TEMPLE ★★
12th C/ Hindu

A great deal of care has gone into the construction of the Kashivisvanatha temple in Lakkundi which deifies Shiva. This temple has a unique feature: a small *surya* shrine faces the main shrine on the west. There is a common platform between both which must have been an open *mandapa* originally. Hence the Kashivisvanatha temple has an entrance on the east side and south side of the *mandapa*. The entrance doorway and the towers are covered with close intricate carving. The *shikhara* is in the North-Indian style and it looks like a lathe must have been used to make the complex circular pillars.

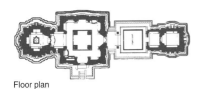

Floor plan

❶ There is an entrance on the south too.
❷ A platform with four pillars inside the *mandapa*.
❸ The later-Chalukyas used Kirthi Mukha (demon faces) in their sculptures .

MANIKESVARA TEMPLE AND STEPPED TANK ★
Hindu

There is an impressive stepped tank of the Chalukya dynasty near the temple. The steps are on three sides of the tank which is flanked on both sides with smaller temples. The approach to the *mandapa* of these temples forms a bridge on the fourth side of the tank.

MALLIKARJUNA TEMPLE ★★
10th C/Hindu

35 km from Haveri, and 30 km from Harihar is Kuruvatti village nestled in the mountains. The narrow road lined with old houses like the pilgrim towns in Spain, is not motorable after a point and has to be covered on foot. The temple is not very large and the tower on the *vimana* is a later addition. But the details on the wall and within, are very precise. The temple has a *garbhagriha*, an *antarala,* a *mandapa* with a porch, also a huge Nandi shrine which is different from others. The pillars inside must have been made by using a lathe. There is no comparison to the richness of this pillar base. The pillar head at the entrance is sculpted with beautiful *apsaras.* This temple reflects the skilled art of the later-Chalukya period.

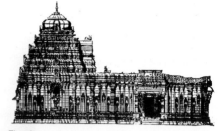
Elevation

Full view of the north type *vimana*

The carvings on the *Vimana*

Up: *Apsara* on the pillar. Down: Pillar base with sculpted *shikharas*

The last great Hindu empire in South India, the Vijayanagara empire ruled from 14-17centuries. Vijayanagara, the city of victory, was their capital. Developed by Krishna Devaraya (1510-1529) it had many temples, palaces and public facilities spread over a wide area. The city walls extended up to 26 km along the Tungabhadra banks and the population was more than 500,000. In 1565 they were overpowered by the Five Muslim Kingdoms' united front and after the Battle of Talikota they shifted to Penukonda and Vijayanagara was abandoned. The Virupaksha temple, where prayers are still offered, is located here and all the ruins are loosely called Hampi. This includes Kamalapuram village and the Anegondi ruins. Hospet town, which is 13 km in the southwest, is the base from which to visit these ruins. The ruins are divided into Temple Area in the north and Palace Area in the south. There is a 700 m long road called Hampi bazaar leading from the Virupaksha temple. Residents live in buildings on both sides of this street. From here to Vitthala and other temples in the north is an enjoyable 1.5 km long walk on the scenic riverbank route.

Up: East end of the 32 m wide Hampi Bazaar.
Down: The view of the palace grounds with the mountains in the background.

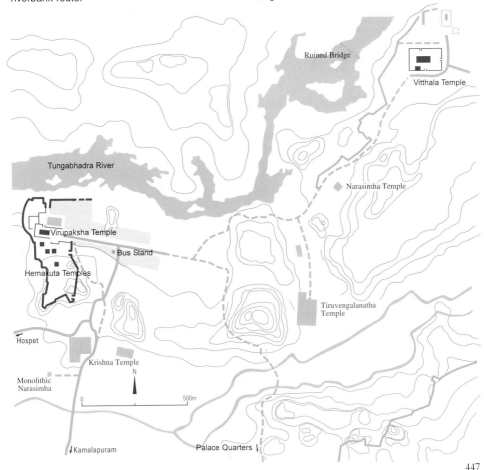

447

HEMAKUTA TEMPLES ★
10th~14th Century/Jain

Hampi was a holy town even before the Vijayanagara dynasty. There is a group of seven temples overlooking the town with their pyramid like spires, sure signs that the-later Chalukyas built them. Now Jain, originally they were all Shiva temples. There are three temples with three *garbhagrihas,* one temple with two *garbhagrihas* and the rest are the usual *garbhagrihas* and *mandapa* design. There are no decorative sculptures on the walls. The hardness of the rocks determined the design that was used for carving.

The *mandapa* of the three-*garbhagriha* temple

Up: Rear view of 3-shrine temple. Down: 2-shrine temple below the hill.

VIRUPAKSHA (PAMPAPATI) TEMPLE ★
13th~17th Century/ Hindu

This temple is situated between the Hemakuta hills. It is a very old construction. It was renovated and additions were made after a long period of time. Virupaksha is another name for Shiva. Since Pampa (wife of Shiva) is also enshrined, it is also called Pampapati temple. The Vijayanagara style *gopura* beckons one from outside. The *gopura* built by Krishna Devaraya is 52 m high. The huge precincts are fenced as is the shrine (*vimana*) inside. The ceiling of the *mandapa* was painted with designs in the 18th century.

Up: View from Hemakuta hills.
Down: The ceiling designs in the *mandapa* (the wedding of Pampa and Virupaksha)

448

RAMACHANDRA TEMPLE ★★
15th C/ Hindu

This temple is in the heart of the palace grounds and is called Hazara Rama. Rama (an incarnation of Vishnu) is deified here. It was a medium-sized temple of the royals. It has entrances in the east and north and has a low wall. The wall has a relief of animals, musicians etc, sculpted on it in many layers. The temple plan is the same as the later Chalukya type square *mandapa* with a three-sided entrance. The *vimana* reflects the southern style with decorations that can only be described as harmonious. Nearby is the Amman *garbhagriha*, which was built later and is richer in sculptures.

Up: The temple from afar. Down: Entrance with relief carving

❶ The external view of the *vimana*. ❷ The pillar in the north porch. ❸ Inside the *mandapa* with its rich sculpting.

449

VITTHALA TEMPLE ★★★
16th C/ Hindu

Vitthala temple at the northeast end of Hampi, is the greatest of Vijayanagara architecture. The exact year of construction is not known, but Krishna Devaraya was the main patron. In the 1000 years that it took for stone construction to evolve, this temple is evidence that it had attained great heights of perfection.

This temple spans 95 m x 164 m with its fence and cirumbulatory. In the centre is the chariot and east *gopura*. The southern side also has a *gopura* and main gate facing the city road. The temple consists of a *garbhagriha* with a pathway around it, a closed *mandapa* and a three-way entrance. There is a large open *mandapa* in the east, with a highly sculpted base platform with pillars. There are 56 pillars,

which again is a group of pillars with deities and *yalis* (mythical horse figures) sculpted on them. These make it all look very complex. This space surrounded by pillars makes a fantastic sight. This is a place that is really worth taking trouble to examine carefully.

There are a number of small shrines on the premises enshrining different deities. The *kalyana mandapa* with its suspended construction on pillars, leaves one speechless. The base is granite while *vimana* and *gopura* are made of bricks. One side is in ruins. Even though stone chariots with elephants or horses drawing them are a common sight in temples in the south, in Vitthala, they are excellent.

❶ Pillars in open *mandapa* ❷ Chariot and Eastern *gopura*
❸ Inside the open *mandapa* ❹ Sculptures at the base
❺ Chariot ❻ The open *mandapa*

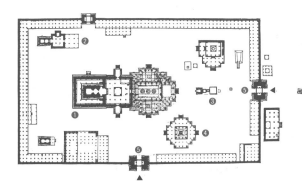

Floor plan
❶ Vitthala temple
❷ Amman shrine
❸ Chariot
❹ *Kalyana mandapa*
❺ *Gopura*

PALACE QUARTER ★
15th~16th C/ Hindu

The palace quarter is 35 km away from Hampi Bazaar. The fort walls and most of the buildings are destroyed but what is left is an entirely different architectural style from the temples. The structures have been finished with plaster.

LOTUS MAHAL
It is a palace for the ladies with an Islamic arch construction and Hindu roof.

SENTINEL TOWERS
There are two sentinel towers near the Lotus Mahal. One is four-sided and the other eight-sided.

ELEPHANT STABLES
It stands in a line with many floors in the middle and five rooms on both sides. The roof of each stable looks different.

QUEEN'S BATH
It is a rectangular construction with no decoration on the outside. The bathplace is 15 m long and from the surrounding gallery there are *jharokhas* or extended windows, that are richly decorated.

STEPPED TANK
It is called Pushkarini and the water is brought from a higher level. There are no shrines on the steps, hence it may not religiously significant.

Up: The fort. Down: The courtyard of Royal ladies bathhouse.

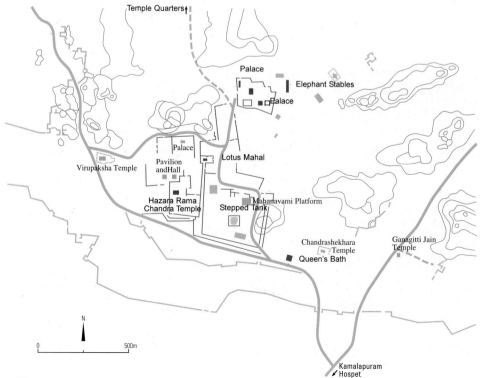

❶ Elephant stables seen from the rectangular building
❷ The eight-sided sentinel tower
❸ The stepped tank
❹ The rectangular sentinel tower and palace platform
❺ Lotus Mahal

Cross section of Elephant stable

HAVERI ⋆

32

SIDDESHWARA TEMPLE ⋆
11th C/ Hindu

A classic example of later-Chalukya style of temple can be seen outside the town of Haveri, 100 km from Gadag and 50 km from Harihar. It has a *garbhagriha*, a front hall and a four-pillared *mandapa* with a porch which has entrances on three sides. The shrine is on the side of the porch. *Vimana* is made of green schist.

The temple as seen from the northeast

KELADI ⋆

33

HINDU TEMPLES
16th C/ Hindu

Keladi, once the Nayaka capital, is 10 km away from Ikkeri. The complex has several small *garbhagrihas* through a long, covered wooden entrance. There is a common *mandapa* for the Ramesvara and Veerbhadra *garbha-grihas*. The simple Parvathi shrine is a later addition. The wooden sculptures and wooden pillars inside are a rarity.

Left: Parvathi temple Right: 2-shrined temple

IKKERI ⋆⋆

AGHORESVARA TEMPLE ⋆⋆
16th C/ Hindu

Small vassal kingdoms of the Vijayanagara dynasty in Madurai, Tanjavur and Ikkeri sprang up around the 16th century. They were called Nayakas. The Nayakas of Ikkeri reigned from 1540 to 1763. The Aghoresvara temple where Shiva is deified is a blend of Hoysala and Dravida style. Vengayya was the architect of this symmetrical temple which is without excessive decoration.

There is an Amman shrine and a unique Nandi shrine inside the laterite wall, in addition to the main shrine. The temple along with Muka *mandapa* and *garbhagriha* is made of black basalt stone. The *mandapa* has six pillars and the entrance to the *garbhagriha* is magnificent. The Vijayanagara style of construction is seen here. The sculptures on the outside entrance belong to the Hoysala style. The tower on the shrine sports an in-between style. This temple is in a field 3 km from Sagar which is 100 km from Haveri.

❶ Temple with sloping eaves and parapets. ❷ Nandi shrine with arch.

❸ The symmetrical Agoreshwara Temple without excessive decoration.

❹ Sculpted ceiling of *mandapa*. ❺ In-between style of the tower. ❻ Inside the wide *mandapa*.❼ Intricately carved sculptures.

KHETAPAI NARAYANA TEMPLE ⋆
17th C/ Hindu

The west coast style of south India starts from here. The roofs of the buildings are steep since it rains heavily on the Western Ghats. They are mostly wooden structures as in Kerala. In Karnataka, stone constructions are prominent. This temple has a circumbulatory around the shrine and a simple sloped roof. The outside wall is made of stone with lattice work, and there are magnificent Vijayanagara style decorations at the entrance.

Temple seen from the entrance   Up: Magnificent sculptured entrance Down: High quality of sculpture

CHANDRANATHA BASTI
17~18th C/ Jain

There are some Jain temples in the old Bhatkal town but the Chandranatha temple is in the new town. The sloping roofs of the *garbhagriha* continue lengthwise and in the front a *mana stambha* has been designed. There is a two-floored turret facing the *stamba*, which is also different from others. The open pillared *pradakshina path* only around the *garbhagriha* is also a rarity.

The temple is being renovated

MANJUNATHA TEMPLE
1068/ Hindu

This temple is at the foot of the Katri hills and generally full of pilgrims. It dates back to the 10th century, but the pyramid like tower belongs to another time. There are wooden lattice screens on the first floor. In startling contrast with the greenery around, the temple is painted white. Pilgrims go round the *garbhagriha* clockwise.

Pillared ambulatory surrounding the shrine

VIDYASHANKARA TEMPLE ★★
14th C/ Hindu

Sringeri is a monastic temple town started by Shankaracharya, who promoted the Advaitha philosophy in the 9th century. The temple was built in the 14th century with the support of Vijayanagara. It is simply called Shankaracharya temple. It has a *garbhagriha* and *mandapa* style. The star-shaped walls on the foundation platform are almost circular and the *shikhara* rises up in four levels. The outer wall has the Hoysala star shape, but the interior is pure Vijayanagara.

The wall surface where deities are placed

❶ Full view. ❷ *Vimana* and wall surface. ❸ *Mandapa* south entrance.

GOMMATESHWARA STATUE
1432/Jain

A group of Jain temples are 15 km away from Mudabidri, on the way to Karkala. These temples are around a *Mana stambha.* Nearby is a simple 13 m high statue of Gommateshwara, who was the son of Adinatha the first *tirthankara.* South India accepted Jainism and these statues have been erected in five places.

Right: Platform built once in 12 years.
Left: Gommateshwara statue.

CHATURMUKHA BASTI ★
1587/Jain

A *chaumukha* (four-side open) temple on the hill faces the Gommateshwara statue. The central shrine holding 12 *tirthankaras,* is open on all four sides. In each side are three statues of *tirthankaras* made of black stone standing with their backs to each other. They are all connected with an cirumbulatory around the cloister.

Temple with a line of pillars.

TEMPLE TOWN (JAINA BASTIS)
Jain

Mudabidri is another Jain town on par with Shravanabelagola. It is 35 km from Mangalore. This small farming town has 18 Jain temples. More than half of them line up on both sides of the road, which makes it a temple town. They all look alike, with steep roofs, a *manastambha* in the front and all are made of stone. The west coast temples can be compared with the temple towns in Japan. Jain temples are called "basti" or "basati" here a word evolved from the Sanskrit word "vasati".

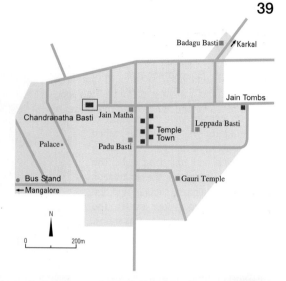

❶ Kallu temple ❷ Leppada temple ❸ Roof of the Guru temple

TOMBS OF JAINA PRIESTS
19th C/ Jain

Jains believed in reincarnation. They believed that the dead would be born again in 49 days. There was no custom of building tombs. But here is a group of Jain memorials made of laterite which resemble the Meru of Bali island with their multi-layered towers. These could be memorials of holy people.

Jain memorials

CHANDRANATHA BASTI ★★
1429/ JAIN

This is the main temple and the largest. Inside is a wide rectangular precinct. There is a beautiful *mana stambha* in front of the long temple at the far end. It has three *mandapas* in front of the *garbhagriha* with a circumbulatory around them. The roof looks complex as if there are a number of rooms inside. There is stone roofing on the first floor and wooden roofing on the second floor with embellishments like those on Nepal temple roofs. Inside too the structure resembles the wooden trabeated or post and beam style of construction. The pillars are circular and rich with Vijayanagara carving.

❶ The top of the 16 m high *manastambha*.
❷ Stone *mandapa* in wooden construction style.
❸ Sculptures on the pillars in the *mandapa*.
❹ The temple. The top floor is used as the relinquary.

HOYSALESVARA TEMPLE ★★★
12th C/ Hindu

The present day Halebid was earlier known as Dvarasamudra, the capital of the powerful Mysore Hoysala kingdom, in the 12th - 13th centuries. Now it is a small village with a group of temples; the fort and palace no longer exist. Hoysalesvara temple reflects the Hoysala style in all its grandeur. They started by improving on the Later-Chalukya construction style and the ultimate Hoysala style with its high quality sculpture is truly breathtaking. The temple platform is carved in horizontal bands. Musicians, animals, fantasy beings and humans, have all been sculpted in a row above another band of sculptures in the same way. Even the eaves are densely carved. The tower over the *vimana* is broken. There are many such Hoysala temples with broken towers. This may be because there was no symmetry in the size and order of the structure. Maybe the people of Hoysala preferred sculptures rich with detail, rather than monolithic monuments.

This large temple has one Shiva shrine and another dedicated to Santelesvara, two *mandapas* and two Nandi shrines. The *mandapa* continues into a wide space where there are high quality carved ceilings, entrance pillars made with lathes and exquisite pillar heads. This type of Hindu temple is very rare.

❶ The four pillars that surround a round platform.
❷ The horizontally accentuated exterior view.
❸ Details on the outer walls and eaves
❹ Outer wall designed with horizontal bands.
❺ Details on the pillar capital inside.

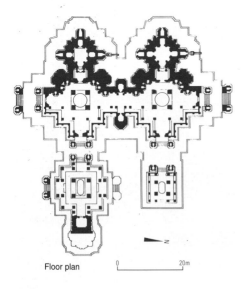

Floor plan   0   20m

JAINA BASTIS
12th C/ Jain

500 m from Hoysalesvara temple is a group of Jain temples and 400 m from there is the Hindu Kedaresvara temple. This Jain group is made up of three temples. When compared to the Hindu temples, they are very simple with few decorations. These temples were built before Jain king Biddiga of Hoysala, converted to Hinduism.

Stamba and temple from North

BELAVADI ★

VIR NARAYANA TEMPLE ★★
116/ Hindu

It is a large Hoysala temple, 12 km from Halebid which gets few visitors. King Biddiga converted to Hinduism under the influence of a philosopher and called himself Vishnuvardhana. At first he built this temple and deified Vishnu in it. It is one of the three temples famous in the Hoysala era. This is the largest temple among the three. The three *mandapas* join and form one large *mandapa* stretching left and right and the *garbhagriha* is at the far end facing a closed *mandapa*. This *garbhagriha* is simple and in contrast, the other two *garbhagrihas* are heavily decorated. All temples are low in height as compared to their length and reflect the horizontal strength of Hoysala style architecture.

Up: Front *vimana*. Down: Full view.

Up: Beautiful sculptures on shrine. Down: *Mantapa* with a low of pillars.

CHENNAKESAVA TEMPLE ★★
1117/ Hindu

This temple is 38 km away from Hassan from where one can visit both Belur and Halebid. It is on par with the Halebid temple, which is 16 km away. It was built by King Vishnuvardhana as a tribute to his victory against the Cholas. Halebid temple was built 10 years later.

Prayers are still offered at Chennakesava temple. The numerous buildings in the precinct gives Belur the look of a temple town. Originally there were three other small shrines in the complex. Maybe that is why the main shrine is a simple *garbhagriha* and *mandapa* type. The main feature of the Hoysala style is that the plan is star-shaped and the *mandapa* has entrances from three sides. There is a huge pillared hall inside the precincts. The latticed stone wall added in the 13th century makes the hall rather dark. Nearby is a Halebid-style shrine, the tower of which has collapsed. As in other Hoysala temples this one is made of green schist, which heightens the precision of the sculptures.

❶ Façade of the south entrance.
❷ *Apsaras* have been sculpted on the axis of the ceiling
❸ The outer wall and miniature shrine
❹ The tank with two small shrines at both sides of the entrance.
❺ The sculpture of deities on the wall

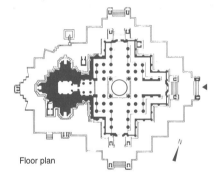

Floor plan

LAKSHMIDEVI TEMPLE ★
1113/ Hindu

This Hoysala temple is 12 km from Hassan. It has shrines on four corners with a low wall enclosing the precincts. The temple has four shrines with one *mandapa* connecting them. There is another small shrine close to these, which has nine towers. Only the east shrine *shikhara* is richly carved. The others are simple stepped pyramids and there are not many sculptures on the wall either. It looks more like the Later-Chalukya style.

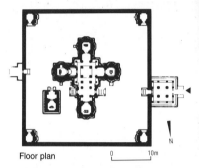

Floor plan   0   10m

N

Up: East shrine entrance. Down: Circular pillars made using lathes.

LAKSHMI NARASIMHA TEMPLE ★
1234/ Hindu

In the 13th century when the Hoysala kingdom was at the peak of its power, a temple was constructed in every area, with detailed sculptures and decorations. The builder of this temple was Maridamma, an architect and sculptor. The plan is similar to that at Halebid. The tower still exists and reflects the in-between style. The vaulted ceiling in the *mandapa* is also richly sculpted on.

Inside the *mandapa*

Vimana seen during dusk

PANCHAKUTY BASTI ★★
10th C/ Jain

During the 9th-10th century, the Jain West Ganga dynasty, ruled Mysore. The Sravanabelagola and Kadambadahalli temples were built before the Hoysala structures. Kadambadahalli has temples with interesting shapes. There are two temples to the left and right facing each other at the entrance. Straight ahead three shrines share a *mandapa*. This makes a total of five shrines altogether and the complex is called *Panchakuta*. *Tirthankaras* have been enshrined in all temples and there are *shikharas* on top of the shrine. They are in the southern style with layers. This type of five-temple complex is very rare. Outside there is another temple called the Shantinatha temple. The *mandapa* has the nine-block ceiling that is popular in this area. In the middle a *tirthankara* image has been carved and on the sides other deities are sculpted.

Floor plan of the complex ▲

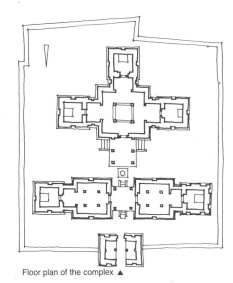

❶ Four of the five *shikharas* can be seen
❷ *Tirthankara* in the niche of the turret
❸ Details of the *vimana*
❹ There are three shrines with a common *mandapa*
❺ Inside the unfinished Shantinatha temple
❻ The sculpture on the ceiling of the Shantinatha temple

Jainism was born in Bihar in East India. When there was a great famine it is said that saint Bhadrabahu along with his followers, came to Karnataka. The ruler of the Maurya empire of the time Chandragupta, who considered Bhadrabahu a saint, followed him and also undertook a fast unto death. This place is the holiest Jain pilgrim centre in Karnataka. With the patronage of the later West Ganga dynasty many Jain temples were built on two rocky hills. The Gommatesvara statue built on Vindhyagiri in 981 attracted a lot of people and became an important pilgrimage centre. It is said that Gommateswara the son of Adinatha, the first *Tirthankara*, stood without moving in meditation for such a long time to uphold the doctrine of non-possessiveness, that white ants built their nest around him. This is the legend around the statue. At the foot of the hill are three noteworthy structures: a large tank, a Jain Matha (monastery) and the Hoysala Akhanda temple.

SHRAVANABELGOLA   46

VINDHYAGIRI AND GOMMATESVARA STATUE
10th~12th C/ Jain

An 18 m high Gommatesvara (Bahubali), many temple groups and a *stamba* are located on a granite hill, which is 143 m high. The hill faces a huge tank. Architecturally they are not spectacular. There is a 12th century three- shrine temple, the tower of which is broken and a *mana stambha* in the 17th century Chyannana temple.

❶ The Gommatesvara statue and the temple group can be seen on the mountain top.
❷ Gommatesvara statue surrounded by temples
❸ *Mana stambha* with the open field in the background.

The temple without the *shikhara*

CHANDRAGIRI AND JAIN BASTIS
★★
10th~12th C/Jain

There are 10 temples with a beautiful *mana stambha* on the Chandragiri hills. Chamundaraya temple dates back to the 10th century, is on par with the Panchakuta temple of Kambadahalli and it reflects the southern style of Karnataka area. The outside walls have pilasters all around. The parapet and the tower have been engraved without the layer pattern. The Jains did not adopt the developing Hoysala style and continued in the original style as seen in the 12th century Parsvanatha temple. As such these temples are not as lively as those in Belur and Halebid.

❶ View of Chamundaraya temple
❷ The group of temples can be seen to the left of Chandragiri hills
❸ The sculptures on the parapet of Chamundaraya temple
❹ *Mana stambha* of Parsvanatha temple

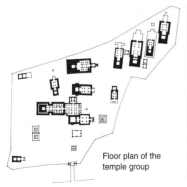

Floor plan of the temple group

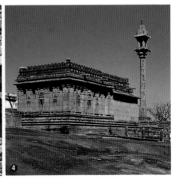

This was the capital of Mysore during British times. It was a highly developed city with a population of 700,000. Between 1760 and 1799 the Muslims, Haider Ali and Tippu Sultan, father and son duo, gained control and shifted the capital to Srirangapatnam in the north. There is a large temple dedicated to Chamunda the protector goddess of the city on a hill south-east of the city. This hill range is called the Chamundi Hills. There is a large statue of Nandi here too. The city is well planned with wide pathways criss-crossing each other, many palaces and colonial constructions.

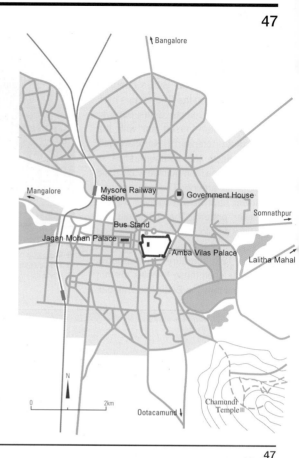

Jagan Mohan Palace (1902)

AMBA VILAS PALACE ★
1897/ Colonial
by Henri Irwin

The palace is in the heart of the city surrounded by a fort, belonging to the Vijayanagar era. When the old wooden palace was burnt in a fire, in 1897, Henry Irwin a skilled architect of the British Viceroy, designed the new palace in the Indo-Saracenic style with a blend of European, Islamic and Hindu architectural styles.

The overall general impression is that of a sweet sugary cake. The most impressive area is the Darbar Hall, the ceiling of which is completely covered with stained glass made in Glasgow.

Façade from East

GOVERNMENT HOUSE
1870/ Colonial
by Thomas Fiott
It was planned by Mark Welks the resident representative of the Viceroy and completed in 1805. It is a small scale building. Thomas Fiott designed the meeting hall and dance hall across the courtyard and completed it in 1807. It has an elegant design with an Italian flavour.

LALITHA MAHAL ★
1930/ Colonial
by E.W. Fritchley
In contrast to the Indo-Saracenic style of the city palace, this palace was designed entirely in the European style in the eastern suburbs. Fritchley's design of the central dome of this building is based on St. Paul's Cathedral in London, as is the interior too. Now this palace is a luxury hotel.

SRIRANGAPATNAM (SERINGAPATAM) ★   48

TOMB OF HAIDER ALI AND TIPU SULTAN ★
1799/ Islamic
River Kaveri flows by Srirangapatnam, which is 16 km north of Mysore. It was the capital of the Muslim Mysore kingdom, which was at loggerheads with the English and the Mysore king. East of the city is the Gumbaz (tomb) of Tipu Sultan who died fighting the British and his father Haider Ali. The tombs resemble the Golconda tombs.

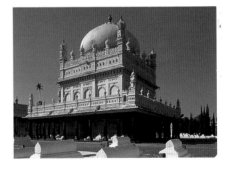

JAMI MASJID (FRIDAY MOSQUE)
1787/ Islamic
Built by Tipu Sultan, the exterior look is different from that of the other mosques. The minarets are finished in plaster and delicately decorated in arabesque and geometric patterns. It looks like there is a low wall surrounding it, but the courtyard is on the second floor. There is no dome over the prayer room and there are only two tall minarets.

Outer View   Minaret

SOMNATHPUR ★★

KESHAVA TEMPLE ★★★
1268/ Hindu

A good example of Hoysala architecture is in Somnathpur, 36 km from Mysore. Here you can see the entire range of the Hoyṣala style. It is a 50 m x 65 m precinct. It has a row of small shrines in the west, in its enclosed corridor, as in Jain temples. The entrance is in the east. There are three *vimanas* with a common *mandapa*, and all three *vimanas* with their towers are very well preserved. They each have the star plan, which is also repeated in the plinth. The 'in-between style' of the *gopuras* reflect the southern style in its horizontal layer and the northern style in its pile-up of miniature *shikharas* on the surface. There are various gods and goddesses lining the walls.

Even the base of the walls is divided horizontally and sculpted closely. Inside is a *mandapa* with a row of pillars. On three sides there are three *garbhagrihas* with their own *mandapas*. The idol inside cannot be seen without illumination which makes it look like a cave. The Hoysala also did not have circumbulatories around the shrine. The interior space is simple.

The view of *vimana* and *mandapa*

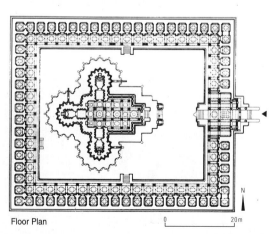

Floor Plan

0   20m

N

The sculpture of a goddess in green slate stone

❶ Circumbulatory around temple. ❷ Tower formation of temples. ❸ The *garbhagriha* and *mandapa*. ❹ Carving on the ceiling

❺ Circular pillars made by using a lathe. ❻ Foundation base is also carved. ❼ Outer wall with six bands of carving.

KALLESVARA TEMPLE
9th C/ Hindu

The Hoysala temples here belong to the last days of the Hoysala dynasty. The Kallesvara temple however, is from the much older Noramba dynasty. The Noramba dynasty ruled the Karnataka region at the same time as the West Ganga dynasty and built a large number of temples here. This is a simple temple with pilasters on the front. Inside, the ceiling has carved images of deities worth seeing.

Outer view of the temple painted white

BHOGANANDISVARA TEMPLE **
9th, 16th C/ Hindu

At the foot of Nandi hill and its fort, 60 km from Bangalore, is a temple built in the Noramba style. In the 16th century there was a large open *mandapa* in the front with small Bhoganandisvara and Arunachalesvara temples reflecting the Vijayanagara style. Only the walls of the tower were sculpted upon. Now these walls are hidden behind the heavily sculpted *mandapa*. Inside the precinct are three square formations and a stepped tank.

❶ Inside the Bhoganandisvara temple.
❷ Two *vimanas* standing next to each other.
❸ The *mandapa* built during the Vijayanagara era.

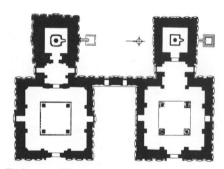

The floor plan of the two temples

The stepped tank at the back

TIPU SULTAN'S SUMMER PALACE
1789/Islamic

Bangalore is the capital of Karnataka. It is at the height of 900 m above sea level. It is not an old city but it has developed as a city of research and production with a population of 4,500,000. The palace of Tipu Sultan, who built Bangalore, is a compact two-storeyed wooden structure with an open styled Persian *Dalan* design.

The half open hall with wooden pillars

VIDHANA SOUDHA (SECRETARIAT) ★
1956/ After Independence

It was designed as the secretariat of the Mysore state after Independence. Since national identity was desired, Kengal Hanumanthaiyya, the governor of the Public Works Department, chose Rajya Mahal of Chandragiri as the model design to build the Vidhan Soudha. A 'New Dravida style' was born.

Vidhana Soudha in the Dravidian style.

INDIAN INSTITUTE OF MANAGEMENT ★
1985/ After Independence
by Balakrishna Doshi

In the sixties four management institutes were constructed. Louis Kahn designed the one in Ahmedabad and Doshi designed the one in Bangalore. On the south suburb of the city this group of large-scale buildings was made with a combination of concrete frame and granite obtained locally. The colour scheme is mainly gray. Space has been divided into exterior and interior and the semi-open space in between, has an ornate framed structure. A man-made environment rich with variety has been created.

Up: The outside of the entrance. Down: the semi-open space

TAMIL NADU

This is the state where South Indian culture is truly reflected and the language spoken is Tamil. The Mughals did not extend their empire this far south, which is why there is little or no trace of Islam in Tamil Nadu. Pure Hindu culture still thrives here.

There are not many old ruins to be found here. Buddhist temples were supposed to have been constructed in every region, but nothing is left of them now. There are a large number of temples and all of them were built in the Dravidian style. Any differences would be only stylistic, reflecting changes down the ages.

The south style developed mostly in north Karnataka and around Mahabalipuram (Mamallapuram) and Kanchipuram. In the 7-8th centuries the Pallava dynasty built the Stone temples. Even now in Mahabalipuram there are many small stone temples and cave temples.

Rock-cut architecture was gradually replaced by structures which were built with brick and stone. The Shore temple at Mahabalipuram is the best example of structural architecture. The evolution of the south Indian style can be seen in the stepped towers. The formation of the *gopura* can be seen in the Ganesha Ratha, a stone sculpture. The mature style of this temple can be seen in the Kailasanatha temple and in the Vaikunta Perumal temple of Kanchipuram.

The Chola Dynasty became stronger in the 9th century and this power is reflected in their architecture which was on a magnificent scale. Two 60m high temples were constructed one in each capital of Thanjavur and Gangaikondacholapuram during the 11th century. The *vimana* or shrine of one was made strong and straight and manlike and the other was made beautiful with feminine curves.

In the 13th century the power of the Cholas weakened and the Vijayanagar Empire rose. Temple architecture development that was taking a straight course changed direction without reason. From then on the temples became larger, more complex with a great number of buildings inside a wide rectangular area. The main shrine became small and could not be distinguished from the outside.The *gopuras* on the outer walls became larger and more magnificent, as can be seen in those at Madurai or Srirangam where the *gopura* stands more than 70m tall. This typical Dravidian architecture can be seen 1000 km away in ancient Egyptian architecture too. The Egyptian Karnak and Edof temples too have small shrines while the Pylon on the outside is as large as the *gopuras* that crown the Dravida temples.

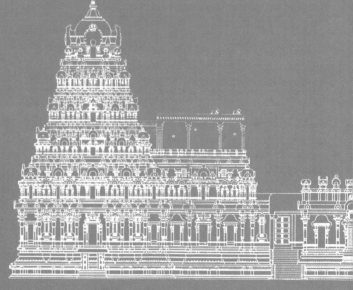

Elevation of Brihadishvara Temple (12th century, Darasuram)

The 2nd *gopura* of Jalakanteshwara Temple (16th century, Vellore)

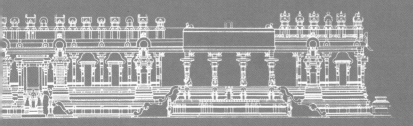

Madras now known as Chennai, is one of the four metropolitan cities of India. It is the capital of Tamil Nadu, developed in 1639 by the British East India Company and called Madraspatnam. Fort St. George, which was the business centre, was completed in 1640, which makes it much older than Mumbai or Kolkata. The whole of India came under the British rule in 1801 after the fourth Mysore war. The present population is 6,000,000 in this city with its greenery and relaxed environment. Inside the city is the old Kapalesvara temple built in the 17th century. The colonial buildings are worth seeing from an architectural point of view since most of them belong to the 19th century, except the Holy Mary Church, which was built in 1680 inside Fort St.George.

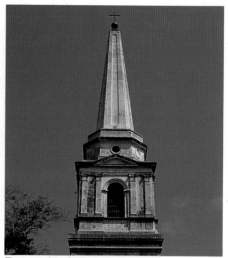

The tower of the St Mary's Church

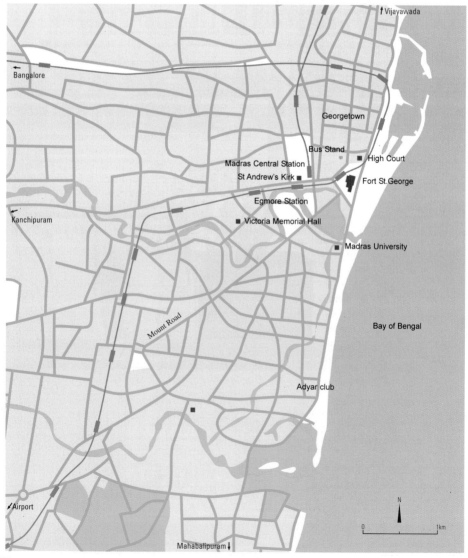

ST.ANDREW'S KIRK ★
1821/Colonial
by Thomas de Havilland and
James Caldwell

This church was designed after completing the Madras Cathedral. It was modelled after the Saint Martin-in-the-Fields Church in London. The two architects completed the circular dome ceiling that the architect of the original church had given up on and thus created an excellent new building which could be termed as the New Model.

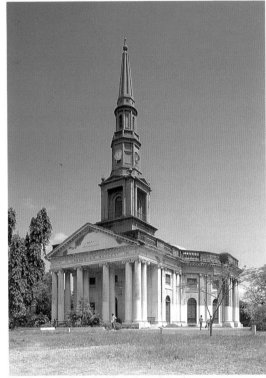

16 pillars support the dome ceiling in the main hall   The church with the Ionic style portico and steeple.

SENATE HOUSE OF MADRAS UNIVERSITY ★
1873/Colonial
by Robert F. Chisholm

Robert F. Chisholm a leading architect in Madras, designed the Senate House on the university campus on the coast road. Chisholm used the Byzantine style of design where he could improvise, unlike other architects who used the Indo-Saracenic style. The four towers with oriental arches and domes have produced a fantastic effect. There is a huge lecture hall inside along with various other rooms. Later he also designed buildings in Vadodara and Trivandrum.

Full view of the towers   An independent design -- Byzantine flavoured tower

HIGH COURT ★★
1892/Colonial
by J.W. Brassington and Henry Irwin
This is a more mature construction in the Indo-Saracenic style at the north of the fort in George Town. It is the best looking High Court with colourful combinations and has become a landmark in Madras. Since the architect Brassington died before completion, Irwin completed the building. With the domes, *chhatris* and minarets it looks distinctly Mughal. The 50 m high central dome also acts as a lighthouse. There is no other structure which bears comparison to this design.

❶ The colourful façade of red and white combination
❷ The brick-building group surrounding the courtyard
❸ The large entrance with many small arches

VICTORIA MEMORIAL HALL ★
1909/ Colonial
by Henry Irwin
Henry Irwin designed this building after completing the High Court. He shows versatility in the design of this building, which is an art gallery, now inside the museum premises. It is made of red sandstone and the plan of this structure is similar to that of the buildings in Fatehpur Sikri.

The Memorial Hall with row of *chhatris*

ADYAR CLUB
1891/Colonial
Adyar Club is located in the green area beside the Adyar river. It is a very old club and is presently called the Madras club. The club has a portico facing it. It has an eight-cornered central hall with a tower-like centre. There used to be many paintings here, but these have disappeared over the years.

The eight-cornered central hall. A circular hall in front with two pairs of pillars

It is a small village 60km from Chennai and 65 km from Kanchipuram. It is an important place for Indian art history and it is a tourist town with motorable roads. The Pallava dynasty ruled this region from 6th to 9th centuries. Their capital was Kanchipuram. They were constantly at strife with the Chalukyas and Pandyas until the Cholas overpowered them. Since the Pallavas had trade relations with many countries and invaded Sri Lanka, it was only understandable that the port city of Mahabalipuram was very prominent. It was built by Mamalla or Narasimhavarman I Pallavamalla (630-668) it came to be called Mamallapuram. Since the Tamil traders travelled far and wide as far as South East Asia, the Pallava architecture boasts of the Champa style .

Since Mahabalipuram was developed on par with Badami and Aihole of Chalukya, the evolution of stone architecture right from cave temples, rock cut temples and the early stone temples can be seen here in sequence.

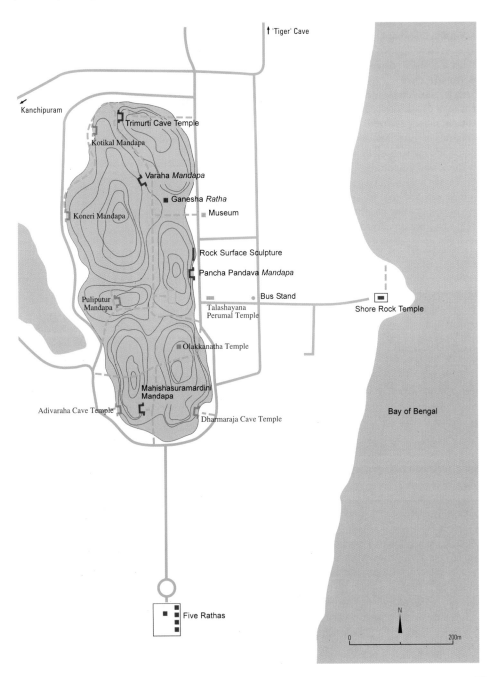

CAVE TEMPLES ★★
7 th C/ Hindu

There are 10 small temples around a granite hillock 400 m from the shore. Extensive constructions have been made in the South Indian style. It will be noticed that the pillars of the Early Ages were four-sided. Also, a typical feature of Pallava structures are sculptures of lions at the base of the pillars.

❶ Pancha Pandava Mandapa
This is the largest cave. The sculptures on this cave were later used on South Indian temples.

❷ Varaha Mandapa
This is small cave with two pillars. It is symmetrical with dense carving.

❸ Trimurti cave
These are three continuous caves with attached pillars with sculptures on them.

❹ Mahishasuramardini Mandapa
This has a *garbhagriha* in the centre with a porch and the walls of both sides are sculpted.

❺ Rock wall sculptures
This is not a cave, but a group of sculptures on a rock wall that tells of Arjuna's penance and the descent of Ganga. The temple architecture of the time is also carved on it.

Lion pillar in Ramanuja cave

The unfinished cave clearly shows methods of sculpture used

PANCHA RATHAS**
7th C/ Hindu

Ratha means chariot. The chariot used in temples is also called *ratha*. Here the five stone temples carved out of rocks one behind the other also came to be called *Pancharatha* or five *rathas*. It is interesting to note that the style of each temple is different and becomes a catalogue of the temple styles of the time. Each temple is named after five Pandava brothers in the Mahabharata and their wife Draupadi.

✦ Draupadi *Ratha* is small square with a sloping roof found in houses.
✦ Nakula Sahadeva *Ratha* has the straight front curved rear *chaitya* style.
✦ Arjuna *Ratha* is a south style *vimana* with a stepped pyramidal roof.
✦ Dharmaraja *Ratha* is one tier higher. It is unfinished and does not have a shrine.
✦ The Bhima Ratha is rectangular with a suspended roof and has a farmhouse look.

❶ From the left--Draupadi, Arjuna, Bhima, Dharmaraja and Nakula Sahadeva *Ratha*.
❷ Nakula Sahadeva *Ratha* with straight front and curved back design.
❸ The lower portion of the Bhima *Ratha* is incomplete.
❹ At the far end is the Dharmaraja *Ratha*.

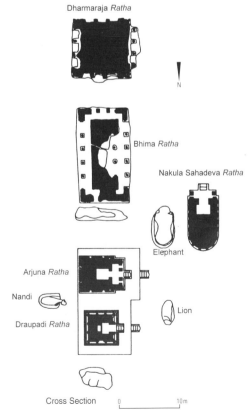

Dharmaraja *Ratha*

N

Bhima *Ratha*

Nakula Sahadeva *Ratha*

Elephant

Arjuna *Ratha*

Nandi

Draupadi *Ratha*

Lion

Cross Section   0   10 m

GANESHA RATHA ★
7th C/ Hindu

This is a rock-cut temple with a shrine at the end of the verandah on the west side. This long temple has the same plan as the Bhima Ratha. On the walls are layers of eave-like structures on top of which is an arched gabled roof. This form evolved into the *gopura*. There are three other unfinished rock temples in the west of the village.

The east side surrounded by a wall

SHORE TEMPLE ★★
8th C/ Hindu

During the reign of Rajasimha (700--728 AD) the Pallavas developed the stone temples earlier than the Pattadakal temples of the Chalukyas. Rajasimha also built the Kailasanatha temple in Kanchipuram. Before that he built the Shore temple and dedicated it to Shiva. In 1000 years it has been slowly eroded by salt, water and wind, but the rare spectacle of the small and large *gopuras* in the south style is fairly well preserved. Another shrine faces the *pradakshina path* around the large shrine. This Vishnu temple probably dates back to the 7th century.

❶ The Shore temple against the dawn skies.
❷ The temple that was close to the water, is now protected by a grove that acts as wind breaker.
❸ The tower of the small temple that has been eroded by salt, water and wind.
❹ The reclining Vishnu statue sculpted here.

Cross-section

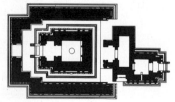

Floor Plan

TIRUTTANI ★

55

VIRATTANESHWARA TEMPLE
9 th C/ Hindu

A temple dedicated to Murugan lies in Thiruthani 40km from Kanchipuram. Pilgrims gather here. It is historically important, as it is a Pallava styled small temple on the other side of the town. Made of stone, not brick, it has the same straight front and circular back style of a *chaitya* temple, yet this has been always been a Hindu temple.

Right: The top portion s similar to the Bhima Ratha in Mahabalipuram.
Left:Straight front and circular at the back.

TIRUKKALIKUNDRAM ★★

56

BHAKTAVATSLESVARA TEMPLE ★★
13th C/ Hindu

It is a large temple 14 km from Mahabalipuram on the way to Kanchipuram. The Vedagrishvara temple on the hilltop is famous since two eagles come flying here at a fixed time twice every day. Yet the sight of the Bhaktavatslesvara temple from the hilltop reflects the ultimate in Dravida architecture. A high wall surrounds the huge rectangular area, with massive *gopuras* on four sides and a tank used for bathing. Inside is another 'inner precinct' surrounded by a wall, which also has a *gopura*. When compared to the outer *gopuras* the central shrine is small. This again reflects the history of the temple where the expansion was done in an orderly manner.

Up: The Bhaktavatslesvara temple. Down left: Base of the east *gopura*. Down right: Shrine with straight front and rounded back.

This temple town was the capital of the Pallava dynasty from 7th to 9th century. It has many ancient stone temples and is famous for the Kailasanatha and Vaikuntha Perumal temples. After the Pallavas, the Cholas, Vijayanagara and Nayaka dynasties added more temples here, Kanchipuram has come to be known as the temple capital.

One can see the evolution of the South Indian style from Mahabalipuram to Kanchipuram; from simple cave temples to baroque style monoliths. Kanchipuram is a small town with a population of 180,000 people and a lot of tiled houses. It is an ideal town to walk about in while visiting the temples. It is simply called 'Kanchi'. During the British rule it was called Kanjeevaram. The area can be divided into three parts. The central area is called 'Shiva Kanchi' with its many Shiva temples. The east area is called 'Vishnu Kanchi' since the large Vaishnavite Varadaraja Perumal temple is here. 'Jaina Kanchi' on the other side of Vegavathi River has Jain temples. It is believed that a "Buddhist Kanchi" also existed in Kanchipuram.

Full view of Kailasanatha Temple

KAILASANATHA TEMPLE ★★
8th C /Hindu

It is a large temple built by the Pallava King Rajasimha, who also built the Shore temple in Mahabalipuram. The south style *vimana* of the Shore temple is built in layers and reminds one of the temples in North India. In contrast this temple looks like a pyramidal type of structure. Inside small shrines surround the area with a row of small shrines in front of the small *gopura* type shrine too. Small shrines even surround the *vimana*. There are a total number of 80 shrines. All of them have pillars decorated with lions or the mythical animal *yazhi*, at their base. There was an independent *mandapa* in front that was later attached to the shrine. The whole temple has been built with sandstone. Hence the quality of the sculpture is the best of its kind and the detailing is complete.

Up: Entrance and small shrines in a row
Down: Precincts with small shrines forming a corridor.

Vimana and *Mandapa* with the protector deities carved on them

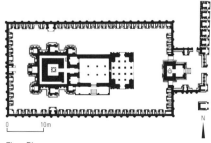

Floor Plan

Sculptures on the wall of the *vimana* (Shiva)

VAIKUNTA PERUMAL TEMPLE ★★
8th C/Hindu

This is a Vishnu temple built by Nandivarman the 2nd of the Pallava dynasty. The *vimana* is similar to the Kailasanatha temple, but the precincts are very different. Instead of the small shrines as in the other temple, this one has a surrounding corridor with lion pillars very near the *vimana*.

The reliefs on the walls are various legends. The circumbulatory bends in places and gives a very interesting dimension of space. Inside the *vimana* there is another circumbulatory round the shrine. As you climb up the stairs, you can go to the roof of the shrine and *mandapa*.

❶ There is an octagonal *vimana* on top of the tower.
❷ The view of the temple from the closed side of the circumbulatory
❸ The corridor with reliefs on the wall and lion pillars.
❹ The wall of the main temple seen from the corridor.

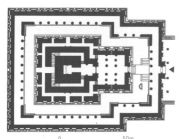

Floor Plan   0   50m

Elevation

486

EKAMBARESVARA TEMPLE ★
16th C-17th C/Hindu

This large Shiva temple, built by the Vijayanagar dynasty is very different from the style of architecture of the Pallava dynasty. One cannot look up and see the *vimana* because it is surrounded by an inner circumbulatory with many shrines that are enclosed by a high wall. Outside the wall is a hall with a row of pillars and a tank which again, is encircled by a wall. There is a large *gopura* at the entrance. Another was later built which is a repeat of the earlier *gopura*. In later ages many replicas of this *gopura* will be seen.

The inside corridor surrounding the main shrine

Up: The west *gopura* inside the precincts. Down: Inside the pillared hall.

VARADARAJA TEMPLE ★
12th C/Hindu

This temple located in Vishnu Kanchi is also known as the Devarajaswami temple. The Cholas designed it, but it was largely built by the Vijayanagara dynasty. There are four walls surrounding the precincts and people of other castes are not allowed inside. The *gopuras* lining the horizon and the play of lights on the water is fantastic as are the pillars with horse and rider statue on the *kalyana mandapa*.

❶ Small shrines and *gopura* around the tank
❷ The second *gopura* at the main entrance
❸ Horse and rider statue pillared Kalyana *mandapa*

Sculptures on the base of the *mandapa*

KAMAKSHI TEMPLE
16th~17th C/ Hindu

This temple dedicated to Parvati, wife of Shiva, is located in the heart of the town surrounded by houses. There are four big *gopuras* around the precincts. The top tier was built in recent times. There is a large tank west of the temple complex. In the middle is a pavilion, which, with the small shrines, makes an idyllic picture. The golden tower rising from the wall is truly impressive.

Pavilion in the tank and *gopura*   The golden tower

VARDHAMANA TEMPLE
12th C/Jain

The Vardhamana temple of the Later-Cholas and Chandraprabha temple of the Pallavas are situated in Jaina Kanchi. There are two *garbhagrihas* with straight front, curved rear style in the Vardhamana temple. Later a common open *mandapa* was erected at the front. The ceilings are adorned with 17th century Jain paintings.

The open *mandapa* with painted ceilings

VELLORE ★★ 58

FORT ★
16 th C/ Hindu

The fort in the business town of Vellore was built by the Nayaka (chieftain), a vassal of the Vijayanagara emperor. The fort changed hands from the Muslims, to the Marathas, to the British and was also the battlefield where the battle of Mysore was fought. There is no palace inside the 1 km long fort. It is encircled by a canal, giving the appearance of a complete whole. There are two layers of fort walls one high and one low with a pathway in between and a bridge entrance to the east.

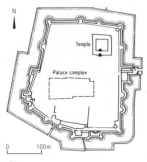

N

Temple

Palace complex

0   100m

Floor Plan

Up: The fort wall and a wide canal. Down: Hindu style engraving

JALAKANTESHWARA TEMPLE ★★
16 th C/ Hindu

A compact Vijayanagara temple of high quality is within the fort area. The *vimana* is enclosed in three layers. The outer layer has a circumbulatory and a *gopura* on the south. The second *gopura* (Page 475) has a new circumbulatory running parallel to the fence and round the shrine. One can look at the peak of the *vimana*. On the wall are statues of Nandi and miniature *gopuras*. There are lovely reliefs on the wall too. The *gopuras* and corridor too have been sculpted on beautifully.

KALYANA MANDAPA ★★

To the left of the big *gopura* is a *kalyana mandapa*. It is an excellent example of Vijayanagara style during their rococo period. *Kalyana mandapa* is the hall used for the marriage festival of the gods and one is usually found in all the big temples. The one in Vellore is very large. Here too as in the Varadaraja Temple the pillar with the horse and rider statue is overwhelming.

Floor Plan

Up: The *gopura* from the northeast. Down: In the Kalyana *mandapa*.

Left: Sculpture at the peak of the small *gopura*. Middle: Glimpse of the *vimana*. Right: Corridor like West European monastery.

ARUNACHALESVARA TEMPLE ★★
16th~17th C/ Hindu

This is a temple town with more than a hundred temples and the holy Arunachal Mountain overlooking the town. This temple is the main attraction here and the whole town is focused on it. Inside, the complex is very wide. The distance between the east and the west *gopuras* will be more than 450 m. If the west *gopura* looks like a high-rise building, the east *gopura* with its 13 tiers at 66 m height, is even higher. All the *gopuras* are painted white and this gives a feeling of purity as compared with the other colourfully painted ones. Shiva and his consort Parvathi are enshrined here. Other than that the large and small tanks, *Amman* shrine, 1000 pillared hall, are similar to other temples.

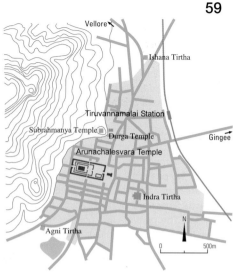

❶ Temple seen from the Arunachala mountain.
❷ The sculpture at the base wall of east *gopura*
❸ Small *gopura* and south *gopura* on the other side of the tank.
❹ Peak of the south *gopura*

GINGEE (SENJI) ★★

60

FORT ★★
15th~18th C/ Hindu

37 km from Tiruvannamalai in Gingee is a huge fort encompassing the hills of Krishna Giri, Chandrayandurg Giri and Raja Giri. The Cholas built the original structure, but the present structure was built by the Vijayanagara dynasty in 1442. From there it went into the hands of the Bijapur Sultan, to the Marathas, to the French army and then into the hands of the British. The outer wall enclosed the three hills. On the plains in between are palaces and public offices which again are surrounded by inner fort walls. The temple, mosque, step tank and storehouse still exist.

KALYANA MAHAL ★

This is a big building surrounded by a wide courtyard in the palace area. The four-sided Kalyana *mandapa* with its tower is impressive. There are verandas on all floors and a multi-tiered tower very similar to Hindu temples. It was used as a lookout tower.

❶ The palace area can be seen from Rajagiri
❷ Kalyana Mahal palace
❸ Inside the storehouse
❹ The palace area and Rajagiri fort seen from the inside the entrance gate.

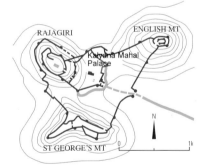

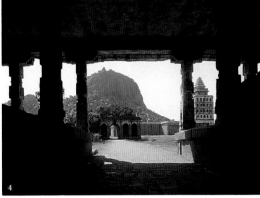

PANAMALAI ★

TALAGIRISHWARA TEMPLE ★
8th C/Hindu

A Pallava temple belonging to the same era at Kanchipuram sits on a hill 7 km west of the Gingee road to the south. There is a square *mandapa* with small shrines on three sides where Shiva is deified. The walls have *yazhi* sculptures and the *vimana* is a pile-up design of small *shikaras* put together. The design is the same as in Kanchipuram.

Mandapa from the Vijayanagara period

CHIDAMBARAM ★★

NATARAJA TEMPLE ★★
9th-13th C/ Hindu

There are many temple towns in Tamil Nadu where pilgrims gather in large numbers. Among them is the temple of Nataraja (Dancing Shiva) where the line of pilgrims never stops. The construction of this temple belongs largely to the Chola era and here is an excellent example of uniformity in style. The *vimana* is small and the *gopura* at the entrance is large and quite excellent. The budding *gopura* that was seen in Mahabalipuram and Kanchipuram during the Pandya dynasty attained style and grew more organized during the Chola period. It came into its own during the Nayaka regime when it became gigantic. The Chidambaram *gopura* falls in the bracket of the 12th - 13th century.

❶ The inner corridor. ❷ The Shivakama Sundari shrine separated by the tank. ❸ The sculpture on the south *gopura* ❹ Siva Ganga tank and north *gopura*

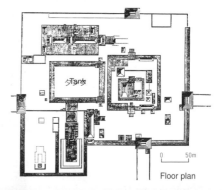

Floor plan

SRI AUROBINDO ASHRAM DORMITORY *
1926
by Antonin Raymond

Raymond designed this concrete building for the new religion's activities. The façade has been designed extremely skillfully and is even now perfectly maintained. In the middle of this Matrimandir (shrine) was a Utopian area where people could meditate and work at the same time.

Garden by Nakajima

AUROVILLE *

64

NEW TOWN *
20th C/ Post Independence

After the death of Aurobindo Ghosh (1872-1950), his main disciple, a French woman called Mirra Alfassa also known as 'Mother', wanted to realize the visions of Aurobindo and started constructing a new town north of Pondicherry from 1968 and called it Auroville.

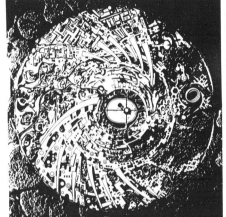

Master plan of the French architect Rositte Ange

❶ Visitors' centre. ❷ *Matrimandir* design by Ange. ❸ Auditorium. ❹ Auroville houses

BRIHADISHVARA TEMPLE ★★★
11th C /Hindu

35 km from Kumbakonam is a towering temple in a huge precinct. Rajendra Chola I (1012-1044) named his new capital Gangaikonda Cholapuram, which means 'the city of the Chola dynasty which took the Ganges'. He built a temple as large as the Brihadesvara temple in Thanjavur, the former capital. This temple was called the Rajendra Cholesvara temple. The temples are not extremely high, but the quality of the architectural finish and beauty of the Brihadishwara temple is greater. The *vimana* of the other is straight and tall and very masculine. In intriguing contrast this *vimana* at Gangaikondacholapuram has elegant bends and graceful curves that make it more feminine. There is an circumbulatory around the main shrine, which ends at the front room or *antarala*, and then continues on to a long rectangular *mandapa*. The wall of the *vimana* has been constructed in two layers. Pillars have been attached with rhythmic regularity and inside the shrine, statues of gods have been sculpted. Previously the same pattern may have been sculpted on the walls of the *mandapa* too. But it has collapsed and the present walls are plain. Inside the complex are two small Shiva temples, built by two of Rajendra's queens. Both temples are called Kailasa.

❶ Full view. ❷ View of the *vimana* from the west. ❸ Uttara Kailasa shrine.

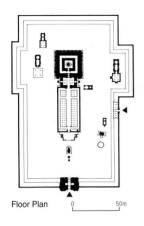

Floor Plan   0   50m

The sculpture of Shiva blessing a devotee   The wall of the *vimana*

❶ ❷ ❸

Kumbakonam has been a temple town from the Chola ages to the present day. There are around 15 temples and prayers are offered in all of them daily. Even though designed by the Cholas, most of the present structures belong to the Vijayanagara dynasty or Nayaka of the area.

Other than the temples there are many tanks. This should be the base and then one can visit Gangaikondacholapuram Dharasuram, Tribhuvanam, etc, which are near. Those who prefer a comfortable visit, should stay in Thanjavur and then go on to Kumbakonam.

KUMBAKONAM   66

NAGESVARA TEMPLE ★
9th C/ Hindu

A very colourful, squat *gopura* can be seen off the road. It has the traditional design of the later Chola period. Inside the precincts are many small *gopuras*. There is also a Nandi shrine with horse and wheels. The main shrine belongs to the early Chola period. There are excellent statues in the niches on the wall of the *mandapa*.

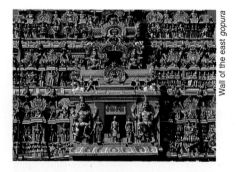

Wall of the east *gopura*

KUMBAKONAM   66

MAHAMAKHAM TANK
17th C/ Hindu

In South India, where it is summer all year long, water is a very important commodity. This tank not attached to any particular temple, is rectangular and is surrounded by steps. People use it daily for bathing and laundering. There are pavilions erected on all four sides that also double as shrines. Once in 12 years this tank becomes the stage for the festival of Kumbareshwara.

The tank surrounded by the steps

SARANGAPANI TEMPLE
13th C/ Hindu

This is the largest Vishnu temple in Kumbakonam. The Kumbeshwara is the largest Shiva temple and between these two temples is a large tank. The Sarangapani temple is shaped like a chariot and it dates back to the last Chola days. Most of the structure belongs to the 17th century Nayaka dynasty. Many *gopuras* are so tall they tower above the walls.

The temple on the other side of the tank

RAMA TEMPLE
16th ~17 th C / Hindu

This is a medium-sized temple built by Raghunatha Nayaka of Thanjavur. Inside the premises is a corridor the walls of which have murals painted on. As you enter the large and small *gopuras* you come to the open *mandapa* on the pillars of which high quality sculptures of the Vijayanagara dynasty have been depicted.

Up: The peak of the Vimana.
Down: The pillar in the *mandapa*.

TRIBHUVANAM ★★ 67

KAMPAHARESHWARA TEMPLE ★
13th C / Hlindu

The last temple of the Chola era lies six kilometres north-east of Thanjavur. Kulotunga the 3rd (1178-1218) built this temple following the Thanjavur temple style. The *vimana* is 32 m high and vertical and this is the last temple that had the *vimana* higher than the *gopura*. However the *vimana* filled with deities is the same as the large *gopuras* constructed later and the strength of the sculptures is also lessened.

Inside the *mandapa* leading to the *gopura*

The colourful *vimana*

DARASURAM ★★

AIRAVATESVARA TEMPLE ★★
12th C / Hindu

This is a Chola temple 4 km from Kumbakonam. It has close and intricate carving from end to end and nothing has been destroyed. This was the third large temple built by the Cholas, but the *vimana* is small at 25 m and not even half the height of the temple in Thanjavur. These were signs of changes in the south Indian temple architecture. They concentrated on making the detailing as elaborate as possible instead of making the vimana huge. Expanding the temple area became important (see elevation on page 474). As in Thanjavur a wall surrounds the temple. The entrance is not from the *mandapa* but from the porch to the left of the *mandapa*. Here a chariot façade has been sculpted with statues of elephants, horses and wheels. In and around 13th century the temples were styled as if they were going around heaven, the largest is in the Surya temple in Kajuraho.

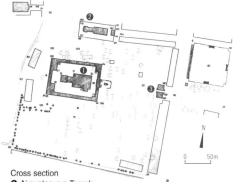

Cross section
❶ Airavatesvara Temple
❷ Amman temple ❸ Unfinished *gopura*

❶ Inside the open *mandapa*. ❷ Sculpture on the wall.
❸ The smaller second *gopura*. ❹ The elephant, horse and wheel pulling the chariot.

The chariot facade of the temple

DAIVANAYAKI AMMAN TEMPLE ★
12th C/ Hindu

Amman temples are generally shrines dedicated to the goddess in the main temple where they stand by the side of another shrine. Here it stands alone with its own fence and is a miniature of the Airavatesvara temple. Since the base of an unfinished *gopura* is right in front of the shrine, a full-fledged temple could have been planned here.

The front façade of the open *mandapa*

THIRUVARUR ★ 69

THYAGARAJA TEMPLE ★
13~17th C/ Hindu

This temple 55 km from Thanjavur is a typical Dravida temple. While the main shrine is small, the temple has been walled with a *gopura* at the entrance and many other shrines have been built. The entire complex is contained within a high wall with gigantic *gopuras* on all four sides. The highest *gopura* is 70 m high, but in front of it, the main shrine is almost buried and cannot be seen from the outside. The Kamaiaya tank is to the west of the temple. The temple construction began with the shrines of Vanmikanataa and Thyagaraja during the Chola days and by the Nayaka era, 1000 pillared *mandapas* and 8 *gopuras* had been added. Thus in 100 years the temple area was extended by 100s of meters on one side; on other sides, even more.

Up: Temple seen from west. Down: Centre of the precincts.

The magnificent and colourful east *gopura*

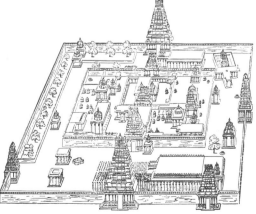

Sketch by Ramraj in the 19th century

Tiruchirapalli (Tiruchi) with its rock fort, was also the stage for the Carnatic war. Now it is the main city of central Tamil Nadu. Nearby the temple town of Srirangam, on an island in the River Kaveri (Cauvery), is surrounded by seven concentric walled courtyards. There are two large temples where a huge number of pilgrims gather. The larger one is the Ranganathasvami temple built in the Chola era belonging to the Vishnu group and the other is the *Shaivite* Jambukesvara temple built later. Most of the buildings in the temples date back to the Nayakas.

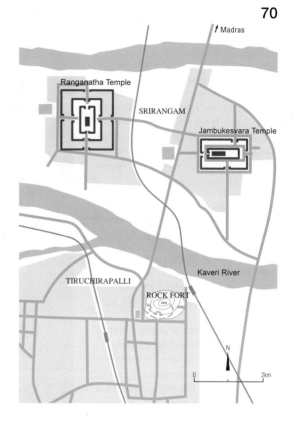

Rock fort and Thepakulam in Tiruchirapalli

JAMBUKESVARA TEMPLE ★★
17th C/ Hindu

There are five high walls around this temple, which is crowned with seven *gopuras*. People of other religions are not allowed in the main sanctum. The outer wall is also as large as the *gopura* and the temple resembles a citadel. It was thus fortified not just to retain its sanctity, but also to defend it from the invading Muslims. Walking on the *pradakshina path* between the wall and the corridor is a religious experience.

The tall *gopura*

Up: The *gopura* is the only opening. Down: Inside the *mandapa*.

RANGANATHA TEMPLE ★★
13th~17th C/ Hindu

The temple complex is surrounded by seven layers of wall and has 21 *gopuras*. Building continued even recently when the incomplete *gopura* was extended to a height of 78 m. The precinct is 5 km long and extends into the temple town. This temple has the largest precincts in India. The large number of pilgrims added to the market atmosphere makes the environment similar to that of the Asakusa temple. Inside the precincts are tanks, small shrines and many pillared halls, all with the Vijayanagara style of sculpture and carving. It was not only a place for praying but was also a place for people to meet.

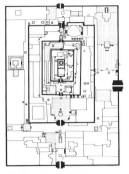

The floor plan up to the 5th surrounding wall

❶ Various *vimanas* and *gopuras* towering above the wall (The golden one is the main shrine)
❷ Temple precincts spill into the shop-lined streets
❸ The inner precinct from the third north tower
❹ Inside the Garuda *mandapa*
❺ The open *mandapa* and horse and rider statue pillar
❻ The sculptures on the wall of the Venu Gopala shrine.

SRINIVASANALLUR ★

71

KORANGANATHA TEMPLE
927/ Hindu

Early Chola temples were small with no walls around them. Koranganatha temple 50 km from Trichy is the *garbhagriha*-and-*mandapa* type with beautiful sculptures on every surface. The base of the wall has a row of sculpted mythical animals called *yazhi* that is a special feature of Chola architecture. The first floor is made of bricks which have been plastered. This temple is a prototype of south-style architecture.

Up: Full view of the 14 m long temple.
Down: The wall surface with the statue of Dakshinamurthy (Shiva) sculpted on it.

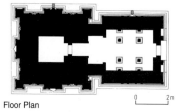

Floor Plan
0   2 m

KODUMBALUR ★

72

MURAKOVIL (TEMPLE) ★
880/ Hindu

Kovil is the Tamil word for temple. This temple dates back to the early Chola days. There were originally three temples of which only two are standing without the *mandapa*. It is built in the typical south Indian style with a four-sided square roof or *shikhara*. A temple built in the 10th century stands just one kilometre away from here.

Up: A Nandi statue sits before the temple
Down: The *yazhi* on the base of the wall is also called *vyala*

Elevation and cross section

Thanjavur is a quiet old city 60 km from Thiruchirapalli. Rajaraja Chola established his capital here and built the huge temple Brihadisvara, which is considered the premier destination for architectural pilgrimage. This temple, above 60 m high is the tallest in South Indian architecture. The land changed hands over the centuries from the Cholas, to Vijayanagara, to the Nayakas, to the Marathas and finally to the British. The British called this place Tanjore.

The walls of the Brihadisvara temple facing the stream were fortified some centuries later

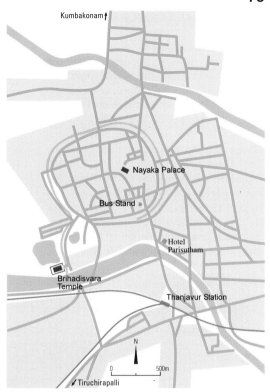

NAYAKA PALACE ★
16th C/ Hindu

The Nayakas were the vassals of the Vijayanagara kings until the Marathas took over from them. The buildings have heavy Islamic influences with arches and domes. The castle tower built during the 17th century looks like the *vimana* of a Hindu temple. In contrast there is another building that is four-sided, has a lot of arches and resembles the Kalyana *mandapa* in Gingee without the Hindu-style roof.

The observation platform (17th century)

The 58 m tall palace tower also has arches within

BRIHADISHWARA TEMPLE ★★★
1010/ Hindu

When Rajaraja Chola I, built the temple dedicated to Shiva in his new capital, he named it after himself. This temple which later came to be called the Brihadishwara temple was an epoch-making building in the history of south Indian architecture. Until then the temples were smaller. This temple was built with the *vimana* towering over 60 m thus taking the south type style to its peak.

It reflected the golden age of the Cholas that was also at its peak. In the precincts measuring 75 m X 150 m encircled by a circumbulatory, two *gopuras*, a Nandi shrine, two *mandapa*s, a front room, and the shrine are all located in a straight line. There are entrances with steps from the left and right of the front room in addition to the main entrance from the *mandapa,* a common basic plan of Chola temple construction. The *vimana* is designed in layers and rises vertically. The dome type of stone right on top of the *shikhara* is simple and is supposed to weigh around 80 tons.

Another important feature that will be developed later is the *gopura* which is the entrance to the temple built into a high wall surrounding the temple. Here it is broader than it is tall and looks squat. Compared with the height of the *vimana* a little more height could be desired here. But no matter; it looks as magnificent as the peacock spreading its plumes.

The entrance *gopura*

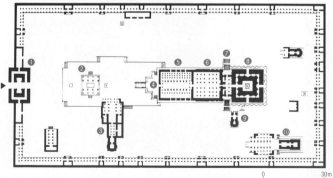

Floor Plan
❶ 2nd *gopura*. ❷ Nandi Shrine. ❸ Devi Shrine. ❹ Porch. ❺ Mukha *Mandapa*. ❻ Ardha *Mandapa*. ❼ Front Room (*Antarala*).❽ The main shrine and pathway. ❾ Chandeshwara Shrine. ❿ Subrahmanya Shrine.

① The *Vimana* towering over the surrounding wall
② Porch in front of the *mandapa* built by the Nayakas
③ 17th century wall design of Subrahmanya tank.
④ The top part of the *mandapa* is not complete.
⑤ Chandeshwara Shrine and Subrahmanya Shrine
⑥ A line of Shivlingas in the corridor.

VIJAYALAYA CHOLEESVARAM TEMPLE ★★
9th C / Hindu

This temple sits on a hill 17 km from Pudukottai and reflects the style that is the transition from the Pallava period to the Chola period. It is small in size and has eight small shrines surrounding it out of which three still stand. The shrine is circular and the circumbulatory is roofless. The outer walls and the tower portion are detached from each other. Behind are a number of rock caves belonging to the same age.

Right: Looking down at the temple
Left: The cave temple has 12 Vishnu statues

RAMALINGESVARA TEMPLE ★★
16~17th C/ Hindu

Rameshwaram is connected with the famous epic Ramayana and is the main city in the island that is nearest to Sri Lanka. The old portion of the temple complex where people from other castes are not allowed to enter was built by the Pandya dynasty. Most of the other parts were built in the 17-18th centuries by the Nayakas. The temples built during this age had circumbulatories around the shrines. The inner corridor with a line of sculpted pillars is 200 m long. It has an overwhelming force of its own.

The 7m high ceiling has been painted

Madurai has a population of 120,000 and is the biggest city in Tamil Nadu after Chennai. This old city is as popular a pilgrim centre in the south as Varanasi is in the north.

The history of the city goes back to the BC years. Between the 7th and 14th century it was the capital of the Pandya dynasty. But no vestiges of that era remain. In the 14th century it came under the control of the Delhi Khilji dynasty and became a Muslim kingdom. Half a century later the Vijayanagar dynasty took it over and again turned it into a Hindu holy land. In 1565 the Nayaka dynasty ruled the land until 1781. Thirumalai was a very prominent Nayaka and the Minakshi temple and the palace that is standing even now were built during his time. He had also built a wall around the city and a moat.

The scale and the lifestyle of Madurai resemble Varanasi in the north. The main difference is that while the centre of activity is on the *ghats* on the Ganges river there, here it is the Minakshi temple. The biggest festival celebrated here is the wedding of Shiva and Parvathi, when the statues of both these deities are taken on a chariot all over the city.

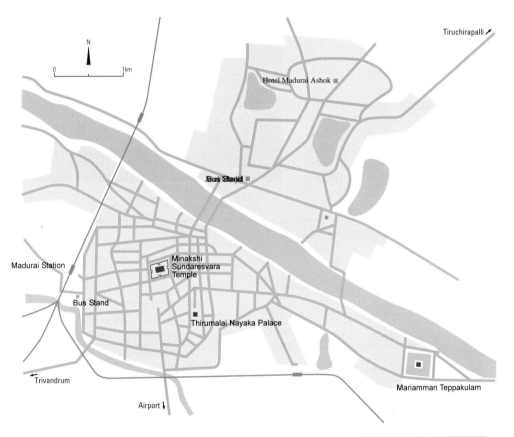

VANDIYUR MARIAMMAN THEPPAKULAM
1646/ Hindu

This is a man-made lake built by Thirumalai Nayaka. It is three kilometres from his other creation, the Minakshi temple. This is a square tank as large as the temple precincts. He built a square island with pavilions on the four corners in the middle of this lake and a *vimana* in the centre. During the Teppam festival, deities from the Minakshi temple are floated here along with lighted lamps.

Festival season: people come here to relax and bathe

MINAKSHI SUNDARESVARA TEMPLE ★★★
17th C/ Hindu

Minakshi means the lady with the eyes like a fish. Minakshi was a local goddess. Later she came to be identified as Parvathi the wife of Shiva. Sundareshwara is another name for Shiva. Two shrines were constructed for both deities right at the start and it became a large temple with 230 X 260 m precincts.

There are 12 gopuras altogether along with the north, south, east and west gopura entrances. The south gopura is the highest at fifty metres. The Pudumandapa is before the east gopura. If it had been completed this gopura would have towered at 80 m. Both were built by the Hindu Pandya kings. They are densely carved and are painted once in 15 or 20 years.

In the precincts are the two main shrines with circumbulatory, a tank of the golden lotus, a thousand pillared hall (actually there are 985 pillars) and many other mandapas and small shrines, the walls of which cannot be called either pillars or walls. The carving on them is similar to the Vijayanagara style of later days. However, the style lacks a little in vitality and is over-sculpted, but what can be called the zenith of styles in India is reflected here. The gold-plated main shrines are small and the turrets tower over the horizon in typical Dravida style.

Porch of Eight goddesses and the East gopura

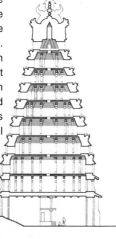

Cross section of the gopura

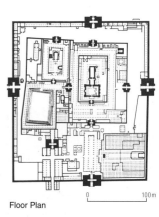

Floor Plan

Inside the porch of eight goddesses

Ceiling of the mandapa

❶ The various shrines and *gopuras* (the golden roofs belong to the shrines of the two deities).
❷ The peak of the north *gopura* (before it was painted).
❸ Small shrine inside (the sunshine slants in through the stairwell).
❹ *Yazhi* pillars on the inner cirumbulatory.
❺ Kambataddi *Mandapa* (18th C)

THIRUMALAI NAYAKA PALACE ★★
1636/ Hindu

Thirumalai Nayaka ruler of the southern half of Tamil Nadu built a marvellous palace which must have been enormous, but now, only a pillared hall and a dance hall surrounded by a courtyard, remain. The style is a blend of Hindu, Islamic and European architecture and completely different from the traditional Minakshi temple. It is said that an Italian architect was asked to do the designing. Maybe he did it along with an architect from the Vijayanagar kingdom.

Up: The top part of the wall of the huge dance hall.
Down: Pillared hall surrounding the main courtyard.

The pillared hall has a lotus motif on the ceiling

KALUGUMALAI ★★ 77

VATTUVAN KOVIL (TEMPLE) ★★
8~9th C/ Hindu

Cave temples were carved in Tamil Nadu too. Rock cut temples are found in Mahabalipuram and Garudamalai. They were all incomplete, but the sculpture is of high quality. Vattuvan Koil means sculptors' paradise. They reflect the south type temple style of the Pandya age. Nearby at a rock, reliefs of Jain *tirthankaras* can be found which highlights the fact that both the religions enjoyed cordial relations.

Up: The sculpting begins at the peak and the lower portion has been left incomplete.
Down: The *shikhara* at the peak.

Jain relief sculptures

PADMANABHAPURAM ★★

WOODEN PALACE ★★★
18th C/ Hindu

Padmanabhapuram where the palace of the Travancore chieftain is located, is now maintained by the government of Kerala. The architecture of the palace is Malabar west coast style and is only 50 km away from Trivandrum; transport too is very convenient. This is the only wooden palace in the whole of India that has been preserved completely and the fact that one can see it from end to end is gratifying. The palace was designed in the 15th century, and most of the present edifice was built by King Marthanda Varma in the 18th century. Because they shifted to Trivandrum in 1790 and this palace became the summer palace, it has thankfully escaped the battles and has been well preserved.

The palace area is 100 m x 150 m. Other than the royal temple which is made of stone, all other buildings here are made of wood. The slate roof is sloping with wooden carving on the gables. The walls are latticed for ventilation. All this has many common elements with the wooden constructions of south east Asia. Unpainted teak wood has been used. The imposing appearance of the combination of white walls and slate brown, is the search for comfort in residential architecture, rather than reflection of grandeur. The meaning of the name of the city Padmanabhapuram is "The land where the lotus flower bloomed".

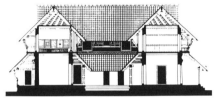

Cross section of the Tai Kottaram

❶ The palace area seen from the front courtyard. ❷ Looking up at the *Uppilika* (King's chambers). ❸ Façade of the audience hall.

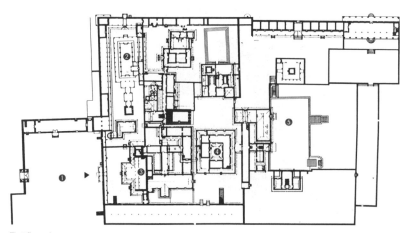

First floor plan
❶ Front courtyard. ❷ *Mandapa* of the temple. ❸ *Mantra Shala.* ❹ *Taikottaram.* ❺ Tank

❹ Mantrashala (1st floor audience room). ❺2nd floor toilet. ❻ King's bedroom mural. ❼ Poomukham (2nd floor audience room).

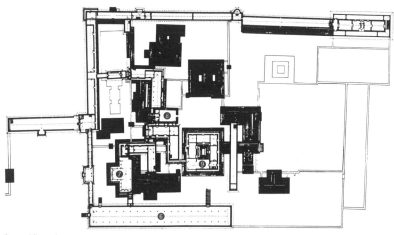

Second floor plan
❻ The large dining hall ❼ *Poomukham* ❽ *Uppilika* ❾ *Taikottaram*

❽King's bedroom. ❾Auditorium that doubles as a *mandapa*. ❿Queen mother's quarters-hall. ⓫ Queen mother's quarters-corridor

KERALA

Kerala in the west and Tamil Nadu in the east make up the southern-most part of India. Kerala is a long, narrow state, sandwiched between the 1000-1500 m high Western Ghats on the east and the Arabian Sea on the west. Moisture laden winds, drop heavy rainfall on the windward side of the mountains. This rich green state is very different in culture from the dry state of Tamil Nadu. Its population comprises 50 percent Hindus and 20 percent each of Christians and Muslims. This diversity of cultures is a result of Kerala's trade with other countries right from ancient times and the consequent exposure to other religions. Churches are visible all over the state, but it is a matter of regret that none of them are of an admirable architectural quality.

It is perhaps, because so many religions co-exist in Kerala, that Hinduism is very rigid. One has to be dressed like a Hindu to enter the temple. Even then, visitors are not allowed to walk freely around the precincts and photography is prohibited. The only place where a visitor's movements are not curtailed and one can look around, is at the Padmanabhaswamy Temple in Thiruvanathapuram. The style of this temple is like the temples in Tamil Nadu; even the language spoken is Tamil, not Malayalam.

While wooden structures are prevalent all over India, they are particularly common in Himachal Pradesh in the north and Kerala in the south, because of the easy availability of wood in these two states. Another common feature in the architecture of the two states, is the tall steeple roof, which is protection against very high rainfall. Kerala has very few wooden temples, but it is interesting to note that there are quite a few wooden mosques like those in Kashmir. J Fergusson has noted the similarity between the wooden constructions in Nepal and those in Kerala. It is perhaps the similar climatic conditions that gave rise to similar architecture. The major difference is that roofs in Kerala are gabled with decorations on them, while Nepal has hipped roofs. Roofs in Kerala are not curved like they are in Himachal Pradesh, but straight like those in Nepal.

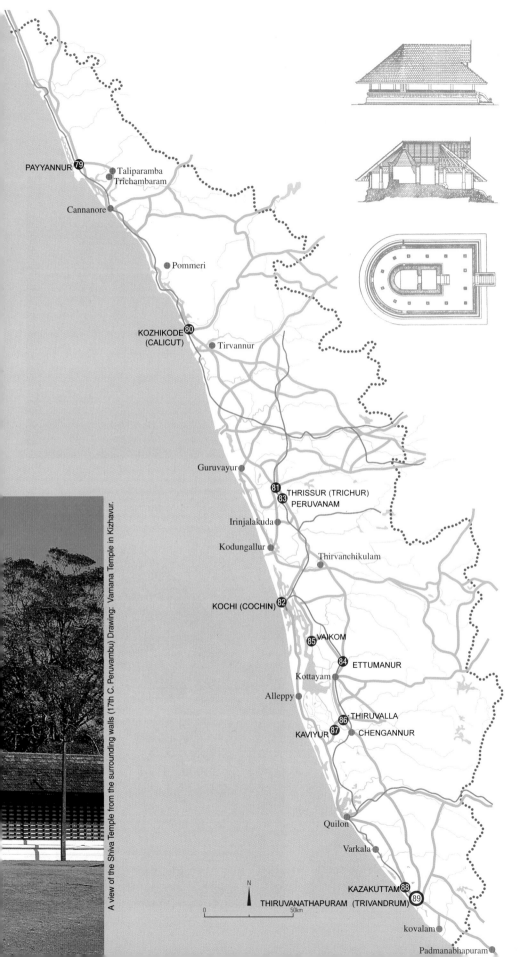

PAYYANNUR 79
Taliparamba
Trichambaram
Cannanore

Pommeri

KOZHIKODE 80
(CALICUT)
Tirvannur

Guruvayur

THRISSUR (TRICHUR) 81
PERUVANAM 83

Irinjalakuda

Kodungallur

Thirvanchikulam

KOCHI (COCHIN) 82

VAIKOM 85

ETTUMANUR 84

Kottayam

Alleppy

THIRUVALLA
86
KAVIYUR 87 CHENGANNUR

Quilon

Varkala

KAZAKUTTAM 88
THIRUVANATHAPURAM (TRIVANDRUM) 89

kovalam

Padmanabhapuram

A view of the Shiva Temple from the surrounding walls (17th C. Peruvambu) Drawing: Vamana Temple in Kizhavur.

N
0   50km

SUBRAHMANYA TEMPLE★
17th C/ Hindu

When entering Kerala from Mangalore, on the Malabar coast, the temples have the west coast style. The first of these, a Buddhist temple with a straight front façade and a circular apse, is seen in Payyannur town. The complex is encircled by a wall made of laterite called *nadambalam* which has a row of oil lamps hanging from its eaves. The gable has decorative carving instead of the customary *chaitya* window.

Up: The low roof over the pathway around the main shrine gives it a double-storeyed look.
Down: Oil lamps around the *nadambalam*.

The main shrine with its circular apse.

WOODEN MOSQUES
17th C/ Islamic

Calicut has the maximum number of Muslims in Kerala, and it has therefore, many mosques. The architectural style of these wooden mosques is similar to that of Hindu temples. The Mishqal Palli Mosque, the largest in Kerala, is a four-storeyed structure with a five-tiered tiled roof. In comparison, the Jami Masjid is small. It has a wooden ceiling over the porch, with floral patterns and verses from the Koran engraved on it.

Up: A wall of the Mishqal Palli Mosque, latticed to provide ventilation.
Down: The carved porch of the Friday Mosque.

The façade of the Muchundi Mosque.

VADAKKUNNATHAN TEMPLE★★★
12th C/ Hindu

One of the finest examples of the Kerala style of temples is the Vadakkunnathan Temple in the heart of Thrissur city. The *srikovil* (main shrine) was built of wood in the 12th century, and has been restored over the years.

Enclosed by the *nadambalam,* with its ambulatories and corridors, in the inner precincts are three *srikovils*, each with their own *namaskara mandapa* or prayer room. Two of these are circular in plan, while the third with the attached *mandapa* is square. All three *srikovils* have walls and pillars of stone and a wooden roof covered with copper sheets. The walls are embellished with sculptures and murals.

The other buildings inside the precincts were built at a later date and none of them are particularly noteworthy. The *nadambalam* has an entrance on each of its four sides. In the outer precincts is a large *kuttambalam* and various other buildings, all surrounded by a wall with large *gopuras* in each of the four cardinal directions. These *gopuras* are different from those seen in Tamil Nadu. The *gopuras* have no embelishments like statues of gods, but are crowned instead with a many-layered, tiled roof.

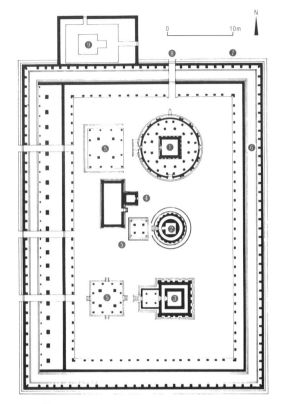

Floor Plan
❶ Vadakkunnatha shrine ❷ Shankara Narayana shrine ❸ Rama shrine ❹ Ganesha shrine ❺ *Namaskara mandapa* ❻ Surrounding pathway ❼ *Nadambalam* ❽ Entrance ❾ Small shrine

The various shrines seen from the outer precincts. On the left is the Rama shrine and on the right is the Vadakkunnatha shrine.

❶Southern *gopura*. ❷The *nadambalam* & *kuttambalam*. ❸ *Namaskara mandapa* in the Rama shrine. ❹ Shrines in the precincts.

KUTTAMBALAM★★
19th C

A *kuttambalam*, usually found in the vicinity of large temples in Kerala, is a traditional theatre used at the time of temple festivities for dance and music performances. The structure has a row of pillars, dividing the space into a hall and corridors. In this *kuttambalam*, which is rather unique, the pillars are connected with a beam surmounted by a hipped roof with trusses. The roof is covered with copper sheets. Since this design is not a traditional one, there is reason to believe it was adopted from a Christian church. A stage in the centre of the hall has circular teak pillars, crafted using a lathe. It has a coffered ceiling, over which is a first floor and the roof. Similar *kuttambalams* can also be found in Irinjalakuda, Harippad and Thiruveggapura.

❺ The *kuttambalam* that looks like a Buddhist palace.
❻ A wide corridor with a row of pillars on the outside and latticed walls.
❼The interior of the hall with the stage.

Vasco-da-Gama opened a trade route between Cochin and Portugal after 1502. It was the capital of the king of Cochin during British rule and was controlled by the British until Independence. Kochi, a port town facing the Arabian Sea is criss-crossed by backwaters. It is a prominent harbour town, and has many colonial buildings.

ST. FRANCIS' CHURCH/ 16th C ❶

St. Francis' church, the oldest in India, is located in Fort Cochin and was built by the Portuguese. Vasco-da-Gama who died in 1524, was buried here until his remains were taken to Lisbon.

MATTANCHERRY PALACE/ 1557 ❷

This palace, built by the Portuguese, was gifted to the king of Cochin. After a century, additions were made by the Dutch and it came to be known as the Dutch Palace. Not heavily embellished, its walls have murals depicting some religious and mythological themes. The murals are a valuable collection of Kerala's temple art.

SYNAGOGUE/ 17th C ❸

The synagogue in the Jewish part of Cochin was burnt in a fire and the present structure was built in 1664.

BOLGHATTY PALACE/ 1744 ❹

Bolghatty palace was built by the Dutch in 1744 and used as a residence for the Viceroy of the British Empire. It has now been converted into a hotel and is run by the state government.

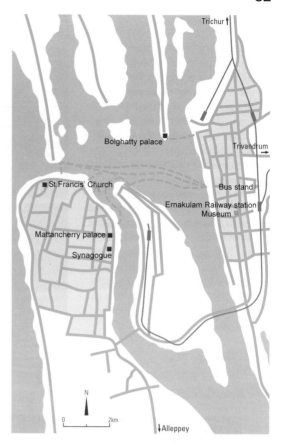

PERUVANAM ★

83

SHIVA TEMPLE★★
12th C/ Hindu

This 12th century Shiva Temple situated in Peruvanam 10 km from Trichur, has a style of construction that is quite unique. As seen from the cross-section, the *srikovil* is on the first floor and the roof over the second floor runs the entire length of the building. The whole edifice is 21 m high and stands apart from the *nadambalam*. The *nadambalam*, though designed in the *vimana* style of stone construction, is executed in wood. The octagonal *shikhara* on top blends with the gabled roof giving it a magnificent appearance.

Full view on page 514

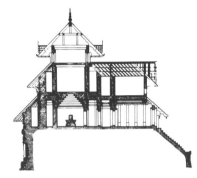

Elevation   Cross Section

ETTUMANUR ★

84

MAHADEVA TEMPLE**
16th C/ Hindu

This temple is located 25 km from Vaikkom and is approximately 12 km from Kottayam. A large temple with a tiled *gopura* in front, its interesting features are 17th century murals on the interior walls. The *padikkal mandapa*, a long, narrow building that leads into the inner precincts, has protruding rafters. Projecting lattice walls, sloping ceiling and unique wooden decorations on the gable, are all characteristic features of the Kerala style of architecture. The *srikovil* is decorated with murals and wooden sculptures.

The painted mural depicting a reclining Vishnu.

The *padikkal mandapa* painted predominantly in blue.

SHIVA TEMPLE★★
16th C/ Hindu

The large Shiva Temple in Ettumanur, 40 km from Ernakulam, has a rare, oval-shaped *srikovil*, 17 m in diameter. The outer walls protected with deep eaves are decorated with beautiful wooden sculptures and colourful 18th century murals. A portion of the temple was destroyed in a fire in 1963. The wooden roof made of rafters and the supporting frame, has carving reminiscent of temples in Nepal.

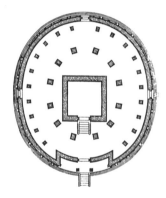

❶ The *nadambalam* as seen from the outer precincts.
❷ Stone pillars in the *padikkal mandapa*, in a style very similar to that of Tamil Nadu.
❸ The *nadambalam* with a row of oil lamps.
❹ The *srikovil* with a conical roof.
❺ Murals on the *srikovil* and sculptures on the eaves.

Floor plan

0   5m

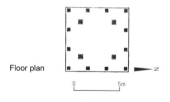

19th C porch with a tiled roof & pillars in a western style.

SRI VALLABA TEMPLE⋆⋆
13th C/ Hindu

The magnificent Sri Vallabha Temple, located in Thiruvalla is approximately 30 km from Kottayam. The circular *srikovil* with its conical roof is 21 m in height. While the walls of the temple are devoid of any embellishment, the *namaskara mandapa* is richly decorated with sculptures. As is the case in the temple in Ettumanur, the *padikkal mandapa* is bigger than the shrine. It has a T-shaped plan, with gables on three sides and serves as the entrance to the inner complex.

Various shrines as seen from the outer precincts.

Padikkal mandapa

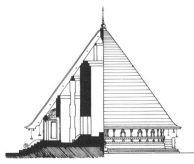

Part section and part elevation

Garuda shrine.

KAVIYUR ⋆

CAVE TEMPLE
8th C/ Hindu

Small cave temples are found in about 10 locations in Kerala. The elaborately sculpted cave temple in Kaviyur near Thiruvalla, has a small veranda with two carved pillars in front of the shrine dedicated to the *shivalinga*. The veranda has sculptures of gods and sants who protect the entrance, including Ganesha, the elephant god.

Left part of the veranda.   The facade.

KAVIYUR

MAHADEVA TEMPLE⋆
18th C/Hindu

This temple with its circular *srikovil* has the ten incarnations of Vishnu on its wall, carved in wood and painted black. The *padikkal mandapa* has some high quality wooden carvings. Around the coffered ceiling, in a design dating back to the 10th century are lacquered sculptures reminiscent of *Kathakali* performers (the traditional dance form in Kerala).

Coffered ceiling of the *padikkal mandapa*

KAZAKUTTAM ⋆

MAHADEVA TEMPLE⋆⋆
14th C/ Hindu

Located 15 km north-west of Trivandrum, in Kazakuttam, is the Mahadeva Temple. This double-storeyed temple with a square ceiling and wooden roof has plastered laterite walls. Wooden sculptures are mounted against these walls. The ceiling of the *mandapa* extends from the *srikovil* and ends in an arched gable. The roof rises over the *nadambalam* that surrounds the precincts. This is a characteristic feature of the architectural style of Kerala.

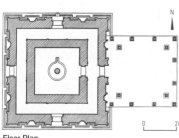

Floor Plan

Up:Square roof with dormer windows. Down:View from the outside.

Thiruvanathapuram, the capital of Kerala was the capital of the former chieftain of Travancore. Known as Trivandrum from the British days, the city has recently reverted to Thiruvananthapuram, its old name, which means "City of the Holy Snake". Padmanabhaswami Temple, is in the centre of the old city south of the railway line, while the northern part of the city was developed during the British *raj*. MG road, leading from the station, has shopping areas, public offices and colonial buildings. Napier museum is in a garden at the end of MG road. The former palace of the Maharaja is on the hilltop beyond.

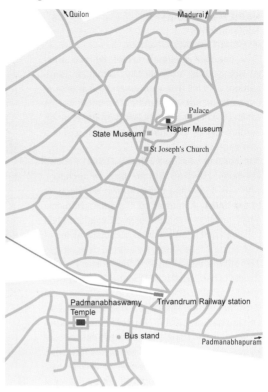

City Library.

PADMANABHASWAMI TEMPLE★
1729/ Hindu

The temple in its wide precinct is situated inside the fort area, where only a part of the fort wall remains. This temple, dedicated to Padmanabha, (Vishnu) the protector, is a blend of architectural styles of Tamil Nadu and Kerala. The entrance *gopura* is in a style commonly found in Tamil Nadu, while the other entrances with tiled roofs on wooden structures are in a style that is typical of Kerala. The latticed *nadambalam* is at the entrance with a circumbulatory. The pillars of the *nadambalam* have a *deepalakshmi* (woman holding a lamp) sculpture. The double-storeyed *srikovil* with its square roof is again in the Kerala style, while the *mandapa* of stone, is in the architectural style of Tamil Nadu. The northern side was burnt in a fire in 1934 and was rebuilt in the original style. The best time to visit is in the early morning, when the ambience inside the complex is wonderfully serene. Photography is prohibited.

Up: Eastern *gopura*. Down: Southern entrance in the Kerala style.

NAPIER MUSEUM★★★
1880/ Colonial
by Robert Fellows Chisholm

This beautiful museum offset by two wide towers stands majestically within a large garden, on a hill. The exterior and the interior of the museum are very ornate. The bright design which covers the entire building on the exterior, borders slightly on the monotonous and is a little oppressive.

The building was designed by Robert Fellows Chisholm (1840-1915), an English architect, who was one of the better known architects of British India. A master at his profession this gifted architect initially designed western style buildings and later turned to traditional styles of architecture. Like Akbar, he started designing in the "Indo-Saracen" style. Though many of his creations can be seen in Chennai and some as far as Vadodara, this museum is one of his most important works. The large exhibition hall is an amalgamation of the western architectural styles and the traditional architectural style of Kerala. This synergy of the two styles has been achieved by a happy coalition of architecture and art, which was brought about by the local artisans involved in the project.

❶ The Kerala style tiled roof, devoid of embellishments.
❷ The carved figures that support the projecting window.
❸ Details of the wooden carving on the gable.
❹ The brick walls of the west wing with stained glass on a window on the second floor.

Facade of the Napier Museum.

A semi-circular wooden window projecting from the surface of a brick wall.

LIST OF SOURCES AND REFERENCES

LIST OF SOURCES FOR SKETCHES
After the Masters—p. 114
Ahmedabad (Marg)—p. 278, 279, 288, 289
Ancient Monuments of Kashmir—p. 39 down
An architectural survey of temples of Kerala
—p. 515, 517, 521, 522, 524
Architecture in India
—p. 222, 236, 238, 274, 341, 512, 513
The Art of India—p. 362
Art and Architecture of Indian Subcontinent—p.153
The Art and Architecture of India—p. 566, 567
The Architecture in the Himalayas—p. 56
The Architecture of Imambaras—p.127
The Art of Ancient India
—p. 181, 273, 305, 364, 368, 369, 443, 460, 463, 464,
485, 502 up, 504
Auroville, The City the Earth needs—p. 493
Balakrishna Doshi—p. 284
Bidar Its History and Monuments—p. 425, 426
The Buddhist Art of Nagarjunakonda—p. 566
Buddhist Monasteries in the Western Himalayas—p. 568
Brick Temples Of Bengal—p. 162, 163, 167, 168, 170, 180
right, 187
The New Cambridge History of India(1-6)—p. 488, 489
The Caves at Aurangabad—p. 378
Cave Temples of the Deccan—p. 373
The Cave Temples Of India—p. 381, 389
The Chalukyan Architecture of the Kanarese district
—p. 445
Charles Correa—p. 100 up
Concepts and Responses—p. 101
Darasuram—p. 474, 498
The Design development of Indian Architecture
—p. 102, 105 right, 421
Early stone temples of Orissa—p. 568
Encyclopedia of Indian Temple Architecture, North India,
Foundations of North Indian Style—p. 38, 40, 329, 343 up
North India, Period of Early maturity
—p. 66, 207, 218, 336, 352
South India, Upper Dravidadesa
—p. 361, 433, 436, 437, 440, 472
South India, Lower Dravidadesa
—p. 482, 486, 495, 502 down
Earthly paradise—p. 36, 94
Essay on the architecture of Hindus—p. 499
Fatehpur Sikri—p. 121 up
Haveli—p. 290
Hindu temple Art of Orissa—p. 196
The History of Architecture in India
—p. 98, 108, 118, 160, 271, 354, 566
History of Indian and Eastern Architecture
—p. 105 left, 180 left, 189, 190, 202, 281, 303, 333, 446,
451, 492
Indian Architecture (Buddhist and Hindu)—p. 39 up
Indian Islamic Architecture—p. 429
The Islamic heritage of Bengal—p. 570
Islamic Sacred Architecture
—p. 116, 117, 121 down, 129, 158
The Jain Stupa And Other Antiquities of Mathura—p. 566
Junagadh (A.S.I.)—p. 566
Le Corbusier Oeuvre Complete—p. 81, 282
Living Architecture
Indian
—p. 195, 200, 206, 221, 243, 348, 390, 414, 470, 508, 566, 569

Islamic India—p. 155, 432
Lothal (A.S.I.)—p. 294
Medieval Temples of Dakhan—p. 382
Mimar 32, (concept media)—p. 201
Modern Architecture of India—p. 100
The Mosque—p. 31, 88
Mughal Architecture—p. 96, 107, 112 middle, 115
Muhammadan Architecture of Bharoch, Cambay, Dholka,
Champaner, and Mahmudabad in Gujarat—p. 292
Mud Architecture of the Indian Desert—p. 308
The Penguin Guide to the Monuments of India
Buddhist, Jain, Hindu
—p. 47, 55, 132, 203, 250,415, 419, 481
Islamic, Rajput, European—p. 90, 357, 379, 413, 422
The Queen's Step well at Patan—p. 266
Raj Rewal—p. 123
Report on the Ellora cave temples—p. 435
Romance of the Taj Mahal—p. 112
The Royal Palaces Of India—p. 224, 335, 339
Shivaji and Facets of Maratha Culture—p. 394
Shri Shatrunjay Giriraj Darshan in Sculptures and
Architecture—p. 297
Somanatha and Other medieval temples in Kathiawad
—p. 566
The Step-wells of Gujarat—p. 287
The Temples Of Himachal Pradesh—p. 59
Temple Architecture in Kerala—p. 523
Temples of Khajuraho—p. 316, 321, 322, 325
The Vijayanagara Courtly style—p. 408, 453
Islamic Architectural Culture
—p. 93, 109, 110, 111, 124, 423
5000 years of Indian Architecture—p. 240, 511
Takeo Kamiya—p. 241, 268, 270, 320, 343, 377, 465, 467
International Architecture-year 1966, August edition
—p. 261
Architecture of Hinduism
—p. 27, 199, 387, 441, 501, 567, 569
Design of Paradise—p. 34
Louis Kahn (a + u special edition)—p. 179, 185, 283

LIST OF SOURCES FOR MAPS
Architecture in India—p. 340
Bishnupur (A.S.I)—p. 165
Bundhi (Maps and publications)—p. 264
Guide map of Gujarat (Govt. of Gujarat)—p. 307
India 4.South (Nells Maps)—p. 515
India 5.North East (Nells Maps)—p. 179
Old Goa (A.S.I)—p. 396
The Penguin Guide to the Monuments of India
Buddhist, Jain, Hindu
—p. 28, 51, 58, 104, 133, 162, 117, 193, 234, 235, 257,
300, 318, 332, 370, 433, 439, 444, 447, 452, 458, 466,
479, 484, 490, 496, 500, 503, 507
Islamic, Rajput, European
—p. 86, 97, 106, 119, 126, 128, 158, 160, 174, 220, 225,
227, 230, 254, 274, 276, 353, 378, 383, 393, 422, 424,
427, 468, 476, 491, 520, 525
Sanctuaries Bouddhiques Du Ladakh—p. 42, 43
Srinagar Guide Map (Survey of India)—p. 26, 27
State map of Sikkim (Survey of India)—p. 144
Tourist Map of Himachal Pradesh (Survey of India)—p. 57
Takeo Kamiya—p. 182

Glossary

* Mark means that the actual explanation is available.
→ Means reference.

A

■ ADINATHA

Legend says that Adinatha was the first *tirthankara* of
Jainism. He was also called Rishabanatha. His son was
called Gomateshwara.

■ AHIMSA

Ahimsa means no killing or non-violence. It was preached
by all the religions in India, but was put to practice most
effectively, by Jains.

■ AJIVIKAS

Ajivikas was a religion started by Makkari Gosala, at the
same time as, Buddhism and Jainism. The features of this
religion were fatalism and austerity. It is said that this
religion was later interpolated into Jainism.

■ AKBAR

Akbar was the third emperor of the Mughal dynasty. In
addition to establishing the empire, he also strove to blend
Hinduism and Islam. He put this into effect in Fatehpur Sikri
and in his own tomb*, in Sikandra.

■ AMALAKA

This is one of the constituent parts of the *shikhara**, in the
north Indian type of temples. It resembles the seed of an
amalok (amalaka in Sanskrit). It is circular in shape and is
symbolically placed at the apex of the shrine.

■ AMMAN SHRINE

This is a shrine adjacent to the main shrine in south Indian
temples, where the consort of the main god is enshrined.

■ ANTARALA

Antarala is a small space or front room between the
garbhagriha (shrine) and *mandapa*, usually found in north
Indian temples.

■ APSIDAL SHAPE

The plan with a rectangular entrance and a circular rear.
This was developed as Buddhist *Chaitya* shrines and can
be seen in very early Hindu temples too.

■ ARCH

An arch is a curved opening, built by placing cut stones or
bricks along a predefined curve. Traditionally, in India,
column and beam structures, corbelled constructions, etc.,
were common. An arch is also called a true arch. →Dome

■ ARYANS

Aryans entered India from the north, in 1500 BC and
settled here. They used to speak an Indo-European dialect.
Entirely different from the Dravidians* of the south, they
introduced the Veda* religion and Brahman* religion into
India.

■ ASHOKA

Ashoka was the ruler of the Maurya dynasty that ruled
during the period 321 BC to 184 BC. He brought most of
India under his control. When he converted to Buddhism,
he built a *stupa** and *stambha** in every region.

■ ASHRAM

An ashram is a training ground for Hinduism. Gandhi also
called the living place of his followers, ashram.

B

■ BAGH

A Persian word, meaning garden.

■ BAHAI FAITH

This is a religion started by Bahaulla, in 1863, in Persia. It
believes that there is only one God, one world and one
people.

■ BANGALDAR ROOF

The roof style commonly seen in Bengali houses. The four corners are bent and fall vertically. Through the Mughals, this style spread as far as west India.

■ BANGLA

The common Bengal-style roof. Since Bengal gets more rainfall, the thatched roofs were bent to face downwards. When this style was incorporated into the brick constructions in temples, the name was retained.

■ BAOLI → Step-Well.

■ BASTI

Jain temples are called Basti, Basati, Vasathi etc. The original Sanskrit word is *vasathi*.

■ BHANDAR

A book house or library of Jain literature. The one in Jaisalmer is very famous.

■ BHUNGA

In Kutch, the houses are circular with round walls made of clay, on top of which is the wooden framework of the roof, which is then thatched with straw. This circular house plan is called Bhunga.

■ BLIND ARCH

An arch without an opening.

■ BRAHMAN

The highest in the caste hierarchy, of the four *Varnas* in Hinduism and Jainism.

■ BRAHMINISM

The predecessor of Hinduism. Based on the *Vedas*, only the Brahmins, the topmost in caste hierarchy could interact with God and man.

■ BUDDHISM

Was started by Buddha who had his own ideals. He took the path of moderation, which was accepted by the ruling class and spread all over India. In the 13th century, it was overwhelmed by Hinduism and all but disappeared.

■ BUTTRESS

A wall designed to reinforce the main wall, so that it will not collapse under pressure.

C-D

■ CAMPANILE

An independent structure like a belfry that developed in Italian churches.

■ CAPITAL

The top most portion of the pillar that is elaborately sculpted with designs. The most popular designs are cushions and the pot and foliage motif *.

■ CARAVANSARAI

Wayside inns, in the Islamic world, for travellers, sometimes simply called *sarai*.

■ CAVE DWELLINGS → CAVE TEMPLES

These are created by hollowing out rocks. There are simple caves and architecturally complex ones with pillars and beams. In Buddhism, the monks' dwellings were called *Viharas* and the shrine caves were called *Chaityas**.

■ CENOTAPH

Is used as a memorial to the dead or a place to pray for the dead, but where the dead are not actually buried. It is a tomb design, with its origin in central Asia. An imitation coffin is kept on the main platform and the actual coffin is kept in a small tomb room underground.

■ CHADDAR

In the Mughal gardens, diagonal waterways were designed in stone, which gave the effect of a waterfall when water flowed over it. The resultant bubble formations were very enjoyable.

■ CHAITYA

This is a common word in Sanskrit for the object of prayer. In Buddhism, this word came to be associated with anything connected to Buddha. Since the most important thing associated with prayer was the *stupa**, the hall where the *stupa* was deified came to be called the *Chaitya* hall.

■ CHAITYA WINDOW

In order to light up the interior of *Chaitya* caves, horseshoe shaped arch windows were constructed and came to be called *Chaitya* windows.

■ CHALA

Hindu temples of Bengal. Every surface of the hipped roof was called *Chala*. Usually, four-sided roofs were called *Char Chala* and a two-tiered roofs of this type were called *Aat Chala*.

■ CHALUKYA STYLE

Fergusson, who chronicled Indian architecture, called the temple architectural style of the Middle Ages, the Chalukyan style, after the dynasty that ruled during that period. This name is not used anymore.

■ CHAR BAGH →The square garden.

Char Bagh, an Islamic design, is a large square garden dvided into four smaller quadrants and water channels.

■ CHATTRI

An umbrella-like, circular disc, at the apex of the *stupa*. Usually made of stones, but wooden ones can be seen in some cave temples.

■CHAUMUKHA/CHATURMUKHA

In Jain temples, four *thirthankara* statues (Chaumukha) are placed together, facing the four cardinal directions, with their backs towards each other. The four sides of the shrines were open and *mandapas* were built on all four sides. Thus Jain temples could be extended on all four sides. Chaumukha shrine →Four-sided shrine

■ CHHATRI

These were decorative elements on the roof of Indian Islamic structures. They were also called small pavilions.

■ CHHATRI

An open structure with a dome supported by four or more pillars. Chhatra means umbrella in Sanskrit. After the advent of Islam, tombs were built and these tomb* structures came to be called *chhatris*.

■ CHORTEN

A *stupa** is called a *chorten*, in Tibet and Ladakh. It started as a mound where Buddha's remains were venerated and was later built in various places, as a symbol of Buddhism.

■ CIRCUMBULATORY

A corridor or pathway that pilgrims use to walk around a shrine.

■ CLOISTER

The courtyard in European monasteries, surrounded by a corridor.

■ COLONIAL STYLE

Buildings erected by the Europeans in the colonies. At first, simple English style buildings were erected in India that were later blended with the Indian traditional architecture that gave rise to the Indo-Saracenic style.

■ CORBELLED STRUCTURE

A construction technique where bricks or slabs of stone are kept one on top of another, horizontally jutting out a little at a time, Arches and domes were constructed using this technique. Since arches and domes built this way are not very strong, large spaces cannot be spanned with this technique.

■ DARGAH

The tomb of a Sufi saint is known as *Dargah*, in Persian. In Arabic it is called *Mazar*. Once in a year, believers collect here in large numbers and hold prayer services, etc.

■ DARWAZA

Entrance gateway in Persian →Pol

■ DELHI SULTANATE

The Islamic dynasties that ruled Delhi until the Mughal dynasty was established. They came from Turkey and Afghanistan. It started with the Slave Dynasty, went on to the Khalji Dynasty, followed by the Tughlaq dynasty, then the Sayyed dynasty and ended with the Lodi dynasty.

■ DEUL

The shrine in an Orissa temple. At times the whole temple is called a Deul.

■ DIWAN-I-AM →Public audience room

The hall where the Muslim emperors gave audience to low ranked officials and common people. It was also used as a courtroom.

■ DIWANI-I-KHAS →Private audience room

The hall in Islamic palaces where the King gave private audience to officials and dignitaries. Meetings were also held here. →Public audience hall.

■ DOME

The ceiling and a roof created by placing bricks or cut stones in a particular fashion and creating a big spherical space without pillars. It came to India along with Islamic architecture. Before that similar domes were constructed in India with corbelled structures. →Double shell dome. Vault.

■ DOUBLE SHELL DOME

In Islamic structures, the dome* and the ceiling are two separate layers with a ceiling support, in between. As a result, the height of the ceiling is perfect from the inside while retaining the majestic appearance on the outside.

■ DRAVIDIAN

The language and people of the four south Indian states are called Dravidians and they are different from the Aryans of the north. The south style * temple construction is also called Dravidian style of construction.

■ DUKHANG

Assembly Hall in a Buddhist Monastery during religious services. The saint is deified in the front and the monks sit in a line and work, on the opposite side. The ceilings are high and the light enters from the top.

■ DURGA

The wife of Shiva* who is worshipped independently. Also called Parvathi, Uma, Gauree, Kali etc.

■ DVARAPALA

These are statues placed at temple entrances, to protect the shrine.

E-G

■ EKA-RATNA

A Hindu temple in Bengal, which has only one tower.

■ EK-BANGLA

The half room in a Hindu temple, in Bengal.

■ FAÇADE

The main elevation of a building - usually the front elevation.

■ FEUDAL KINGDOM

Semi-independent states, under the control of the British. It is said that in 1927, there were 562 such states. The chief of these states was generally called Maharaja.

■ FOUR IWAN STYLE

The Persian style mosque has four iwans surrounding a courtyard and facing each other. They are called the four iwan style Mosque. →Pillared hall

■ FRIDAY MOSQUE

The large mosque, where all believers in the area gather. This is also called the Jami Masjid (Friday mosque) or Jama Masjid.

■ GANDHARA

At present in northwest Pakistan. Buddhist art, with a heavy influence of Hellenic culture is prominent here. The architectural style of monasteries was also developed here.

■ GANGA

The river Ganges, is a holy river that is supposed to have the power of purification. The sculptures of Ganga and Yamuna can be seen at times on the entrance gateways of temples.

■ GARBHAGRIHA

The sanctum sanctorum. In Hindu temples, statues of gods are deified in a shrine.

■ GELUGPA

A new Buddhist group in Tibet also called the Yellow Cap. Sionkpa started it in the 14th century, as a rigid religion based on virtuous conduct, but it was merged into the Kagyu group, in the 17th century. The two groups coexist in Ladakh.

■ GHAT

Stone steps usually leading down to a river, or a lake. They descend in steps making bathing possible. Even if there was no temple near by, the water source was a religious space.

■ GOMMATESHWARA

The son of the first *tirthankara,* Adinatha. He is also called Bahubali and is worshipped in south India. His gigantic statue has been sculpted on a monolithic rock.

■ GOMPA

The Tibetan word used in Ladakh and Sikkim to mean temples or monasteries. The monks and the young novice monks, live together, self-sufficiently in the gompas.

■ GOPURA

In south India, a fence surrounds the precincts of a temple and tall turret-like entrances are built on all four sides. These turrets are called gopuras. Usually, they rise above the fence and are sometimes as tall as 60 m.

■ GOTHIC REVIVAL

It was started around the 18th century, in England, when Gothic architecture of the Middle Ages was revived. At that time, architects in India too, built colonial buildings with Gothic influences.

■ GOVERNOR GENERAL OF INDIA

The top-most official who ruled India for the British. At first he was the head of the British East India Company, in Bengal, in 1774. In 1834, he became the Governor General of the whole of India. In 1854, when the King of England also became the King of the Indian nation, he became the royal representative and ruled by proxy.

■ GOVINDADEVA

God who looks after the cows. Another name for Krishna.

■ GUMBAD

A dome in Persian. The tombs with a dome for a roof, also

came to be called Gumbad. The same is called Gubba in Arabic. →*Chhatri, Rauza*

■ GUMPHA

The cave temples of Orissa are called Gumphas.

■ GURUDWARA

The prayer hall and the surrounding buildings of the Sikh religion are called Gurudwara. Guru means teacher and Gurudwara means a teacher's house. Gurudwaras resemble the Mughal palaces in their architecture and are usually painted completely white.

H-I

■ HAMIRUKA →Harmika

■ HAMMAM

The bathing house in Mughal architecture, equipped with a steam bath.

■ HARMIKA

A box like structure on top of the *stupa*. On top of this, an umbrella-like circular disc is erected

■ HAVELI

A residence made of wood or stone, in Persian. The word corresponds to the word mansion in English.

■ HELLENISM

Is a culture that is a blend of the Grecian culture and the eastern culture after Alexander came to conquer the east. The effect of Hellenism spread from Gandhara to Kashmir, but there is not much remaining now.

■ HINDUISM

Brahmanism or the Indian religion. It would be more apt to call it an aggregate of the life style, customs and thinking process of Indians in general.

■ HOYSALA STYLE

The architecture developed by the Hoysala dynasty in south India. It was an in-between style with mature looking, step designs. There is more than one shrine, with a star shaped plan and a profusion of sculptures.

■ ICON

Any sculpted statue used in prayer, be it of a God, human or animal. In India, statues are aplenty. Islam frowns upon idol worship thus there are neither murals nor statues in a mosque.

■ IDGAH

Idgah is an outdoor prayer area, where all Muslims meet during the ID festival. Along with the *mihrab* and minarets, the *Quibla* wall faces Mecca.

■ IMAMBARA

The Sufi saint, Imam Hussain attained martyrdom in Karbala, in Iraq, in the year 680. Since then, this day is celebrated in his memory. *Imambaras* are used during the Muharram festival.

■ INDO-SARACENIC STYLE

Many colonial style buildings were built during the British era. Later, the traditional Indian style and the Mughal style were incorporated into this. This blended style is called the Indo-Saracenic style.

■ IRIMOYA

Irimoya is a type of roof style traditionally predominant in Japan, where two sloping roofs are placed either parallel to each other or angled to each other, with a small roof placed on top of them

■ ISLAM

Islam means, "absolute obedience to the only God, Allah".

Islam was started by the prophet Muhammad*, in Arabia, in the 6th century. The religion came to India in the 11th century. In 1206, Islamic rule was established in Delhi.

■ IWAN

Iwan is an element of design from Persia. A large arched opening is constructed on the façade of the building and a square framework is built around it, which is called, Iwan. It is a half open space with a vaulted ceiling on the inner side of the arch.

J-L

■ JAGAMOHAN

The *mandapa* (prayer room in front of the shrine)* in Orissa.

■ JAINISM

Mahavira started this religion with the doctrine of *Ahimsa* (non-killing, non-violence) in the 5th- 6th century, BC. Most of the believers are very rich businessmen, who have built many temples.

■ JALI

Stone latticework on walls and entrances through which, one could look outdoors and let in sunlight and air. Usually 3 to 5 cm thick, with arabesque or geometric patterns.

■ JAMI MASJID →Friday mosque.

■ JANTAR MANTAR

These are astronomical observatories built by Raja Sawai Jai Singh, who was a Rajput chieftain and an astronomer.

■ JHAROKHA

This is a decorative window or projecting balcony made with a *jali*. Generally Rajputs adopted this style.

■ JINA

The *tirthankaras* of the Jain religion were called Jina because they have attained victory over worldly passions. *Jaina* is a person who teaches Jina.

■ JOR BANGLA

Hindu temples in Bengal with two *banglas* were called Jor Bangla.

■ KAGYUPA

A Buddhist group in Tibet, also called the Red Cap Group. In the 11th century.

■ KAILASA

A legendary mountain where Shiva is said to be residing. Shiva temples are built as an analogy to the mountain and were sometimes called Kailasa.

■ KALYANA MANDAPA

The hall in south India, which was used for the wedding ceremony of gods.

■ KOVIL

Temples in Kerala and Tamil Nadu are called kovil.

■ KRISHNA

One of the incarnations of Vishnu, who advised Arjuna, through the verses in the Bhagawad Gita. Krishna, known by many other names is most adored in India, and his pictures and statues are aplenty.

■ KSHATRIYA

The second in the hierarchy of the Hindu Varna (caste) system or warrior class. The king and his soldiers were Kshatriyas. Buddha and Mahavira were born Kshatriyas.

■ KULU LAGAN

A Buddhist shrine in a monastery.

■ KUND

Kunds are reservoirs and tanks with steps, found mainly in west India and south Karnataka. At times they were constructed inside the temple precincts.

■ KUTTAMBALAM

A large building, in a Kerala temple complex that is used for religious discourses, music, etc. Inside the structure is a stage that resembles the Noa stage, in Japan.

■ LHAKANG

The name of the halls in the *Gompas** of Ladhakh. Also a Mahayana Buddhist temple in Ladakh and HP. There are various types of Lhakang →Dukhang

■ LINGA

Linga is the symbol of Shiva. It is a phallus and is deified in Shiva temples, as standing on a female genital organ. The worship of a Shiva lingam continues from the days of the Indus Valley Civilization for whom genital worship was a form of ensuring fertility and productivity.

M

■ MADRASSA

Is an Arabic word meaning school, educational facility, etc. High-level education based on the Quran* is imparted here. Since this system started in Arabia, the building is usually in the Arabian style, with four *iwans.* *

■ MAHA MANDAPA

A large mandapa. When there are many mandapas* in a temple, the main mandapa is called the Maha Mandapa.

■ MAHABHARATA

One of the two great epics of India, along with the Ramayana*. It is based on the 'Bharatha War' that took place around the 10th century BC. Reliefs of scenes from the Mahabharatha can often be seen sculpted on the walls of temples.

This literally means the Great King. The chieftains of Hindu feudal kingdoms* were called Maharajas. The Muslim chief was called a *Nawab.* Depending on the area, they were called *Maharana, Maharawat, Maharao* etc.,

■ MAHAVIRA

The founder of Jainism*. He is the 24th and the last in the line of *tirthankaras.** Mahavira was born a prince, who left the house at the age of 30, after long meditation became a Jina (victor) and at the age of 42, started Jainism and came to be called Mahavira (Great warrior).

■ MANASTAMBHA

A stambha* found in south India, in front of Jain temples. Usually, a four faced Jina* statue is placed at the very top. At times, statues of Brahma, who is supposed to be the protector of the area, is also found on top and it is then called a Brahma Deva Stambha.

■ MANDAPA

The prayer hall right in front of the shrine. The basic construction of a Hindu temple is 'shrine and mandapa style'. In large temples there will be many mandapas and they will have their own names. →Maha mandapa, Ranga Mandapa, Meghanath Mandapa, Namaskara Mandapa, Kalyana Mandapa, Open Mandapa, Jagamohan.

■ MANDIR

Generally means temple, regardless of religion. Important buildings and palaces may also be called thus.

■ MAQBARA

A Persian word that means tomb or tomb gardens *
→ Rauza, Gumbad

■ MARATHA

People whose mother tongue is Marathi are called Marathas. Shivaji, who was a Maratha, fought vehemently with the Mughals* and formed the Maratha Hindu kingdom. Later he fought three Maratha battles with the British.

■ MASJID →Mosque

■ MASONRY CONSTRUCTION

A method of construction that uses stones or bricks piled one on top of the other. In principle, it is the opposite of wood construction.

■ MATHA

A Hindu monastery. A Buddhist monastery is called a *Vihara**

■ MAUSOLEUM

Originally there was no custom of erecting tombs in India. It was brought into India along with the Muslims and the Hindu Rajputs in west India also adopted it. Mausoleum architecture is one of the features of Indo Islamic architecture.

■ MECCA

The Arabian city where Muhammed was born. The Quaba temple is the centre of the Islamic world. All the mosques in the world face Mecca.

■ MEGHANATHA MANDAPA

A large shrine seen in large Jain temples.

■ MIDDLE STYLE

The architectural style of the Middle Ages, was a style that was a blend of the style of North India * and South India *. It came to be called the *Vessara* style. There are many examples of this style in Karnataka.

■ MIHRAB

Niche in the *Quibla** wall designed in the mosque*. It is built in the direction of Mecca.

■ MIMBAR

The platform near the central *Mihrab** in the mosque*. Usually, it is very decorative, with a roof and stairs. This platform is used for preaching.

■ MINARET

A tower attached to the mosque*. From here, the believers are called to come to pray for 'Azan'. At times these minarets stand independently. It is also attached as a decoration on tombs and entrances.

■ MITHUNA

Statue of an amorous couple. At times, in temples, couples in intimate postures were sculpted, which was thought to bring good luck. At times, it is found in Buddhist and Jain temples too.

■ MONOLITH

Anything that has been sculpted out of one single rock, like a *stambha,* etc. Rock cut temples are monolith temples.

■ MOSQUE

The prayer house of Muslims. In Arabic, it is called *Masjid,* which means the place to prostrate oneself. The main places inside the mosque are the *Quibla* wall, *Mihrab.* Minaret, and the water jet to purify oneself→Friday mosque

■ MUGHAL

A dynasty started by Babur in 1526, which later controlled most of India. Mughal means Mongol and the Mughals are the blood descendants of Ghenghis Khan of the Timur Empire.

■ MUHAMMAD

The founder of Islam*. Muhammed. He proclaimed himself to be equivalent to Moses of the Jews and Jesus of the Christians. His name was anglicised to Mahomad.

■ MUKHALINGA

The face of Shiva sculpted on the *Linga*. It may be one face or many faces. If four faces are sculpted then it is called *Chatur Mukha Linga*.

■ MUSLIM

A follower of Islam. Most of the Indian Muslims belong to the *Sunni* sect. Around Lucknow, there are more *Shias*.

N-P

■ NADAMBALAM

A fence with a roof, that encloses the temple in Kerala. At times it becomes a corridor with latticed walls.

■ NAGARA STYLE

Nagara means city or belonging to a city. It is an architectural style of temples in north India.

■ NANDI

A bull and a *vahana* (vehicle) of Shiva*. Also found as a statue in front of Shiva temples. At times independent Nandi shrines can also be seen.

■ NARASIMHA

One of the ten incarnations of Vishnu. He has the body of a human being and the head of a lion. The main Narasimha Temple is located in Ahobilam in south India.

■ NATARAJA

The King of dance, also another name for Shiva*. Usually seen in a dancing posture. The Chidambaram Temple in the south is a famous Nataraja Temple.

■ NAVA RATNA

Hindu temples in Bengal that had nine small towers. 9 tower style →Ratna.

■ NAVE

The main space inside Christian churches in Europe. Usually, there are two rows of columns in the hall. Of the three spaces thus created, the centre is called the main aisle and the sides are the left and the right aisles.

■ NAYAKA

The Governors who ruled the area on behalf of the Vijayanagar Empire. As the empire weakened, the Nayakas became independent and formed their own kingdoms. This era is called the Nayaka era (dynasty).

■ NEO-CLASSICAL

The restored style of old European, Greek and Roman architecture.

■ NICHE

A cavity on the wall. A *Mihrab* is also a type of a niche.

■ NIRVANA

Ultimate aim of Buddhists, final release from the cycle of existence.

■ NORTHERN STYLE

Temple architecture in India is broadly divided into the North style and the South style. The *shikhara* or tower on top of the shrine in the North style is vertical and strong. They can be classified as the Orissa type, Khajuraho type, west India type and can also be called the Nagara type.

■ PAGODA

The origin of the word is unknown, but Europeans called the Buddhist *stupa** and tiered towers, pagodas. The five-storied tower of Japan is also called a pagoda.

■ PANCHA- RATNA

The Bengal temples with five towers were called Pancha ratna

■ PANCHA YATANA See Pancha ratna

■ PANCHRATNA

A style where four shrines are added in the four corners of the main shrine, thus creating five shrines. If three more shrines are added it becomes an eight-shrine temple.

■ PAPIER-MACHE

An art form that uses paper pulp and glue to create a shape. When dry it is varnished and painted on. It is used to make household artefacts.

■ PARAPET

A low wall is built on the roof to protect the ends of the roof and to make it water proof.

■ PARSHVANATHA

The 23rd *thirthankara* who lived 250 years before Mahavira. It is said that the Parshva religion was the predecessor of Jainism.

■ PAVILION

An arbor, or a summerhouse.

■ PIDHA-DEUL

The structure with pyramidal roofs in Orissa temples, usually the prayer hall. Pidha is the flat part from where the pyramidal tower is built. It resembles the temple architecture of the south India.

■ PILLARED HALL

A space with rows of pillars, usually found in Arabian mosques. Since the construction of true arches and domes was not known, most Hindu temples had large halls that were lined with columns.

■ PLAN

Plan usually means the floor plan of the building. The structure and style of the whole building is also called plan.

■ POL

A derivative from Sanskrit language that means doorway .
→Darwaza

■ PORCH

The entrance of a building. The roof is supported by the wall on one side and two pillars on the other side.

■ PORTAL

The area around the entrance of a room or a building. Especially in temples, the entrances of the *mandapa* * and shrine* have statues of *Dwarapalas* and are sculpted and decorated with lively designs.

■ PORTICO

A corridor with pillars.

■ POST AND BEAM STRUCTURE

This is a style of trabeated construction where a beam is placed over two pillars. Originally, it was a style used for wooden constructions, but in India, this technique was adopted for stone constructions, too.

■ PRADAKSHINA PATH

Circumbulatory or pathway around the shrine of the temples by keeping time is a common form of prayer in India. This pathway made of stone around the shrine is called Pradakshina path.

■ PYLON

The tower at the entrance of an Egyptian temple. There have many features similar to the *gopura** of South India.

Q-S

■ QUIBLA WALL

The straight line facing Mecca* is called the Quibla. The wall facing Mecca in the mosque* is called the Quibla wall. Believers pray facing this wall.

■ QURAN (Koran)

Actually called *kur-an*, it is the holy book of the Muslims, in which the sayings of Muhammad that were given to him as revelations from God were compiled after his death.

■ RAILING

The fence that surrounds the circumbulatory around the *stupa*. Originally built in wood, later this style was adopted in stone fences that can be seen even today.

■ RAJPUT

Rajputs, migrated from central Asia, during the 5th century, settled in west India and blended with the locals. They were a warrior class and established their kingdom in west India.

■ RAMAYANA

A very popular epic with Rama and Sita as the main characters. It has been depicted profusely in paintings and sculptures. There are also many temples dedicated to Rama, who is one of the incarnations of Vishnu.

■ RANG MAHAL.

Means a colourfully painted palace. It usually denotes the building in the palace used for entertainment.

■ RANGA MANDAPA

When there is more than one mandapa in a temple, the main mandapa is called a Ranga mandapa. It is a place where people collect.

■ RANN

Forms a large part of Kutch in west India. It is a marshy swamp with salty layers and cannot be used at all.

■ RATHA

A wagon or horse carriage. The chariot used in temples to take God out during festivities is also called a Ratha. At times, the shrine is also called a Ratha.

■ RATNA

In Bengal, the towers in the temple are called Ratna, which means a jewel. →Eka Ratna, Pancha Ratna, Nava Ratna.

■ RAUZA

An institutionalised tomb rather than a religious place. Most of them are located in the middle of gardens or tomb gardens. →Gumbad, Maqbara, Darga

■ REKHA

The part of the tower that portrayed the slope of the *shikhara* in Orissa temple architecture.

■ ROCK CUT TEMPLE

These are temples where huge rocks were sculpted from the top downwards and the temple created, looked exactly like any other temple made with masonry work. These are called rock cut temples, to distinguish them from cave temples.

■ ROCOCO

The phase in European architecture, after the Baroque, where there was a surplus of decorations.

■ SAFAIENCE TILE

This is a tile with an enamel design on top of it, made by baking earthen slabs. These colourful designs are usually some holy writings or arabesque patterns which are decoratively attached to a wall surface.

■ SAGAR

Means lake and is usually used for man-made lakes. →Tank

■ SAMSARA

Ancient India believed that any living being, regardless of caste, would be reborn on the 49th day of their death. This was not considered romantic, but was bondage and the main aim or ideal of the religion was to cut the soul free from this bondage.

■ SAMVARANA

A pyramidal roof found in Gujarat, with countless small glass pieces stuck on it. The special feature is that contrary to the square plan, these are at an angle of 45 degrees.

■ SANCTUM SANCTORUM →Garbhagriha

■ SANGHA

Community or order of Buddhist priests, or Buddhist Monastery

■ SCHIST

Is a construction material mostly used in Karnataka. It is a fine textured stone, green in colour that was easy to sculpt on. The exterior is hard and it is also called crystal schist.

■ SEDGE HAT

A broad brimmed hat used in places where there is a lot of rainfall especially in south east Asian countries by farmers working in fields

■ SHAHJAHAN

The 5th emperor of the Mughal dynasty. He built many buildings like the Taj Mahal, Red Fort, Delhi, Jami Masjid, Delhi, etc. Old Delhi was previously called Shahjahanabad after him.

■ SHAIVITE

Devotee of Lord Shiva

■ SHIA

A large group that put Ali, a family member of prophet Muhammad in the rank of Caliph, are the Shia Ali (Ali school of thought) group and are called Shias. The 12 Imam group forms the national religion of Iran.

■ SHIKHARA

Usually the roof of a shrine is made to look like a mountain, with a tower formation. The whole edifice, including the shrine walls, is called shikhara in north India. In south India, only the rounded stone on the peak is called shikhara, which means mountain peak.

■ SHIVA

Shiva and Vishnu are the two main gods of Hinduism. Parvati (Durga*) is his consort. In Shiva temples, his symbol, *Linga* is deified. In front of the Shiva temple a Nandi statue* can be found. →Nataraja.

■ SHRI KOVIL

The sanctum sanctorum in Kerala. They are usually square, round and apsidal in shape. Sometimes oval shapes are also found.

■ SHRINE →Garbhagriha

■ SIKHISM

A religion started in the 16th century, by Guru Nanak, mainly in the state of Punjab, opposing the caste system in Hinduism. He took the belief of one God and equality from Islam and blended Sufism and Bakthi (belief in God) in his religion.

■ SOUTHERN STYLE

The architectural style of temples in the Middle Ages, can be divided into the North type* and the South type. The main feature of the South style is that the towers on the shrine are made of horizontal layers. This is also called the Dravidian style.

■ STAMBHA

Stambha means pillars that are independent o the building and were built as memorials. Emperor Ashoka built one in every area. Later, Jainism in south India, adopted this feature and built Maha Stambhas in front of their temples.

■ STEP-WELL

A Step-well, is a well, where steps lead down to the level of the water. It is frequently seen in west India, where it is called a *vav* and in north India, it is called a *baoli*. The step-wells built by kings, were rich underground structures, so heavily decorated with sculptures that they looked like palaces.

■ STUPA

Stone monuments over earthen mounds, shaped like half domes, built in India, in the olden days. These were developed specially by Buddhists. The remains of Buddha* were deified here and this custom spread all over the country. In Tibet and Ladakh they are called chortens* .

■ SULTAN

The head of the Islamic kingdom of the Sufi group* was called Sultan.

■ SUNNI

Muslims are divided into two groups, the Shia group and the Sunni group. Those who believe in abstinence and penance, which is a fairly large group, are called Sunni.

■ SURYA

The Sun God of India, from the Rig Vedic era. Surya Temples can be found in Konark, Martand and Modhera.

T-Z

■ TANK

A lake, pond etc., in Sanskrit is called a tadaka. In Gujarati it was called talao, which means man-made lake. It was changed to tank which meant reservoir, lake etc., and was incorporated into English language too. →Kund, Sagar, Teppakulam.

■ TEPPAKULAM

Tanks* in south India that are connected to the temple. During the Teppam festival, statues of Gods are taken on a float to the middle of the tank, where there will be a shrine, on an island.

■ TERRACOTTA

Slabs of clay that are swifty carved on when they are still wet and then baked in the kiln. They were used as decorations on the surface of the brick temples in Bengal.

■ TIRTHANKARA

Mahavira * was the founder of Jainism. Before him, there is said to have been 23 thirthankaras and Mahavira is believed to be the 24th.

■ TIRTHA

A holy place and pilgrim centre in India. It is usually on the banks of a river. Tirtha means going from the world of daily life to the eternal world. Usually pilgrim centres in India are located on the banks of rivers or near the sea. →Ghat

■ TOMB GARDEN

The royal tomb area of the Muslim and Rajput chieftains that were developed as public gardens or tomb gardens.

■ TORANA

A memorial entrance of pillars, beams and braces. Specially used as the entrances to stupas*, in Buddhist temples. It can be seen in some middle age Hindu temples, too. In the earlier times, there must have been wooden structures built as entrance gates of villages.

■ TRABEATED

Pillar and beam construction style where a beam is placed across the top of two pillars

■ TRACERY

A European architectural detail of lattice decoration around window frames. It is similar to the Indian Jali*.

■ TRIMURTHIS

Shiva *, Vishnu * and Brahma, three Gods unified together make the force of the universe. Can be seen at times in sculptures.

■ TYMPANUM

The semi-circular or triangular decorative wall surface on top of the window or gable in European architecture is called tympanum.

■ VAULT

A ceiling and roof constructed in masonry is called a vault. Islamic constructions used many vaults and domes.

■ VEDA

The sacred book of the Hindu religion. There are four Vedas, the Sama Veda, Rig Veda, Yajur Veda and Atharva Veda.

■ VESARA STYLE

The in-between style of south Indian architecture during the Middle Ages.

■ VIHARA

Vihara, in Sanskrit, means a long walk or a place to take a long walk. Buddhist and Jain monks left their home and lived in cave temples*. The monks' quarters in these cave temples were called viharas.

■ VIJAYANAGARA STYLE

The Vijayanagar dynasty was the last Hindu dynasty to rule India. The architectural style of the Vijayanagar dynasty was different from that of the Chola dynasty. Their main shrines were small and the surrounding gopuras were huge. The sculptures were also complex and had details of the Baroque style.

■ VIMANA

The main the architectural style of south Indian is called Vimana. The word Moolaprasada is used in north India. Usually, there is a tower on top of the garbhagriha (shrine).

■ VISHNU

In the Hindu religion, Vishnu along with Shiva, are the most important Gods. With them as the patron, there is the Shaivaite group and the Vaishnavaite group. Vishnu has 10 incarnations Rama, Krishna etc.

■ WEST COAST STYLE

In the long, thin state of Kerala, sandwiched between the Arabian Sea and the Western Ghats, rainfall is plenty. Hence the wooden roofs on the buildings here are sloping. This style is called the West Coast style.

■ YAZHI

Yazhi is a mythical beast, which looks like a lion with horns. It is usually sculpted in a row on the base platform of the temple or at the base of pillars. It is also called Vyala.

■ ZENANA

Harem, the ladies quarters in an Islamic palace. The men's quarters were called mardhana.

BIBLIOGRAPHY

The book with the * mark has a list of reference literature that is related to the theme.

India - General and Archaeology

■ THE WONDER THAT WAS INDIA
A.L.Basham, 1954,
Singwick and Jackson.

■ ARCHAEOLOGICAL SURVEY OF INDIA,
A. Cunningham, 1971-87, 24 volumes,
Reprinted edition, 1966-72,
Indological Book House, Varanasi.

■ A GUIDE TO TAXILA
Sir John Marshall, 1960,
Reprinted edition 1972,
Indological Book House, Varanasi.

■ SIR ALEXANDER CUNNINGHAM AND THE BEGINNINGS OF INDIAN ARCHAEOLOGY
Abu Imam, 1966,
Asiatic Society of Pakistan, Dhaka.

■ THE CAMBRIDGE ENCYCLOPEDIA OF INDIA
Francis Robinson (ed), 1989
Cambridge University Press, Cambridge.

Indian Fine Arts and its History

■ THE ART OF INDIA*
Stella Kramerisch, 1954,
Phaidon Press, London.

■ THE ART OF INDIA*
Kalambur Shivaramamurthy, 1977
Harry N. Abrams, New York.

■ THE IDEALS OF INDIAN ART
E.B. Havell, 1911,
John Murrey, London.

■ A HAND BOOK OF INDIAN ART
E.B. Havell.1920, London,
Reprinted edition, 1972,
Indic Academy, Varanasi.

■ THE ART OF INDIAN ASIA,
Its Mythology and Transformations.
Heinrich Zimmer, 1955,
2 Vol. Text and Illustrations
Princeton University Press, Princeton , New York.

■ A HISTORY OF FINE ART IN INDIA AND CEYLON*
Vincent A. Smith, 1911,
Reprinted Edition 1969,
D.B. Taraporewala, Bombay.

■ THE ART AND ARCHITECTURE OF INDIA
The Pelican History of Art
Benjamin Rowland, 1953,
Penguin Books, London.

■ THE ART AND ARCHITECTURE OF the INDIAN SUBCONTINENT*
J.C. Harle,1986,
The Pelican History of Art
Penguin Books, London.

■ THE ART OF ANCIENT INDIA*
Susan L. Huntington, 1985,
Weather Hill, New York, Tokyo.

■ INDIAN SCULPTURE
Stella Kramerisch ,1933,
Y.M.C.A. Publishing House Calcutta.

■ HELLENISM IN ANCIENT INDIA*
Gauranga Nath Banerjee, 1919,
Amended Edition, 1920 Calcutta,
Probsthain, London.

■ L'INDE ET L'ORIENT CLASSIQUE
Gisbert Combas, 1937,
Libriarie Orientaliste, Paul Gauthner, Paris.
Two separate volumes (the text and illustrations)

■ ANCIENT INDIAN ARTS AND THE WEST*
Irene N. Gajjar, 1971,
D.B. Taraporewala, Bombay.

■ BASIS OF DECORATIVE ELEMENT IN INDIAN ART
K.C.Aryan, 1981,
Rekha Prakashan, New Delhi.

■ GODS, GUARDIANS AND LOVERS*
Temple Sculptures from North India
Vishaka N. Desai, Darielle Mason (ed), 1993
Mapin Publishing, Ahmedabad.

■ TRIBAL INDIA
Saryu Doshi (ed), 1992,
Marg Publications, Bombay.

■ NATIONAL HANDICRAFTS AND HANDLOOMS MUSEUM*
Jyotindra Jain, Aarthi Agarwala, 1989
Mapin Publishing, Ahmedabad.

Indian Architecture and its history

■ HISTORY OF INDIAN AND EASTERN ARCHITECTURE
James Fergusson, 1876, Two volumes,
revised by J. Burgess, and R.P. Spiers, 1910,
London, Reprinted edition, 1972
Munishram Manoharlal, New Delhi

■ THE ANCIENT AND MEDIEVAL ARCHITECTURE OF INDIA
E.V. Havell, 1915, London
Reprinted Edition 1972
S.Chand, New Delhi.

■ INDIAN ARCHITECTURE
E.V. Havell, 1913, London
Reprinted Edition
S.Chand, New Delhi.

■ INDIAN ARCHITECTURE
First Volume, Buddhist and Hindu period,
Percy Brown, 1941
Second Volume, Islamic Period 1956.
E. C. Taraporewala, Bombay.

■ THE ARCHITECTURE OF INDIA
Buddhist and Hindu
Satish Grover 1990,
Vikas, New Delhi.

■ THE HISTORY OF ARCHITECTURE IN INDIA
From the dawn of civilization to the end of Raj
Christopher Tadgell, 1990, paper 1994,
Phaidon Press, London.

■ INDIAN LIVING ARCHITECTURE
Andreas Volhasen, 1969, paper 1993,.
Benedict Taschen, Cologne.

■ ISLAMIC INDIA-LIVING ARCHITECTURE
Andreas Volhasen, 1971, paper-1993,
Benedict Taschen, Cologne.

■ ORIENTAL ARCHITECTURE
Mario Bussagli, 1973,
Henry s. Abrams, New York.

■ ARCHITECTURE IN INDIA
Association Francaise d' Action Artistique, 1985,
Electa Moniteur, Paris.

■ FORMAL STRUCTURE IN INDIAN ARCHITECTURE
Kluas Herdeg, 1990,
Rizzoli, New York.

■ STUDIES IN INDIAN TEMPLE ARCHITECTURE
Pramod Chandra (ed), 1975,
American Institute of Indian Studies

■ ENCYCLOPEDIA, INDIAN TEMPLE ARCHITECTURE
Michel M. Meister and M.A. Dhaky (eds),
American Institute of Indian Studies,1983-1991
University of Pennsylvania Press,
VOL 1, PART 1 SOUTH INDIA
Lower Dravidadesa, 200 BC-1324 AD, 1983
VOL 1, PART 2 SOUTH INDIA, 1986
Upper Dravidadesa, early phase, 550-1075 AD,
VOL 2, PART 1 NORTH INDIA1988,
Foundations of North Indian style, c. 250 BC-1100 AD,
VOL 2, PART 2 NORTH INDIA
Period of early maturity, c. 700-900 AD, 1991

■ A STUDY ON VASTUVIDYA OR CANONS
ARCHITECTURE OF INDIA
Trapada Bhattacharya, 1947, Patna.

■ SILPA PRAKASA
Medieval Orissan Sanskrit text on Temple Architecture
Ramachandra Kaulacara, 1966,
E.J.Brill, Leiden.

■ THE MORTUARY MONUMENTS IN ANCIENT
AND MEDIEVAL INDIA
Ratan Lal Mishra, 1991,
B.R.Publishing, Delhi.

■ THE DESIGN DEVELOPMENT OF
ANCIENT ARCHITECTURE
Claude Batley, 1973,
Academy Editions, London.

■ ELEMENTS OF INDIAN ARCHITECTURE
Jose Pereira, 1987,
Motilal Banarsidass, Delhi, Varanasi.

■ THE IMPULSE TO ADORN
Saryu Doshi,(ed), 1982,
Marg Publications, Bombay.

■ ANCIENT AND MEDIEVAL TOWN PLANNING
IN INDIA*
Prabhakar V. Begde, 1978,
Sagar Publications, New Delhi.

■ RURAL INDIA,Villages Houses in Rammed Earth
Popposwamy, 1979,
Kienste in Bersee, Stuttgart.

■ THE ANCIENT BRIDGES OF INDIA*
Jean Deloche, 1984,
Sitaram Bhartia Institute of Scientific Research,
New Delhi.

Ancient Times/ Buddhist Architecture

■ EARLY INDIAN ARCHITECTURE-Palaces
Ananda K. Coomaraswamy, 1991,
Munshiram Manoharlal, New Delhi.

■ EARLY INDIAN ARCHITECTURE,
Cities and City Gates.
Ananda K. Coomaraswamy, 1991,
Munshiram Manoharlal, New Delhi.

■ LA VIE PUBLIQUE ET PRIVEE DANS
L'INDE ANCIENNE
Jeannine Auboyer, Jean Francois Enault, 1969,
Presses Universitaires de France, Paris.

■ THE SYMBOLISM OF THE STUPA
Adrian Snodgrass, 1985,
Cornell University Southeast Program,
reprinted edition-1992, Motilal Banarsidass, Delhi.

■ BUDDHIST ART IN INDIA
Albert Grunwadel, 1901, Reprinted edition 1974,
Bharatiya Publishing House, Varanasi.

■ BUDDHIST MONUMENTS*
Debala Mitra, 1971,
Sahitya Samsad, Calcutta.

■ EARLY BUDDHIST ARCHITECTURE OF INDIA
H.Sarkar, 1966, 2nd (ed), 1933,
Munishram Manoharlal, New Delhi.

■ THE BUDDHIST ART OF GANDHARA
John Marshall, 1960,
Government of Pakistan, Karachi.

■ THE BUDDHIST CAVE TEMPLES OF INDIA
S.R. Wouchap, 1933, Calcutta,
reprinted edition 1981,
Cosmo Publications, New Delhi.

■ BUDDHIST CAVE TEMPLES OF INDIA
Owen C. Kail, 1975,
Taraporevala, Bombay.

■ BODH GAYA, The site of enlightment
Janice Leoshko (ed), 1988,
Marg Publications, Bombay.

■ THE BUDDHIST ART OF NAGARJUNAKONDA
Elizabeth Rozen Stone, 1994,
Motilal Banarsidass, Delhi.

Hindu Architecture

■ THE HINDU TEMPLE- 2 volumes,
Stella Kramerisch, 1946, 6th publication 1996,
Motilal Banarsidass, Delhi.

■ ESSAY ON THE ARCHITECTURE OF THE HINDUS
B.Ram Raz, 1834,
Royal Asiatic Society of Great Britain & Ireland, London.

■ MANASARA SERIES
Prasad Kumar Acharya, 1934-46, London,
Reprinted edition 179-81,
Oriental books Reprint Corporation, New Delhi.

■ A DICTIONARY OF HINDU ARCHITECTURE,
Vol.1 1934, reprinted edition 1981.

■ INDIAN ARCHITECTURE ACCORDING TO
MANASARA-SHILPASHASTRA, Vol.2
1934, Reprinted edition 1981.

■ MANASARA ON ARCHITECTURE AND
SCULPTURE, Vol.3 (Sanskrit Text), 1934,
Reprinted Edition 1979,

■ ARCHITECTURE OF MANASARA, Vol.4
(Translation into English), 1934,
Reprinted Edition 1980,

■ ARCHITECTURE OF MANASARA, (Illustrations of
Architectural and Sculptural Objects), Vol.5
1934, Reprinted Edition 1980,
154 illustrations included

■ HINDU ARCHTECTURE IN INDIA AND ABROAD,
Vol.6 1946,
Reprinted Edition 1979.

■ BHARATIYA VASTU - SHASTRA SERIES
D.N. Shukla,
Vastu Vanmaya Prakasana Sala, Lucknow.

■ HINDU SCIENCE OF ARCHITECTURE,
Vol.1, 1960.

■ HINDU CANONS OF ICONOGRAPHY AND
PAINTING, Vol.2
1958, reprinted edition 1993,
Munshiram Manoharlal, New Delhi.

■ STUDIES IN INDIAN TEMPLE ARCHITECTURE
Pramod Chandra (ed), 1975,
American Institute of Indian Studies.

■ TEMPLES OF NORTH INDIA
Krishna Deva, 1969,
National Book Trust, India, New Delhi.

■ TEMPLES OF SOUTH INDIA
K.R. Srinivasan, 1972,
National Book Trust, India, New Delhi.

■ INDIAN TEMPLE STYLES
The Personality of Hindu Architecture
K.V. Soundara Rajan, 1972,
Munshiram Manoharlal, New Delhi.

■ INDIAN TEMPLE ARCHITECTURE*
Form and Transformation
Adam Hardy, 1995,
Abhinav Publications, New Delhi.

■ ROYAL PATRONS AND GREAT TEMPLE ARTS
Vidhya Dehejia (ed), 1988,
Marg Publications , Bombay.

■ RITUAL ART OF INDIA
Ajit Mukherji, 1985,
Thames and Hudson, London.

■ THE DEVELOPMENT OF HINDU ICONOGRAPHY
Jitendra Nath Banerjea, 1941,
University of Calcutta.

■ A DICTIONARY OF HINDUISM*
Its Mythology, Folklore and Development
Margeret and James Stutley, 1977,
Allied Publishers, Bombay.

Architecture of Jainism

■ JAINA ART AND ARCHITECTURE, 3 Volumes
A.Ghosh (ed), 1974,
Bhartiya Jnapith, New Delhi,

■ ASPECTS OF JAINA ART AND ARCHITECTURE
U.P. Shah and M.A. Dhaky (ed), 1975), Gujarat State
Committee, L.D. Institute of Indology, Ahmedabad

■ JAINA SHRINES IN INDIA
O.P. Tandon, 1986,
Ministry of Information and Broadcasting, Government
of India.

■ SHREE 108 JAIN TIRTH DARSHANAWALI
Palitana,

■ JAINA TEMPLES OF WESTERN INDIA*
Harihar Singh, 1982,
Parshvanath, Vidyashram Reserch Institute, Varanasi.

■ PANORAMA OF JAIN ART
C.Sivaramamurti, 1983,
Times Of India, New Delhi.

■ INVITING DEATH*
Historical Experiments on Sepulchral Hill
S.Settar, 1986,
Karnatak University, Dharwad.

■ JAINA-RUPA-MANDANA Jaina Iconography
Uma Kant P. Shah, 1987,
Abhinav Publications, New Delhi.

■ JAINA ART
Ananda K. Coomaraswami, 1994,
Munshiram Manoharlal, New Delhi.

■ JAIN ART FROM INDIA*-The Peaceful Liberators
Pratapaditya Pal, 1995,
Thames and Hudson, London.

■ THE JAIN COSMOLOGY
Collette Cailatt, Ravi Kumar, 1981,
Jaico Publishing House, Bombay.

The architecture of Islam

■ ISLAMIC ARCHITECTURE
John G. Hoag, 1977,
Harry N. Abrams, New York.

■ ARCHITECTURE OF THE ISLAMIC WORLD
George Mitchell, (ed), 1978, paper 1995,
Thames and Hudson, London.

■ ISLAMIC SACRED ARCHITECTURE*
-A stylistic History
Jose Pereira, 1994,
Books And Books, New Delhi.

■ JHAROKHA
Illustrated Glossary of Indo Muslim Architecture
R.Nath, 1986,
Jaipur.

■ THE MOSQUE, HISTORY, ARCHITECTURAL
DEVELOPMENT OF REGIONAL DIVERSITY
M.Frishman and H.U. Khan (ed),1994,
Thames and Hudson, London.

■ THE MANARA IN INDO MUSLIM ARCHITECTURE*
A.B.M. Hussain,1970,
The Asiatic Society of Pakistan, Dhaka.

■ THE GREAT MUGHALS*
Bamber Gascoigne 1971,
Time Book International, New Delhi.

■ MUGHAL ARCHITECTURE*
An outline of its history and development
Ebba Koch, 1991,
Time Books International, New Delhi.

■ ARCHITECTURE OF MUGHAL INDIA*
{The New Cambridge History of India1-4}
Catherine B. Asher, 1992,
Cambridge University Press, Cambridge.

■ SOME ASPECTS OF MUGHAL ARCHITECTURE
R. Nath, 1976,
Abhinav Publications, New Delhi.

■ HISTORY OF DECORATIVE ART IN MUGHAL
ARCHITECTURE*
R. Nath , 1976,
Motilal Banarsidass, Delhi.

■ BUILDING CONSTRUCTION IN MUGHAL INDIA
Ahsan Jan Qaisar, 1988,
Oxford University Press, Delhi.

■ INDIAN ISLAMIC ARCHITECTURE*
The Deccan 1347- 1686
Elizebath Schotten Merklinger, 1981,
Aris and Phillips, Warminister.

■ EARTHLY PARADISE, GARDEN AND COURTYARD
IN ISLAM
Jonas Lehrman, 1980,
Thames and Hudson, London.

■ THE GARDENS OF MUGHAL INDIA
Sylvia Crowe and Sheila Haywood, 1972,
Thames and Hudson, London.

■ THE WORLD OF ISLAM, FAITH, PEOPLE,
CULTURE
Bernard Lewis (ed), 1976, Paper 1992,
Thames and Hudson, London.

Rajput and the Architecture of the Middle Ages

■ RAJPUT ART AND ARCHITECTURE*
Hermann Goetz, 1978,
Franz Steiner Verlag, Weiabaden.

■ RAJPUT ARCHITECTURE
G.S.Ghurye, 1968,
Popular Prakasan, Bombay.

■ THE RAJPUT PALACES*
G.H.R. Tillotson, 1987,
Yale University Press, New Haven.

■ THE FORTS AND FORTRESSES OF GWALIOR
AND ITS HINTERLAND*
B.D. Misra, 1993,
Manohar Publishers, New Delhi.

■ ORCHHA
Kalyan Kumar Chakravarthy, 1984,
Arnold Heinnemann, New Delhi.

■ ART AND ARCHITECTURE OF JAISALMER
Sureshwara Nand 1990,
Research Publishers, Jodhpur.

■ A GUIDE TO THE OLD OBSERVATORIES IN
DELHI, JAIPUR, UJJAIN AND BENARES
G.R. Kaye, 1920,
Superintentant Government Printing, Calcutta.

■ JANTAR MANTARS OF INDIA
Prahlad Singh, 1986,
Holiday Publications, Jaipur.

■ SHIVAJI AND FACETS OF MARATHA CULTURE
Saryu Doshi, (ed) 1932,
Marg Publications, Bombay.

■ SIKH ARCHITECTURE IN PUNJAB
Pradeep. S. Arshi, 1986,
Intellectual Publishing House,

■ SIKH RELIGION (DOCTRINE AND HISTORY)
Cole and Sanbee.

The Age of English rule and the Architecture after Independence

■ STONES OF EMPIRE- Buildings of British India
Jan Morris, 1983, Paper 1984,
Penguin Books, London.

■ SPLENDOURS OF THE RAJ*
British Architecture in India.1660-1947
Phillip Davies, 1985. Paper 1987
Penguin Books, London.

■ EUROPEAN ARCHITECTURE IN INDIA, 1750-1850
Sten Nisson,1968,
Faber and Faber, London.

■ AN IMPERIAL VISION, INDIAN ARCHITECTURE
AND BRITIAN'S RAJ
Thomas R. Metcalf, 1989,
Faber and Faber, London.

■ ARCHITECTURE IN VICTORIAN AND
EDWARDIAN INDIA
Christopher W. London (ed) 1994,
Marg Publications, Bombay.

■ THE TRADITION OF INDIAN ARCHITECTURE
G.H.R.Tillotson,1989,
Yale University Press, New Haven.

■ INDIAN SUMMER*,
LUTYENS BAKER AND IMPERIAL DELHI
Robert Grant Irwing, 1981, Paper 1982,
Yale University Press, New Haven, London.

■ THE INDIAN METROPOLIS*
Norma Everson, 1989,
Yale University Press, New Haven, London.

■ MODERN ARCHITECTURE IN INDIA
Sarbjit Bahga, Surinder Bahga, Yashinder Bahga, 1983,
Galgotia Publishing Company, New Delhi.

■ AFTER THE MASTERS, Contemporary Indian
Architecture
Vikram Bhatt and Peter Scriver, 1991,
University of Washington Press, Washington.

■ CONTEMPORARY ARCHITECTURE
BANGLADESH
Shah Alam Zahiruddin et.al., 1990,
Institute of Architects, Bangladesh.

■ LOUIS KAHN THE WORLD OF ARCHITECTURE
D.B.Brownly, D.G.DeLong, 1992,
Delphi Research Centrre.

■ BALAKRISHNA DOSHI
William J.R.Curtis, 1988,
Mapin Publishing, Ahmedabad.

■ CHARLES CORREA
Hasan Uddin Khan, 1984, revised edition. 1987,
Concept Media, London.

■ RAJ REWAL
Brian Brace Taylor, 1991,
Concept Media, London.

■ DAWNING PLACE OF THE REMEMBRANCE OF
GOD, The Bahai house of Worship, 1987
Bahai Publishing Trust, New Delhi.

■ CONCEPTS AND RESPONSES,
International Architectural design Competition for the Indira
Gandhi National Centre for the Arts, New Delhi, 1992,
Mapin Publishing, Ahmedabad.

Architecture of North India

■ ARCHITECTURE IN THE HIMALAYAS
William Simpson, 1883, Reprinted Edition 1970,
Susil Gupta, New York.

■ THE HIMALAYAS IN INDIAN ART
E.B. Havell, 1924,
John Murray, London.

■ BUDDHIST MONASTERIES IN THE WESTERN HIMALAYAS*
Romi Khosla, 1979,
Patna Pustak Bhandar, Kathmandu.

■ SANCTUARIES BOUDDHIQUES DU LADAKH
Genevieve Tchekhoffet Yvan Comolli, 1984,
White Orchid Press, Bangkok.

■ ANCIENT MONUMENTS OF KASHMIR
Ram Chandra Kak, 1933,
The India Society, London

■ ART AND ARCHITECTURE OF ANCIENT KASHMIR
Pratapaditya Pal (ed). 1989
Marg Publications, Bombay.

■ PANDRETHAN, AVANTIPUR AND MARTHAND
Dabela Mitra1977,
Archeological Survey of India, New Delhi.

■ ART AND ARCHITECTURE OF HIMACHAL PRADESH*
Mian Govardhan Singh,1983,
B.R.Publishing Corp., Delhi.

■ ANTIQUITIES OF HIMACHAL
M. Postel, A. Neven and K. Mankod,1985
Franco Indian Pharmacueticals, Bombay.

■ THE TEMPLES OF HIMACHAL PRADESH
Shantilal Nagar,1990,
Aditya Prakashan ,New Delhi.

■ HIMALAYAN TOWERS*
Temples and Palaces of Himachal Pradesh
Ronald . M. Bernier,1989,
S.Chand and Company, New Delhi.

■ ANTIQUITIES OF CHAMBA STATE
Archeological Survey of India,New Imperial series 36,
J P H Vogel, 1911, Calcutta, Reprinted Edition, 1990
Buckingham Books, London.

■ THE EARLY WOODEN TEMPLES OF CHAMBA
Hermann Goetz, 1955, E.J Brill, Leiden.

■ THE SEVEN CITIES OF DELHI
Gordon Risley Hearn, 1906,
W. Thaker, London.

■ REBUILDING SHAHJAHANABAD,
The Walled City of Delhi
Jagmohan, 1975,
Vikas, Delhi.

■ DELHI AND ITS NEIGHBOURHOOD
YD Sharma, 2nd ed, 1990,
Archeological Survey of India, New Delhi.

■ AN HISTORICAL SURVEY OF QUTB DELHI
Memoirs of the Archeological Survey of India
Government of India Central Public Branch, Calcutta.

■ DELHI, HUMAYUNS TOMB AND ADJACENT BUILDINGS
S.A.A. Naqvi, 1947,
Manager of Publications, Delhi.

■ MANSIONS OF DUSK,
THE HAVELIS OF OLD DELHI
Pavan .K. Varma 1992,
Spantek Publishers, New Delhi

■ THE JAIN STUPAS AND OTHER ANTIQUITIES OF MATHURA
Archaeological Survey of India, New Imperial Series 20
Vincent A. Smith, 1901, Allahabad.

■ URBAN GLIMPSES OF MUGHAL INDIA*
Agra, The Imperial Capital
IP Gupta, 1986,
Discovery

■ ROMANCE OF THE TAJ MAHAL*
P. Pal, .J. Leoshko, J.M.Dye and S.Markel, 1989,
Thames and Hudson, London.

■ FATEHPUR SIKRI
Saiyid Athar Abbas Rizvi, 2nd ed, 1992
Archaeological Survey of India, New Delhi.

■ FATEPUR SIKRI [OPUS 5]
Attilio Petticioli et al, 1992,
Ernst and Sons.

■ THE MUGHAL ARCHITECTURE OF FATEHPUR SIKRI
Edmund W Smith 1894,
Reprinted edition 1985,
Caxton Publications, Delhi.
4 Volumes,

■ FATEHPUR SIKRI
Michel Brand and Glenn D. Lowry (eds), 1987
Marg Publications, Bombay.

■ THE ARCHITECTURE OF IMAMBARAS
Neeta Das, 1991,
Lucknow Mahotsav Patrika Samithi, Lucknow.

■ THE TEMPLE OF BHITARGAON*
Mohammed Zaheer,1981,
Agam Kala Prakashan, Delhi.

Architecture of East India

■ LIST OF ANCIENT MONUMENTS PROTECTED UNDER ACT VII OF 1904 IN THE PROVINCE OF BIHAR AND ORISSA
Archeological survey of India Report,
New Imperial series 5.1
Maulvi Muhammed Hamid Kureishi 1931
Government of India, Calcutta.

■ KUMRAHAR

Vijayakantha Mishra, 1976,
Archaeological Survey of India, New Delhi.

■ NALANDA

A Ghosh, 6th ed.1986,
Archaeological Survey of India, New Delhi.

■ RAJGIR

Muhammed Hamid Kuraishi,
Revised by A. Ghosh, 5th ed.,1987,
Archaeological Survey of India, New Delhi.

■ MAHABODHI or The Great Buddhist Temple under the Bodhi Tree in Bodh Gaya.

A.Cunningham, 1982,
Revised edition 1982.

■ BRICK TEMPLES OF BENGAL*

George Mitchell, 1983,
Princeton University Press, Princeton.

■ BISHNUPUR

S.S. Biswas, 1992,
Archaeological Survey of India, New Delhi.

■ BIRBHUM TERRACOTTAS

Mukul Dey, 1959,
Lalit Kala Academy, New Delhi.

■ INDIAN TERRACOTTA ART

O.C. Ganguly, 1959,
MayFlower, London.

■ THE ISLAMIC HERITAGE OF BENGAL

Protection of the Cultural Heritage, Research Papers 1,
George Mitchell (ed), 1984,
UNESCO, Paris.

■ CALCUTTA, Changing Visions,

Lasting Images through 300 years
Pratapaditya Pal (ed), 1990,
Marg Publications, Bombay.

■ ARCHITECTURE OF ASSAM

P.C. Sarma, 1988,
Agam Kala Prakashan, Delhi.

■ HINDU TEMPLE ART OF ORISSA*

Thomas E Donaldson,
3 Volumes, 1985-1987,
E.J. Brill, Leiden,

■ EARLY STONE AGE TEMPLES OF ORISSA*

Vidya Dehejia, 1979,
Vikas Publishing House, New Delhi.

■ BHUBANESHWAR

Debala Mitra , 5th ed, 1984,
Archeological Survey of India, New Delhi.

■ KONARAK

Debala Mitra , 4th ed, 1992,
Archaeological Survey of India, New Delhi.

West Indian Architecture

■ THE ARCHITECTURAL ANTIQUITIES OF WESTERN INDIA

Henry Cousens, 1926,
The India Society London.

■ WESTERN INDIAN ART

Umakant .P. Shar, Kalyan K. Ganguli (ed), 1966,
Indian Society of Oriental Art, Calcutta.

■ MUD ARCHITECTURE OF THE INDIAN DESERT

Kulbhushan Jain and Minakshi Jain, 1992,
AADI Centre, Ahemadabad.

■ HISTORY, ART AND ARCHITECTURE OF JAISALMER

Ram Avatar Agarwala, 1979,
Agam Kala Prakashan, Delhi.

■ ABU TO UDAIPUR

John Singh Mehta, 1970,
Motilal Banarsidass, Delhi.

■ MUHAMMEDAN ARCHITECTURE OF BHAROCH, CAMBAY, DHOLKA, CHAMPANER, AND MAHMUDABAD IN GUJARAT

Archaeological Survey of Western India 6,
New Imperial series 23
J. Burgess, 1896, London.

■ SOMANATHA AND OTHER MEDIAEVAL TEMPLES IN KATHIAWAD

Archaeological Survey of India, Imperial Series 45
Henry Cousens, 1931,
Government of India, Calcutta.

■ NOTES OF A VISIT TO SOMNATH, GIRNAR, AND OTHER PLACES IN KATHIWAD

J. Burgess, 1869,
Bombay, Reprinted edition, 1976,
Kishore Vidya Niketan, Varanasi.

■ THE STEP WELLS OF GUJARAT

In Art-Historical perspective
Jutta Jain - Neubauer,1981,
Abhinav Publications.

■ THE QUEEN'S STEP WELL AT PATAN

Kirit Mankodi 1991,
Franco Indian Research, Bombay.

■ HAVELI, WOODEN HOUSES AND MANSIONS OF GUJRAT

V.S. Pramar, 1989,
Grantha Corporation, U.S.A.
Mapin Publishing, Ahmedabad.

■ AHMEDABAD

K.V. Soundara Rajan, 1980,
Archaeological survey of India, New Delhi.

■ AHMEDABAD
George Mitchell and Snehal Shah (eds), 1988
Marg Publications, Bombay.

■ LOTHAL
S.R.Rao, 1985,
Archaeological Survey of India, New Delhi.

■ THE TEMPLES OF SHATRUNJAYA
James Burgess, 1869, Bombay.
Reprinted edition 1977, Gandhinagar.

■ JUNAGADH
K.V. Soundara Rajan, 1985,
Archaeological Survey of India, New Delhi.

■ SOMANATHA TEMPLE
V.V. More, 1948,
Aryavrata Sanskrit Samaj, Calcutta.

■ ARCHITECTURAL AND ARCHEOLOGICAL
REMAINS OF THE PROVINCE OF KACHH
Dalpatram Pranjivan Kakhar, 1879, Bombay,
Reprinted Edition 1978,
Indian India, Patna.

■ ARCHITECTURE IN PAKISTAN
Kamil Khan Mumtaj, 1985,
Concept Media, Singapore.

Architecture of Central India

■ TEMPLES DE L'INDE CENTRALE ET
OCCIDENTALE MEMOIRS ARCHEOLOGICS 11, 2
VOL, Text & Illus.
Odette Viennot, 1976,
E'cole Francaise d' Extreme Orient,
Librairie Adrien Maissenneuve, Paris.

■ TEMPLES OF THE PRATIHARA PERIOD
IN CENTRAL INDIA
Architectural Survey of Temples No. 4
R.D. Trivedi , 1990,
Archaeological Survey of India, New Delhi.

■ GWALIOR FORT
Kalyan Kumar Chakravarty, 1984,
Arnold Heinemann, New Delhi.

■ CHANDERI MONUMENTS OF MADHYA PRADESH
AND THEIR ENVIRONS,
CONSERVATION SERIES 2, 1985,
Environmental planning and Coordination Organization,
Madhya Pradesh.

■ KHAJURAHO
Krishna Deva 6th (ed) 1980,
Archaeological Survey of India, New Delhi.

■ TEMPLES OF KHAJURAHO, Vol. 2)
Architectural Survey of Temples 5.

Text and Illustrations
Krishna Deva,1990,
Archaeological Survey of India, New Delhi.

■ DIVINE ECSTASY - THE STORY OF
KHAJURAHO
Shobita Punja, 1992,
Viking, New Delhi.

■ KHAJURAHO
Kalyan Kumar Chakravarty, 1985,
Arnold Heinmann, New Delhi.

■ SANCHI
Debata Mitra, 6th ed., 1992,
Archaeological Survey of India, New Delhi.

■ MANDU
D.R.Patil 2nd ed., 1992,
Archaeological Survey of India, New Delhi.

■ THE CAVE TEMPLES OF INDIA
James Fergusson and James Burgess, 1880,
London, Reprinted Edition 1988,
Munshiram Manoharlal, New Delhi.

■ AJANTA
Debata Mitra, 10th ed., 1992,
Archaeological Survey of India, New Delhi.

■ NOTES ON THE BUDDHA ROCK TEMPLES OF
AJANTA-Their paintings and sculptures,
Archaeological Survey of Western India 9,
James Burgess, 1879,
Reprinted edition, 1970, Bombay.

■ REPORT ON THE ELLORA CAVE TEMPLES
AND THE BRAMINICAL AND JAINA CAVES IN
WESTERN INDIA
Archaeological Survey of Western India 5,
James Burgess 1883, Reprinted Edition, 1970
Indological Book House, Varanasi.

■ THE CAVES OF AURANGABAD
Early Buddhist Tantric Art In India
Carmel Berkson, 1986,
Mapin Publishing, Ahmedabad.

■ MEDIAEVAL TEMPLES OF THE DAKHAN
Archaeological Survey of India report,
New Imperial Series 48.
Henry Cousens, 1931,
Reprinted Edition, 1985,
Cosmo Publications, New Delhi.

■ GOA, Cultural Patterns
Saryu Doshi, (ed), 1983
Marg Publications, Bombay.

■ OLD GOA
S. Rajagopalan, 2nd ed, 1982,
Archaeological Survey of India, New Delhi.

South Indian Architecture

■ ISLAMIC HERITAGE OF THE DECCAN
George Mitchell, (ed), 1992,
Marg Publications, Bombay.

■ GOLCONDA AND HYDERABAD
Shebaz H. Safrani, (ed). 1982,
Marg Publications, Bombay.

■ BIDAR, ITS HISTORY AND MONUMENTS
G. Yazdani, 1947,
Oxford University Press, London

■ NAGARJUNAKONDA
H. Sarkar, B.N. Misra, 3rd ed. 1987,
Archaeological Survey of India, New Delhi.

■ AMARAVATI
H. Sarkar, S.P. Nainar, 1992,
Archaeological Survey of India, New Delhi.

■ THE SIMHACHALAM TEMPLE
K. Sundaram, 1969,
Simhachalam Devasthanam.

■ ENTRE ALAMPUR ET SRISAILAM*
Publications de l'Institut Francais d'Indologie 67-1,2
Bruno Dagens, 1984, 2 Vol (text and Illustrations)
l'Institut Francais d'Indologie, Pondichery.

■ EARLY TEMPLE ARCHITECTURE
IN KARNATAKA AND ITS RAMIFICATIONS
K. V. Soundararajan, 1969,
Karnataka University, Dharwar

■ THE CHALUKYAN ARCHITECTURE OF THE
KANARESE DISTRICT
Archaeological survey of India report, Imperial Series 42,
Henry Cousens, 1926, Government Of India, Calcutta

■ IN PRAISE OF AIHOLE, BADAMI,
MAHAKUTA, PATTADAKKAL
1980, Marg Publications, Bombay.

■ THE ART AND ARCHITECTURE OF AIHOLE
R.S. Gupta, 1967,
D.B. Taraporevala, Bombay.

■ ARCHITECTURE AND ART OF SOUTHERN INDIA*
The New Cambridge History of India, 1-6
George Mitchell, 1995,
Cambridge University Press, Cambridge.

■ HAMPI
D. Devakunjari, 3rd ed,. 1992,
Archaeological Survey of India, New Delhi.

■ HAMPI RUINS
A. H. Longhurst, 1917,
Madras Government, Madras.

■ THE VIJAYANAGARA COURTLY STYLE
George Mitchell, 1992,
Manohar Publications, New Delhi.

■ RAMACHANDRA TEMPLE AT VIJAYANAGARA
Anna. Dallapiccola, John M. Fritz,
George Mitchell and S. Rajashekara, 1992,
Manohar Publications, New Delhi,

■ HAMPI-VIJAYANAGAR,
THE TEMPLE OF VITHALA
Pierrae -Sylvan Fillozat and Vasundara Fillozat 1988,
Sitaram Bhartia Institute of Scientific Research,
New Delhi.

■ THE HOYSALA TEMPLES*
S.Settar, 1992,
Kala Yatra Publications.

■ TEMPLES OF THE GANGAS OF KARNATAKA
Architectural Survey of Temples 6,
I.K. Sharma, 1992,
Archaeological survey of India, New Delhi.

■ HOMAGE TO SHRAVANA BELAGOLA
Saryu Doshi, (ed) , 1981,
Marg Publications, Bombay.

■ MYSORE, The Royal City
T. P. Issar, 1991,
UNESCO

■ CAVE TEMPLES OF THE PALLAVAS
Architectural Survey of Temples 1,
K.R.Srinivasan, 1964, 2nd ed, 1993,
Archaeological survey of India, New Delhi.

■ TEMPLES PALLAVA CONSTRUITS
[Memoires Archeologiques 9.]
Jacques Dumacay et Francoise l'Hernault, 1975,
Ecole Francaise d'Extreme-orient,
Librarie Adrien- Maisonneuve, Paris.

■ MAHABALIPURAM
B. Shivamurthy, 5th ed. 1992,
Archaeological survey of India, New Delhi

■ TIRUPPARUTTIKUNDRAM AND ITS TEMPLES
T.N.Ramachandran, 1934,
Madras.

■ AUROVILLE, A DREAM TAKES SHAPE
Alain G. (ed). 1992

■ TEMPLE TOWNS OF TAMIL NADU
George Mitchell,
Marg Publications, Bombay.

■ TEMPLE GATEWAYS IN SOUTH INDIA*
Architecture and Iconography of Chidambaram Gopuras
James C. Harle, 1963,
Bruno Cassier, Oxford.

■ EARLY CHOLA ARCHITECTURE AND
SCULPTURE 866~1014 AD
Douglas Barrett, 1974,
Faber and Faber London

■ MIDDLE CHOLA TEMPLES
S. R. Balasubramaniam, 1975,
Thomson Press, Faridabad.

■ THE CHOLA TEMPLES
C. Sivaramamurthy, 5th ed. 1992,
Archaeological Survey of India, New Delhi.

■ TEMPLE ART UNDER THE CHOLA QUEENS
B. Venkataraman, 1976,
Thomson Press, Faridabad.

■ DARASURAM
Francoise l'Hernault, 1987,
Ecole Francaise d'Extreme-orient,
Librarie Adrien- Maisonneuve, Paris.

■ KAMPAHARESHWARA TEMPLE AT
TRIBUVANAM
H. Sarkar, 1974, Department Of Archaeology,
Government Of Tamil Nadu, Madras.

■ LIVING WOOD, SCULPTURAL TRADITIONS OF
SOUTHERN INDIA
George Mitchell, 1994,
Marg Publications, Bombay.

■ MONUMENTS OF KERALA
H. Sarkar, 1973,
Archaeological Survey of India, New Delhi.

■ SPLENDOURS OF KERALA
Ronald M. Bernier et al. 1979,
Marg Publications, 1994, Bombay.

■ DRAVIDA AND KERALA IN THE ART OF
TRAVANCORE
Stella Kramrisch, 1953,
Artibus Asiae, Switzerland.

■ THE ARTS AND CRAFTS OF KERALA
Stella Kramrisch, J. H. Cousins and R. Vasudeva
Poduval, 1970,
Paico Publishing House, Cochin.

■ TEMPLE ARCHITECTURE IN KERALA
K. V. Soundararajan, 1974,
The Government Of Kerala, Trivandrum.

■ AN ARCHITECTURAL SURVEY OF TEMPLES OF
KERALA (ARCHITECTURAL SURVEY OF TEMPLE 2)
H. Sarkar, 1978,
Archaeological survey of India, New Delhi.

■ TEMPLE ART OF KERALA*
Ronald M. Bernier, 1982,
S. Chand & Co. Ltd. New Delhi.

■ TRAVEL GUIDE AND ARCHITECTURAL GUIDE
Indo [Blue Guide World 28]

■ INDIA -A TRAVEL SURVIVAL KIT
HughFinley, Tony Wheeler, Bryn Thomas, Michelle
Coxall, et al. 6th ed. 1996.

■ LONELY PLANET,
Australia.

■ BANGLADESH -A Travel Survival Kit
Jon Murrey, 2nd ed. 1991,
Lonely Planet, Australia.

■ THE PENGUIN GUIDE TO THE
MONUMENTS OF INDIA
Penguin Books , London,
First Volume, Buddhist, Jain ,Hindu
George Mitchell, 1989.
Second Volume, Islamic Rajput ,European
Philip Davies.

■ GREAT MONUMENTS OF INDIA BHUTAN, NEPAL,
PAKISTAN AND SRI LANKA
Shobita Punja, 1994,
The Guide Book Company, Hong Kong.

■ DISCOVER THE MONUMENTS OF BANGLADESH
Nizamudin Ahmed, 1984,
The University Press, Dhaka.

■ THE FORTS OF INDIA
Virginia Fass, Rita and Vijay Sharma, Christopher
Tadgell, 1986,
Collins, London.

■ THE PALACES OF INDIA, MAHARAJA OF
BARODA
Virginia Fass , 1980,
The Vendome Press, New York.

■ THE ROYAL PALACES OF INDIA
George Mitchell, 1994,
Thames and Hudson, London.

■ HILL STATIONS OF INDIA
Gillian Wright, 1991,
Odessey, HongKong.

■ MUSEUMS OF INDIA, AN ILLUSTRATED GUIDE
Shobita Punja,1990,
The Guide Book Company, Hong Kong.

Maps Of India

■ A HISTORICAL ATLAS OF SOUTH ASIA*
Joseph E. Schwartzberg (ed), 1992
Oxford University Press, New York.

■ AN HISTORICAL ATLAS OF INDIAN PENINSULA
D.Collin Davies, 2nd ed. 1959,
Oxford University Press, Madras.

INDEX OF ARCHITECTS

[ ] shows the name of the place and the page published in

■ **Aliwal Khan (India, 16th C)**
Worked for Sher Shah
Tombs of Sher Shah and Hassan Khan [Sasaram p155]

■ **ARCOP (India, 20th C)**
Architects group of Ramesh Khosla, Ray Afleck, etc.
Mughal Sheraton Hotel [Agra, p114]

■ **Ata Aula (India, 17th C)**
Bibi ka Makabra [Aurangabad, p379]

■ **Balakrishna Vithaldas Doshi (India 1927)**
Was a disciple of Le Corbusier, made Ahmedabad his base and represents contemporary Indian Architecture
Gandhi Labour Institute [Ahmedabad, p284]
Indian Institute of Management [Bangalore p473]

■ **Charles Correia (India, 1930)**
Is an architect who represents present day India
Jeevan Bharathi Building [New Delhi p100]
Cidade de Goa Hotel [Goa p401]

■ **Charles Martin (France, 1735-1800)**
Army Major General Architect born in Leon
Old Town Hall and the New Palace [Kholapur, p395]
Mayo University [Ajmer, p226]

■ **Depaka (India 15th C)**
Adinatha Temple [Ranakpur, p248]

■ **E.W. Fritchley (England, 19th-20thC)**
Lalit Mahal Palace [Mysore, p469]

■ **Edwin Lutyens (England, 1869-1944)**
An architect who excelled in arts and crafts

■ **Farubuz Sabha (Iran 20th C)**
Bahai House of Worship [New Delhi-p100]

■ **Fredrick William Stevens (England 1848-1900)**
Victoria Terminus and Churchgate Terminus and the Municipal Buildings [Bombay p385]

■ **George Gilbert Scott (England 1811-1878)**
An architect who represented Gothic Revival
The Lecture Hall and Library in Bombay University [Bombay, p384]

■ **George Wittet (England, 1880-1926)**
He was the consulting architect for Bombay Jurisdiction
Prince of Wales Museum and Gateway of India [Bombay p386]

■ **Gunda (India, 8th C)**

Virupaksha Temple [Pattadakkal, p437]

■ **Henry Alexander Nesbitt Medd (England, 1892-1977)**

Anglican Cathedral [New Delhi, p99]

■ **Henry Conybeare (England-1873)**

He worked as an engineer in Bombay city.

He was dismissed in 1850.

Afghan Memorial Church [Bombay p384] Page 548

■ **Henry Irwin (England 1841- 1922) His speciality are the designs with use of various styles.**

Rashtrapati Nivas (Former Vice Regal Residence) [Shimla P. 72]

Amba Vilas Palace [Mysore, p468]

Victoria Memorial Hall and High Court [Madras p 478]

■ **Herbert Baker (England, 1862-1946)**

Helped designing New Delhi on invitation from his friend Lutyens

Secretariat and Parliament House [New Delhi, p99]

■ **J.W. Brassington (England, 19th-20th C)**

High Court [Madras p478]

■ **James Agg (England, c1758- 1828)**

Architect of Army first lieutenant

Saint John's Church [Calcutta, p175]

■ **James Augustus Fuller (England, 1828-1902)**

High Court [Bombay, p386]

■ **James Lillyman Caldwell (England, 1770-1863)**

Army admiral and Architect

St. Andrew Kirk [Bangalore p 477]

■ **John Garstin (England 1756-1820)**

Technician of Army major general

Golghar [Patna, p150]

■ **John Theophilus Boileau (England, 1805-1886)**

Worked as the Chief Engineer in the Indian North West Jurisdiction

Christ Church [Simla, p72]

■ **Louis Kahn (America 1901-74)**

Was a great architect, whose architectural ideas had great effect on the world

Ayub National Hospital [Dhaka, p184]

National Assembly Hall [Dhaka, p185]

Indian Institute of Management [Ahmedabad, p283]

■ **Malik Sandal (Persia, 17C)**

Ibrahim Tomb [Bijapur, p430]

■ **Mallitamma (India 13th C)**

Lakshmi Narasimha Temple [Harnahalli, p464]

■ **Mirak Mirza Ghiyas (Persia 16thC)**

Worked for the Mughals

Humayun's Tomb [Delhi, p92]

■ **Nek Chand (India 20thC)**

Works for the Roadways of the State of Punjab.

Rock Garden (Sculptors' Paradise) [Chandighar p85]

■ **Otto H. Koenigsberger**

Designed the new city of Bhubaneshwar, in the recent age even before Chandigarh was designed. [Bhubaneshwar p193]

■ **Pierre Jeanneret (France, 1896-1967)**

Helped Le Corbusier in designing the city of Chandigarh

University and the buildings in the business district [Chandigarh, p81-84]

■ **Robert Fellowes Chisholm (England 1840-1915)**

Was consultant architect for the Madras Jurisdiction. Returned to England in 1900.

Senate House of Madras University [Madras p477]

Senate house of Baroda College [Baroda, 291]

Napier Museum [Trivandrum, p526]

■ **Samuel Swinton Jacob (England 1841-1917)**

He worked as the Chief Engineer of the King of Jaipur.

Mubarak Mahal Palace

Albert Hall Museum [Jaipur, p221, 223]

Lalghar Palace [Bikaner, p227]

■ **Satish Grover (India 20th C)**

Is also an Architectural Historian

Oberoi Hotel [Bhubaneshwar, p201]

■ **Sawai Jai Singh II(India 1686- 1744)**

Feudal Lord of Jaipur and Astronomer

Built the Astronomic Observatory in Jaipur, Delhi and Ujjain called Jantar Mantar

[Jaipur, p222] [Delhi, p 96] [Ujjain, p352]

■ **Thomas Fiott de Havilland (England, 1775-1866)**

St. Andrew's Kirk [Madras, p447]

Govt. House (former Vice Regal Lodge) [Mysore, p469]

■ **Thomas Lyon (England, 18thC)**

Came to India in 1780 and started his designing activities

INDEX OF PLACES AND BUILDINGS

K

L

GENERAL INDEX

T

U

V

W

Y-Z

	BC	**1st-3rd century AD**
NORTH INDIA	Kaushambi City Ruins Old Stupa and Monastery of Sarnath	Jain Stupas in Mathura
EAST INDIA	Stupa and Stambha of Vaisali Kumarahal Ruins of Patna Lomas Rishi Caves on Barabar Hills Cave Temple Groups of Khandagiri and Udaygiri	City Ruins of Shishupal Ghar
WEST INDIA	Indus Civilization city of ruins of Lothal	Cave Temple Groups of Junagadh
CENTRAL INDIA	Stupa and Torana in Sanchi Cave Temple Groups in Baja Cave Temple Groups of Early Age in Ajanta Cave Temple Groups in Pitalkora Pandolena Cave Temple Groups	Cave Temple Groups of Bedsa Cave Temple Groups of Aurangabad Cave Temples of Karli Cave Temple Groups of Kanheri Trivikrama Temple of Ter
SOUTH INDIA	Cave Temple Groups in Gundo Palle	Stupa of Amravathi Kapotheshwara Temple of Chezarla
GENERAL HISTORY	Indus Civilization at its height 2300BC-1800BC Rig Veda was established 1200-BC-1000BC Aryans settled on the Gangetic plains 1000BC Birth of Buddhism and Jainism 6th C, BC Advent of Alexander 326 BC Unification of India under Emperor Ashoka of Maurya Dynasty 3rd C, BC	Kushana dynasty ruled over northern India Satavahana dynasty ruled over central India The 3 dynasties of Chola, Chera, Pandya ruled over southern India The Buddhist Philosopher Nagarjuna was active Trade relations between India and the Roman Empire The great mythological epic *Ramayana* came into existence

4th-6th century AD	7th century	8th century
Dhamekh Stupa of Sarnath Brick Temple of Pittalgaon		Lakshana Devi Wooden Temple in Bharmaur Stupa and Monastery in Paraspora Shankaracharya Temple in Srinagar Surya Temple in Martand Mahesha Temple in Jagasik Wooden Temple in Chatrali
Buddhist University and Monastery in Nalanda	Shiva Temple in Mundeshwari Parashurameshwara Temple in Bhubaneshwar Stupas and Monasteries in Ratnagiri Mahabodhi Temple in Bodhgaya	Vittal Deol Temple in Bhubaneshwar Madakeshwara Temple in Mukhalingam Somapura Vihara in Paharpur Mainamathy Monastery in Comilla (12th century)
Vishnu Temple at Gop	Shiva Temple in Vireshwar.	Hindu Temple Group and Kund in Rodha. Hindu Temple Groups in Osian. Mahavira Temple in Osian. Fortress and Palace Groups of Chittorgarh
Cave Temple Group at Damnar Cave Temple Group in Udaygiri Parvathi Temple at Nachna Kankari Devi Temple at Tigawa Sanchi Temple 17 Cave Temple Group of the later age at Ajanta Hindu Cave Temple Groups at Ellora (~9C) Cave Temples at Elephanta Island Dashavatara Temple at Devgarh	Buddhist Monasteries in Sirpur Lakshmana Temple in Sirpur Buddhist Monastery Group in Sanchi Buddhist Cave Temple Groups in Ellora	Kailasa Temple in Ellora (16th cave) Rajivalochana Temple in Rajim Teli Temple in Gwalior Dharmanatha Temple Damnar Hindu Temple Groups in Naresar.
Stupa and Monastery at Nagarjuna Konda Stupa and Monastery at Sankaram Cave Temple Group in Badami Cave Temple Group in Aihole	Cave Temple Groups in Mahabalipuram Five Rathas in Mahabalipuram Meguti Temple in Aihole Hindu Temple Groups in Badami Hindu Temple Groups in Mahakuta Hindu Temple Groups in Aihole Hindu Temple Groups in Alanpur CaveTemple Groups in Bhairavakonda	Shore Temples in Mahabalipuram Shiva Cave Temple in Kaviyur Tarakeshwara Temple in Panamalai Kailasanatha Temple in Kanchipuram. Ramalingeshwara Temple in Satyavolu Vaikuntaperumal Temple in Kanchipuram Hindu Temple Groups in Pattadakal Rock-cut Temples in Garudamalai.
Gupta Empire was established (320-550) Vakataka dynasty was prominent in Central India Pallava dynasty ruled over south India (9th C) Poet and philosopher Kalidasa became active Mythological epic *Mahabarata* was established Early Chakukya dynasty of Badami (8th C) Maitraka dynasty arose in West India (8th C) Kalachuri dynasty came in Central India (circa 12th C)	King Harshavardhana ruled over north India Hieun Tsang came on a study tour of India. Karkota dynasty became prominent in Kashmir. Islam took birth in Arabia. East Chalukya dynasty ruled Andhra Pradesh.	Pratihara dynasty ruled over north India. (11th C) Arabian army of Umaiya dynasty attacked Sind region. Rashtrakuta dynasty came into existence. (10th C) Para dynasty came into being in East India (12th C) The philosopher belonging to the Vedanta school of thought Sankara became active.

		9th century	10th century	11th century
NORTH INDIA		Rock-cut Shiva Temple in Masrur Rock-cut Buddhist Statue in Murbek Visveswara Temple in Bajavara. Avantiswamin Temple in Avantipur	Hindu Temple Groups in Parmol Vishnu Temple in Buniyar	Shiva Temple in Payal Sumtsek gompa in Alchi Gompa in Tabo
EAST INDIA		Siddeshwara Temple in Barakar Stupa and Temple in Udaygiri Rega Deol of Orissa (left: early age, Right: later age)	Varahi Temple in Chaurasi Mukteshwara Temple in Bhubaneshwar	Raja Rani Temple in Bhubaneshwar Paramesvara Temple in Bhubaneshwar Chausatt Yogini Temple in Hirapur Lingaraja Temple in Bhubaneshwar
WEST INDIA		Ghateshwara Temple in Baroli Kund (Stepped Tank) in Abhaneri	Sas Bahu Temple In Nagda Ambika Mata Temple In Jagat Hindu Temple Group in Kiradu Mountain Temple City in Shatrunjaya	Surya Temple and Tank in Modhera Mahanalesvara Temple in Menal Queen's Step-well in Patan Jain Temple Group in Kumbaria Vimla Vasahi Temple in Mount Abu Sachiya Mata Temple in Oshian Hindu Temple Group and Tank in Bijolia
CENTRAL INDIA		Jain Caves and Temple Groups in Ellora Chaturbhuja Temple in Gwalior Kadarmal Temple in Padpatri Maladevi Temple in Gyaraspur Chaturmukha Mahadeva Temple in Nachna Chausatt Yogini Temple in Khajuraho	Matangeshwara Temple In Khajuraho Jain Temple Group in Khajuraho Lakshmana Temple in Khajuraho Hindu Monastery in Chandrehi	Visvanatha Temple in Khajuraho Kondesvara Temple in Sinnar Kandaria Mahadeva Temple in Khajuraho Udayesvara Temple in Udaipur
SOUTH INDIA		Moovar Kovil in Kodumbalur Vijayalaya Cholishwara Temple in Narthamalai Virattaneshwara Temple in Tiruttani Navalinga Temple In Kukkanur Kaleshwara Temple In Aralaguppe Bhoganandeshwara Temple in Nandi Jain Temple in Pattadakkal	Koranganatha Temple in Srinivasanallur Panchakoota Temple in Kambadahalli Mallikarjuna Temple in Kuruvatti Chamundaraya Temple in Shravanabelgola Manjunatha Temple in Mangalore Hemakuta Temple Group in Hampi	Brihadisvara Temple in Thanjavur Siddesvara Temple in Haveli Temple in Gangaikondacholapuram Jain Temple in Lakkundi
GENERAL HISTORY		The most Prosperous period of Pratihara dynasty in north India Cholas who grew strong again defeated the Pallavas Utpala dynasty in Kashmir (10th C)	West Ganga Dynasty became prominent in West India Jainism spread in West India Solanki Dynasty started in West India (13th C) Palmara dynasty started in Central India (13th C) Chauhan Dynasty started in north-west India (12th C)	Muhammed of Ghazni dynasty attacked West India The Golden Age of Cholas in South India (mammoth temples were built) Chandela Dynasty became prominent in Central India The later Chalukya age in Kalyani (~12th C)

568

12th century	13th century	14th century
Gompa in Lamayuru Gompa in Likir Qutb Minar and Mosque in Delhi	Vaidyanatha Temple in Baijnath. Iltutmish Tomb in Qutb area of Delhi Cave Temples of Saspol	Tughlaqabad Fort in Delhi Ghiyasuddin Fort in Delhi Lakshminarayana Temple Group in Chamba Firoz Shah Kotla in Delhi Khirkee Mosque in Delhi
Bhaskaresvara Temple in Bhubaneshwar Jagannatha Temple in Puri	Surya Temple In Konarak Ramesvara Temple in Bhubaneshwar	Adhina Mosque in Pandua
Neminatha Temple In Girnar Neminatha Temple In Kumba Hindu Temple Gate in Wadnagar Navlaka Temple in Sejakpur Vikia Step-well in Kumli Rukmini Temple in Dwarka Ajithanatha Temple in Taranga	Runa Vasahi Temple in Abu Mountain Parsvanatha Temple in Girnar Arai Mosque in Ajmer Kirthi Stamba In Chittorgarh Mada Step-well in Wadhwan	Taragarh Fort and Palace
Hindu Temple Group (South Group) in Khajuraho		Fort City in Daulatabad

Scene where a huge stone for construction is being transported

12th century	13th century	14th century
Mahadeva Temple in Ittagi Chennakeshava Temple In Belur Irawatesvara Temple in Darasuram Shiva Temple in Hanamkonda(Thousand Pillar temple) Kashi Vishwanatha Temple in Lakundi Hoysalesvara Temple in Halebid Dodda Basappa Temple in Dambal Kamala Narayana Temple in Degamve Vadakkunnada Temple in Trichur	Nataraja Temple in Chidambaram Ramappa Temple in Palampet Kambaharesvara Temple in Tribhuvanam Lakshmi Narasimha Temple in Haranahalli Keshava temple in Somnathpur Varaha Narasimha temple in Simhachalam Ranganatha Swamy temple in Srirangam(17th C) Sarangapani Temple in Kumbakonam(17th c) Sri Vallaba Temple in Thiruvalla	Thyagaraja Temple in Thiruvarur Vidhya Shankara Temple in Sringeri Mahadeva Temple in Kazhakkuttam Friday Mosque in Gulbarga Baktavatsala Temple in Thirukalikkundram
Hoysala dynasty started in south India (12th C) Ramanuja who advocated Vedanta philosophy became active Kakatiya dynasty started in Central India(14th C) Jain Scholor Hemachandra became active East Ganga dynasty of the later ages grew prominent in East India(14th C) Muhammed of Ghori Dynasty attacked North India	Vikramasheela dynasty was destroyed (1203) Buddhism all but disappeared from India. Sultan dynasty, north India (1206-90) Genghis Khan's army entered India (1221) Chola dynasty in South India ceased to exist (1279)	Tughlaq dynasty in Delhi(1320-1413) For some time he shifted his capital to Daulatabad Ibun Patouda of Iran stayed in India for some time Vijayanagara empire in South India (17th C) Bahmani empire in South India (1347-1527) Timur army from Mongolia entered India (1398)

	15th century	16th century	17th century
NORTH INDIA	Atala Mosque in Jaunpur Al Abidin's mother's tomb in Srinagar Gompa in Tikse Group of Tombs of Lodi Dynasty in Delhi	Purana Quila in Delhi Hidimba Devi temple in Manali Gompa of Phiyang Red Fort and palace groups in Agra (17th C) Humayun's Tomb in Delhi Akbar Bridge in Jaunpur Palace Quarters in Fatehpur Sikri Friday Mosque in Fatehpur Sikri Govinda Deva Temple in Brindaban	Akbar's Tomb in Sikandra Shalimar Gardens in Srinagar Itimudaula Tomb in Agra Nishad Gardens in Srinagar Lal Quila (Red Fort) in Delhi Taj Mahal Tomb in Agra Friday Mosque in Delhi Fort and Palace In Leh Friday Mosque In Srinagar
EAST INDIA	Eklakhi Tomb in Pandu Dahir Gate and Rattan Mosque in Gaur	Goaldi Mosque in Sonargaon Kadam Rasul Mosque in Gaur Sher Shah Tomb in Sasaram Friday Mosque in Kusumba Begunia Temple Group in Barakar	Rasa Mancha In Vishnupur Chotti Dargah in Maner Terracotta Temple groups in Vishnupur Ananta Vasudeva Temple in Panchberia Lal Bagh Fort in Dacca Jagannatha Temple in Comilla Gopinatha Temple in Pabna Tank Tomb and Mosque Complex in Vardhaman Gompa in Tashiding
WEST INDIA	Friday Mosque in Ahmedabad Victory Tower in Chittorgarh Adinatha Temple in Ranakpur Fort of Bikaner Dada Harir's Step-well in Ahmedabad Digambara Temple in Sanganer Jain Temple Groups in Jaisalmer(16th C) Tank, Mosque,Tomb, Palace complex in Sarkej Fort Town of Kumbarghar	Ruda step-well in Adalaj Rani Mosque and Tomb in Ahmedabad Friday Mosque in Champaner Dwarkadisha Temple in Dwarka Junagadh Fort in Bikaner Akbar Palace in Ajmer Sayyed Mubarak Tomb in Mehmedabad City Palace in Udaipur(19th C) Fort and Churches in Diu	Ana Sagar and Pavilion group in Ajmer Jain Temple in Loderva in Jaisalmer Royal Chhatris at Ahar in Udaipur Manmade Lakes and Ghats in Rajsamand Royal Chhatris in Mandor Fort Palace in Amber Mehrangar Fort in Jodhpur Royal Chhatris in Bhuj
CENTRAL INDIA	Indra Mahal Palace in Mandu Chand Minar in Daulatabad Hoshian Shah Tomb and Friday Mosque in Mandu Koshk Mahal (Palace) in Chanderi Batar Mahal Gate in Chanderi Mosque Group in Dhar Jahaj Mahal Palace in Mandu Man Mandir (Fort Palace) in Gwalior	Muhammed Ghaus Tomb in Gwalior Convent of St. Francis of Assisi Fort Palace in Orcha (~17th C) Jain Temple City in Sonagiri	Chaturbhuja Temple in Orchha Fort Palace in Dhatia Royal Chhatri Groups in Orchha Friday Mosque in Gwalior Bibi's Tomb (Maqbara) in Aurangabad Se Cathedral in Goa Saint Cajetan Convent in Goa Fort of the Maratha Kingdom in Raigarh
SOUTH INDIA	Haft Gumbad in Gulbarga Mallikarjuna Temple in Srisailam Chandranatha Temple in Mudabidri Gingee Fort (18th C) Palace Quarters and Temples in Vijayanagara Fort and Temple in Bidar Royal Tombs in Bidar Narasimha Temple in Ahobilam(~16th C) Palace of the Vijayanagara dynasty in Penukonda	Vittala Deva Temple in Lepakushi Vittala Temple in Vijayanagara Aghoresvara Temple in Ikkeri Fort and Jalakandesvara Temple, Vellore Chaturmukha Temple in Karkal Char Minar in Hyderabad Mahadeva Temple in Ettumanur Shiva Temple in Vaikkom Big Temple in Thiruvannmalai	Palace of the Nayaka Dynasty in Thanjavur Fort and Royal Tombs of Golconda Ibrahim Tomb in Bijapur Minakshi Temple in Madurai Vijayanagara dynasty palace in Chandragiri Thirumalai Nayakan Palace in Madurai Gol Gumbad in Bijapur Ketapai Narayana Temple in Bhatkal Subramania Temple in Payyanur
GENERAL HISTORY	Ahmed Shahi dynasty in West India. (16th C) Mandu became an important city of the Marwar kingdom. Lodhi dynasty in Delhi.(1451- 1526) Religious philosopher Kabir became active. Namgyal dynasty started in Ladakh. Vasco-da-Gama landed in Calicut.	Founder of the Sikh dynasty, Nanak became active. Golconda dynasty started in Golconda.(1518-1687) Babur won the battle of Panipat.(1526) Akbar became the Emperor of the Mughal dynasty (1542-1605) Vijayanagar kingdom were defeated by the Muslim army and retreated to Penukonda. Nayaka rule started in all regions of south India.	British East India Company was established. Agra became prominent as the capital of the Mughals. Bijapur city became prominent in the south India. Ladakh kingdom developed under King Seng Namgyal. Shivaji started the Maratha kingdom. (-1818) French East India Company acquired Pondicherry.

18th century	19th century	20th century
Ramnagar Fort in Varanasi	Royal palace in Stok	Designing of the city of New Delhi and important facilities
Jantar Mantar (Observatory) in Delhi	Gompa in Rizong	Anglican Cathedral in New Delhi
Adi Brahma Temple in Khokhan	Friday Mosque in Lucknow	Designing of the city of Chandigarh and important facilities
Golden Temple in Amritsar	Raghunatha Temple In Lucknow	Rock Garden in Chandigarh
Shah Hamadan Mosque in Delhi	Royal Palace in Sainj	Mughal Sheraton Hotel in Agra
Safdarjang's Tomb in Delhi	Muir College in Allahabad	Jeevan Bharathi Building in New Delhi
Great Imambara Complex in Lucknow	Rashtrapathi Niwas in Simla	Bahai House of Worship in New Delhi
Bhima Kali Temple in Sarahan	All Saint's Cathedral in Allahabad	Indira Gandhi National Centre for Arts
La Martiniere's Boy's School in Lucknow		STC Building in New Delhi
Katra Mosque in Murshidabad	Indian Vice-Regal Lodge in Kolkata (Calcutta)	Rama Krishna Math in Kolkata (Calcutta)
Terracotta Temple groups in Vishnupur	Terracotta temple groups in Puthia	Victoria Memorial in Kolkata (Calcutta)
Terracotta Temple groups in Karna	Terracotta temple groups in Pathar Narayanpur	Gompa In Rumtek
TerracottaTemple groups in Baranagar	Imambara and palace in Murshidabad	Shanthi Stupa in Dhauli
Gompa in Pemayangtse	Dakshineshwara temple in Kolkata (Calcutta)	New City of Bhubaneshwar
Writers Building in Kolkata (Calcutta) (~1800)	Sheetalanatha Temple in Kolkata (Calcutta)	Legislative Assembly in Dacca
Golghar in Patna	High Court In Kolkata (Calcutta)	Oberoi Hotel in Bhubaneshwar
Saint John Cathedral in Kolkata (Calcutta)	Rajbari in Sonargaon	
Designing of Jaipur City and City Palace	Hathi Singh Temple in Ahmadabad	Ranjit Vilas Palace in Wankaner
Jantar Mantar (Observatory) in Jaipur	Mayo College in Ajmer	Government office, High Court and Temple Complex
Queen's Step-well in Bundi	Albert Hall museum in Jaipur	Rebuilding of Somanatha Temple, Somnathpur
Senate House of Baroda College in Baroda	Baktawar Singh Tomb in Alwar	Umaid Bhavan Palace in Jodhpur
City Palace and Sagar in Alwar	Haveli Group and New Palace in Jaisalmer	Mill Owner's Association Building in Ahmedabad
Royal Chhatris in Jaipur (Gaitor)	Maqbara in Junagadh (royal Chhatris)	Sanskar Kendra Building in Ahmedabad
Udai Vilas Palace in Dungarpur	Jaswant Dada Tomb in Jodhpur	Indian Institute of Management in Ahmedabad
City Palace in Deeg	Mahendra Desai Haveli in Vaso	New Town and Secretariat in Gandhinagar
		Gandhi Labour Institute in Ahmedabad
Tomb of Emperor Aurangazeb in Kurdabad	New Palace in Satara (wada)	Taj Mahal Hotel in Mumbai (Bombay)
Jantar Mantar (Observatory) in Ujjain	Afgan Memorial Church in Mumbai	India Gate in Mumbai (Bombay)
Vishvweshwara Temple in Mauli	Jai Vilas Palace in Gwalior	Prince of Wales Museum in Mumbai
Shanwar Wada Palace in Pune	Bombay University Library in Mumbai	National Centre for Performing Arts
Shanti Durga Temple in Ponda	High Court in Mumbai	Bharat Bhavan Culture Centre in Mumbai
Mangesha Temple in Mardol	New Palace in Kolhapur	Cidade De Goa Hotel in Goa
Parvathi Temple In Pune	Victoria Terminus Railway Station in Mumbai	
Rebuilding of Bom Jesus Basilica in Goa	Government offices in Mumbai	
Ramalingesvara Temple in Rameshwaram	Jain Tombs in Mudabidri	Thyagaraja Temple in Thiruvarur
Wooden Mosque Group in Calicut	Government House in Mysore	Vidhya Shankara Temple in Sringeri
Padmanabhaswami Temple in Trivandrum	Lalitha Mahal palace in Mysore	Mahadeva Temple in Kazhakkuttam
Padmanabhapuram Palace	Shri Aurobindo Ashram and Dormitory in Pondicherry	Friday Mosque in Gulbarga
Mahadevi Temple in Kaviyoor	Vidhana Soudha (government building) In Bangalore	Baktavatsala Temple in Thirukalikkundram
Mosque and Tomb in Srirangapatnam	Indian Institute of Management in Bangalore	
Tipu Sultan Summer Palace in Bangalore	Auroville New Town	
British built Fort William in Kolkata (Calcutta).	Ranjit Singh built the Sikh Kingdom (1802-49)	Decision to shift the capital from Kolkata (Calcutta) to Delhi (1911)
Maratha alliance was formed (1708-1818)	Britain brought India under its control (1849)	Poet Rabindranath Tagore received the Nobel Prize for Literature (1913)
Warren Hastings became first Governor General of India	War of Indian Independence (1857-59)	First World War (1914-18)
Nadir Shah of Iran conquered Delhi (1739)	India came under British (1858)	Nonviolent Satyagraha struggle led by Gandhi
Carnatic War between the British and French (1744 - 1761)	50,00,000 people died in the great Indian Famine (1876-78)	Second World War (1939-1945)
Mysore war that ran into 4 wars (1767-99)	Queen Victoria of England proclaimed herself Empress of India.	India & Pakistan get Independence (1947)
Maratha war that ran into 4 wars (1775-1818)	Indian National Congress was formed (1885)	Bangladesh got Independence from Pakistan (1971)

Postscript

The world has been steadily demarcated by the three-point structure of Europe, America and Asia. The reason for this at the present time, may be economically related. On a cultural basis the importance of Asia will gradually increase. Architectural development comes just a step behind economic development. The Asian age of architecture will come soon. The sleeping giant, India, whose economy had stagnated after Independence has started showing steady activity with the opening up of its economy. On the basis of the size of the country, India will become the focus of economic and cultural developments along with China in the 21st century.

It is an actual fact that, even in the field of architecture, architects who have a very deep understanding of American architecture know almost next to nothing about Indian architecture or traditional Islamic architecture. Everyone knows that a well-developed civilization flourished in India and China from ancient times and that through Buddhism, India made a great impact on Japan too. But if asked what comes to mind about the architecture of India from ancient times to the present day, there are not many who can even conjure up an image.

This book tries to narrow that gap by introducing architecture of the Indian subcontinent including Bangladesh in great detail and entice the traveller to make a tour of South Asia. This area has a great architectural culture that is richly different from that in Japan, Europe and America.

It is difficult for those who cannot take long vacations, to make an extensive tour of India. This book is aimed at giving these people a visual feast with a large number of photographs, which will transport the reader to the site without having to actually travel to these magnificent but far-flung monuments.

This book introduces Indian architecture through the ages, from ancient times to the present day, with Islamic architecture and Colonial style architecture during the British rule also included.

It is usual for this kind of book to include only one photograph of the exterior of the building. This book has many pictures of important buildings, of their details and interiors, which along with the explanations and illustrations bring about a better sense of belonging. With 1800 photographs and 300 maps and illustrations, and notes and characters the book ran into 400 pages and was a little too big for an ordinary volume. This book is the equivalent of something like three ordinary volumes. Since India is historically and geographically equal to West Europe, it is impossible to introduce this country in one volume.

This book is the fruit of 20 years of study and photographic tour done by the author. The first time he came to India was by bus on the Asia highway from London to Kathmandu when it was a comparatively peaceful time with the Vietnam War just over and the strife in Afghanistan and the Iranian revolution just beginning. Now the rupee rate is 3 yen to a rupee. But at that time it was as much as 35 yen to the rupee and it was very hard on the author who was young and poor; the tour was not at all a pleasant one. It was difficult because sufficient information was also difficult to obtain. Despite this, the author energetically toured the architecturally important sites for three months. The differences in culture sprang new surprises every day. With all this hardship when the author reached the site at last, the appearance of the architectural construction never failed to make a deep impression on him. It was an intense emotional experience for the author and also the fact that here was architecture that was completely alien to him, made him decide that he would like to introduce this architecture to Japan by writing a book about it some time. To make this a reality took almost 20 years. In the 12 photographic tours undertaken the number of photographs taken in India alone would exceed 20,000 slides. Since the same building was photographed many times over, the difference in colouring of Kodak Chrome and the later Belvia was mixed. The books collected in this context also increased. The literature catalogue with simple explanations has exceeded 100,000 words.

The author is deeply obliged to *The Penguin Guide to the Monuments of India* written by George Mitchell and Phillip Davies. He purchased this book before starting the tour, and was surprised at the details in it and carried it with him all the time he was touring India. Both the authors did not visit all the sites but wrote the articles reading other literature and hence there were instances where they must have found it very difficult to visualize the actual building. *A Guide to the Monuments of India* has even been updated based on the modification or addition of areas, cities etc. Those who want to make a detailed study tour of Indian architecture are recommended to use the two volumes along with this book.

Another book written by the author called *Indian Architecture* has also been published around the same time. It will be ideal if one were to read the book along with the others. For convenience in reference of buildings, the inscriptions and groupings have been put together. Thus the book, where Indian Architecture has been introduced in geographical order and where the peculiarities of Indian Architecture have been pondered on, became a reality.

Next the author wants to write a book about the history of Indian architecture and his long cherished dream, a book on Jain architecture for which he wants to do an extensive and relaxed study tour. This depends on the opinion and criticism this book, *A Guide To the Architecture of the Indian Subcontinent* attracts.

Author's Personal History

TAKEO KAMIYA

1946	Born in Tokyo, Japan.
1969	Graduated from the Tokyo University of Fine Arts and Music (Architectural course in the Art Faculty).
1971	Worked in the firm of Kazumasa Yamashita, architects and associate.
1980	Established the firm, Takeo Kamiya, architect and associate.

Member of the Japanese Institute of Architects
Member of the Institute of Architecture in Japan

Important Architectural Works

- Town House, Yokohama (Grand prix award for the Kanagawa Architectural contest, 1983).
- Cloisters (Award for the SD review contest).
- Paradise Garden (Kisarazu, won the GID competition, 1991).
- Coei Building, Tokyo, 1990.
- A house with a Hanging Garden, Tokyo.
- Morita Building, Tokyo, 1991.
- Hisago Tokyo Branch Office, 1994.
- Shiokawaya Building, Yokohama, 1995.

Books

Authored
- The Architecture of India, 1996, Touhou Shuppan Publications.

Translated
- Architecture d' Islam, 1978, by Henri Stierlin, Hara Shobo Publications.
- Design of Paradise, Garden Culture of Islam, 1989, by John Brooks, Kajima Shuppan Publications.
- Hindu Temples, 1993, by George Michell. Kajima Shuppan Publications.

Present Address
3-1-8-506, Takinogawa, Kitaku, Tokyo 114-0023
http//www.ne.jp./asahi/arc/ind/engl.htm

Publisher's Profile

GERARD DA CUNHA

1955	Born in Gujarat State, India
1979	B. Arch. School of Planning and Architecture, New Delhi.
1974-75	Apprentice to Laurie Baker
1979-81	Delhi Development Authority.
1982	Private Practice.

Main Works
- Nrityagram Dance Village - Bangalore
- Library & Main Building for Kannada University - Hampi
- Palacio de Aguada - Goa
- Kuteeram Tourist Resort - Bangalore
- Nisha's Play School - Goa
- Tourist Village - Kumarakom
- Siolim House (Restoration) - Goa
- JVSL Township - Bellary
- Inn With A View - Goa

Awards

1991	Commendation Award for "Rural Architecture", Architect of the Year Award.
1993	Designer of the year, Interiors India Design Annual
1998	Prime Minister's National Award for Excellence in Urban Planning and Design
2000	Nerul Gymkhana - Mumbai, Best Design Competition.

Exhibition

1996	"Roots" Fujitsu Center, Tokyo "Innovative Architecture in Asia" Exhibition, Osaka
1998	"Innovative Architecture in Asia" Exhibition, Bangalore
1999	"Houses of Goa", Panjim, Porto, Lisbon, Mumbai, Delhi
2000	"East Wind", Tokyo
2001	"City Nestling in the Forest", Fukushima

Editors Profiles

ANNABEL LOPEZ

1966	Born in Goa, India
1988	B. Arch. Goa College of Architecture,
1988	Apprenticeship, Kulbhushan Jain.
1988-89	National Institute of Design.
1990-92	Building Centre, Delhi
1992-96	Architecture Autonomous
1996	Private Practice.

Publications

- Researched and authored a book *Churches and Convents of Goa,* for India Book House
- Researched and authored a book *GOA,* for Roli Books, (P) Ltd.
- Authored the section on 'GOA' for Dorling Kindersley's *Eyewitness Guide to INDIA.* Published in December 2002
- Authored a section on Churches and Convents of Goa in *Speaking Stones - World Cultural Heritage Sites in India* for Eicher publications.
- Co-authored the book, *Houses of Goa,* published in 1999.
- Content writing for 'britannica india.com' on architecture and conservation.

Architectural Conservation

- Consultant to Taj Mahal Conservation Collaborative for the restoration and conservation of the Taj Mahal, Agra.
- Consultant to INTACH for World Heritage Site Assessments of Agra Fort and Taj Mahal, for the year 1999.
- Consultant architect to INTACH, for the Jaipur Heritage Trail Project, funded by American Express.

Present Address

B 17/4, n.e.a., Rajinder Nagar, New Delhi 60.
Tel: 011 2576 5653, 2574 5260
Fax: 011 2582 2756
email: annabel@eth.net

Acknowledgements

Amba, Amu, Anurag, Ashok Sharma, Babu, Balbir Verma, Benu Joshi, Caetano, Guru Bhat, J P Malhotra, J K Tandon, K N Patel, K T Ravindran, Kidar Nath Sahani, Komal Vazirani, Manas Patnaik, Narendra P, Naveen Krishna, Nirmala De Mello, Paul, Sanjay Singh, Raman Madhok, Ravi, Sajjan Jindal, Sandhya, Satoshi Asakawa, Shirley, Sukbir, Sumedha Kumar, Tara Sharma, TOTO, V L Rao, Vinu.

BEVINDA COLLACO

1954	Born in Goa, India
1975	Literature Major, Bachelor of Arts, Bombay University,
1976	Post Graduate Diploma in Journalism, from Bombay School of Journalism
1977-78	Regular writing assignments for Times of India publications, Junior Statesman (Statesman Group), The Sunday Standard, Super Magazine, Cine Blitz.
1978-82	Joined Cine Blitz; coined the word "Bollywood", which is now included in the Oxford Dictionary.
1982-95	Travelled widely, freelanced.
1995-2002	Magazine editor of WEEKENDER, (Gomantak Group of Publications, Goa)
2002-2003	Editing, feature writing, media consultancy, copywriting, guest lecturing, ghost writing.

Present Address:

460, Rua de Natal, Panjim - 403001, Goa, India.
Tel: 91- 0832 - 2220855
email: bcollaco@sancharnet.in

Translator's Profile

GEETHA PARAMESWARAN

1959	Born in Bangalore, India
1978	Sociology Major, B. A, University
1996	On call interpretor/translator for Immigration Department, Japan for Sri Lankan Tamil refugees.
1998	Translation of Tamil films to Japanese Translation of Tamil TV programmes on South India from Tamil, Malyalam, Kannada and Hindi.
2001	Administered the Japan Desk of a software company in Bangalore.
2003	Private practice with freelance assignments

Present Address

Kodandarama Layout, Osborne Road, Bangalore 560042
Mobile: 98442 52466
email: s_parameswaran@sify.com